THE POLITICS OF EXODUS

PERSPECTIVES IN CONTINENTAL PHILOSOPHY
John D. Caputo, Series Editor

THE POLITICS OF EXODUS

Søren Kierkegaard's Ethics of Responsibility

MARK DOOLEY

Fordham University Press
New York
2001

Perspectives in Continental Philosophy No. 20
ISSN 1089-3938

Library of Congress Cataloging-in-Publication Data

Dooley, Mark.
    The politics of Exodus : Søren Kierkegaard's ethics of responsibility / Mark Dooley.—1st ed.
       p. cm. — (Perspectives in continental philosophy ; no. 20)
    Includes bibliographical references and index.
    ISBN 0-8232-2124-5 — ISBN 0-8232-2125-3 (pbk.)
    1. Kierkegaard, Søren, 1813–1855—Ethics.
    2. Derrida, Jacques—Ethics. I. Title. II. Series.
B4378.E8 D66   2001
170'.92—dc21   2001033347

Printed in the United States of America
01 02 03 04 05 5 4 3 2 1
First Edition

To Laura,
for making my dreams come true

CONTENTS

ACKNOWLEDGMENTS

I wish to thank Jack Caputo, Jacques Derrida, Richard Kearney, Brendan Purcell, and Vanessa Rumble for their generous advice and help throughout the writing of this book.

Many thanks also to four of my students—Brian Garvey, Neil Brophy, Liam Kavanagh, and Eoin O'Connell—for their assistance in preparing the manuscript.

I would also like to extend my gratitude to my colleagues in the Department of Philosophy, University College Dublin, for their constant support of my work. A very special acknowledgment is owed to Mary Buckley and Ann O'Dwyer for all their expert secretarial assistance and guidance.

Without the support and fellowship of Madeline and James Dooley this book would surely not have seen the light of day.

Finally, and most importantly, I wish to thank my wife, Laura, for her inspiration and friendship.

ABBREVIATIONS FOR WORKS BY KIERKEGAARD

CA   *The Concept of Anxiety.* Trans. Reidar Thomte in collaboration with Albert B. Anderson. Princeton: Princeton University Press, 1980. (*Begrebet Angest,* by Vigilius Haufniensis, ed. S. Kierkegaard, 1844)

CI   *The Concept of Irony,* together with "Notes on Schelling's Berlin Lectures." Trans. Howard V. Hong and Edna H. Hong. Princeton: Princeton University Press, 1989. (*Om Begrebet Ironi,* 1841)

CUP   *Concluding Unscientific Postscript to the Philosophical Fragments.* Trans. Howard V. Hong and Edna H. Hong. 2 vols. Princeton: Princeton University Press, 1992. (*Afsluttende uvidenskabelig Efterskrift,* by Johannes Climacus, 1846)

DODE   *De Omnibus Dubitandum Est.* Trans. Howard V. Hong and Edna H. Hong. Princeton: Princeton University Press, 1985.

EO   *Either/Or.* Trans. Howard V. Hong and Edna H. Hong. 2 vols. Princeton: Princeton University Press, 1987. (*Enten/Eller 1–2,* ed. Victor Eremita, 1843)

FSE   *For Self-Examination.* Trans. Howard V. Hong and Edna H. Hong. Princeton: Princeton University Press, 1990. (*Til Selvprøvelse,* 1851)

FT   *Fear and Trembling.* Trans. Howard V. Hong and Edna H. Hong. Princeton: Princeton University Press, 1983. (*Frygt og Bæven,* by Johannes de Silentio, 1843)

JFY   *Judge for Yourself!* Trans. Howard V. Hong and Edna H. Hong. Princeton: Princeton University Press, 1990. (*Dømmer Selv!* 1852)

JP   *Søren Kierkegaard's Journals and Papers.* Ed. and trans. Howard V. Hong and Edna H. Hong, assisted by Gregor Malantschuk. Bloomington: Indiana University Press, 1967–78. (From *Papirer* 1–11 and 12–13, and *Brev og Akstykker vedrørende Søren Kierkegaard,* ed. Niels Thulstrup, 1–2, 1953–54)

PC   *Practice in Christianity.* Trans. Howard V. Hong and Edna

H. Hong. Princeton: Princeton University Press, 1991. (*In-døvelse I Christendom*, by Anti-Climacus, ed. S. Kierkegaard, 1850)

PF   *Philosophical Fragments* and *Johannes Climacus*. Trans. Howard V. Hong and Edna H. Hong. Princeton: Princeton University Press, 1985. ("Johannes Climacus eller de omnibus dubitandum est," written 1842–43, unpublished, *Papirer* 4)

POV   *The Point of View for My Work as an Author*. Trans. Walter Lowrie. London: Oxford University Press, 1939. (*Synspunktet for min Forfatter-Virksomhed*, posthumously published 1859; *Om min Forfatter-Virksomhed*, 1851)

R   *Repetition: A Venture in Experimenting Psychology*. Trans. Howard V. Hong and Edna H. Hong. Princeton: Princeton University Press, 1983. (*Gjentagelsen*, by Constantin Constantius, 1843)

SLW   *Stages on Life's Way*. Trans. Howard V. Hong and Edna H. Hong. Princeton: Princeton University Press, 1988. (*Stadier paa Livets Vej*, ed. Hilarius Bogbinder, 1845)

SUD   *The Sickness unto Death*. Trans. Howard V. Hong and Edna H. Hong. Princeton: Princeton University Press, 1980. (*Sygdommen til Døden*, by Anti-Climacus, ed. S. Kierkegaard, 1849)

TA   *Two Ages: The Age of Revolution and the Present Age: A Literary Review*. Trans. Howard V. Hong and Edna H. Hong. Princeton: Princeton University Press, 1978. (*En literair Anmeldelse: To Tidsaldre*, 1846)

WL   *Works of Love*. Trans. Howard V. Hong and Edna H. Hong. Princeton: Princeton University Press, 1995. (*Kjerlighedens Gjerninger*, 1847)

INTRODUCTION: LOOSENING THE LUTHERAN THREAD

IN THIS BOOK, I argue that the work of Søren Kierkegaard contains a strong social, political, and ethical dimension that is often overlooked or simply ignored by contemporary commentators. Until quite recently, Kierkegaard was appraised as a champion of isolated subjectivity, individuality, and, in the words of Theodore Adorno, "objectless inwardness."[1] From this perspective, Kierkegaard's contribution was judged solely in "existential" or "subjectivist" terms. Such constricted readings inevitably resulted in his being accused of promoting a "totally abstract, utterly indefinite, and completely incomprehensible" notion of selfhood.[2] My fundamental objective is to dispute these claims by arguing that Kierkegaard's notion of the self does not result in isolated subjective interiority divorced from all social interaction, but rather one that seeks to engender a notion of community existence, and which therefore has much to offer the contemporary reader.

However, this study is not the first to make such claims. We have recently seen a proliferation of texts endeavoring to make a case for Kierkegaard's inclusion in mainstream ethical and political debate. Authors like Merold Westphal, Stephen Crites, C. Stephen Evans, Bruce Kirmmse, John Elrod, Robert Perkins, Edward Mooney, Martin Matustík, and George Pattison have contributed to this area of scholarship. Their analyses are a welcome addition to the ever-burgeoning body of secondary literature on Kierkegaard.

This study builds upon the work of these commentators by drawing out the ethical and political implications of Kierkegaard's work by coming at his writings from a specifically Derridean perspective.

---

[1] Theodore W. Adorno, *Kierkegaard: Construction of the Aesthetic*, trans. Robert Hullot-Kentor (Minneapolis: University of Minnesota Press, 1989), 24–46.

[2] Mark C. Taylor, *Journeys to Selfhood: Kierkegaard and Hegel* (New York: Fordham University Press, 2000), 274.

Although there has been much groundbreaking work undertaken in this respect by Mark Taylor, Louis Mackey, and John D. Caputo, I will go a step further by showing that to read Kierkegaard from a Derridean perspective not only teaches us much about Kierkegaard's literary methods, but also elucidates what this characteristically nineteenth-century philosopher can offer us in a concrete ethical and political sense in the contemporary milieu.

There are, of course, obvious differences between Kierkegaard and Derrida, not the least of which is the fact that Kierkegaard is a Christian thinker and Derrida is not. However, as John Caputo has argued for many years, the radicalness of Kierkegaard's religious thought is similar in structure to many of the themes that have preoccupied Derrida, especially in his more recent incarnation. That is, for a decade now Derrida's thinking has been more sensitive to ethical, religious, and political matters in a way that echoes in many respects Kierkegaard's own responses to what he called "the plagues of the age." The main thrust of my argument, therefore, is that to align Kierkegaard with Derrida will not obfuscate the rich insights of both thinkers at an ethical and political level, but rather ensure that their originality is underscored and appreciated.

In brief, I will argue in this context that reading Kierkegaard from a Derridean perspective not only helps us understand the implications of Kierkegaard's "proto-ethics" (as instanced in *Fear and Trembling*, e.g.), but that it also helps us appreciate the rich significance of Kierkegaard's social and political thought in a way we might not have otherwise been able to.

I am aware that such a reading of Kierkegaard will not sit well with those who interpret his work simply as an endeavor to liberate the genuine spirit of Luther from the grip of those nineteenth-century Danish ecclesiastics for whom he had a particular loathing. While I acknowledge that Kierkegaard was responding in his authorship to problems specifically endemic to his own cultural matrix, I am nevertheless committed to the task of demonstrating how those writings can and ought to be reconsidered in the light of contemporary philosophical, political, and cultural developments. Such a reconsideration will no doubt provoke the criticism from certain quarters (especially from those whose objective it is to render Kierkegaard politically ineffective) that the thesis I advance is of dubious merit, one that is obviously the product of unrestrained hermeneutic violence. Although it is true that I have taken certain liberties in my reading of Kierkegaard, and that I do on occasion push him in a direction he himself might not have favored, I do not believe this amounts to hermeneutic violence. First, I see a real tension in Kierkegaard's work between, on the one hand, his tendency to advance the strictly Lutheran idea that the individual's private salvation is realized through an "absolute relationship" to God, and on the other, his more radically liberating idea of identifying the God-man as ethical prototype par excellence, the imitation of which engenders a sensitivity toward the other qua neighbor. It is this latter idea, developed in such texts as *Practice in Christianity* and *Works of Love,* that I wish to emphasize and develop throughout this book. My contention is that the political message contained in these and related texts is the one most suited for our purposes today. In giving this message a contemporary application by reading it from a Derridean perspective, we loosen the thread of Kierkegaard's Lutheran straitjacket, thus making him more useful as a fellow traveler as we begin a new millennium.

This brings me to my second reason for refuting the charge that my reading of Kierkegaard is hermeneutically violent. I will respond by using for my own ends the answer Richard Rorty has given those who have accused him of doing a similar type of violence to John Dewey throughout his writings:[3] every writer who stands in the shadow of a great philosophical forebear is obliged to make a distinction between the spirit and the letter of that forebear's work. This is so because each great thinker is the product of his or her time—that is, no philosopher can take up a neutral standpoint to assess the quandaries of the age. If Kierkegaard has taught us anything, it is that even philosophers are subject to time and chance, and are thus incapable of rising up on eagles' wings (in the spirit of Hegel) to assume a godlike position. Kierkegaard, that is, realized that philosophers, as existing individuals, never succeed in having the last word.

In the case of Kierkegaard himself, there were many who were not convinced by what he said, many who did not share his convictions. So it is left to those of us who *have* been convinced to suggest why

---

[3] See Rorty's rejoinder to James Gouinlock on this point in *Rorty and Pragmatism: The Philosopher Responds to His Critics,* ed. Herman J. Saatkamp (Nashville and London: Vanderbilt University Press, 1995), 91–99.

we think he failed to win widespread approval. Consequently, we
have to concede, if the thinker we admire is to continue to be read
and if his spirit is to stay alive, that perhaps the way in which Kierkegaard framed things was not always the best way. This is why I want
to distance myself from the Kierkegaard who speaks of "the absolute
relationship to the absolute" (the one in the Lutheran straitjacket)
while making the most of the Kierkegaard who speaks of selfless love
for the other as the basis of genuine community life (the one who
loosens the Lutheran thread). By emphasizing this latter point, and
by showing how it has taken hold in the influential work of some of
our leading contemporary theorists, one is able to make a strong
case for keeping Kierkegaard on the curricula of many schools and
universities irrespective of ethos or denomination, and not merely
on the bookshelves of their respective libraries as relics of yesteryear.
Despite the protestations of those who would privilege the letter
over the spirit of Kierkegaard's work, I want to say that if the said
thinker is to have relevance in our contemporary context, conces-
sions have to be made for the sake of his survival as someone who
can still inspire and impassion.

   In short, I want to do for Kierkegaard what Hubert Dreyfus has
done for Heidegger, Richard Rorty for Dewey, and Terry Pinkard and
Robert Solomon for Hegel—that is, attempt to suggest what each
thinker might have said if he or she had the benefit of foresight. Just
as Rorty endeavors to articulate what Dewey might have said had he
been around long enough to appreciate the full impact of the linguistic turn, and just as both Rorty and Dreyfus try to take the steam
out of Heidegger's overwrought Continental language so as to render
him more digestible for those with a pragmatist orientation, I strive
to make Kierkegaard palatable to a contemporary audience by guess-
ing how he might have applied his trenchant wit and humor to our
current dilemmas. My aim, in other words, is to imagine the use to
which Kierkegaard would have put his irony and religious sensitivi-
ties had he come after deconstruction. Whether we like it or not, a
thinker can only survive if we are willing to separate his or her most
original insights from those that have no practical utility today.

   If the reading of Kierkegaard I advance in this text sticks in the
throat of those purists and disciples who would unreservedly privilege the letter over the spirit of his work, I am equally cognizant that
there are many within the ranks of contemporary European thought

for whom it will also prove unsatisfactory. I attribute this to the immense impact the thought of Emmanuel Levinas has had on those currently engaged in this field of inquiry. While there is no denying the value and worth of Levinas's contribution writ large, his critique of Kierkegaard has only served to obfuscate the rich ethical and political character of the latter's work.

Levinas's essay "Existence and Ethics" was first published in 1963, and was followed a year later by a dramatic and stinging intervention at a conference dedicated to Kierkegaard sponsored by UNESCO. For Levinas, "the suffering truth" of which Kierkegaard speaks at many junctures throughout his authorship "does not open out to others, but to God in isolation."[4] This interpretation is symptomatic of the view that Kierkegaard advocates an "absolute relationship to the absolute" to the detriment of the existing individual's relationship to society and others. It is predicated upon the erroneous belief that a philosophy that emphasizes subjectivity "participates in the violence of the modern world, with its cult of Passion and Fury." On this reading, Kierkegaard is a militant whose thought "brings irresponsibility in its wake and a ferment of disintegration."[5]

There is one outstanding reason for Levinas's aversion to Kierkegaardian thought: the latter's insistence that a "suspension of the ethical" is required as a means of overcoming the despair of the age. For Levinas, Kierkegaard's appropriation of the Genesis narrative of Abraham and Isaac in *Fear and Trembling* is deeply perturbing. Levinas considers the attempted sacrifice of Isaac nothing less than a violent abomination, an act of unrestrained religious fanaticism. For him, Abraham's suspension of his familial and civic ties is a wanton violation of the primacy of the ethical. Consequently, the feature of the story that most interests Levinas is Abraham's reclamation of the ethical, his return from Moriah with his son safely in hand.

What Levinas seems to overlook in his reading of *Fear and Trembling* is the fact that Kierkegaard does not simply demand a "suspension of the ethical," but a "*teleological* suspension of the ethical." In other words, for Kierkegaard it is never a case of merely abandoning what he calls the "sphere of the universal" by abdicating

---

[4] Emmanuel Levinas, "Existence and Ethics," in *Kierkegaard: A Critical Reader,* ed. Jonathan Ree and Jane Chamberlain (Oxford: Blackwell, 1998), 30.

[5] Ibid.

one's social and civic responsibilities. The aim of the teleological suspension of the ethical is to reinforce the fact that our ethical codes are ineluctably open to revision, since they are the formulations of existing individuals who are always in the process of becoming, forever subject to the vagaries of time and contingency. This does not imply, however, that everything is up for grabs or that our most hallowed and hoary values are rendered worthless. The fundamental objective of Kierkegaard's teleological suspension is neither to raze everything to the ground nor to let chaos ravage the land; rather, it is a means by which both the laws of the state and those fundamental ethical principles that govern our actions are sufficiently loosened up so as to prevent them from becoming dogmatic, rigid, and insensitive to those whose welfare they are supposed to guarantee and safeguard.

For Kierkegaard, laws and norms do not, as Hegel would have us believe, unfold in accordance with some divine design; if such were the case, it would be reasonable to assume that those laws that have caused more harm than good, or those that have been put in place to protect the interests of the few over the many, have been sanctioned by God. Consequently, any forms of injustice perpetrated in the name of the law would have divine warrant.

On the contrary, Kierkegaard maintains that ethics and law are the products of historical change and mutation; that is, they are not static, ideal forms that are immanently recollected. Because existing individuals are continually in the process of becoming, their truths and values are no less subject to temporal variation. To say that one is in possession of the truth (epistemic, ethical, etc.) suggests that one has somehow managed to twist free from the grip of history and time. Existing beings, however, are unavoidably situated in a temporal flux from which there is no escape. Hence truth is not something they possess with certainty, but is rather contingent. "Everything that becomes historical is contingent," Kierkegaard insists, "inasmuch as precisely by coming into existence, by becoming historical, it has its element of contingency, inasmuch as contingency is precisely the one factor in all coming into existence" (CUP, 98). Consequently, truth is not something one can take hold of in its purity, but "is only in the becoming, in the process of appropriation" (CUP, 78).

In looking at the teleological suspension of the ethical from this perspective, we can conclude that Kierkegaard is not in the business of perpetrating irresponsibility and social disintegration. Rather, by emphasizing existence, becoming, and contingency, or by taking time seriously, he shows that genuine responsibility requires us to keep both the law and our dominant ethical codes open to revision so as to serve the interests of existing individuals and not the reverse. In other words, suspending the ethical is for Kierkegaard a matter of privileging the needs of singularity above those of the universal, of making the universal *responsive* to the singular. As such, the "suspension" amounts, not to a leveling of the ethical, but to its teleological reconfiguration.

Levinas fails to appreciate the subtleties of Kierkegaard's reading of the Abraham story. He fails, that is, to catch the spirit of *Fear and Trembling*, to see it in the broader context of Kierkegaard's authorship. Had he studied it from this perspective, he might have realized that the one abiding concern throughout is how to release the ethical from the sclerosis of dogma so as to keep it focused on what is essential and primary in all ethical considerations, that is, the single individual. Otherwise stated, had Levinas not stuck so closely to the letter, had he not read Kierkegaard's text through the lens of the Old Testament, he might have cultivated a greater appreciation for the radicalness of Kierkegaard's critique of traditional approaches to ethical questions. He might, that is, have tapped into the strain of Kierkegaard's thinking that emphasizes the importance of love toward the neighbor, and especially to "those who labor and are burdened" (PC, 13)—fundamental themes and features, ironically enough, of Levinas's own work.

In short, I am aware that the argument I advance in this book will encounter opposition from those who consider it disadvantageous to place Kierkegaard within the "postmodern" context, that is, those who would continue to confine him in a Lutheran straitjacket, and from those within that context who subscribe to the type of criticisms proffered by Levinas. I believe, however, that there is a line of thought in Kierkegaard that confounds both of these theses, a thread with the potential to keep this thinker at the cutting edge of contemporary ethical and political debate. I will exploit this particular strain in rendering Kierkegaard politically useful today.

As intimated at the outset, I have derived much benefit from the work of John Caputo, a thinker who has in no small measure helped to consolidate the Kierkegaard-Derrida alliance. What one finds so original in this individual's work is his persuasive belief that Christian philosophy of the Kierkegaardian sort is not synonymous with the philosophy espoused and promoted by mainstream Christianity today (which is more akin to what Kierkegaard called "Christendom"), but resembles to a greater extent contemporary postmodern thought. In other words, Caputo has shown that Kierkegaard's legacy has been preserved more richly by those with whom he is ostensibly least associated than by those who claim to be his direct heirs and descendants.

Caputo maintains that postmodernism is not, as many argue, a form of neo-Nietzschean nihilism, but a movement that has its roots in the very soil Kierkegaard plowed so many years ago. That is, Caputo contends that there is a strong biblical impulse driving both Kierkegaard and his late-twentieth-century fellow travelers. In a recent work Caputo encapsulates the essence of his argument: "The right comparison of Derrida to Kierkegaard is not, as Derrida's critics imagine, to the Kierkegaardian aesthete in the papers of 'A' in *Either/Or, Volume I*. The right comparison of deconstruction with Kierkegaard is to the religious sphere."[6]

The theme of responsibility, as the title of this book indicates, is a central motif running through what follows. Like Caputo, I believe that Kierkegaard's religious bent amounts to an ethics of responsibility strikingly similar in tone to that evoked by Derrida of late. As I suggested above, "responsibility" in this context means an obligation to the singular other that overrides one's obligation to the universality of the law. In other words, responsibility for Kierkegaard and Derrida amounts to a response to the other whose singularity is not guaranteed by the prevailing orthodoxy. This requires that one must, while responding to the other, sacrifice one's own security in the established paradigm so as to champion the cause of the "poor existing individual" (CUP, 189–90) who has no place in the system.

This is, of course, a political gesture, for to challenge the dominant order in the name of singularity is always a politically motivated action. It is not, however, a conventional political response, but one that is politically defiant. This is why I call the ethics of responsibility

---

[6] John D. Caputo, *Demythologizing Heidegger* (Bloomington: Indiana University Press, 1993), 210.

defended by both Kierkegaard and Derrida a "politics of exodus" or of the émigré—a politics, that is, of one who places the needs of the singular over those of the universal, of one who takes up the cause of the outcast and the marginalized, the victims of injustice, the lepers and the lame, as a means of destabilizing the establishment.

It was Kierkegaard's lifelong vocation to impart in his writings how essential it is to cultivate passion in matters so essential to one's life as an existing being. This involves a continual process of self-questioning with the aim of submitting to critical appraisal the prevailing philosophical, ethical, political, and religious currents of one's time. It demands that the individual not merely reflect on what he or she takes to be the truth of ethics or religion, but to "doubly reflect," as Kierkegaard argues, on the efficacy of such truths. This means that in order to become genuinely responsible, one needs to become engaged to such a degree that one's critical reflection resolves in committed action by way of ethically guided decision. At such moments, one is called to emigrate from the sphere of the universal by suspending one's obligation to it, with the aim of making it more responsive or sensitive to the needs of the other. So rather than being a form of irrationalism, the ethics of responsibility is grounded in what I will call, following Kierkegaard, a "doubly reflected" reason. This is not the reason of speculative philosophy, nor is it enlightened reason, but it is a form of ethical or religious reason, or reflection, that is guided by the appeal from the other for a response to his or her plight. The ethics of responsibility does not give up on reason, but seeks rather to make it more liberating and engaged and less dispassionate and impartial.

For both Kierkegaard and Derrida, I will contend, the ethics of responsibility and the politics of the émigré need to be cultivated if genuine community is to emerge. Derrida's recent pronouncements on democracy and what he calls "an *open* 'quasi'-community of people"[7] help us greatly in trying to understand the type of social philosophy that one can find echoes of throughout Kierkegaard's authorship. It must be stated, however, that neither Derrida nor Caputo has identified how close Kierkegaard's radical politics is to his own ideals. Indeed, I will show in chapter 6 just how much Kierke-

---

[7] Jacques Derrida, *Points . . . : Interviews, 1974–1994*, ed. Elizabeth Weber, trans. Peggy Kamuf et al. (Stanford: Stanford University Press, 1995), 351.

gaard anticipated both authors in this respect. I must note, however, that Caputo, as a Christian thinker, comes closer than Derrida to recognizing this facet of Kierkegaard's oeuvre, although he has yet to make any direct comparison between his notion of a postmodern Christian community and Kierkegaard's Christian "community of neighbors," a theme I will discuss in detail in the closing stages of this work.

So this book has, in effect, two central aims: first, to make a case for Kierkegaard as a committed thinker who had an ethico-political sensitivity; and second, to show how far in advance of their time were the ethical and political ideals he espoused. In so doing, I hope to press the case for Kierkegaard as a "proto-deconstructionist" further by arguing that, if studied from the point of view of an ethics of responsibility, the Kierkegaard-Derrida relationship is indeed much stronger than has been hitherto suspected.

I begin in chapter 1, therefore, with an analysis of *Two Ages*, Kierkegaard's most overtly political text, and one that most commentators wishing to extrapolate a political message from Kierkegaard's writings turn to. My reading of this work will underline what Kierkegaard considers the most dangerous impediments to genuine community existence and set out what he considers the most effective antidotes to these ills. I will also take the first tentative steps toward a comparison of Kierkegaard's and Derrida's similar critiques of the present age by focusing on their equally trenchant attacks on the press and public opinion.

In chapter 2, I examine Hegel's philosophy of identity and his related *Philosophy of Right*, and suggest that if looked at as a reaction to the dangerous implications of the Hegelian ethical scheme (*Sittlichkeit*), the raison d'être of both the Kierkegaardian and Derridean enterprises becomes easier to identify and understand. For it is precisely against Hegel's assertion that the law of the state is Spirit's (*Geist's*) "divine design" on earth, and against the related belief that there is a teleological force driving history toward the realization of the absolute state, that Kierkegaard and Derrida react. Responsibility, I will argue, requires much more from the individual than merely adhering to the laws of the state.

Chapter 3, entitled "The Ethics of Irony," focuses on the dangers for the individual and for singularity if the established order or *Sittlichkeit* has no criterion other than itself to judge the efficacy of its laws and principles. In order to avoid the ultimate danger of the state's self-deification, Kierkegaard proposes that each individual regulate his or her actions in accordance with a higher ethical criterion or "idea," in the manner of those whom he identifies as ethical exemplars or "prototypes." In this context I examine why Kierkegaard turns to both Socrates (as a negative ironist) and Abraham (as a positive ironist) as exemplars of this type. Such a study will, of course, involve a comprehensive analysis of the vexed and complex issues surrounding Kierkegaard's notion of the teleological suspension of the ethical in *Fear and Trembling*.

Chapter 4 introduces what I believe to be the most central and significant of all Kierkegaardian categories, "repetition." An understanding of repetition in Kierkegaard's work provides the reader not only with a means of identifying a linear structure to his rather disparate authorship, but also with the greatest evidence that Kierkegaard's project is a responsible form of deconstruction. By examining repetition from the point of view of Kierkegaard's complex notion of selfhood, I show that repetition is the means by which the individual comes to appropriate God as the highest ethical ideal. The Kierkegaardian God is the incarnation, the God-man who challenges the prevailing order in the name of those laid low. He is therefore not an object of knowledge in the sense of the traditional God of Scholastic ontology, or indeed the Old Testament God, but one who calls for each individual to "respond" to him by bringing to life anew (repetition) his ideals of mercy and forgiveness. This requires that the individual have faith, as hope in and affirmation of what offends the establishment. Responsibility is faith to the degree that one consistently hopes for the type of justice the God-man so passionately sought to engender.

Chapter 5 deals comprehensively with the nature of the God-man as described in Kierkegaard's writings, most especially in *Practice in Christianity*. It analyzes Kierkegaard's fundamental contention that to imitate the God-man is the way to become genuinely responsible, and indeed the way to establish concrete relationships with the other.

Finally, in chapter 6, which is divided into two parts, I show how congruous all of the preceding are with the current spirit of deconstruction in the work of Jacques Derrida. While the first part of this chapter considers the strong parallels that exist in their mutually compatible responses to systematization, the second part argues in favor of both Kierkegaard and Derrida as thinkers whose scrupulous attention to the needs of singularity does not stop them from holding a concrete political philosophy. By situating Kierkegaard in relation to Derrida in this way, I show how Kierkegaard's insights can have practical political utility. It also provides the opportunity to show how Kierkegaard's "community of neighbors," as developed in *Works of Love* (1847), anticipated many of the themes central to the ethical and political writings of both Caputo and Derrida.

THE POLITICS OF EXODUS

1

What the Age Demands

IN THIS FIRST CHAPTER I will provide a general outline of Kierke-gaard's critique of society as enunciated primarily in *Two Ages* (1846).[1] Until quite recently, Kierkegaard's thought was considered somewhat devoid of any form of social analysis. Because of the stress he places on the role of "the single individual" throughout his corpus, and as a result of commentators' tendency to appraise his writings either in terms of their existential import or their theological significance alone, scant attention has been devoted to the not-so-obvious social and ethical currents that run throughout Kierkegaard's work. In the last decade, however, this traditional portrayal has given way to a wide panoply of readings, each sensitive to this central facet of the Kierkegaardian authorship. Common to nearly all of these assessments is the importance each one attributes to Kierkegaard's sardonic and trenchant diagnosis of the ills of contemporary society developed in *Two Ages* under the title "The Present Age." Indeed, it could be argued that many of the present-day attempts[2] to persuade the philosophical community of Kierkegaard's

---

[1] For an analysis of this text in relation to the rest of Kierkegaard's authorship, see Bruce Kirmmse, *Kierkegaard in Golden Age Denmark* (Bloomington: Indiana University Press, 1990), 265–78. This is the most exhaustive study available of Kierkegaard's work in relation to the politics of nineteenth-century Denmark.

[2] See George B. Connell and C. Stephen Evans, eds., *Foundations of Kierkegaard's Vision of Community: Religion, Ethics, and Politics in Kierkegaard* (Atlantic Highlands, N.J.: Humanities Press, 1992); William John Cahoy, "The Self in Community: Søren Kierkegaard's Thought on the Individual and the Church" (Ph.D. diss., Yale University, 1989); Stephen Crites, "*The Sickness unto Death*: A Social Interpretation," in Connell and Evans, *Kierkegaard's Vision of Community*, 144–60; Mark Dooley, "Risking Responsibility: A Politics of the *Emigré*," in *Kierkegaard: The Self in Society*, ed. George Pattison and Steven Shakespeare (London: Macmillan, 1998), 139–55; John W. Elrod, *Kierkegaard and Christendom* (Princeton: Princeton University Press, 1981); Ronald L. Hall, *Word and Spirit: A Kierkegaardian Critique of the Modern Age* (Bloomington: Indiana University Press, 1993); James L. Marsh, "Kierkegaard and Critical Theory," in *Kierkegaard in Post/Modernity*, ed. Martin J. Matustík and Merold Westphal (Bloomington: Indiana University Press, 1995), 199–215; Martin J. Matustík, *Postnational Identity: Critical Theory and Existential*

relevance to mainstream social, ethical, and political debate stem originally from an early collection (1984) in *The International Kierkegaard Commentary* series (vol. 14) devoted to *Two Ages*. In the introduction to this volume, Robert Perkins endeavored to counter the prevailing trend in Kierkegaard studies:

> With the publication of this volume of essays on Kierkegaard's *Two Ages* a myth should die. Whether the myth will die or not will depend upon the intellectual integrity of the academy, the professors, of whom Kierkegaard has a very low opinion.
>
> The myth is to the effect that Kierkegaard presents his concept of the individual in a social and political vacuum, that Kierkegaardian inwardness and subjectivity is so pervasive and unqualified that for the Kierkegaardian individual (*hiin Enkelte*) there is no social and historical context, that society and history stop and cease to have an effect on the individual who chooses himself before God. Consequently, since the individual is stripped of his social relations, is a bare particular, the Kierkegaardian analysis of the individual must fail. Such a view can be justified by a select reading of Kierkegaard's works, but it cannot be justified by a balanced and thorough reading of the whole authorship. A reading of *Two Ages* shows this select and partial reading to be humorous.[3]

Each essay that followed took the form of sensible and articulate reading of Kierkegaard from the perspective of his indictment of the

---

Philosophy in Habermas, Kierkegaard, and Havel (New York: Guilford Press, 1993), and "Kierkegaard's Radical Existential Praxis, or: Why the Individual Defies Liberal, Communitarian, and Postmodern Categories," in Matustík and Westphal, *Kierkegaard in Post/Modernity*, 239–64; John Douglas Mullen, *Kierkegaard's Philosophy: Self-Deception and Cowardice in the Present Age* (New York: New American Library, 1981); Jane Rubin, "Too Much of Nothing: Modern Culture, the Self, and Salvation in Kierkegaard's Thought" (Ph.D. diss., University of California, Berkeley, 1984); Merold Westphal, *Kierkegaard's Critique of Reason and Society* (Macon: Mercer University Press, 1987).

[3] Robert L. Perkins, ed., *The International Kierkegaard Commentary*, vol. 14, "*Two Ages: The Present Age and the Age of Revolution*," *A Literary Review* (Macon: Mercer University Press, 1984), xiii. Articles of particular interest in this volume include John W. Elrod, "Passion, Reflection, and Particularity in *Two Ages*," 1–18; Lee Barrett, "An Immediate Stage on the Way to the Religious Life," 53–71; Patricia Cutting, "The Levels of Interpersonal Relationships in Kierkegaard's *Two Ages*," 73–86; Robert L. Perkins, "Envy as Personal Phenomenon and as Politics," 107–32; Merold Westphal, "Kierkegaard's Sociology," 133–54; James L. Marsh, "Marx and Kierkegaard on Alienation," 155–74; John M. Hoberman, "Kierkegaard's *Two Ages* and Heidegger's Critique of Modernity," 223–58. For a collection of related studies see Robert L. Perkins, ed., *International Kierkegaard Commentary*, vol. 13, "*The Corsair Affair*" (Macon: Mercer University Press, 1990).

present age, thereby confounding those who, in spite of all the evidence to the contrary, continued to defiantly render Kierkegaard politically and socially ineffective.

Following the lead taken by Perkins et al., I wish to contend that the spirit and purpose of "The Present Age" are not unique to this text alone, but are evident, albeit in different forms, at each stage of Kierkegaard's philosophical trajectory. In other words, Kierkegaard's authorship is a critical response to certain perennial and pernicious features of social and political life.

In order to appreciate the insights and significance of this remarkable little essay from 1846, I begin with an examination of what separates "subjective" from "objective" reflection. This will allow me, in turn, to define more perspicuously the meaning of some pivotal concepts that are developed in an elementary way in "The Present Age" but which subsequently become central tenets in Kierkegaard's later works. To satisfy this demand, let us turn briefly to his discussion of these themes in the *Concluding Unscientific Postscript*.

SUBJECTIVE VERSUS OBJECTIVE TRUTH

The question of "subjective truth" preoccupies the pseudonymous author, Johannes Climacus, throughout the *Concluding Unscientific Postscript*. For Climacus, existing beings are temporally bound, embedded in particular historical contexts, and are therefore incapable of acquiring a purely objective idea of truth; that is, "objective reflection" presupposes that truth is something that can become an "object" divorced from an existing subject who thinks. The idealist tendency to conflate thought and being, for Kierkegaard, "proves to be nonsense, unless it is perhaps intended only for fantastical beings" (CUP, 191). Objective reflection not only "turns existence into an indifferent, vanishing something," but transforms truth itself into something "indifferent":

> All essential knowing pertains to existence, or only the knowing whose relation to existence is essential is essential knowing. Essentially viewed, the knowing that does not inwardly in the reflection of inwardness pertain to existence is accidental knowing, and its degree and scope, essentially viewed, are a matter of indifference. That essential

knowing is essentially related to existence does not, however, signify the above-mentioned abstract identity between thinking and being, nor does it signify that the knowledge is objectively related to something existent [*Tilværende*] as its object, but it means that the knowledge is related to the knower, who is essentially an existing person [*Existerende*], and that all essential knowing is therefore essentially related to existence and to existing. (CUP, 197–98)

Climacus, therefore, is less concerned with the content of "what" we know than with "how" we come to know what we know; stated otherwise, the pseudonym views objective reflection as being disinterested and disengaged, while in subjective reflection the existing individual realizes that what he or she holds to be truth might in fact be erroneous. Unless the subject is actively engaged with what he or she knows by continually testing its veracity and its truthfulness, he or she is entangled in the web of objective reflection.

So-called objective truths, according to Climacus, have little to do with existing beings who are situated in the inexorable tide of temporal becoming, and because truth is an issue only for existing individuals, it too "becomes." That is, truth, being related to particular beings in existence, is subject to the same degree of mutation and metamorphosis as the individuals for whom it is an issue. This is not to suggest that there are no objective truths as such; mathematical truths, for example, are objectively true to the extent that they are held universally. Kierkegaard, however, is less concerned with this type of knowledge than with "ethical and ethical-religious knowing," which he defines as "essential knowing" (CUP, 198). In other words, the truths of ethics—and indeed those of religion—being directly related as they are to the lives of "poor existing individuals," must be continually rethought and reassessed by the subjective beings for whom such truths matter. Being concerned with the welfare of the singular individual, which he prioritizes over the universal (established orthodoxy), Climacus endeavors to bring the existing being to the point where he or she can evaluate the prevailing ethical and religious standards, with a view to determining if they are in the service of the prevailing order or if they guarantee the needs and rights of individuals. Becoming ethically responsible, for this thinker, is not a matter of merely adhering to the requirements of state law or established mores alone, but of responding to the call of the singular other whom the law neither protects nor serves. This is why, as we shall see, Kierkegaard's ethical exemplars (Socrates, Abraham, and the God-man) are outlaws to a degree, on the margins of all established ethical and religious paradigms.

The question, then, is one of "relation": how does the individual relate to truth (ethical, religious, and indeed political)? If the individual relates to ethical truth objectively, it becomes for him or her only a universally sanctioned program to be deferred to in all circumstances, which amounts to empty conformism and, at times, irresponsibility; for is it not the case that legal, ethical, and religious orders sometimes lose their vocation by oppressing rather than protecting rights and freedom? However, if the individual relates to truth subjectively by making it an issue *for him or her,* he or she then critically questions the efficacy and merits of the prevailing ("universal") ethical and religious currents in the name of those individual subjects whom the law (ethical and religious) does not accommodate. Subjective reflection is, therefore, passionately engaged reflection, while objective reflection is apathetic and disengaged. Subjective reflection leads to action and decision, while objective reflection leads to inactivity, indecision, and indolence.

It is necessary at this point to make a further distinction to which I shall return throughout the course of this work—that between "inwardness" and "outwardness." It has often been supposed that what Kierkegaard means by "inwardness" amounts to an abdication of social responsibilities in favor of a solitary and isolated existence before God. Such an interpretation amounts to a serious misrepresentation, however. "Inwardness," simply defined, is the movement the individual makes while becoming subjective; that is, in order to transform impersonal objective reflection into engaged and passionate subjective reflection, the individual is required to adopt a critical distance from the prevailing ethical, political, and religious truths governing his or her reality, with the object of responding to the claims of singularity. The subjective thinker, in other words, "is essentially interested in his own thinking, is existing in it" (CUP, 73). "His thinking," therefore, "has another kind of reflection, specifically, that of inwardness, of possession, whereby it belongs to the subject and to no one else" (CUP, 73). The ethically and religiously motivated subject must break free of the web of immediate reflection, of public or established opinion, with the objective of establishing the worthiness of such objectively held standards of truth.

According to Climacus, the subjective thinker comes to understand
that in matters of ethics, religion, and (as we shall see) politics there
can be no rigid criteria of evaluation, for the demands of subjectivity,
of singular individuals in time, are always changing according to the
requirements of specific historical circumstances that could not have
been foreseen by preceding generations:

> Whereas objective thinking invests everything in the result and assists
> all humankind to cheat by copying and reeling off results and answers,
> subjective thinking invests everything in the process of becoming and
> omits the result, partly because this belongs to him, since he possesses
> the way, partly because he as existing is continually in the process of
> becoming, as is every human being who has not permitted himself to
> be tricked into becoming objective, into inhumanly becoming specu-
> lative thought. (CUP, 73)

When the subjective thinker reflects, therefore, the "reflection of
inwardness" amounts to what Kierkegaard calls "double reflection,"
or a form of reflection that is not disinterested or immediate, universal or objective, but a form of passionately engaged reflection that
resolves in action and decision. That is, the individual who practices
the art of double reflection goes beyond the mere immediate expression of truth in an objective form by asking what relevance such
knowledge has for existing beings. Double reflection grants the individual freedom from the hegemony of popular opinion by enabling
him or her to "teleologically suspend" the objective sphere of public
discourse so as to respond in a genuinely ethical sense to the suffering of the "poor existing individual":

> Objective thinking is completely indifferent to subjectivity and
> thereby to inwardness and appropriation; its communication is there-
> fore direct. It is obvious that it does not have to be easy. But it is
> direct; it does not have the illusiveness and the art of double-
> reflection. . . . [I]t can be understood directly; it can be reeled off.
> Objective thinking is therefore aware only of itself and is therefore no
> communication. . . . The form of a communication is something dif-
> ferent from the expression of a communication. When a thought has
> gained its proper expression in the word, which is attained through
> the first reflection, there comes the second reflection, which bears
> upon the intrinsic relation of the communication to the communica-
> tor and renders the existing communicator's own relation to the idea.
> (CUP, 75–76)

Ethical truth, which each individual is responsible for striving after, cannot be communicated directly. The reason for this is clear: if one were to communicate ethical—or indeed religious—truths in an objective form, or through public channels, one would run the risk of having such truth become the object of apathetic and disinterested reflection. In order to communicate that ethical truth is not a matter for speculation, but for actively engaged individuals who are constantly in the process of becoming, it is necessary, according to Climacus, to "negatively" or "indirectly" help the other; that is, because ethical truth is not abstract knowledge, but something that affects the lives of individuals, each subject has to be brought to the truth in such a way that he or she does not merely reflect on its content, but doubly reflects on what it means for his or her life. For Climacus, thus, truth is not (speculative) knowledge, but the way in which one cultivates passionate inwardness:

> In order to clarify the divergence of objective and subjective reflection, I shall now describe subjective reflection in its search back and inward into inwardness. At its highest, inwardness in an existing subject is passion; truth as a paradox corresponds to passion, and that truth becomes a paradox is grounded precisely in its relation to an existing subject. In this way the one corresponds to the other. In forgetting that one is an existing subject, one loses passion, and in return, truth does not become a paradox; but the knowing subject shifts from being human to being a fantastical something, and truth become a fantastical object for its knowing. (CUP, 198–99)

It is essential to keep in mind here that when Kierkegaard talks of subjective truth, he is referring to truth of an ethical kind, which, because of its time-bound character (values do change over time), is paradoxical to objective knowledge. In other words, to be ethically engaged in a passionate and interested (*inter-esse*) manner suggests that human beings cannot take up a godlike view from nowhere, but experience the world and their relationships with others from where they stand. Once this is realized, the individual comes to see that any attempt to lay down objective ethical standards without taking cognizance of the fact that each individual's needs and wants vary from situation to situation and from age to age is simply paradoxical. Subjective ethical truth demands that attention be paid to the particularity or singularity of each individual situation.

This is not to suggest that Kierkegaard is advocating some form of relativism or perspectivalism; he is suggesting, rather, that the demands of the singular should always outweigh those of the universal. This is why, as we shall see, the case of Abraham's teleological suspension of the universal is such a central consideration for Kierkegaard. Universal ethical and juridical paradigms are products of their time, the creations of historically situated subjects. Because existing individuals are always subject to change and contingency, ethical dilemmas inevitably arise that the prevailing schema is unable to respond to adequately. This in turn calls for the reformulation of the objectively held universal principles so as to respond to the unique and singular appeal for what Derrida calls "justice."[4] Ethical truth thus keeps evolving in accordance with the singularity of events.[5]

Having highlighted the nature of the difference between subjective and objective truth, and that between apathetic and double reflection, let me return at this juncture to Kierkegaard's reflection on the ills of the age—and his proposed antidotes—in *Two Ages*.

THE PRESENT AGE

In his biting and satirical assessment of the problems endemic to the age, Kierkegaard argues that only through the cultivation of "genuine" community existence, in which "the coiled springs of life-relationships" regain "their resilience" (TA, 78), can there be social harmony. The particular, ideal community he seeks to generate is composed of ethically responsible and committed individuals or selves, each of whom has critically challenged the basic assumptions underlying the philosophical, political, and ethical paradigms that have heretofore determined the manner in which both the individual and society have been defined; that is, for Kierkegaard, self-awareness requires that individuals reevaluate what they formerly believed to be the truth about both themselves and their relationships with

---

[4] I shall return to this Derridean/Levinasian concept in chapter 6.

[5] See John D. Caputo, "On Being Inside/Outside Truth," in *Modernity and Its Discontents*, ed. John D. Caputo, James L. Marsh, and Merold Westphal (New York: Fordham University Press, 1992), 45–63, for a contemporary Kierkegaardian approach to the question of ethics, and one from which I have drawn much inspiration.

others. This pursuit is deemed "ethical" to the extent that the individual, and indeed society, begins to take responsibility for what it is and indeed what it can become.

At one point in *Two Ages*, Kierkegaard enunciates what he believes must be required of each individual in society if "strong communal life" is to be engendered:

> In our age the principle of association (which at best can have validity with respect to material interest) is not affirmative but negative; it is an evasion, a dissipation, an illusion, whose dialectic is as follows: as it strengthens individuals, it vitiates them; it strengthens by numbers, by sticking together, but from the ethical point of view this is a weakening. Not until the single individual has established an ethical stance despite the whole world, not until then can there be any question of genuinely uniting; otherwise it gets to be a union of people who separately are weak, a union as unbeautiful and as depraved as a child-marriage. (TA, 106)

The problems that beset the age, according to Kierkegaard, derive from a negative "principle of association" (TA, 106). This takes the form of individuals acquiring a sense of identity with one another solely on the basis of satisfying their mutual material interests. Such an alliance is not a genuine unity, since each individual member has no sense of personal identity, but acquires a knowledge of the self through participation solely within the group.[6] That is, the individual

---

[6] While I intend to argue in this work that the social critique undertaken by Kierkegaard anticipates to a considerable extent those leveled by postmodern thinkers against the "established order" or prevailing orthodoxy, there are equally illuminating discussions and analyses of the manner in which Kierkegaard paves the way for Heidegger's response to the crisis of modernity. See Hubert Dreyfus and Jane Rubin, "Appendix: Kierkegaard, Division II, and Later Heidegger," in Dreyfus, *Being-in-the-World: A Commentary on Heidegger's "Being and Time," Division 1* (Cambridge: MIT Press, 1991), 283–340; Hoberman, "Kierkegaard's *Two Ages* and Heidegger's Critique of Modernity," 223–58; Patricia J. Huntington, "Heidegger's Reading of Kierkegaard Revisited: From Ontological Abstraction to Ethical Concretion," in Matuštík and Westphal, *Kierkegaard in Post/Modernity*, 43–65. Although Huntington's article is incisive in its attempt to argue for Kierkegaard as a mediating force in contemporary ethical and political debate, it fails to appreciate the nature of the deeply postmodern strain in Kierkegaard's oeuvre. The following is an example of the type of reading this book is endeavoring to counter: "Even though Derridean deconstruction strives to counteract Heideggerian quietism by politicizing theory, this does not automatically alleviate the problems of stoicism and decisionism. Postmodern conceptions of positionality offer at best weak versions of agency that repeat the Heideggerian turn away from motivational questions (since bound

internalizes the values and ethos of the society in which he or she is embedded without subjecting these to a critical diagnosis. Thus, for Kierkegaard, this type of community is sustained by its numerical strength only, not by any form of authentic communication between subjects. Not until each subject has risked the responsibility of adopting an "ethical stance" (described in detail below) and has chosen to become *self*-aware "can there be any question of genuinely uniting" (TA, 106).

The notion of community Kierkegaard is tentatively sketching in *Two Ages* privileges the idea that we are, from the beginning, situated in a complex network of relationships that antedate any claims to autonomy that the subject might make. As such, the individual is always already embedded in a particular historical matrix. Being in the process of temporal becoming, we have no way of taking up a neutral standpoint beyond or outside time. Consequently, when Kierkegaard recommends that we take up an "ethical stance," he is not suggesting that there is some way of transcending the cultural networks that determine our beliefs and practices, as well as our truths and values. Rather, he is saying that through double reflection (passionate, subjective scrutiny) we can test the efficacy of the beliefs, truths, and values we currently privilege. In other words, breaking the spell of objective, disinterested reflection does not demand that we take a back door out of the social structures into which we have been thrown, but rather obliges us to relativize what we heretofore unquestioningly considered as truth. In critically challenging the dominant norms and codes of the community, the Kierkegaardian individual is not intent on destroying all that is held valuable and sacred; his or her objective is merely to underscore the contingent and provisional nature of such norms and codes and, in so doing, to keep them from becoming arid tools for the perpetuation of the established order.

In short, the self for Kierkegaard is not acontextual, but rather the product of multifarious contextual forces that precede it. This does not, however, suggest that the self has no means of appraising its

---

to paradigms of consciousness). The turn to positionality tends to lose the category of inwardness and its dialectical relation to the world (or to language) theorized by Kierkegaard" (62). See finally Lawrence Vogel, *The Fragile "We": Ethical Implications of Heidegger's "Being and Time"* (Evanston: Northwestern University Press, 1994).

context. The whole point of Kierkegaard's work, I contend, is to demonstrate how the self can and must challenge the modus operandi of the prevailing political order so as to render it more sensitive to those for whom it is responsible.

In the language of the pseudonym Anti-Climacus, each individual is a synthesis of the "finite" and the "infinite"; being ineluctably bound up with others in institutional life, the self is concretely or finitely situated. However, it is always possible for me to imagine both myself and my sociopolitical framework otherwise—indeed, the capacity to imagine thus is the stuff of which progress is made. That is, while Kierkegaard operates according to the assumption that we are always already subject to the constraints of the prevailing social order, we can nevertheless loosen up those constraints in accordance with the requirements of the subjective individual.

The imagination—the "infinite" component—enables us, therefore, to extend the bounds of our communal horizon; it frees us from the circumscribing grip of a tradition in need of revivification, not by permitting us to take refuge in subjective isolation, but by making it possible to envisage alternatives to the dominant political and social ethos. The objective for each individual, according to Anti-Climacus, is to strike a balance between one's finite and infinite components, that is, between identifying oneself either in terms of one's social role alone or as one who can negate his or her embeddedness by way of an imaginative flight into the seclusion of some interior space. We are always already inside sociopolitical structures, and yet we all have the propensity to take up a critical distance in relation to them, to momentarily suspend our affiliation with such frameworks so as to render them more applicable to the demands of the age. The pseudonym underscores the importance of achieving the right equilibrium between concrete existence and the "infinitizing process" of the imagination, a process equivalent to double reflection: "To become oneself is to become concrete. But to become concrete is neither to become finite nor to become infinite, for that which is to become concrete is a synthesis. Consequently, the progress of the becoming must be an infinite moving away from itself in an infinitizing of the self, and an infinite coming back to itself in the finitizing process" (SUD, 30).

Kierkegaard is forever at pains to stress that his philosophy does not privilege empty interiority, in which the subject stands alone before God to the detriment of his or her relationships with others. To subjectively establish what he calls a "God-relationship," one must, through the process of double reflection, or by means of an imaginative appropriation, see how the religious can actually affect the concrete affairs of the individual. Otherwise such matters become merely the focus of objective, disinterested reflection; becoming subjective, that is, does not demand that one divorce oneself from all social intercourse, but is rather the way in which the subject forges a genuine relationship with those things he or she formerly related to only objectively or abstractly.

Relating to something subjectively thus means concretizing the object of reflection or imagination in such a way that it becomes significant for one's *actual* life *in the world*, or in time. It does not (as I argued with reference to Levinas's reading of Kierkegaard in the introduction) lead to violent fanaticism. For subjective reflection/ imagination, on this telling, is never an end in itself, is never mere fantasy, but must always be followed by a finitizing movement:

> Take the religious sphere, for example. The God-relationship is an infinitizing, but in fantasy this infinitizing can so sweep a man off his feet that his state is simply an intoxication. To exist before God may seem unendurable to a man because he cannot come back to himself, become himself. Such a fantasized religious person would say (to characterize him by means of some lines): "That a sparrow can live is comprehensible; it does not know that it exists before God. But to know that one exists before God, and then not instantly go mad or sink into nothingness!" (SUD, 32)

The objective for one who chooses to relate to God is to juxtapose the ideals of the status quo (the state, the nation—the finite) against those embodied in the actual life of Christ (the infinite). As we shall see in chapter 5, Kierkegaard considers the social and political ideals of what he calls the "God-man" as exemplifying to the optimum degree what is required in order to keep the established order from deifying itself. Moreover, in imaginatively appropriating the ideals of justice for the lame and the leper, the poor and the marginalized, the prostitutes and the tax collectors, the subjective individual ensures that religion does not lose its liberating force, does not become yet another means of strengthening the stultifying grip that the strong have on the weak, the universal on the singular.

In selecting the God-man as one's ethical paradigm, one thus identifies the process of infinitizing the finite not as a fanatical abdication of the social world and its responsibilities, but as a potent means of identifying with the victims of the prevailing orthodoxy, or with those who have been cast to the margins for not cultivating what Anti-Climacus calls "the philistine-bourgeois mentality" (SUD, 41). Such a mentality is characterized by its narrowness of vision, its devotion to maintaining the current state of affairs, and its uncritical stance in relation to ethical, religious, and political convictions. The philistine-bourgeois has no goal beyond the possible; that is, he or she has no aspiration to reach beyond the given so as to contribute to the realization of the hopes and dreams of those who are without worldly privilege. As such, he or she is not in the business of dreaming, as Johannes de Silentio says, of "the impossible," or of what far exceeds the limited and narrow purview of the guardians of the state. Being devoid of a God-awareness, the philistine-bourgeois becomes a prisoner of necessity and finitude; he or she is "bereft of imagination," and lives, as a result, "within a certain trivial compendium of experiences as to how things go, what is possible, what usually happens." What such an individual lacks is the hope to render "possible that which surpasses the *quantum statis* [sufficient standard] of any experience" (SUD, 41).

It would not be incorrect to infer from this that the philistine-bourgeois mentality epitomizes most thoroughly the frame of mind of the present age. For this age scorns subjective interiority, or the process of engendering a balanced synthesis between the finite (one's social and political matrix) and the infinite (the imaginative appropriation of the God-man as one's ideal ethical prototype). This is so because such double reflection poses the most significant threat to the means by which the established order perpetuates itself. In challenging the state to account for the injustices perpetrated by its guardians, the subject takes the first serious steps toward a genuine and fundamental critique of his or her own society and inherited identity.

For Kierkegaard, a primary target of this critique ought to be one of the state's most subtle inventions, "the public." James Marsh defines "the public" as a "collection of inauthentic individuals living amorally as a mass or crowd and expressing itself anonymously, abstractly, passionlessly, and irresponsibly." "The public," he continues, "is the expression of a conformist society in which individuality has lost all depth and social life all ethically defensible mediation. Nothing is sacred, everything is for sale and no one is willing to take seriously anything besides her own pleasure and profit."[7] It is Kierkegaard's contention that the illusion of "the public" is sustained by way of "the press": as a medium that has widespread circulation, the press shapes popular opinion by convincing its body of readers that what it presents to them is an impartial summary of the facts. The consequence of this process is that those who defer to the press in order to become "informed" end up conflating journalistic opinion with truth and fact. The dangers here are manifold, in that when individuals internalize such unfounded and uncorroborated "opinion" (*doxa*), they fail to cultivate the critical capacity to submit to rigorous scrutiny the objective codes that have hitherto shaped the prevailing beliefs and values.[8] Consequently, Kierkegaard concludes, community life and social interaction in the present age have been reduced to the level of mediocre and meaningless externality:

> Only when there is no strong communal life to give substance to the concretion will the press create this abstraction "the public," made up of unsubstantial individuals who are never united or never can be united in the simultaneity of any situation or organization and yet are claimed to be a whole. The public is a corps, outnumbering all the people together, but this corps can never be called up for inspection; indeed, it cannot even have so much as a single representative, because it is an abstraction. (TA, 91)

With this perspicacious observation, Kierkegaard anticipates the subsequent indictment of "the press" and "public opinion" developed in the later work of Jacques Derrida. As the latter half of this book is devoted to forging greater links between these two thinkers at an ethical and political level, I will take a brief excursus through the latter's denunciation of certain insidious types of journalistic endeavor. In so doing, the strong social impulse of Kierkegaard's work will come even more sharply into focus.

In like manner to Kierkegaard, Derrida describes "public opinion"

---

[7] Marsh, "Kierkegaard and Critical Theory," 209.

[8] See Jacques Derrida, "Call It a Day for Democracy," in *The Other Heading: Reflections on Today's Europe*, trans. Pascale-Anne Brault and Michael B. Naas (Bloomington: Indiana University Press, 1992), 84.

as "the silhouette of a phantom";[9] that is, "public opinion" is not,
as it should be, "the forum for a permanent and transparent discussion" that "would be opposed to non-democratic powers, but also to
its own political representation."[10] Rather, public opinion is nothing
less than "the ubiquity of a specter" in that "the *daily* rhythm essential to it presupposes the widespread distribution of something like
a *newspaper*, a *daily*."[11] According to Derrida, the press, or the daily,
is supposed to act as the medium through which we are informed.
The truth of the matter is, however, that the press is never neutral
with regard to what it considers worthy of publication; because
media moguls control what is reported in their dailies, there is inevitably a censoring of the stories of the day. If a particular news item
has the potential to offend the newspaper owner or editor, or indeed
his or her patrons and sponsors, not to mention those politicians
who give either overt or covert support to the daily, then the facts
will be tampered with until such time as the story becomes a crude
imitation of its former self. Consequently, the public is fed, under
the guise of undistorted fact, opinions and, on occasion, lies.

It is Derrida's conviction that the greatest threat to democracy is
this tendency to "filter" or "screen" public opinion, for the " 'freedom of the press' is democracy's most precious good."[12] The press,
that is, has long since ceased to represent actuality, but is now in the
business of producing what he terms "artifactuality": "These days,
anyone who wants to think their time, especially if they want to talk
about it too, is bound to pay heed to a public space, and therefore
to a political present which is constantly changing in form and content as a result of the tele-technology of what is confusedly called
news, information or communication."[13] The public space, in which
all information is collected, is artificial to the extent that it is controlled by forces—technological, political, and economic—that ultimately determine what is and is not newsworthy. On this reading,
actuality is "actively produced; it is sorted, invested and performa-

---

[9] Derrida, "Call It a Day for Democracy," 84. The connection between Kierkegaard's indictment of the press and Derrida's equally sardonic and stinging commentary on the pernicious effects of the dailies has, to my knowledge, received no
critical attention to date.

[10] Ibid., 85.

[11] Ibid., 87–88.

[12] Ibid., 98.

[13] "The Deconstruction of Actuality: An Interview with Jacques Derrida," *Radical
Philosophy* 68 (Autumn 1994): 28.

tively interpreted by a range of hierarchising and selective procedures—*factitious* or *artificial* procedures which are always
subservient to various powers and interests of which their 'subjects'
and agents (producers and consumers of actuality, always interpret-
ers, and in some cases 'philosophers' too), are never sufficiently
aware."[14] Reality thus becomes somewhat of a "fiction" when it is
filtered through the "public space."

Now, just as Kierkegaard endeavors to stimulate critical scrutiny
of the established order (one's given actuality) and the means by
which it maintains itself (the public, press, and objective channels
of all varieties), Derrida is also sensitive to the fact that what is required is a type of "double reflection," or what he calls "vigilant
counter-interpretation"; the latter demands a "work of resistance"
that obliges us "to find out how news is made, and by whom: the
daily papers, the weeklies, and the TV news as well."[15] Through the
acquisition of such information, one is empowered to "strengthen
knowledge, truth and the cause of future democracy."[16] It is only
when one becomes imprisoned by artifactuality—to "images, simul-
acra, and delusions"—that one loses one's sense of critical perspective, which, in turn, desensitizes one to the actuality of events. The
danger here is that for such an individual the image may become so
conflated with reality that "a denial of events—even violence, suffering, war and death—is said to be constructed and fictive, and constituted by and for the media."[17]

In the spirit of Kierkegaard, Derrida thus admonishes the subject
to adopt a critical standpoint in relation to one's tradition or one's
sociolinguistic matrix; one must resist, as far as possible, the insidious forces that the prevailing orthodoxy manipulates and harnesses
in an effort to sustain itself. That is, relating critically to the press,
or to that which fantastically engineers public opinion, is the best
way—according to both Kierkegaard and Derrida—to effect positive
change in the public sphere. For in breaking the spell of public opinion in this way, individuals impede the progress of the press, that
spurious entity which thrives on "consuming everything in its path,
turning everything into grist for its mill, [and] making everyone a

---

[14] Ibid.
[15] Ibid.
[16] Ibid., 29.
[17] Ibid.

celebrity for fifteen minutes."[18] Through such "work of resistance," one imaginatively appropriates what Derrida calls, again following Kierkegaard, the "singularity of the event," or that in the event which cannot be artifactualized by the public, qua universal order. Such "vigilant counter-interpretation" or "double reflection" is what allows one to keep a watchful eye on singularity at the expense of universality, on what lies beyond the realm of "actuality" in a non-public time and space.

Through their strikingly similar appraisals of the press and public opinion, both Kierkegaard and Derrida are striving to encourage conscientious and responsible critiques of prevailing political structures with the aim of sensitizing us to what lies beyond the virtual space of the public. For both thinkers, the essential ingredient in any critique of this kind—what will alert the subject to the fact that the social space is in fact governed and determined by a ubiquitous and spurious specter—is an awareness of those whose very singularity prevents them from being artifactualized. I am, of course, referring here to victims of all types, not least to those who have been victimized by the exploitative tendencies of those who control "actuality," or those who make the actual artifactual. In other words, the objective of critical vigilance and resistance is not simply to appraise the dominant codes governing reality, but more importantly, to affirm those whose welfare is not guaranteed by such codes. This is why counter-interpretation of the kind advocated by both Kierkegaard and Derrida should never be an end in itself, but should open us "to otherness, to the priceless dignity of otherness, that is to say to justice."[19]

The objection that will no doubt be raised to this contention is that while Derrida might make much of "justice" as being that which "refuses to yield to deconstruction," qua vigilant counter-interpretation, Kierkegaard has no such conception. The most effective way to rebut such a charge is simply to highlight once more the fact that while Kierkegaard does not use the word "justice," his notion of "the religious" approximates in no small measure to the intent of this pivotable Derridean category. For on Kierkegaard's telling, to strike the right synthesis between the finite and the infi-

---

[18] Marsh, "Kierkegaard and Critical Theory," 209.
[19] "The Deconstruction of Actuality," 36.

nite requires that one adopt as one's unconditioned ethical goal and criterion the Christ-figure. This is not simply a matter of admiring the God-man from afar, but of striving to imitate him and his life to the best of one's ability through the process of imaginative appropriation. For Kierkegaard, therefore, God is not a *what,* or the subject of disinterested objective analysis; God is, rather, a *how,* or a practical and active engagement with others in the world. Put otherwise, to imitate Christ requires me to stand contemporaneously with him, to walk in his sandals, and to take a stand against the powers that be. It obliges us to interpret the life of the God-man, not as a propaedeutic to an "afterlife," but as a means of enacting ethical and social reform in the here and now. Because no existing being has ever had access to God in his glory, since each one is temporally bound, the only way I may truly appropriate this figure as ethical exemplar is to do as the God-man did *in time.* Anti-Climacus tells his reader that all we have to go on when attempting to do so is the word of "the abased one," the figure who rallied to the cause of all those who labor and are burdened. To infinitize the finite for Kierkegaard thus amounts to envisioning a time when those who are marked by their exclusion are liberated from the strictures of outmoded customs and laws, when social justice will be available for the lepers and the lame and not just for those who have been dealt a good hand by the system. Hence, those who opt to take the side of the "abased one" cannot make "a compromise with this world"—cannot, that is, come to some arrangement with the orthodox powers. If such a thing were to happen Christianity would simply be abolished, for on Kierkegaard's telling, Christianity is always on the lookout for those who have not triumphed, and as such it is always a militant force in the midst of political and religious complacency. Put simply, as long as injustice endures there will be a need for critical resistance and for the type of militancy favored by the God-man. This is why Anti-Climacus underscores the fact that "the Church militant is related, feels itself drawn, to Christ in his lowliness" (PC, 209); while "Christendom *is,* is not becoming," the "Church militant," on the other hand, "is in the process of becoming," or is acutely cognizant that the time of those whom Christ in his lowliness championed "is certainly a kingdom *in* this world, but not *of* this world" (PC, 211; my emphasis).

In short, Kierkegaard does not recommend that we recoil from practical responsibility in an effort to behold God *in abstracto;* rather, he urges that through the imaginative appropriation of the God-man in his lowliness we can keep the state sensitive to its own shortcomings by focusing attention on those who are down and out. Howard Johnson convincingly articulates what is at issue:

> Kierkegaard is convinced that if only each human being could be helped to become conscious of himself as standing "before God," [then] [i]nstead of anonymous, irresponsible masses, there would be persons personally related to the personal God, a God of justice and love who demands the transformation of society and provides re-sources for its renewal. Such people . . . would become critical and constructive citizens of the state, not fanatical devotees of the State.[20]

What is required as a means of generating a genuine ethics of re-sponsibility is that "every generation must begin from the beginning with Christ and then set forth his life as the paradigm" (PC, 107). This in turn guarantees that the given actuality will always be treated with a certain degree of circumspection, that its sovereign claims will be challenged on the basis of its having caused unjustifiable inequity.

If what I have been arguing thus far is correct, then I do not con-sider it too great a leap to go one step further and say that the type of God that Kierkegaard enjoins his reader to imitate is one that approximates in no small measure the God of liberation theology and, indeed, the picture of the "historical Jesus" drawn by many latter-day Jesus scholars, such as John Dominic Crossan. The reason why I do not consider such a comparison misguided is simply that Kierkegaard believes that since as we are ineluctably situated in time, the only access we have to Christ is through his abasement. To con-sider him as ethical goal and exemplar requires that we focus on the actual life of the individual. It is enough for Kierkegaard that we have such a life, for through it we can bring to fruition a form of social change that is perennially demanded.

Following Crossan, and indeed John Caputo, who has made much of Crossan's insights, I want to claim that when Kierkegaard, through the pen of Anti-Climacus, says that the type of kingdom that those who constitute the Church militant dream of "is certainly a kingdom in this world, but not of this world," he presages what Crossan argues

[20] Howard A. Johnson, "Kierkegaard and Politics," in *A Kierkegaard Critique*, ed. Howard A. Johnson and Niels Thulstrup (New York: Harper, 1962), 80.

in one of his most significant chapters of the groundbreaking *Jesus: A Revolutionary Biography,* entitled "A Kingdom of Nuisances and Nobodies."[21] For Crossan, the Kingdom of God is not a "place" but a "process"; it is "what the world would be if God were directly and immediately in charge."[22] One paragraph that succinctly encapsulates the essence of Crossan's approach, and one that I believe illuminates a rich comparison between his interpretation of the Christ-figure and that which is furnished by Kierkegaard, takes the following form:

> An alternative to the future or apocalyptic Kingdom is the present or sapiential vision. The term *sapiential* underlines the necessity of wisdom—*sapientia* in Latin—for discerning how, here and now in this world, one can so live that God's power, rule, and dominion are evidently present to all observers. One enters the kingdom by wisdom or goodness, by virtue, justice, or freedom. It is a style of life for now rather than a hope of life for the future. This is therefore an ethical kingdom. . . . Its ethics could, for instance, challenge contemporary morality to its depths.[23]

For both Kierkegaard and Crossan, the Jesus-figure does not signal the immanent coming of the Kingdom; rather, the Kingdom for these individuals is a process, something that—as long as there is social inequality—has always to be realized. This is why Kierkegaard is intent on underlining the fact that the Church militant is unremittingly "in the process of becoming" (PC, 211). This is not to suggest, however, that the Kingdom is not of this world, that it will be ours only after we have cast off this mortal coil. What it does imply, however, is that the Kingdom of God comes to fruition through the exercise of wisdom, a striving after justice, and the realization of freedom. The Kingdom, in other words, is ours for the taking. Analogously, Kierkegaard says that the Church militant "endures by struggling"—endures, that is, by way of dedicated and committed social praxis, the objective of which is to establish what Crossan calls "radical egalitarianism."

So, on my reading, the object of the teleological suspension of the

---

[21] John Dominic Crossan, *Jesus: A Revolutionary Biography* (San Francisco: Harper, 1994), 54–74.
[22] Ibid., 55.
[23] Ibid., 56.

ethical (qua *Sittlichkeit*), as described by Kierkegaard, is to promote a proto-ethics of the Kingdom, one that, to invoke the words of Crossan once more, could "challenge contemporary morality to its depths." If looked at from this perspective, Kierkegaard's conception of "the religious" and Derrida's notion of justice have more than a little in common in that both lift the burden of the universal order so as to affirm "the priceless dignity of others." In so doing, each hopes to affect "human beings at their very roots, activating their hope principle and making them dream of the kingdom, which is not an entirely different world but this world completely new and renewed."[24]

CONCLUSION

I conclude this chapter by relating the above analysis to Kierke-gaard's central thesis in *Two Ages*. I have shown how Kierkegaard believes that those who populate the leveled age of reflection associate with each other merely at the level of "meaningless externality." In such a society—and here Kierkegaard suggests that all societies endemically experience these problems—there is scant attention paid to ethical truth as defined above; subjects simply regulate their lives according to ritualized norms and empty duty. As such, inter-personal relations take the form of "a fossilized formalism which, by having lost the originality of the ethical, has become a dessicated ruin, a narrow-hearted custom and practice" (TA, 65). If an age is without subjective passion, "it has no assets of feeling in the erotic, no assets of enthusiasm and inwardness in politics and religion, no assets of domesticity, piety, and appreciation in daily life and social life" (TA, 74). Consequently, Kierkegaard concludes, individuals act merely according to rules, programs, laws, and habits without ever testing the veracity of these structures that regulate their lives in the social milieu.

In a significant passage from *Two Ages*, Kierkegaard underscores the dialectical basis of what he believes genuine social behavior con-sists of:

---

[24] Leonard Boff, *Jesus Christ, Liberator: A Critical Christology for Our Time* (Mar-yknoll, N.Y.: Orbis, 1978), 79.

> Purely dialectically the relations are as follows, and let us think them through dialectically without considering any specific age. When individuals (each one individually) are essentially and passionately related to an idea and together are essentially related to the same idea, the relation is optimal and normative. Individually the relation separates them (each one has himself for himself), and ideally it unites them. Where there is essential inwardness, there is a decent modesty between man and man that prevents crude aggressiveness; in the relation of unanimity to the idea there is the elevation that again in consideration of the whole forgets the accidentality of details. Thus the individuals never come too close to each other in the herd sense, simply because they are united on the basis of an ideal distance. (TA, 62–63)

The main distinction between the present age and the type of community Kierkegaard is proposing is that in the former, "individuals relate to an idea merely *en masse*," or "without the individual separation of inwardness" (TA, 63); in the latter, however, relationships are founded upon *each* individual's relation to "an idea." Merold Westphal offers this explanation of Kierkegaard's "idea":

> An initial indication of what he means by the idea can be found by recalling an oft-quoted passage from the Gilleleie journal of 1835: "the crucial thing is to find a truth which is truth *for me,* to find *the idea for which I am willing to live and die.* . . . What is truth but to live for an idea?" (JP, 5: 5100). The animal lives out of instinct; man, as spirit, can live for an idea. The animal dies out of necessity; man, as spirit, can give his life because there is something worth dying for. To live, not out of habit but because one knows why life is worth living, and to die, not out of necessity, but because one values something more than life itself—that is to be related to the idea. The idea is a truth that claims me for its own in life and in death and, in claiming me, gives meaning to both life and death.[25]

The "idea" being referred to here is, of course, that of "God" or the "divine." Genuine community life is founded upon each individual's passionate relationship to the God-man who brings both speculative reason and metaphysics to grief. As I have been arguing, to relate to such an idea as the goal of one's life, and then to relate to others with the same degree of ethical intensity and passion, is the means by which relations become "optimal and normative." This is so be-

---

[25] Westphal, "Kierkegaard's Sociology," 137.

cause through the relationship to the idea, or through the cultivation of inwardness and double reflection, individuals no longer come together on the basis of their common affiliation to the state or the established order alone, but they also unite "on the basis of an ideal distance." As such, "the harmony of the spheres is the unity of each planet relating to itself and to the whole" (TA, 63). The God-man, being one who challenged the established order in the name of the nuisances and nobodies, in the name of justice and radical egalitarianism, is the ideal to be imaginatively appropriated if "the originality of the ethical" is to be prevented from becoming "a dessicated ruin" and "a narrow-hearted custom and practice" (TA, 63).

In the remainder of this book I will show how the individual comes to self-knowledge on the basis of relating to the idea, and consequently how this inward relationship (imitation of the unconditioned ethical prototype) can form the basis of genuinely free and just social relations.[26] I will leave the last word in this chapter, however, to Merold Westphal, who succinctly and incisively explains why such a Kierkegaardian ethics of responsibility is as pertinent and as relevant for us today as it was for those in nineteenth-century Denmark:

> The society that becomes its own point of reference absolutizes itself. . . . Within this framework there is the ethics of socialization by which the individual learns to subordinate instinct and private interest to social requirements. But Eichmann and Mengele were good Germans in this sense, and apartheid is what the age demands for Afrikaners. This is why Johannes Climacus says the system has no ethics. . . . Perhaps there will be those who dismiss him and Kierkegaard, who stands behind him, as irrationalists because they are insufficiently reverent toward the amoral rationality and inoffensive piety that modernity calls Reason. We would do well to remember that Socrates and the early Christians were accused of atheism because they did not worship at the shrines of the self-absolutizing cultures in which they lived.[27]

---

[26] In chapter 6 I will show how central the work of Kierkegaard is for those who have committed themselves to the development of a postmodern ethic.

[27] Westphal, *Kierkegaard's Critique*, 125.

2

The Centrality of Hegel

IN THIS CHAPTER I will pave the way for a more sustained development of the contentions put forward in chapter 1 by outlining the
central distinctions separating the Kierkegaardian from the Hegelian
paradigm. In so doing, I will argue that Kierkegaard's notion of an
ethics of responsibility can make greater sense if one understands it
primarily as a reaction to the Hegelian model of ethical life (*Sittlichkeit*).[1] This, of course, is not to suggest that Kierkegaard is totally
opposed to the Hegelian ideal of social and ethical becoming; it is
clear from the dialectical model of consciousness[2] he employs that

---

[1] For a thorough and engaging account of Kierkegaard's relationship to Danish
Hegelianism, see Kirmmse, *Kierkegaard in Golden Age Denmark*, "Section II: Politics
and Religion in 'Golden Age' Culture," 77–247. For a more philosophical approach
to this question, see both Gregor Malantschuk, *Kierkegaard's Thought*, trans. Howard V. Hong and Edna Hong (Princeton: Princeton University Press, 1971), and
Niels Thulstrup, *Kierkegaard's Relationship to Hegel*, trans. George L. Stengeren
(Princeton: Princeton University Press, 1980). Mark Taylor's early work is indispens-
able for an illuminating and convincing textual juxtaposition of the work of these
two thinkers; see especially *Journeys to Selfhood* and *Kierkegaard's Pseudonymous
Authorship: A Study of Time and the Self* (Princeton: Princeton University Press,
1975). For the first sustained study on the Hegel-Kierkegaard debate in English, and
one that had a profound influence on the formation of Taylor's thought, see Stephen Crites, *In the Twilight of Christendom: Hegel vs. Kierkegaard on Faith and
History* (Chambersburg, Pa.: American Academy of Religion, 1972). For a discussion
not unrelated to my own in this chapter, consult Robert L. Perkins, "Kierkegaard
and Hegel: The Dialectical Structure of Kierkegaard's Ethical Thought" (Ph.D.
diss., Indiana University, 1965). For more recent critical appraisals see Alastair Hannay, *Kierkegaard* (London: Routledge, 1991), 19–53, and Westphal, *Kierkegaard's
Critique*, 61–84. The relevance of the Kierkegaard-Hegel relationship to contemporary Continental ethical issues is discussed in John D. Caputo, *Against Ethics: Contributions to a Poetics of Obligation with Constant Reference to Deconstruction*
(Bloomington: Indiana University Press, 1993), 1–19, and Mark C. Taylor, *Altarity*
(Chicago: Chicago University Press, 1987).

[2] It is not within my ambit here to analyze in detail the precise nature of the
Kierkegaardian phases of consciousness. For exemplary analyses of this type see
Stephen N. Dunning, *Kierkegaard's Dialectic of Inwardness* (Princeton: Princeton
University Press, 1985); George B. Connell, *To Be One Thing: Personal Unity in
Kierkegaard's Thought* (Macon: Mercer University Press, 1985); John W. Elrod,
Being and Existence in Kierkegaard's Pseudonymous Authorship (Princeton:

the basic structure of Hegelian thought exerted a heavy influence. What I will argue, however, is that Kierkegaard rejects the Hegelian assumption that to be ethical and responsible demands merely fulfilling one's civic obligations as prescribed by the established order or the state; that is, in privileging the God-man as unconditioned ethical goal and criterion, Kierkegaard endeavors to resist the state's autodeification—which, he believes, Hegelianism propagates at the expense of singularity and responsibility.

HEGEL'S THEORY OF IDENTITY

Hegel's logic is founded on a radical reformulation of the most fundamental principles of conventional logical reflection. His theory sought to challenge the traditional presuppositions of a logic whose primary principle was that of noncontradiction. Such abstract formulations could never, he claimed, achieve a wholly rational understanding of the actual. In reaction, Hegel endeavored to emphasize how experience dialectically unfolds according to a speculative logic that challenges the principle of noncontradiction. For the speculative logician, it is necessary to rethink the ideas of identity and difference, with the objective of elucidating the contradictions that inhere in experience, while concomitantly showing how such contradictions can be rationally explained. Otherwise expressed, Hegel argued against the conviction that identity and difference were mutually oppositional in order to develop his conviction that there is an "internal relation between identity and difference in such a way that each term passes into the other."[3] In so doing, Hegel gives expression to the famous formulation upon which his entire logic depends: identity amid difference.

At its most basic, the idea of identity amid difference suggests that the opposition that seemingly emerges between two mutually

---

Princeton University Press, 1975); Adi Shmuëli, *Kierkegaard and Consciousness*, trans. N. Handelman (Princeton: Princeton University Press, 1971); M. C. Taylor, *Kierkegaard's Pseudonymous Authorship* and *Journeys to Selfhood*; Sylvia Walsh, *Living Poetically: Kierkegaard's Existential Ethics* (University Park: Pennsylvania State University Press, 1994); and Josiah Thompson, *The Lonely Labyrinth: Kierkegaard's Pseudonymous Works* (Carbondale: Southern Illinois University Press, 1967).

[3] M. C. Taylor, *Journeys to Selfhood*, 145.

exclusive entities can be surmounted and overcome in a positive third that is constituted through the dialectical mediation of both. In order to acquire a more concrete understanding of what is at issue here, it is necessary to briefly sketch the main contours of Hegel's argument in his *Science of Logic*.

In the *Science of Logic*, Hegel became acutely aware that identity is not exclusive of difference; that is, for identity to be identity, or for identity to be identified as selfsameness, it must be juxtaposed with its opposite, difference. In other words, identity can only be recognized *as such* when related to its other. Thus, identity and difference can only be what they are by virtue of being in relation to one another. We could say that identity and difference are wholly dependent upon one another; as identity is identity by being in opposition to difference, so too difference is difference by being in opposition to identity. The conclusion Hegel draws from this quite radical assumption is that because identity requires difference in order to be identity, difference constitutes identity's identity. Difference, that is, rather than being other to identity, is somewhat the same. To be in relation to the other is to be in relation to oneself, for without the other one could not identify oneself *as* oneself. As Hegel remarks, "identity, therefore, is *in its own self* absolute non-identity."[4] In pursuing this a step further, Hegel says that it is the notion of "the other" or of "otherness" that sustains identity: identity, that is, is preserved in and by the relationship to the other. However, if identity is to be maintained, the other must constantly be negated. Another way of expressing this is to say that if "I" am to affirm that "I" am this particular individual, "I" can only do so by saying what "I" am not. The other's nonbeing is the condition for my being. This is not to suggest that the relation between the two terms is negated or nullified. For although identity requires that the other be negated, the very act of negation is a positive affirmation of the other; the other, we can say, must *be* if it is to become the other of identity. Identity, we may conclude, is relational: the self requires its other (difference) if it is to come to a realization of *who* it is. As Mark C. Taylor remarks:

> One of the guiding principles of Hegel's system is that negativity is the structure of constitutive relationality. Determinate identity emerges

---

[4] G. W. F. Hegel, *Science of Logic*, trans. A. V. Miller (New York: Humanities Press, 1969), 413.

through a process of double negation in which opposites become themselves through relation to one another. Affirmation and negation are inseparable. Instead of "to be or not to be," the sum of the matter for Hegel is to be *and* not to be, for to be is not to be, and not to be is to be. Hegel agrees with Jacob Böhme's definition of the speculative task as the effort "to grasp the no in the yes and the yes in the no."[5]

Thus stated, it is clear that the term "abstract identity" is oxymoronic, for in determining that something is identical to itself one is implicitly marking it off from difference. One is affirming in this instance that identity is not its other, or is different from difference. In denying difference, therefore, the exponents of abstract identity, contrary to their expressed findings, affirm difference negatively.

What can be concluded from all the above is that self-consciousness for Hegel is ineluctably bound up with consciousness of the other; for the self to move from the most immediate stage of conscious development through to full self-certainty, it must continually do battle with its other. Consequently, the self is wholly relational.

The broader ramifications of these theoretical reflections can be observed by turning our attention to Hegel's early formulation of his theory of self-identity in the *Phenomenology of Spirit* (1807). In this context, the young Hegel sought to locate the ideal for an emerging consciousness, or as he more idiomatically called it, "Spirit" (*Geist*). His belief amounted to the following: only after *Geist* has extricated itself from the sphere of sense-immediacy and has oriented itself philosophically, which is its highest task and actuality, could it be said to have achieved its teleological aim. For those who seek "mere edification" rather than scientific truth, such a moment is unlikely to become manifest: "Whoever seeks mere edification, and whoever wants to shroud in a mist the manifold variety of his earthly existence and of thought, in order to pursue the indeterminate enjoyment of this indeterminate divinity, may look where he likes to find all this. He will find ample opportunity to dream up something for himself. But philosophy must beware of the wish to be edifying."[6] In contrast, *Geist* seeks to reveal a determinate divinity, one that is not the object of blind faith or pagan ritual, but a living and true God

---

[5] M. C. Taylor, *Journeys to Selfhood*, 149.

[6] G. W. F. Hegel, *Phenomenology of Spirit*, trans. A. V. Miller (Oxford: Oxford University Press, 1977), 5–6.

with whom we can positively identify. The aim of *Geist* or consciousness, therefore, is to move from one sphere of understanding (in
contemporary parlance, a particular conceptual framework) to the
next, after which the truths held in the former sphere, while containing the seed for development, yield to a more positive notion of the
essence of truth *as such:*

> When we wish to see an oak with its massive trunk and spreading
> branches and foliage, we are not content to be shown an acorn instead.
> So too, science, the crown of a world of spirit, is not complete in its
> beginnings. The onset of the new spirit is the product of a widespread
> upheaval in various forms of culture, the prize at the end of a compli-
> cated, tortuous path and of just as variegated and strenuous an effort.
> It is the whole which, having traversed its content in time and space,
> has returned into itself, and is the resultant simple *Notion* of the
> whole.[7]

This, of course, is not to suggest that the world that once showed up
for emerging consciousness is negated entirely once this higher level
of truth comes into being. For science (at least its Hegelian variant)
must hold in place all previous forms of consciousness if it is to come
to an absolute and infinite understanding. Thus, for Hegel, "the
wealth of previous experience is still present to consciousness in
memory." Self-becoming, on this account, implies that one can only
become what one is essentially by retaining the past; that is, for the
truth of *Geist* to be revealed, all moments of consciousness must be
retained.

Hegel's theory of substance as subject bears the previous remarks
out. Unlike substantialistic models of the Spinozistic variety, in which
God can be equated with the one, true substance, Hegel espouses a
theory of "living substance" or "subject." This should not be confused
with any form of isolated subjectivity that attempts to divorce itself
from objectivity. For Hegel, such distinctions are inadequate for a
genuine theory of knowledge in that for knowledge to occur one must
presuppose that subject and object are related dialectically, or that
the identity of the subject depends on its association with, or relation
to, objectivity. "Subject," in the Hegelian lexicon, can be defined as a
movement in which the identity of the self (conceived as being selfsame by alienated consciousness) comes to be through its relationship
with the other, or what is different to selfsameness. For self to be

---

[7] Ibid., 7.

affirmed it needs to be recognized by the other (the different) as a self, and it also needs to recognize the other (difference) in itself. For without this "self-othering," a positive notion of the self—one that aspires to think philosophically and achieve as universal a perspective as is allowed—is impossible to conceive. Being intrinsically social due to its relational structure, the self, as subject, comes to be what it is essentially by jettisoning the notion of pure selfsameness in favor of a dialectical account which specifies that identity is conceived in and through the mediation of identity and difference:

> The living Substance is being which is in truth *Subject*, or, what is the same, is in truth actual only insofar as it is the movement of positing itself, or is the mediation of its self-othering with itself. This Substance is, as Subject, pure, *simple negativity*, and is for this very reason the bifurcation of the simple; it is the doubling which sets up opposition, and then again the negation of this indifferent diversity and of its antithesis [the immediate simplicity]. Only this self-*restoring* sameness, or this reflection in otherness within itself—not an *original* or *immediate* unity as such—is the True. It is the process of its own becoming, the circle that presupposes its end as its goal, having its end also as its beginning; and only by being worked out to its end, is it actual.[8]

Because the self is intrinsically relational, it becomes what it is through the other; that is, in order for the self to positively affirm itself, it must recollect (**Erinnerung, relever**) itself, or retrieve itself from the dialectical exchange it has with its other. Stated in Kojévian,[9] or indeed Lacanian,[10] terms, the self *desires* the affirmation of

---

[8] Ibid., 10.

[9] See Alexandre Kojève, *Introduction to the Reading of Hegel: Lectures on the "Phenomenology of Spirit,"* trans. James H. Nichols, Jr. (Ithaca: Cornell University Press, 1969), 7, where the author remarks: "Man's humanity 'comes to light' only in risking his life to satisfy his human desire—that is, his Desire directed toward another Desire. Now, to desire a Desire is to want to substitute oneself for the value desired by this Desire. For without this substitution, one would desire the value, the desired object, and not the Desire itself. Therefore, to desire the Desire of another is in the final analysis to desire that the value that I am or that I 'represent' be the value desired by the other: I want him to 'recognize' my value as his Value. I want him to "recognize" me as an autonomous value. In other words, all human, anthropogenetic Desire—the Desire that generates Self-Consciousness, the human reality—is, finally, a function of the desire for 'recognition.'" For a related study substantially influenced by Kojève's analysis, see Mark C. Taylor, *Deconstructing Theology* (New York: Crossroads, 1982).

[10] Jacques Lacan, *Four Fundamental Concepts of Psycho-Analysis*, trans. Alan Sheridan (New York: Penguin, 1977). For more on the Lacan-Hegel connection, see Jo-

the other. In order to achieve this, it must acquire recognition from the other as a self. Lacan would say, while drawing on the principle of identity amid difference, that the self desires the desire of the other. More simply put, the self desires that the other, through the process of mediation, be negated or sublated into a higher union. Hegel's notion of *Erinnerung* is founded on the premise that being in relation to the other does not signal a loss of self. The other, to the contrary, is a necessity for the realization of selfhood. Division, according to this scheme, is resolved ultimately in coming back to oneself after the opposition, which in immediacy separated the self from the other, is negated. To borrow from the language of Christianity (for it is in these terms that Hegel poses his own questions and reflections): out of loss or death (of self to the other) comes life (*Geist*). The loss of autonomy that results from the self's having to acknowledge the other as constitutive of one's identity is, for Hegel, a long-term gain. For, having surrendered oneself to the other through a "bifurcation of the simple . . . which sets up opposition," the self reappropriates itself through the process of what Hegel calls "this self-*restoring* sameness." The self, that is, presupposes that reappropriation results from disappropriation, that the beginning is presupposed in the end, and the end in the beginning:

> The result is the same as the beginning, only because the *beginning* is the *purpose*; in other words, the actual is the same as its Notion only because the immediate as purpose, contains the self or pure actuality within itself. The realized purpose, or the existent actuality, is movement and unfolded becoming; but it is just this unrest that is the self; and the self is like that immediacy and simplicity of the beginning because it is the result, that which has returned into itself, the latter being similarly just the self. And the self is the sameness and simplicity that relates itself to itself.[11]

That is, immediacy, or the immediacy of consciousness, contains within itself the potential to realize absolute self-consciousness through the process of dialectical unfolding or becoming.

---

seph Smith and William Kerrigan, eds., *Interpreting Lacan* (New Haven: Yale University Press, 1983); Mark C. Taylor, "Real," in *Altarity*, 83–115, and "Refusal of the Bar" in *Lacan and Theological Discourse*, ed. Edith Wyschogrod, David Crownfield, and Carl A. Raschke (Albany: SUNY Press, 1989), 39–59.
    [11] Hegel, *Phenomenology of Spirit*, 12.

SOCIAL ETHICS (*SITTLICHKEIT*)

In rejecting the substance model of the self, Hegel advances a theory of identity that endorses the belief that the self is structured dynamically and dialectically.[12] He rejects the philosophy of the *cogito*, what Paul Ricoeur entitles *idem* identity, or that hierarchy which insists that "permanence in time constitutes the highest order," in favor of *ipse* identity, or that form which "implies no assertion concerning some unchanging core of the personality."[13] Hegel explains: "Self-consciousness is faced by another self-consciousness; it has come out of itself. This has a twofold significance: first, it has lost itself, for it finds itself as another being; secondly, in doing so it has superseded the other, for it does not see the other as an essential being, but in the other sees its own self."[14] Such is what Hegel calls the operation of "recognition." In this description, Hegel is attempting to determine how an individual can become identified as an integrated self in and through the acknowledgment of other such selves. In so doing, he is proffering an analysis of the origins and features of civil society. A person becomes self-conscious, according to Hegel, by risking death; that is, the person strives to become a fully integrated self by looking to others for recognition as someone who, by virtue of his or her willingness to relate, is deserving of liberty and freedom. Thus, Hegel's self is an " 'I' that is 'We' and 'We' that is 'I.' "[15] It is only as a consequence of such dialectical mediation and integration that "truth" and "freedom" can be realized.

It may be assumed at this juncture that for Hegel, becoming self-conscious involves dialectically overcoming the opposition of abstract objectivity by relating oneself to oneself as a member of community or society; otherwise stated, self-consciousness involves the recognition of oneself as a citizen through the acknowledgment of

---

[12] For some excellent studies on Hegel's ethical thought, see Perkins, "Kierkegaard and Hegel"; Charles Taylor, *Hegel and Modern Society* (Cambridge: Cambridge University Press, 1979); Allen W. Wood, *Hegel's Ethical Thought* (Cambridge: Cambridge University Press, 1990), and "Hegel's Ethics," in *The Cambridge Companion to Hegel*, ed. Frederick C. Beiser (Cambridge: Cambridge University Press, 1993), 211–33.

[13] Paul Ricoeur, *Oneself as Another*, trans. Kathleen Blamey (Chicago: University of Chicago Press, 1992), 2.

[14] Hegel, *Phenomenology of Spirit*, 111.

[15] Ibid., 110.

this fact by fellow citizens. When Hegel says that freedom results from this process, he is suggesting that through recognition and acknowledgment the individual acquires independence from the state of pure immediacy, a state in which the individual has only the "capacity for rights," without having any "formal rights." Becoming self-conscious is thus the means by which the individual obtains civic rights, which is what it means to be free.

Having established that freedom is consequent upon self-conscious beings recognizing themselves "as mutually recognizing each other,"[16] Hegel enunciates what he considers the nature of ethical life. For him, the "ethical life is the concept of freedom developed into the existing world and the nature of self-consciousness."[17] This suggests that in order to be ethical, subjective individuals must uphold the "ethical order," or the institutions of the state, for it is only in and through this objective order that selves can relate to one another harmoniously as subjects under the law. That is, what individuals identify themselves to be, by virtue of having been acknowledged in this role by fellow citizens, can be sanctioned only within the larger framework of state relations. From this Hegel concludes that "the ethical order is freedom or the absolute will as what is objective, a circle of necessity whose moments are the ethical powers which regulate the life of individuals. To these powers individuals are related as accidents to substance, and it is in individuals that these powers are represented, have the shape of appearance, and become actualized."[18]

One could plausibly argue that Kierkegaard, in his analysis of the transition the individual makes from the aesthetic to the ethical sphere of existence, follows Hegel's assessment of the developmental passage from the immediate to the more ethically informed phase of consciousness (**Geist**). Kierkegaard, however, fundamentally diverges from Hegel at the point where the latter argues that the laws and powers of the ethical order—that objective paradigm which regulates the lives of individuals—constitute "an absolute authority and power infinitely more firmly established than the being of nature." For on this account, the particular individual acquires freedom by making

---

[16] Ibid., 112.

[17] G. W. F. Hegel, *Philosophy of Right*, trans. T. M. Knox (London: Oxford University Press, 1967), 105.

[18] Ibid.

his or her will fully congruent with the will of the universal. Being dutiful and abiding by the laws as enshrined in the constitution of the ethical order are the requirements to ensure that such a harmonization of wills is engendered:

> But the subjective will also has a substantial life—a reality—in which it moves in the region of essential being, and has the essential itself as the object of its existence. This essential being is the union of the subjective with the rational Will: it is the moral Whole, the State, which is that form of reality in which the individual has and enjoys his freedom; but on the condition of his recognizing, believing in, and willing that which is common to the Whole. . . . [T]he State is the actually existing, realized moral life. . . . It must further be understood that all the worth which the human being possesses—all spiritual reality, he possesses only through the State.[19]

Truth is the "unity of the universal and the subjective Will," which is concretized in the state, or the "Divine Idea as it exists on Earth."[20]

Hegel's idea of the rational state, in which subjects become conscious of themselves through laws and objective institutions, reveals to the reader that becoming self-conscious necessitates becoming conscious of divine reason (*Geist*), which in its most concrete form is "God." God's divine design unfolds as the history of the world, the history of reason evolving in the form of universal will. *Geist* is, therefore, the underlying teleological coherence to the ostensibly contingent mutations in world history. In essence, Hegel is positing that God's divine plan for the world is revealed through the systematic history of laws that regulate the life of each self.

MORALITY (*MORALITÄT*)

Having outlined the nature of what Hegel refers to as ethical life (*Sittlichkeit*), I now extend my analysis by looking at what this thinker has to say concerning the negative moment in the dialectical emergence of the ethical state, what he terms "morality" (*Moralität*), or subjective responsibility. For Hegel, "morality" is the nega-

---

[19] G. W. F. Hegel, *Philosophy of History*, trans. J. Sibree (New York: Dover, 1956), 38–39.
[20] Ibid., 39.

tive moment, or the particularization of the universal standpoint, in the ethical dialectic. I mentioned in the previous section that Hegel considers the mediation of the universal and subjective wills the means of guaranteeing truth and freedom. This is realized at a practical level by means of the individual's striving to regulate his or her life according to state law. As the law is the tangible manifestation of God's "divine design" on earth, and that to which all individuals must conform in their proper perfection, it is the instrument by which one can gauge the evolution of the world-historical plan.

Following the development of individual consciousness, the consciousness of the state dialectically unfolds when each individual member makes sense of the law or, alternatively, makes present to consciousness what initially, at the level of pure immediacy, appeared abstract and alien. As Hegel says in his discussion of world history in the *Philosophy of Right*:

> A nation does not begin by being a state. The transition from a family, a horde, a clan, a multitude, &c., to political conditions is the realization of the Idea in the form of that nation. Without this form, a nation, as an ethical substance—which is what it is implicitly, lacks the objectivity of possessing in its own eyes and in the eyes of others, a universal and universally valid embodiment in laws, i.e. in determinate thoughts, and as a result it fails to secure recognition from others. So long as it lacks objective laws and an explicitly established rational constitution, its autonomy is formal only and is not sovereign.[21]

Now the problem that emerges at the level of morality is that the subjective individual conflates his or her own inner will with that of the universal will. In order to understand this point sufficiently, it is necessary to juxtapose what Hegel defines as "freedom" and what he terms "the real aspect of the concept of freedom."[22] As I have shown, Hegel defines "freedom" as that which the individual realizes after his or her subjective will has been mediated with the universal will; that is, Hegel believes that fundamental liberty can be experienced only after the subject has become a full member of the state. "The real aspect of the concept of freedom," however, may be defined as freedom is normally understood, that is, liberty from all oppressive constraint. Having conflated this second form of freedom with the

---

[21] Hegel, *Philosophy of Right*, 218–19.
[22] Ibid., 75.

only genuine sense of freedom, at least as Hegel determines it, the individual believes that liberty can only be truly experienced at the level of subjectivity: "This process is accordingly the cultivation of the ground in which freedom is now set, i.e. subjectivity. What happens is that subjectivity, which is abstract at the start, i.e. distinct from the concept, becomes likened to it, and thereby the Idea acquires its genuine realization. The result is that the subjective will determines itself as objective too and so as truly concrete."[23]

The subjective will thus appeals to no higher objective order to determine how one should practically act in concrete intersubjective situations. Being totally subjective, and insofar as it fails to recognize the binding power of the law, it is "abstract, restricted, and formal."[24] Hegel is conflating here what he terms "the self-determination of the will" with the Kantian deontological notion of the will, which is made good by appealing to formalistic laws of reason. As such, "the general characteristics of morality and immorality alike, rest on the subjectivity of the will."[25] The individual's subjective will therefore becomes in matters of moral concern the sole objective standard or criterion against which one judges the rightness or wrongness of external states of affairs.

In the introduction to the *Philosophy of Right*, Hegel abbreviates his discussion of the nature of subjective will as follows:

> If the will's determinate character lies in the abstract opposition of its subjectivity to the objectivity of external immediate existence, then this is the formal will of mere self-consciousness which finds an external world confronting it. As individuality returning in its determinacy into itself, it is the process of translating the subjective purpose into objectivity through the use of its own activity and some external means. Once mind has developed its potentialities to actuality [*wie er an und für sich ist*], its determinate character is true and simply its own.[26]

In this way, the aim of the subject who confuses his or her own will with that of the universal is to affirm his or her freedom by engendering results that reflect the subject's own needs and purposes, not

---

[23] Ibid.
[24] Ibid., 76.
[25] Ibid.
[26] Ibid., 24.

those sought by universal consensus. In effect, what is being asserted
here is that the individual who regulates his or her life for the purpose of realizing subjective freedom is one who strives only for a
particularized happiness, not for the general welfare of the objective
community. The freedom or right that such a subject experiences
is illusory, since one becomes a prisoner to an abstract and vague
conception of reason.

It is within the context of a discussion of "Good and Conscience"
that Hegel teases out his criticisms of the subjective disposition indicative of morality (*Moralität*). With the Kantian paradigm firmly
in mind, Hegel argues that any model that has as its central tenet
the belief that "the *good* alone is the essential," without giving the
idea of the good any specific determinations, is essentially flawed.
Kant argues in both his *Groundwork for a Metaphysics of Morals*[27]
and *The Critique of Practical Reason*[28] that the will is made good
once the intention of the subject is to act in accordance with duty
out of reverence for the law of reason. Autonomy is characterized in
these texts as freedom from the whim of irrational desire and in-
stinct, which can be achieved through a determination to adhere to
the claims of reason to govern one's practical existence. Hegel, however, directs his critique at the theory of duty Kant provides, stating
that because "the good is characterized to begin with only as the
universal abstract essentiality of the will, i.e. as duty," and "because
every action explicitly calls for a particular content and a specific
end, while duty as an abstraction entails nothing of the kind, the
question arises: what is my duty?"[29] In response, Hegel maintains
that because duty is "abstract universality" it is totally indeterminate
and therefore without any specific content. What he is attempting
to emphasize here is that when prominence is given "to the pure
unconditioned self-determination of the will as the root of duty,"
the only measure of justification for one's practical actions is a law
of reason, an absolutely indeterminate concept that is at variance
with Hegel's concretization of the law as external manifestation of
the rational idea in the constitution of the state.

---

[27] Immanuel Kant, *Groundwork of the Metaphysics of Morals*, trans. H. J. Paton
(New York: Harper Torchbooks, 1964).

[28] Immanuel Kant, *Critique of Practical Reason*, trans. Lewis White Beck (Indianapolis: Bobbs-Merrill, 1977).

[29] Hegel, *Philosophy of Right*, 89.

Hegel, I have argued, considers objective freedom to derive from the ability to recognize and acknowledge the nature of one's relationship to the absolute or universal, and considers how this can be practically consolidated through concrete action. The individual, that is, being a linguistic, relational, and social entity, internalizes the determinate laws that guide and regulate action. When situations that demand moral attention arise, therefore, the subject refers to his or her "conscience" (*Gewissen*), which Hegel defines as "the disposition to will what is absolutely good." In its non-Kantian form, conscience "has fixed principles and it is aware of these as its explicitly objective determinants and duties." The content of conscience is thus the "truth" qua the good, since it is the objective code by which all self-conscious, rationally engaged agents direct their lives. As such, conscience provides rules "for a mode of conduct which is rational, absolutely valid, and universal."[30] However, when the nature of duty is taken to be so formal that it is incapable of guiding the subjective will to realize concrete good, it cannot be sanctioned by the state "any more than science can grant validity to subjective opinion, dogmatism, and the appeal to a subjective opinion."[31] This leaves open, according to Hegel, the possibility of evil: "Once self-consciousness has reduced all otherwise valid duties to emptiness and itself to the sheer inwardness of the will, it has become the potentiality of either making the absolutely universal its principle, or equally well of elevating above the universal the self-will of private particularity, taking that as its principle and realizing it through its actions, i.e. it has become potentially evil."[32] In this passage, Hegel contends that if conscience is taken to be an element of formal subjectivity only, without the application of universally valid laws, then the individual will act according to "desire, impulse, and inclination." In order to glean a precise understanding of what is at issue in this statement (and here I wish to emphasize the importance of this passage for our treatment below of Kierkegaard's *Concept of Irony*), it is necessary to comment on Hegel's distinction between the inner and outer regions of conscious life.

For Hegel, the inner realm is that interior space in which the sub-

---

[30] Ibid., 91.
[31] Ibid.
[32] Ibid., 92.

ject wills the good without any objective or universal criteria to measure the nature or level of the good so willed. As this form of subjective willing has a totally "contingent character," and is divorced from the sphere of objective universality, it is regulated by what the subject alone determines as satisfactory methods of justification. Because the subject has no higher point of reference than the interior self, Hegel concludes that the standard of good the subject appropriates is based on personal predilection and impulse. Having no universal court of appeal to provide aid in determining what one ought to do in practical situations, the subject could indeed will either good or evil.

It follows from the above that Hegel takes the outer realm to be the objective sphere, wherein the reflective consciousness wills in accordance with the manifold of concrete laws that preserve the good as constituted universally. Evil is therefore a possibility that derives from a form of particularity that "is set in opposition to the universal as inner objectivity, to the good, which comes on the scene as the opposite extreme to immediate objectivity, the natural pure and simple, as soon as the will is reflected into itself and consciousness is a *knowing* consciousness."[33]

"True conscience," therefore, will guide the actions of the individual in accordance with the normative standards laid down in the constitution of the state. As such, account will be taken of the possible consequences and ramifications of one's actions for the lives of others. According to Hegel, the form of conscience that instructs out of respect for the indeterminate good of Kant's paradigm, or merely on the basis of subjective interior willing, might result in wrongdoing or evil. The self alone cannot be the sole standard of legitimation in ethical matters.

It is in this context that Hegel devotes a paragraph to the notion of irony. At the end of his discussion of subjective conscience in the *Philosophy of Right*, Hegel briefly attends to the Socratic technique of pretended ignorance. According to Hegel, Plato employed the term "irony" (from the Greek *eiróneia*) to describe the manner in which Socrates undermined the credibility of the Sophists. Socrates' aim was to reveal the paucity of the conceptions of truth, knowledge, and justice upheld by sophistic teaching. For Hegel, however, irony

---

[33] Ibid., 93.

is the highest form of inauthentic subjectivism, especially that form practiced by the romantic movement. In saying this, Hegel appears not to be pointing a finger at Plato, for his thought did not seek to encourage the supreme form of subjectivism Hegel has in mind. The Greeks, he asserts, used irony "only as a manner of talking against *people*," and "not as a substitute for the Idea [of truth]."[34] Indeed, they, like Hegel, stressed that "the essential movement of thought is dialectic, and Plato was so far from regarding the dialectical in itself, still less irony, as the last word in thought and a substitute for the idea, that he terminated the flux and reflux of thinking, let alone of a subjective opinion, and submerged it in the substantiality of the Idea."[35] To those who ascribe a more profound role to irony in the quest for truth, however, Hegel has this to say:

[The ironic disposition] consists in this, that it knows the objective ethical principles, but fails in self-forgetfulness and self-renunciation to immerse itself in their seriousness and to base action upon them. Although related to them, it holds itself aloof from them and knows itself as that which wills and decides thus, although it may equally well will and decide otherwise. You actually accept a law, it says, and respect it as absolute. So do I, but I go further than you, because I am beyond this law and can make it suit myself. It is not the thing that is excellent, but I who am so; as the master of the law and thing alike, I simply play with them as with my caprice; my consciously ironical attitude lets the highest perish and I merely hug myself at the thought. This type of subjectivism not merely substitutes a void for the whole content of ethics, right, duties, and laws—and so is evil, in fact through and through and universally—but in addition its form is a subjective void and in this knowing knows itself as absolute.[36]

The importance of this passage for analyzing the efficacy of Kierkegaard's critique of Hegel's theory of society and ethics cannot be overestimated, for it is here that Hegel denounces irony as a form of ethical irresponsibility, while Kierkegaard in response will champion this disposition as one of the most effective ways for the subject to become earnest, ethical, and responsible. Indeed, it could be argued that Kierkegaard's entire authorship is a meditation on this passage from the *Philosophy of Right*.

---

[34] Ibid., 101.
[35] Ibid.
[36] Ibid., 103.

I have undertaken so far in this chapter an analysis of the Hegelian theory of the ethical life (*Sittlichkeit*) and the contrasting nature of morality (*Moralität*). It is necessary, by way of a conclusion, to draw out some of the implications raised by Hegel's thesis. In so doing, I will begin to identify the inherent shortcomings of the Hegelian paradigm, before considering whether or not Kierkegaard's rejoinder is plausible and effective.

SITTLICHKEIT: AN ETHICS OF RESPONSIBILITY?

Hegel's theory of society and the ethical life is inspired by his belief that social cohesion can be generated only when universal freedom is the primary political objective. Although Hegel successfully illuminates many of the intellectual inconsistencies of the Kantian paradigm, he nevertheless (and this is where Kierkegaard's critique hits the mark) remains hostage to many of the same shortcomings he considered endemic to Kant's model of morality. I will follow Ernst Tugendhat[37] in arguing that the type of freedom Hegel espouses in his discussion of *Sittlichkeit* is subjectively defined. I employ the expression "subjectively defined" because Hegel defines true freedom as a surrendering by the individual of his or her particular and subjective autonomy for a type of freedom that is dependent upon one's submission to the universal will as instantiated in the law of the state. It must also be recalled that Hegel founds his criticisms of the subjective condition on the fact that there appears to be no objective standard, point of reference, or regulative criterion that could justify or legitimate the actions of the moral individual. In his description of this individual and the Kantian moral agent, Hegel presupposes, however, that the laws of the state are sufficient to act as regulatory principles against which one can judge the truth of one's

---

[37] See Ernst Tugendhat, *Self-Consciousness and Self-Determination*, trans. Paul Stern (Cambridge: MIT Press, 1986). In citing Tugendhat here, I do not wish to give the impression that the type of "Kierkegaardian" critique of Hegel that is being proffered throughout this work is motivated by the spirit of Critical Theory. As we shall see, our reading of Kierkegaard takes a patently postmodern form. It is my belief, however, that Tugendhat succeeds in identifying the main shortcoming of Hegel's ethical theory in a way most contemporary commentators have failed to do. For a reading of Kierkegaard that makes more use of Tugendhat's work, see Matustík, *Postnational Identity*.

actions. If we take it as given that no state has yet succeeded in constituting laws that do not in some way or another violate the rights of certain minorities, or in some obvious cases the rights of the majority, then we can only deduce that Hegel's theory of the state is an ideal one that has no concrete equivalent. However, if we assume that Hegel did take this idea to be more than an ideal thought experiment, then we encounter the difficulty that presents itself once we recognize that laws which serve as methods for justification in one state might act as tools of oppression in the next. This does not have to take any definite or obvious form, in that the law might safeguard the rights of all, but at the same time favor the privilege of the few. In either case, the picture presented here leaves one in no doubt that Hegel must succumb to much the same criticism he leveled at Kant; that is, if the laws in one state are distinct from those in the next, and if the law is supposed to be the manifestation of the divine design, then the divine harmony thesis is somewhat confounded.

Furthermore, if the law is the standard the individual must appropriate in order to determine the moral worth of a particular decision, and if that law does not in fact accord with the universal will of the people, then the responsibility for the consequences of that action must necessarily lie at the feet of the lawmaker. These criticisms are intended to demonstrate that a state is vulnerable to the same subjective ethical miscarriages that Hegel condemns the Kantian and the ironist, among others, for propagating.

In the light of these reflections, Hegel seems correct in ascertaining that freedom is enjoyed once the individual observes the code of law and objectively participates in the institutional infrastructure of the state, but this is surely not enough to ensure the type of ethical harmony this model proposes. For to act merely in accordance with the law, in order to safeguard one's civil liberty alone, cannot be considered truly responsible and ethical behavior, at least not to the degree Hegel maintains it does. Responsibility, as Kierkegaard and Derrida have both observed,[38] is not a matter of ritually observing the law without—at the same time—critically questioning its foundations. It is a matter, however, of scrupulously testing the methods of justification the state uses to ensure its legitimation. This does

---

[38] See my "Risking Responsibility."

not mean that the idea of responsibility I am supporting aims to destabilize the existing status quo; if anything, this would be irresponsible. Rather, it is a matter of acquiring the critical skills to enable one to ask whether the ideals and criteria by which the state justifies its existence are both reasonable and ethical. If not, then it is a case of broadening one's frame of reference to make them so. Tugendhat lends support to this argument when he remarks:

> Let us assume that Hegel had developed a conception of the state that is as good and just as one could imagine. Would it then be justified to demand unconditional obedience to the state and to require the surrender of responsibility on the part of the citizens? In both instances there is a disregard for the fact that a state cannot be good or rational, much less liberal, if it demands an unconditionally affirmative relation from its citizens. In contrast, it follows from the conception of responsibility that a community only deserves to be designated as rational if its highest end is the responsibility of all its citizens; and this also applies precisely in the relation of the citizens to the community itself.[39]

This idea of responsibility, one that I believe Kierkegaard works tirelessly to ensure that his reader practices, is suspicious of any normative framework that claims to know exactly what the conditions are for the realization of an absolutely good life. As Kierkegaard will show, in matters of ethical concern we can never have certainty, only fear and trembling, trial and error. By constantly questioning the standards of justification to which we appeal, we come to realize that, like Socrates, "we can attain an outlook upon the good in the knowledge of our ignorance."[40] This is why, in spite of Hegel's assurances to the contrary, irony, for both Kierkegaard and Derrida, has everything to do with being genuinely responsible.

---

[39] Tugendhat, *Self-Consciousness and Self-Determination*, 319–20.
[40] Ibid., 323.

3

The Ethics of Irony

IN THE PREVIOUS CHAPTER I examined the nature of the Hegelian notion of the ethical life (*Sittlichkeit*) and the disposition Hegel perceives as being the negative moment in the universal dialectic leading to such an authentic existence, morality (*Moralität*). In so doing, I determined that the type of ethical existence upon which Hegel is insisting is not "ethical" in the sense of being a truly responsible and committed attitude both to the nature of the self and what it means to live a good life. I concluded by arguing that Hegel's model preserves the existing order, irrespective of how that order is constituted. It was not, of course, Hegel's intention to give rise to the totalitarian state (*pace* Popper), as he is often accused of having done. Moreover, it would be unfair to suggest that he could be used to justify either Communism in its most brutal form or, indeed, Nazism. Hegel's vision of a spiritually integrated state, one whose laws protect the freedoms and liberties of all those committed to their maintenance, is indeed commendable in the main. However, the preservation of the "established order" should not be considered ethical in itself. Many keep the law, but whether their lives can be deemed ethical is another issue. When the state has no objective critical standard other than itself to justify its legitimacy, the freedom and liberty of its citizens, rather than being safeguarded, are indeed circumscribed and challenged.

In this chapter I will define precisely what Kierkegaard's notion of an ethics of responsibility demands. I propose to do this by examining the critique Kierkegaard forged against the Hegelian model of the ethical self. In so doing, I will determine in general terms the nature of the ethical point of view Kierkegaard considers necessary if genuine community life is to be engendered. In order to best realize these aims, I shall scrutinize Kierkegaard's critique of the Hegelian model in his earliest publication, *The Concept of Irony,* and Johannes de Silentio's contribution in *Fear and Trembling.* This, in turn, will enable me to advance some of the key ideas put forward in chapter 1.

A Reconsideration of *Sittlichkeit*

It is Kierkegaard's contention that by not encouraging each individual to individually relate to "the idea" (the unconditioned ethical criterion), and thereafter to each other in an engaged and passionate fashion, the Hegelian model of ethical life (*Sittlichkeit*) is one in which individuals relate to each other merely "in a herd-like" manner; that is, because the citizens of the state see it as their fundamental ethical goal to will the universal by adhering to the demands of the law only, they fail to consider whether observing these demands is in itself sufficient to guarantee genuine ethical integrity. Becoming self-conscious, for Kierkegaard and his pseudonyms, requires more than merely adhering to the letter of the law and living out one's social role. It enjoins each individual to cultivate a more responsible standpoint from which to determine both the merits and the demerits of the established ethical and political order. Tugendhat crystallizes what I take Kierkegaard to be saying:

> If we conceive of the individuals of a society as responsible, that is, as placing themselves, each other (reciprocally), and their society into question, they must certainly reciprocally recognize one another; and they are mutually directed toward harmony as a regulative idea in the same sense that they are directed toward truth as a regulative idea. Nevertheless, they do not *find* themselves in a harmony, much less in an identity. Hegel has an essentially closed model, and the idea of responsibility requires an essentially open one.[1]

We saw in the previous chapter how Hegel considers the individual who reduces the universal will to his or her own subjective will to be one who prioritizes the "inner" world of personal harmony, à la Kant, over the "outer," external world of state and spiritual harmony. We also saw, in chapter 1, how Kierkegaard suggests that one way of responding to the dilemmas of the age is to cultivate "passionate inwardness," which I defined as an intensified reflective disposition—"double reflection" or "vigilant counter-interpretation"—

---

[1] Tugendhat, *Self-Consciousness and Self-Determination*, 321–22. We should stress here that Kierkegaard does not subscribe to a strong rational "regulative idea" of a Kantian or Habermasian sort. As we saw in chapter 1, Kierkegaard's "idea" takes the form of the Christ-figure. This quote from Tugendhat does, however, help us make a crucial point at this stage of our analysis.

aimed at establishing social cohesion and harmony through involved critical praxis. This disposition requires that the individual not assume that what the established order promulgates in the law is the best way to live a life, but rather adopt a critical posture in order to verify and legitimate the methods of justification the state appropriates to sustain itself. In so doing, each individual who has taken this ethically responsible initiative attempts to relate to others at this new level of discernment and understanding.

Kierkegaard sees this "inner" life, therefore, as being essential to the realization of a responsible social ethic. This concurs also with his belief, articulated in *Two Ages*, that individuals fail to realize their full potential as selves—and in many cases never even come to ask the fundamental questions concerning personal and social identity—when they are "externally oriented" alone, or when they relate to each other "merely *en masse*." Thus, when the individual conflates being a member of the state with having an identity, and when he or she further believes that the existing order is a social harmony founded on responsibility, without ever putting the fundamental tenets of that society into question, then "the established order continues to stand" and "passionless reflection is reassured" (TA, 80). As Johannes Climacus remarks: "The longer life goes on and the longer the existing person through his action is woven into existence, the more difficult it is to separate the ethical from the external, and the easier it seems to corroborate the metaphysical tenet that the outer is the inner, the inner the outer, the one wholly commensurate with the other" (CUP, 138).

In a probing, satirical meditation on the nature of the established order in *Practice in Christianity*, Anti-Climacus takes Hegel's postulation concerning inner moral conscience to task. In the *Philosophy of Right*, Hegel maintained that the individual who regulates his or her life according to conscience (*Gewissen*) is guilty of confusing the law, objectively considered, with his or her own subjective interpretation, and further that this may give rise to evil. In response the pseudonym inquires: "Why has Hegel made conscience and the state of conscience in the single individual 'a form of evil' (see *Rechts-Philosophie*)? Why? Because he deified the established order. But the more one deifies the established order, the more natural is the conclusion: ergo, the one who disapproves of or rebels against this divinity, the established order—ergo, he must be rather close to imagining that he is God" (PC, 87). Anti-Climacus contends that Hegel, in composing his social ethics, "ignored" the origins of the state; that is, in claiming that the individual's personal autonomy and integrity are dependent upon an unwavering observance of the law, as the objectification of Spirit (*Geist*), Hegel overlooked the fact that the state was founded by individuals and is for individuals, not vice versa; in other words, the pseudonym reminds the reader that the state is a product of the initiative of single individuals, people who recognized that in human affairs nothing could be deemed absolute or established for good. I take it that Anti-Climacus is here objecting to Hegel on the grounds that responsibility demands an open model of society, one in which there is no certainty or reassurance that what one takes to be freedom or truth can be justified simply by appealing to the belief that the state is another moment in God's design. In raising the question of what it takes to become genuinely responsible and earnest about one's own life and that with others, one needs to acquire a sense of "fear and trembling," or the feeling that accompanies the realization that identity is not something immanently conceived. Rather, fundamental self-knowledge can only be realized by transcending the current order through engaged double reflection or vigilant counter-interpretation. As such, "fear and trembling signify that we are in the process of becoming; and every single individual, likewise the generation, is and should be aware of being in the process of becoming" (PC, 87).

"The process of becoming" suggests for Kierkegaard that identity is nothing static, but rather something forever being approximated. In opposition to the full self-certainty the Hegelian epistemic model guarantees, the Kierkegaardian paradigm is founded on the belief that, in true Socratic fashion, identity is always something yet to be established. Thus, when individuals relate to each other at an objective level only, as they do in Hegel's state, passionate inwardness is not cultivated. Consequently, the subject who believes in the "closed model" of society Hegel develops takes it for granted that harmony and identity already exist. That is, the individual relates to him- or herself and to others at the level of externality alone. Hence, when this type of "commensurability and congruity are accomplished and the established order has been deified, then all fear and trembling is abolished" (PC, 90).

We have seen, therefore, that what is required for an ethics of responsibility to be engendered is an essentially "open model" of society, where individuals are mutually directed in fear and trembling toward an idea that exceeds that of the state. The alternative is a closed model of society, or what Anti-Climacus has termed the "self-deification" of the established order.

Now, it is necessary at this juncture to introduce a vital distinction Kierkegaard draws at many points both in his directly signed texts and in the pseudonymous works—that between "self"-knowledge, or that form of "subjective" knowing we have been describing in our portrait of the ethical and responsible individual to date, and "human" knowledge (see JFY, 105). "Human" knowledge can be equated with what I called in chapter 1 "objective" knowledge, or what Kierkegaard tends to call a "secular" mentality. This form of knowing equates being ethical or responsible with simply upholding the law in Hegel's objective sense. As such, it is a type of world-historical knowledge that sees no reason to cast a hermeneutically suspicious eye on the dominant codes governing reality, since they are the realization of the divine design. "Human" knowledge identifies truth and freedom with the state's definition of these goods. From a purely human point of view, thus, individuals take it for certain that they have a predetermined identity. They fail, therefore, to scrutinize the origins of the established order and the reasons why they relate to one another in a particular way. They further fail to acquire the skills required to test the veracity of the opinions they espouse through the process of passionate inward double reflection. For those with the human point of view, the state is its own final court of appeal, its own criterion for the realization of truth: "The deification of the established order, however, is the smug invention of the lazy, secular human mentality that wants to settle down and fancy that now there is total peace and security, now that we have achieved the highest" (PC, 88).

This distinction between the "human" and the "self" is of particular importance for our argument. Becoming a self—and this is a point I will stress continually—does not demand an irrational and totally subjectivistic leap. Rather, the individual is encouraged to expand the scope of his or her rational potential by becoming *self*-reflective. Kierkegaard is not railing against objective human knowing per se, but against a reflective orientation that fails to translate into critically engaged action. Becoming self-aware is a process whereby each individual breaks the spell of objective reflection by asking how such knowledge can actually affect one's life and the lives of one's neighbors. It could be said simply that subjective knowledge is a process of putting things into question. As we saw in chapter 1, reflection ought to be the occasion for acting more intensely. Hence "the ethical is not only a knowing; it is a doing that is related to a knowing, and a doing of such a nature that a repetition of it can at times and in more ways than one become more difficult than the first doing" (CUP, 160–61).

"Human" knowledge, we can now say, has no real "interest" in questions of truth. It lures the individual into believing that what is objectively (in the Hegelian sense) knowable is in fact the sum total of knowledge. It deals, therefore, with what Kierkegaard calls "the probable"—that is, it does not subject to rigorous examination the truth of its own basic hypotheses:

> The person who inquires about the probable and only about that in order to adhere to it does not ask what is right and what is wrong, what is good and what is evil, what is true and what is false. No, he asks impartially: which is the probable, so that I might believe it— whether it is the true is a matter of indifference or is at least of less importance; which is probable, so that I can adopt it and side with it—whether it is evil or wrong is a matter of indifference or is at least of less importance, if only it is probable or something that offers the probability of gaining power. Familiarity with the probable, and the more profound it is, does not in a more profound sense lead a person closer to himself but further and further away from his deeper self, brings him closer and closer to himself only in the sense of selfishness. (JFY, 104–5; see also SUD, 41–42)

The established order is thus a body of subjects who communicate with one another at the level of pure externality only. In so doing, they interact with one another directly. What Kierkegaard is attempting to generate, however, is a state of affairs in which each individual risks responsibility by becoming *self*-reflective. This calls for a passionately intensified engagement with the question of (ethical and religious) truth. We have ascertained that this is what Kierkegaard calls the movement inward so as to emphasize and illuminate the distinction with the external and objective points of view. Indirect communication, therefore, is the manner in which all genuine selves relate to one another; that is, when two individuals have suc-

ceeded in acquiring the inward disposition, the emphasis is not on
what they say, but on *how* it is said. For those with the human mentality, concerned only with probability, all that is of consequence in
interpersonal relations is *what* is enunciated superficially. Authentic
selves, however, attempt to probe the truth of what they know and
say before engaging the other in dialogue. For these individuals, the
perspective from which they communicate is what is essential; that
is, *how* they speak—whether it is from the objective or subjective
point of view—is of crucial significance. For "objectively, the question is only about the categories of thought, subjectively, about inwardness" (CUP, 203). Climacus reiterates this point when he says
"the inwardness of the existing person is truth" and "subjectivity,
inwardness is truth" (CUP, 204, 209).

In this section I have demonstrated that Kierkegaard takes Hegel's
model of *Sittlichkeit* to be an essentially closed model, one that has,
without questioning its own origins, deified itself. This deification
was the "smug invention" of the "human mentality," which, unlike
the responsible self, does not put its own assumptions into question.
In taking for granted that they have found identity and social harmony just by being members of the state, such individuals fail to
acquire the inward disposition or the critical standpoint from which
they can scrutinize the efficacy of what they take to be both true and
good. To affirm that identity and harmony are ideals toward which
one has to strive means that the individual accepts that truth is not
something immanently received but is rather something one must
become, something that demands one to transcend one's current
beliefs (what chapter 1 referred to as "public opinion"). In fear and
trembling evoked by the knowledge that responsibility requires sacrificing one's "total peace and security" in the established order, the
individual develops a "residual incommensurability," to borrow a
phrase from Johannes de Silentio, or a sense of inwardness. In so
doing, one acknowledges that there is a higher ethical task for the
individual than simply honoring one's duty to the state. This, as we
shall see, does not mean that the subjective individual withdraws
from all state dealings. If anything, for Kierkegaard, inwardness requires that the individual become more passionately engaged with
others. The difference is, however, that with this greater level of self-
awareness the subject does not see his or her objectives only in terms
of one's social or state role. When the ethical is considered little

more than a passionless observance of social norms, "there is no inward decency that decorously distances the one [individual] from the other; thus there is turmoil and commotion that ends in nothing." "In the relation of unanimity to the idea," however, "there is the elevation that again in consideration of the whole forgets the accidentality of details" (TA, 62–63).

Socrates As Ethical Prototype: Ironic Inwardness I

I remarked in the previous chapter how Hegel, in his section of the *Philosophy of Right* entitled "Good and Conscience," proclaims that irony is the most extreme form of subjectivism. He does not, however, condemn Plato, or indeed Socrates, for being a practitioner of this art. Although Hegel claims in *The Philosophy of History* that Socrates is the founder of morality (*Moralität*), he nonetheless ascribes to him a positive content. Hegel looks favorably on Socrates because he considers him from the standpoint of universal history, or what Kierkegaard calls "the world-historical process"; that is, Socrates represents for Hegel a positive moment in the development of *Geist* in that he signifies the transition from morality to the ethical life (*Sittlichkeit*). When Hegel declaims irony in the context of his critique of morality in the *Philosophy of Right,* therefore, he has the romantic movement in mind. The one point on which Hegel and Kierkegaard do agree is that the romantic movement—with its emphasis on the belief that only in imaginative life-forms can a fully comprehensive life be led—is responsible for a widespread ethical apathy.[2] The antidotes both thinkers recommend, it can easily be guessed, vary in their import considerably. It is not my objective to examine the Kierkegaardian response to the romantic conception of irony. I mention it only to dispel any belief that Kierkegaard can be considered a representative of the romantic spirit.

---

[2] For more on Kierkegaard and the Romantic movement, see Harvie Ferguson, *Melancholy and the Critique of Modernity: Søren Kierkegaard's Religious Psychology* (London: Routledge, 1995), 34–56; David Gouwens, *Kierkegaard's Dialectic of the Imagination* (New York: Peter Lang, 1989), 13–93; George Pattison, *Kierkegaard: The Aesthetic and the Religious: From the Magic Theatre to the Crucifixion of the Image* (London: Macmillan, 1992); Walsh, *Living Poetically,* 43–63.

It is my intention, however, to examine closely how Kierkegaard defends irony against the Hegelian attack and, in so doing, renders it apparent to the reader why Socrates, at least on this account, should be considered an exemplar of the ethical point of view. Consequently, it should become clear why Kierkegaard considers a certain form of irony an essential ingredient for the responsible subject.

Kierkegaard's Socrates is a figure who, believing that "the whole given actuality had lost its validity" (CI, 264), ventured to alienate himself from the "substantial world." In taking his distance from the given actuality, Socrates lived as a "stranger and a foreigner" (CI, 246) in his own land—a motif Kierkegaard plays on considerably throughout the authorship and something to which I shall return when discussing his use of both Abraham and Christ. To become an alien in one's own land, to resign from the given actuality, is the very process of inwardness—not a total withdrawal from or abdication of one's cultural matrix, but rather the adoption of a critical posture in relation to the prevailing sociopolitical structures. Kierkegaard's antiheroes—and one thinks primarily of Socrates in this instance— are as much a part of the state as they are dissenters. Their objective is to undermine the power of the state to delude its citizens into believing that singularity must always be sacrificed on the altar of universality.

Now, since the usual methods of disseminating knowledge are governed and controlled by the state, the "knights of inwardness" appropriate techniques outside its control or shunned by the state. We saw above how Hegel condemns irony as the most subjectivistic form of communication, and how, in the larger framework, it is totally extraneous to the sphere of social ethics. Ironists do not intend, therefore, to counter the "human" or "secular" mentality with the usual forms of rebellion and revolution; rather, they strive to bring each self to a level of awareness that will provide him or her with the know-how to live a more engaged and harmonious existence. But the kernel here is that the ironist endeavors to make each one responsible for his or her own self-becoming, for if the learner was instructed *directly* on what to do, at the level of externality, he or she would once more be merely following a program, a set of rules, or a fossilized custom. Thus, "in an era of negativity the authentic ironist is the hidden enthusiast" (TA, 81).

Socrates epitomizes the role of the hidden enthusiast for Kierke-

gaard in *The Concept of Irony*. Not only did he purposely alienate
himself from the world of immediate ("external") actuality, but
through the use of irony he also "destroyed Greek culture" (CI, 264).
In leading his interlocutors from sophistic knowledge to a comprehensive knowledge of truth, he began to corrode the fabric of Greek
society without actually posing any direct affront to the establishment. That is,

> the whole substantial life of Greek culture had lost its validity for him,
> which means that to him the established actuality was unactual, not
> in this or that particular aspect but in its totality as such; that with
> regard to this invalid actuality he let the established order of things
> appear to remain established and thereby brought about its downfall;
> that in the process Socrates became lighter and lighter, more and
> more negatively free. . . . But it was not actuality in general that he
> negated; it was the given actuality at a particular time, the substantial
> actuality as it was in Greece, and what his irony was demanding was
> the actuality of subjectivity, of ideality. (CI, 271)

This extract is particularly important for the efficacy of the argument
being put forward in this work: in saying that Socrates, through his
use of irony, became negatively free, Kierkegaard is appealing to the
type of freedom Hegel condemned in his analysis of *Moralität* in *The
Philosophy of Right*. There Hegel asserted that the individual can
become positively free only after he or she has fully recognized the
law as the objectification of truth in world history. Hence, by taking
up one's social role and observing the demands the state makes upon
the self, the individual secures rights and civic liberties.

Negative freedom, alternatively, is required if truly ethical and responsible behavior is to be engendered, according to Kierkegaard. In
Tugendhat's assessment of Hegel's social ethics, we saw that the
closed model Hegel develops "is consciously and explicitly the philosophy of the justification of the existing order, quite irrespective
of how this existing order may be constituted."[3] With the aim of
generating a type of freedom that is more than that provided by the
existing order, each individual is encouraged to call into question
the criteria and ideals upon which the order depends for its perpetuation. This in turn will ensure a genuine sense of personal identity,

---

[3] Tugendhat, *Self-Consciousness and Self-Determination*, 315.

in that the subject takes responsibility for the type of existence he or she wishes to live.

Socrates thus does not seek to generate a spirit of anarchy, with the purpose of destroying all actuality and social cohesion, but rather aims to negate the given actuality of the time, the existing order, by educating his interlocutors to become ethically oriented. That is, Socrates encourages his listeners to suspend belief in relative notions of the Good, or what constitutes the good life, so as to inquire in the nature of the Good-in-itself. By means of irony, as the disposition that orients the individual toward the ethical in a negative sense, Socrates made the Good an objective to be realized by the efforts of responsible agents, not something revealed to the law-abiding citizen by necessity. This is what Hegel failed to grasp in his treatment of the role of Socrates, and indeed in his critique of the concept of irony. As David Gouwens remarks:

> Socrates' irony endeavored to move his contemporaries from the concrete to the abstract, from the confusing limits of custom to the true idea of the good as ethical passion. For Kierkegaard, Socrates establishes the validity of ironic negativity in a way that Hegel cannot allow, and opens the way to a continuing non-Hegelian role for irony in the life of an individual person. . . . For Kierkegaard, irony is not a surpassed moment on the way to objectivity, but is a continuous factor in each individual's ethical subjectivity. Irony is indeed, the beginning of subjectivity.[4]

For Kierkegaard, Socrates' life constituted a "self-sacrifice," meaning that he sacrificed his life in the state, or that he "teleologically suspended" his "everyday" existence in order to acquire an understanding of what constitutes the good life. Striving toward the Good as an absolute *telos* in this manner allows the individual to negate the given actuality while bringing forth a state of affairs that will renew and make more vibrant that same actuality. The "actuality of ideality" which Kierkegaard says Socrates was demanding in his irony suggests that the aim of all responsible, conscientious, and vigilant subjects is to make concrete the ethical ideals that encouraged the move from externality to inwardness to begin with. That is, the subject is admonished never to take for granted that ethical harmony and personal identity can be realized without constant striving and

---

[4] Gouwens, *Kierkegaard's Dialectic of Imagination*, 58.

determination to test the validity of the state's methods of justification. This, again, does not require that the individual withdraw from all societal relations, or that society as one knows it be overthrown. Rather, it contends that each subject, by practicing irony and by developing an ethical disposition and orientation—or "by broadening one's frame of reference"—relativizes what is inconsequential to the individual's absolute and infinite ethical task of determining the self. If this ideal is sought after by enough subjects, then the established order, by necessity, loses actuality in the same sense as Socrates' Greece. So subtle is this disestablishment that Socrates "let the established order of things *appear* to remain," and by this very ploy "brought about its downfall" (CI, 271; my emphasis).

Johannes Climacus reflects on the ironic disposition in the following manner:

> The [ironic/negatively free] individual does not cease to be a human being. . . . He lives in the finite, but he does not have his life in it. His life, like that of another, has the diverse predicates of a human existence, but he is within them like the person who walks in a stranger's borrowed clothes. He is a stranger in the world of finitude, but he does not define his difference from *worldliness* by foreign dress (this is a contradiction, since with that he defines himself in a worldly way); he is incognito, but his incognito consists in looking just like everyone else. (CUP, 410)

But even though the ironist is a stranger in the world of "finitude" (one can take this to mean "externality"), it is only to the degree that the ironist does not consider him- or herself free while being mediated in an absolute sense by the universal will; that is, for Kierkegaard, the ironist considers it an obligation to become passionate in ethical matters, and for this reason he or she recognizes that the given order (actuality) is not an essentially closed model. With this realization, in fear and trembling, the master of irony begins to see his or her art as something that "manifests itself in its truth precisely by teaching how to actualize actuality, by placing the appropriate emphasis on actuality." Consequently, and here we can see how essential irony is to the project of engendering "strong communal life" (TA, 91), actuality "acquires its validity, not as a purgatory—for the soul is not to be purified in such a way that stark naked, so to speak, it runs blank and bare out of life—but as history in which consciousness successively matures, yet in such a way that salvation consists not in forgetting all this but in becoming present in it. Actuality, therefore, will not be rejected, and longing will be a sound and healthy love, not a weak and sentimental sneaking out of the world" (CI, 328–29).

All the ironist is rejecting is the deification of the existing or established order. The ironist is incognito, or inward, only to the extent that he or she sees the need to escape the purely human point of view in order to become passionately self-aware. By raising the question of what is ethical and what it means to have an awareness of who one is, the ironic individual hopes to transform the given actuality into a "higher actuality whose fullness the soul craves." This means that the aim is not to evade social and ethical responsibility, but rather to raise the general level of consciousness, both individual and communal. In this way, history is not taken to be the account of the evolution of an objective divine design; rather, history from this new point of view is subjective history, or the account of how actuality matured from being merely a given state of affairs to being a process of becoming generated by the will of each subjective individual.

In a journal entry from 1845, Kierkegaard provides a definition of irony that draws together the many themes currently under discussion: "Irony is the unity of ethical passion, which in inwardness infinitely accentuates the private self, and of development, which in outwardness (*in association with people*) infinitely abstracts from the private self. The effect of the second is that no one notices the first; therein lies the art, and the true infinitizing of the first is conditioned thereby" (JP 1745, vol. 2, p. 276; my emphasis). The art of irony, or the essential and ethical movement of inwardness, is anything but a withdrawal from the world; inwardness, or that critical disposition in which each individual teleologically suspends the relationship to the purely external world, is the means by which that same individual can acquire a more profound sense of one's identity in that world. At no time in either the pseudonymous or the directly signed works is there the suggestion that authenticity can be found only in solitariness. Ironic becoming is, for Kierkegaard, the manner in which relations between individuals in society are made more comprehensive and resilient.

Abraham As Ethical Prototype: Ironic Inwardness II

In discussing Kierkegaard's Socratic irony throughout this section, I have emphasized how "negative freedom"—the type of liberty Hegel condemns in his formulation of concrete objective ethical standards—is in fact a most responsible and positive form of ethical practice. Asking critical questions of the state, and inquiring into the nature of the relationship one has with it, is in itself being radically ethical in this sense. To live life according to standard conventions of morality and customs alone is a form of ritualized behavior that should not, according to Kierkegaard, be termed "ethical" in the sense of earnest and passionate engagement with one's life tasks. It is only after the subject has become *conscious* of why he or she acts in a certain way, and according to certain standards, that the ethical (inwardness, irony, earnestness) can be deemed a central feature of the individual's existence.

Kierkegaard, however, does not subscribe entirely to the Socratic paradigm as a guide to ethics; we shall see in chapter 5 why he ultimately rejects Socrates as the supreme ethical prototype in favor of the Christ-figure. For the problems that beset Kierkegaard called for a religious solution rather than a pagan one. And indeed, it was Kierkegaard's intention that this religious, or radical Christian, solution would be operable as a means of critiquing ideology in any form and at any time. It was not intended to be merely a Danish answer to a Danish problem. This is the view I will be supporting throughout the remainder of this work, and the reason why I contend that the Kierkegaardian Christian ethic is as viable as any alternative being argued for in moral and political philosophy today.

Before I go on to argue in defense of these claims, however, it is important to return to an issue I have already touched on in some detail above—the use of Abraham as ethical prototype and antihero.[5] *Fear and Trembling* is undoubtedly the most debated text in the Kierkegaardian corpus. Commentators from all corners of philosophical and theological scholarship have found in it endless resources: some use it as a archetypal example of how not to proceed ethically,

---

[5] This study of *Fear and Trembling* is a propaedeutic to a much more extensive analysis of this text and its implications for contemporary ethical theory in chapter 6.

while others, such as John Caputo, Jacques Derrida, Edward Mooney and Mark Taylor, have discovered amidst its intriguing pages much to validate a postmodern ethic.[6] What much of this fertile debate has failed to address, however, is how the rich insights developed by the pseudonym of this work, Johannes de Silentio, can enrich the reader's understanding of the Kierkegaardian project writ large. The key to breaking the code of this "dialectical lyric" is to examine how the argument for faith as a way of teleologically suspending one's absolute attachment to the established order—or as the pseudonym calls it in this particular context, "the universal"—is used at many critical junctures throughout the authorship. Upon so doing, one notices that faith is not a wild and irrational response to a divine ordinance, but rather a passionate way of taking cognizance of what it means to be a responsible and ethical self in one's daily life.

In the previous section I noted how Socrates ironically opposed the self-deification of the existing order by encouraging the individual to become negatively free. This, I concluded, is how responsible aspirants can establish a critical distance in relation to the claims

---

[6] See Paul B. Armstrong, "Reading Kierkegaard—Disorientation and Reorientation," in *Kierkegaard's Truth: The Disclosure of the Self*, ed. Joseph H. Smith (New Haven: Yale University Press, 1981), 23–50; Olivia Blanchette, "The Silencing of Philosophy," in *International Kierkegaard Commentary*, vol. 6, *"Fear and Trembling" and "Repetition,"* ed. Robert L. Perkins (Macon: Mercer University Press, 1993), 29–65; John D. Caputo, *Radical Hermeneutics: Repetition, Deconstruction, and the Hermeneutic Project* (Bloomington: Indiana University Press, 1987), *Against Ethics*, and "Instants, Secrets, and Singularities: Dealing Death in Kierkegaard and Derrida," in Matustík and Westphal, *Kierkegaard in Post/Modernity*, 216–38; Jacques Derrida, *The Gift of Death*, trans. David Wills (Chicago: University of Chicago Press, 1995); Hent De Vries, "Adieu, à dieu, a-Dieu," in *Ethics as First Philosophy: The Significance of Emmanuel Levinas for Philosophy, Literature, and Religion*, ed. Adriaan T. Peperzak (New York: Routledge, 1995), 211–20; Mark Dooley, "Murder on Moriah: A Paradoxical Representation," *Philosophy Today* 39 (Spring 1995): 67–83, "Playing on the Pyramid: Resituating the 'Self' in Kierkegaard and Derrida," *Imprimatur* 1, nos. 2–3 (Spring 1996): 151–62, and "Risking Responsibility"; C. Stephen Evans, "Faith as the Telos of Morality: A Reading of *Fear and Trembling*," in *International Kierkegaard Commentary*, vol. 6, *"Fear and Trembling" and "Repetition,"* ed. Perkins, 9–27; Hannay, *Kierkegaard*, chapters 3 and 4; Edward F. Mooney, *Knights of Faith and Resignation: Reading Kierkegaard's "Fear and Trembling"* (Albany: SUNY Press, 1991), and "Art, Deed, and System," in *International Kierkegaard Commentary*, vol. 6, *"Fear and Trembling" and "Repetition,"* ed. Perkins, 67–100; Robert L. Perkins, ed., *Kierkegaard's "Fear and Trembling": Critical Appraisals* (University: University of Alabama Press, 1981); Mark C. Taylor, "Transgression," in *Altarity*, 305–55; Merold Westphal, "Levinas's Teleological Suspension of the Religious," in Peperzak, *Ethics as First Philosophy*, 151–60.

that the universal, or state law, makes upon the individual. Responsi-bility of this type calls for an open model of society in which each participant attempts to become more self-engaged by earnestly striv-ing to relativize the regulative criteria, or objective standards of justi-fication, by which the state is legitimated. All the while, however, the individual is attempting to keep a focus on the "unconditioned" principle or idea (for Kierkegaard, the God-man), one that will serve to constantly keep in check the state's autodeifying pretensions. In relation to this, I underscored the vital distinction between such self-knowledge and the type of understanding that those living passion-less, wholly "external" lives have—the "human" point of view. This latter type of knowledge is epitomized by the disinterested reflective disposition of the leveled public, described so trenchantly in *Two Ages* and set forth here in chapter 1. Another expression Kierkegaard tends to use in relation to this categorially circumscribed mentality is "sensibleness." According to Kierkegaard (and here he is not con-demning the **individuals** who are sensible, but rather the rational system that has leveled the vital distinctions between each individ-ual, which he believes is a prerequisite if harmonious social relations are to obtain), the sensible life is one that sees itself only in terms of universal and objective (rather than subjective, singular, and particu-lar) categories. As such, "sensibleness is mutiny against the uncondi-tioned" (JFY, 157): "But it is eternally certain that nothing so offends sensibleness as the unconditioned, and to continue in the same vein as before, the immediately obvious mark of this is that sensibleness will never unconditionally acknowledge any require-ment but continually claims itself to be the one that declares what kind of requirement is to be made" (JFY, 155).

For those with the purely human point of view, therefore, the unconditioned "is basically madness," and is anathema to any rule-based morality. Hence it appears both offensive and absurd.[7] While striving to become incommensurable with the existing order, one is indeed bound to offend and appear paradoxical to those who are guided, as C. Stephen Evans says, by "imperialistic understanding."[8]

---

[7] See John D. Caputo, "Reason, History, and a Little Madness: Towards a Herme-neutics of the Kingdom," *Proceedings of the American Catholic Philosophical Associ-ation* 68 (1994): 27–44.

[8] C. Stephen Evans, *Passionate Reason: Making Sense of Kierkegaard's "Philosoph-ical Fragments"* (Bloomington: Indiana University Press, 1992), 79.

However, the new ethical vision Kierkegaard has in mind is not one that, unlike the given actuality, "threatens to make a fetish of thoughtless, passionless conformity."[9] It seeks, rather, to widen reflection's scope so that the presumptions made on behalf of the sensible order's belief in its own capacity to regulate the lives of its citizens are debunked.

I want to argue at this point that "faith," as Kierkegaard defines it, is precisely the individual's transformation of the sensible and reflective human point of view into self-knowledge. That is, faith is the process of becoming negatively free. The faithful individual is one who recognizes that the truth of *what* one knows is predicated upon *how* one knows it; that is, if the subject is not *self*-reflective, what he or she determines as being good or true will be either public opinion or objective knowledge, neither of which has a direct bearing on the individual's life. Taking the standpoint of faith requires that one learn the nature of the unconditioned ethical criterion; this, in turn, demands the cultivation of a passionately engaged personality, one that decisively strives in fear and trembling to actualize new possibilities, believing as it does in an open model of society. In order to realize these aims, the faithful individual must develop an inward disposition. In this way, the self dies to the given actuality, or immediacy, with the objective of establishing whether or not one's beliefs and values can be justifiably held. Such is what risking responsibility entails. As Johannes Climacus attests: "Without risk, no faith" (CUP, 204).

Johannes de Silentio considers Abraham the exemplar for the individual willing to risk the security of the existing order, or the state, with the objective of ascertaining just what the nature of the "unconditioned" idea is. At face value, this seems absurd: how can the story of a father's sacrifice of his son in response to a putatively divine call assist the agent in determining how one should act ethically? Does this not give credence to fundamentalists and extremists who justify terrorism, assassination, and the like by saying that they are acting in accordance with the will of God? Furthermore, how can this assist Kierkegaard in generating the type of authentic commu-

---

[9] Edward F. Mooney, *Selves in Discord and Resolve: Kierkegaard's Moral-Religious Psychology from "Either/Or" to "Sickness unto Death"* (New York: Routledge, 1996), 48.

nity existence he seeks? These claims notwithstanding, however, I
do believe we can make sense of de Silentio's radical call, following
Abraham, to teleologically suspend the ethical if we take cognizance
of what we have been suggesting thus far: Kierkegaard's conception
of a genuine social harmony deriving from each individual's adoption
of the ethical point of view is a reaction to closed models of society
(in this case the Hegelian paradigm) that consider freedom positively
or have as a fundamental tenet the belief that to be ethical enjoins
the individual to adhere to state law alone. Thus the ethics Kierkegaard and de Silentio are enjoining their readers to suspend is not
ethics per se, but rather the type of model that is merely rule-based
and which thus does not take account of personal motivation, or one
which believes that such essentially "ethical" ideals as harmony and
identity can be immanently realized. As Edward Mooney has incisively explained, "mere rule following, however desirable as training,
is primarily premoral behaviour. . . . Constraints on liars and cheats
are essential, but the larger issue remains the question of motivation." And with reference to Kierkegaard's appeal to the story of
Abraham as a correction to this type of inauthentic ethic, he says:

> As Johannes will unveil it, the story is a chilling metaphor away from
> the simple "outward" code of morality toward a more complex moral
> stance where purity of heart, purity of will, becomes its central focus.
> It is a metaphor of transformation any person can (and should) un-
> dergo, not a test reserved for heroes. Serving maids and shopmen can
> undergo inner struggles in the midst of which it may seem to them
> that codes are broken, that civic virtue falls flat, that ethics and moral
> identity are at risk *en masse*. . . . In the end, Johannes brings us back
> to ethics properly understood, to a "post-suspension ethics."[10]

Hence being truly ethical—at least according to the definition proffered by Kierkegaard and his pseudonyms—does not require a move
from the world of "everydayness." It does demand, however, that
one have the courage to suspend one's security in that world in order
to vigilantly assess the merits of one's guiding principles. This, as
seen in the case of Socrates, requires an ironic standpoint, and to
this I shall return later in this section.

For the moment, it is important to keep in mind that Abraham
metaphorically exemplifies this type of ethical crisis in which the

---

[10] Ibid., 46–47.

individual responds to an obligation to radically question the hypotheses upon which his or her moral convictions are based. Such questioning is how self-determination begins: by deliberating on why one acts in a certain way, and to what end, the question of ethical motivation and responsibility, as well as the usefulness of one's normative ideas, becomes an issue for the self. Abraham's plight, the pseudonym maintains, epitomizes the "madness" of such a passionate disposition.

From the very outset of his "dialectical lyric," Johannes de Silentio, describing himself as a "supplementary clerk who neither writes the system nor gives promises of the system, who neither exhausts himself on the system nor binds himself to the system" (FT, 7), makes a clear demarcation between the "external" and "internal" worlds, the latter of which he refers to as the "world of spirit." It may be assumed that this pseudonym considers "inwardness" as being in some way "spiritual." We might consider this a play on Hegel's notion of *Geist*, qua world-historical consciousness. Such a conclusion is, however, far from certain. A good indication of what is at issue here can be gleaned by analyzing Anti-Climacus's definition of the self rendered in *The Sickness unto Death*. Although I will be depending on this definition substantially in succeeding chapters, it is worthwhile quoting it in full at this juncture:

> A human being is spirit. But what is spirit? Spirit is the self. But what is the self? The self is a relation that relates itself to itself or is the relation's relating itself to itself in the relation; the self is not the relation but is the relation's relating itself to itself. A human being is a synthesis of the infinite and the finite, of the temporal and the eternal, of freedom and necessity, in short, a synthesis. A synthesis is a relation between two. Considered in this way, a human being is still not a self.
>
> In the relation between two, the relation is the third as a negative unity, and the two relate to the relation and in the relation to the relation; thus under the qualification of the psychical the relation between the psychical and the physical is a relation. If, however, the relation relates itself to itself, this relation is the positive third, and this is the self. (SUD, 14)

Despite its seemingly impenetrable and imponderable character, this definition supplies the reader with much to help determine the meaning of so many facets of the authorship. We can see clearly from even a cursory reading, for instance, that Kierkegaard is quite explicit in his juxtaposition of what he terms "a human being" and the self. This distinction has already been drawn in relation to the various levels of ethical comprehension Kierkegaard identifies: objective and reflective "human" knowing (opinion) and subjective self-knowledge. It can be further determined from the above extract that a human being has the *potential* to become spirit or a self; to return to my analysis of *The Sickness unto Death* in chapter 1, all human beings for Anti-Climacus are composed of a finite, temporal, and necessary element and an infinite, eternal, and free element. From the fact that human beings possess these attributes it does not by necessity follow that they are selves; that is, Kierkegaard, in response to the Hegelian notion of the self, believes in a "transcendent" rather than an "immanent" model in both the ethical and epistemological realms. This suggests that identity and ethical consciousness, from the viewpoint of responsibility, are not located naturally in the human being, but are to be realized through individual striving and the transcending of one's particular context. Until the human being begins to "relate itself to itself," it will not become a self.[11] The implication here is that unless and until the human being becomes *self*-reflective (rather than being merely reflective in the sense of the apathetic reflection of the present age), genuine truth and freedom will not gain a foothold in the lived reality of each individual. The human being has the ability, however, to acquire a passion for what lies beyond the purview of the state or the established order, for what cannot be teleologically predetermined by the world-historical process. This capacity, which I will examine in more detail when we come to discuss Kierkegaard's theory of repetition in chapter 4, empowers each individual to make concrete—through decisive resolution—what has hitherto been merely an abstract ideal. Thus, by transforming apathetic reflection into engaged and committed reflection, the individual succeeds in challenging the conception of the self that obtained at the level of human knowing. Such is what occurs when the merely human understanding confronts the infinite and eternal dimension of the self-system.

The world of spirit is thus the world in which individuals strive to realize their full potential as committed and responsible selves. De

---

[11] I will examine the meaning of this notion more extensively in chapter 4.

Silentio asserts that in this world "an eternal divine order prevails," one where "it holds true that only the one who works gets bread, that only the one who was in anxiety finds rest, that only the one who descends into the lower world rescues the beloved, that only the one who draws the knife gets back Isaac" (FT, 27). The suggestion here seems to be that in contradistinction to the objective ethical order, which is also the manifestation of a divine design, what de Silentio is speaking of can only be effectuated through the ethical trials Kierkegaard takes to be indicative of the risk demanded by radical responsibility. This is what the pseudonyms refer to as a "spiritual trial"; that is, the fear and trembling one undergoes in the transition from "a fossilized formalism which, by having lost the originality of the ethical, has become a desiccated ruin, a narrow-hearted custom and practice," to the point where one critically estimates the value of the guiding ideas and methods of justification, which have served as rules for moral guidance heretofore. Such a transition requires the "sacrifice" of those things in life that have greatest significance. De Silentio thus calls on his reader to deny the self anything that is inconsequential to the absolute task of challenging the given actuality by becoming self-reflective, even to the point of offering up one's son.

Johannes believes that although many in the present age find the story of Abraham remarkable, few actually understand it. To have such a comprehension requires that the individual experience the anxiety that the spiritual trial generated in Abraham's own experience. Indeed, it is more than anything a vexed and fraught *ethical* crisis because "to the son the father has the highest and holiest" obligation, and yet what is being asked of the father contravenes all sense of good conscience. Ethically speaking (and here the pseudonym is referring to the positive social ethics of *Sittlichkeit*), Abraham's actions cause grave concern, for he attempts murder in God's name.

Religiously speaking, however, Abraham "meant to sacrifice Isaac" (FT, 30). It is important to note at this point that, for Kierkegaard, the religious attitude is synonymous with what I have been calling "the ethics of responsibility." When looked at from this perspective, it becomes clear that Abraham's pain is meant to be analogous to that experienced by the individual who surrenders or suspends the peace and security of the age in order to become more passionately attuned to what it is required to respond to others' claims. For in the story of Abraham, Kierkegaard is placing before his reader the requirements for what it takes to cultivate inwardness, and hence the genuinely responsible point of view. He is endeavoring to allegorically demonstrate the fear and trembling occasioned when the individual comes into conflict with the age in such a manner. "Sacrifice" (and here I refer the reader back to what I said in a similar sense of Socrates) in this context means, therefore, the relinquishing of the objective human mentality, or of disinterested reflection. Ironically remaining within the state while at the same time undermining its tendency toward self-deification, by striving to establish an unconditioned and extraneous standard of justification, is what suspending the ethical, or dying to the world, implies throughout the authorship:

> To have to shatter one's fulfilled desire, personally to have to deprive oneself of the dearly desired one who is now one's own: that means to wound selfishness at the root, as it was with Abraham when God demanded that Abraham himself . . . should sacrifice Isaac—Isaac, the so long and so longingly awaited gift, indeed, a gift from God, for which Abraham felt he should give thanks the rest of his life but would never be able to give thanks enough—Isaac, his only child, the child of his old age, the child of promise! Do you think death can be as painful as this? I do not think it can. In any case, when it is death, then it is definitely over, but dying to is not over in this way, because he does not die, indeed, perhaps a long life lies before him, the one who has died. (FSE, 79)

To understand what is required in order to "die to" the world in this way, or to comprehend the movement from externality to inwardness, necessitates "faith," what we have described as passionately engaged double reflection leading to resolute responsible action in the life of the individual. Ordinary human understanding—what de Silentio calls "human calculation"—must be checked so that the individual can begin to acquire a more fundamental (doubly reflected) knowledge of the world and his or her relationship to it. Kierkegaard is not suggesting that individuals retreat from the world of everyday experience so as to establish some form of radical solitary individualism. He *is* saying, however, that if real and genuine relations are to be realized between selves, each individual must develop a self-understanding that will, in turn, afford him or her a critical perspective from which to examine the state's methods of justification. That is, when Kierkegaard suggests that dying to the world is the only means of realizing the responsible point of view, he is asserting that if a sincere apprehension of one's self and others is to be gleaned, one needs to suspend one's "everyday" calculation in order to develop a more conscientious understanding. In this way, the world, as the milieu in which the individual engages with others, is anything but lost with the inward movement. What is occurring here is what M. Jamie Ferreira calls a "transformation of vision"[12] in which the individual intensifies his or her relationship with the world as a consequence of having asked critical questions of what one had previously taken for granted at an ethical, religious, and political level. "Sacrifice" in this context, therefore, means a yielding up of the "human" understanding with the aim of strengthening subjective knowledge. As such, the existing order, or the immediate actuality, is challenged from within.

The movement of faith is a double movement in the sense that when the individual resigns from the existing order, it is with the objective of returning to the world with a more engaged and passionate disposition. The subject, that is, in becoming more responsible and passionate in his or her appraisal of what appears to be reality, and consequently by forming the realization that harmony and identity have yet to be engendered, strives to regulate his or her life in accordance with the requirements of an "unconditioned idea."

Faith—at least as defined in the Kierkegaardian paradigm—is this movement from complete identification with the state or the universal to the point where one has become free by virtue of having developed a residual incommensurability with the immediate order. Resignation thus is only resignation from the sphere of inauthentic externality, and by no means demands a withdrawal from the world or from one's participation in it. Inwardness constitutes taking a critical stance in relation to the dominant codes that govern reality. Rather than being a withdrawal from personal and social responsibility, it is an intensification of both.

---

[12] See M. Jamie Ferreira, *Transforming Vision: Imagination and Will in Kierkegaardian Faith* (Oxford: Clarendon Press, 1991). Ferreira's text is undoubtedly one of the most incisive and original works to have emerged in recent years. Particularly appealing is its willingness to take for granted that Kierkegaard is a partner in mainstream philosophical and theological debate, not a nineteenth-century figure whose writings have little to teach the present age.

If, however, faith is a broadening of the scope of reflection, rather than its circumscription, it is the double movement of reflection and action that functions "by virtue of the absurd." That is, the movement of faith "is not the spontaneous inclination of the heart but the paradox of existence" (FT, 47). It is paradoxical and absurd to believe—at least for the purely *human* objective mentality—that sacrifice and resignation can enhance and fulfill the life of the responsible individual. The "natural" self (and it is vital to keep this distinction in focus) who has yet to enter the spiritual order in the manner described by Anti-Climacus—that is, one who has yet to become a self qua spirit—finds it offensive to hear de Silentio remark: "By faith I do not renounce anything; on the contrary, by faith I receive everything" (FT, 48). Resignation must lead to faith. The two movements, the pseudonym informs the reader, are inextricable; for if the movement of resignation is undertaken without the belief that one is attempting to achieve a teleological suspension of the ethical, qua *Sittlichkeit,* in favor of a more just and ethical society— one where conformity and unquestioned obedience to the established order are not considered truly responsible behavior—then the individual does indeed renounce and deny the world. The "courage of faith," however, is that after the individual has resigned from the given actuality, he or she once again grasps "the whole temporal realm"—this time, however, with an enlarged or, to appropriate Ferreira's phrase once more, "transformed vision." Such is what confounds and seems absurd to the human mentality; ordinary human calculation is incapable of comprehending the paradox implicit in the statement that as a result of dying to or sacrificing the world, an act that is always a madness to human calculation, one will receive that world back to an even greater degree. For only after the individual comes to know *why* he or she performs or acts in a certain way, and in accordance with what ideals, can there be a totally genuine sense of self:

> When the believer has faith, the absurd is not the absurd—faith transforms it, but in every weak moment it is again more or less absurd to him. The passion of faith is the only thing which masters the absurd—if not, then faith is not faith in the strictest sense, but a kind of [human] knowledge. The absurd terminates negatively before the sphere of faith, which is a sphere by itself. To a third person the believer relates himself by virtue of the absurd; so must a third person

judge, for a third person does not have the passion of faith. . . . Therefore, rightly understood, there is nothing at all frightening in the category of the absurd—no, it is the very category of courage and enthusiasm. (JP 10, vol. 1, p. 7)

What appears absurd to those with the human point of view, or to those who conflate Hegelian (positive) freedom with Socratic (negative) freedom, is truth to those who are prepared to make the movement of faith.

It is true that Johannes de Silentio, with his rendering of the story of Abraham, does not develop a social ethic *stricto sensu*. This, I suggest, is because *Fear and Trembling* is an account of how each *individual* should appropriate the subjective (ethical) point of view, rather than a description of the type of community life that results from such responsible and concerted action.[13] By suggesting that faith requires a more intensive involvement with the world, the text does reinforce the main Kierkegaardian claim that becoming subjective is the way to enhance community relations. But by taking Abraham as the ethical exemplar in this case, Kierkegaard is only discussing "the formal definition of faith" without demonstrating exactly how this can generate a social ethic. Such a discussion, which will be a major feature of succeeding chapters, will have to wait until faith is situated in a Christian context. For the moment it is enough to state that de Silentio takes the Abraham story to represent how each individual should go about challenging the methods of justification employed by the established order. It aims to expose the reader to what suspending the ethical demands, while at the same time demonstrating that this movement is a transformation of actuality rather than its denial. And this it does by way of the extreme example of how a father revokes his parental duties. I remarked at the outset how this should be interpreted as a metaphor for how difficult it is for one with the human point of view to sacrifice that peace and security provided by the passionless age of reflection. Responsibility is not merely following rules, but a process of subjecting to vigilant scrutiny the hypotheses upon which such rules rest. Be-

---

[13] We will see in chapter 6, however, that Abraham's teleological suspension of the ethical can be adequately defended as a "politics of the *émigré*," which in turn founds the "open quasi-community"—which I will argue, following Derrida and Caputo, Kierkegaard anticipates.

coming responsible therefore requires that the subjective individual doubly reflect on the efficacy of those moral precepts that bind individuals together, and on how these should be revised so as to accommodate the will of a more self-conscious public. This is the ineluctable "double bind" that responsibility demands: how to change the law without actually breaking the law, or how to become more responsible while staying within the broad parameters of the ethical. Mooney rationalizes the dilemma in the following way:

> A suspension of ethics does not need to be a suspension of a specific ethical prohibition, say, against killing one's son. It can mark suspension of a general moral orientation. If the willingness to sacrifice Isaac is roughly equivalent to a willingness to suspend a broad moral stance, then some of the terror of the upraised knife will be diffused. The more general ethics meant to be suspended could be a Hegelian assimiliationist view of ethics. Furthermore, if we link this suspension of a broad ethical stance to faith's double movement, then we can expect that the apparent suspension of parental duty (and other duties generally) is linked to the simultaneous assurance that parental duties (and Isaac) will be returned. One believes every moment that one has *not* forfeited one's status as a parent, or as a moral being. . . . Ethics can be suspended only on the presumption that it will not be lost.[14]

This reading by Mooney can be substantiated if one looks to the second of de Silentio's "problemas," where he asks if there is "an absolute duty to God." In stating that the paradox of faith is that the single individual is higher than the universal—meaning that the individual who becomes passionately self-reflective and who thereby begins to critically assess the state's (qua universal objective ethical order—*Sittlichkeit*) claim to be the concrete realization of a divine design—de Silentio clarifies that "from this it does not follow that the ethical should be invalidated; rather, the ethical receives a completely different expression, a paradoxical expression, such as, for example, that love to God may bring the knight of faith to give his love to the neighbor—an expression opposite to that which, ethically speaking, is duty" (FT, 70). The objective, therefore, of a teleological suspension of the ethical is not to nullify one's everyday ethical obligations. Rather, by developing a more engaged and conscientious mode of double reflection—what de Silentio at one point refers to

---

[14] Mooney, *Selves in Discord and Resolve*, 57.

as "passionate concentration" or "intense consciousness"—the individual becomes capable of establishing the nature of a guiding ethical idea or principle (in this case God), which paradoxically collides with what is deemed dutiful to observe in the sphere of the universal. This, in turn, translates into practical ethical action, such as loving one's neighbor.[15] For although "the absolute duty can lead one to do what ethics would forbid," it can never "lead the knight of faith to stop loving" (FT, 74). Let me reiterate that for Kierkegaard, to have faith is to suspend "desiccated formalism" in favor of a guiding idea that emphasizes inwardness as the means of establishing genuinely harmonious and comprehensive community relations.

CONCLUSION

Abraham personifies the trauma of passionate concentration. As an "emigrant from the sphere of the universal," he "*cannot* speak" (FT, 115). In emphasizing this, the pseudonym is implying that the individual who makes the movement of faith and inwardness "speaks no *human* language" (my emphasis), but rather speaks "in a divine language"; that is, Abraham does not communicate directly, but in an ironic and oblique fashion. For if he were to make sense of his spiritual trial by explaining it in a disinterested and objective fashion, it would no longer be the trial that it is. The story of the sacrifice would become just another object of exegetical scrutiny.

De Silentio is here playing on Kierkegaard's distinction—drawn most poignantly in *Two Ages*—between "chattering" and "essential speaking." I have shown how the knight of faith withdraws or resigns from the world only insofar as he or she returns to that world with a heightened sense of personal and passionate responsibility. As in the case of Socrates, therefore, the knight adopts a critical distance from the universal (*Sittlichkeit*), with the object of challenging the premises upon which the state claims the authority to deify itself. By transcending the immediate given actuality, the individual acquires an engaged disposition by which he or she can surmount the leveling generated by the passive assimilation of public opinion. Conse-

---

[15] In chapter 6, I will return to the theme of a "community of neighbors" formed through "selfless" love.

quently, he or she begins to treat all knowledge directly transmitted through public channels with suspicion, recognizing the illusory nature of the apparent (vigilant counter-interpretation).

Unlike Socrates, however, Abraham is not in pursuit of truth in the form of the Idea of the Good; his guiding "idea" forces him to reflect on how his relationships with actual others can be made more concrete and ethically based. He begins this reflection by relating to the other (in this case Isaac, Sarah and Eliezer) ideally and not immediately; that is, when individuals relate to one another in an immediate sense, they are "in a relation of [passive] reflection" and "are oriented to externalities" only (TA, 97–98). Kierkegaard calls such external communication "chatter," a purely external mode of discourse that gives "utterance to [passive] reflection" and as a consequence "has a weakening effect on action by getting ahead of it." With reference to our discussion of the present age in chapter 1, we might say that the chattering public is composed of individuals who "relate to an idea merely *en masse*" and "consequently without the individual separation of inwardness" (TA, 63).

"Essential speaking," on the other hand, is based on the "passionate disjunction between being silent and speaking" (TA, 97). The category of silence in the work of Kierkegaard, like most categories in this context, should not be interpreted literally. It does not mean a refusal to speak or, as the pseudonyms term it, a form of "inclosing reserve" (see SUD, 63–67, 72–73; CA, 123–35). Rather, "silence is inwardness." The individual transforms *human* knowledge (passive reflection) into *self*-knowledge (engaged and passionate concentration or double reflection) by taking a critical stand in relation to all objective truths (metaphysical, ethical, and political) that appear to govern reality (inwardness). Throughout this discussion I have urged that such a movement not be interpreted, as Adorno and others would contend, as a flight from the real concerns of the everyday into the solitary seclusion of an objectless world, but rather as the way to achieve a genuine and wholesome relationship to the actual world and those with whom it is shared. Kierkegaard calls the establishment of this more concrete engagement with reality "certitude," in contradistinction to "probability":

> Certitude and inwardness are indeed subjectivity, but not in an entirely abstract sense. . . . Abstract subjectivity is just as uncertain and

lacks inwardness to the same degree as abstract objectivity. When it is spoken about *in abstracto*, this cannot be seen, and so it is correct to say that abstract subjectivity lacks content. When it is spoken about *in concreto*, the content clearly appears, because the individuality who wants to make himself into an abstraction precisely lacks inwardness, as does the individuality who makes himself into a mere master of ceremonies. (CA, 141)

Kierkegaard, therefore, makes a clear demarcation between abstract and concrete subjectivity; the inward subject has developed a mode of understanding (passionate reflection/concentration) that is fully concrete and certain of reality in a way that abstract, probable speculation is not. Moreover, the concrete subject, in order to become *self*-reflective, begins to question the foundations and premises upon which the content of his or her knowledge is based. Inwardness is thus a mode of more concrete and passionate understanding of the external world, rather then an irrational exit from the concrete actuality:

Inwardness is an understanding, but *in concreto* the important thing is how this understanding is to be understood. To understand a speech is one thing, and to understand what it refers to, namely, the personal, is something else. The more concrete the content of consciousness is, the more concrete the understanding becomes, and when this understanding is absent to consciousness, we have the phenomenon of unfreedom that wants to close itself off against freedom. (CA, 142)

I have defined "inwardness" also as a mode of engaged action; I have attempted, that is, to demonstrate how the responsible individual—one who has succeeded in developing a form of intense subjectivity by relating to the "idea"—transforms the manner in which he or she engages with actuality. It could be argued, in accordance with the definition of the self provided by Anti-Climacus above, that inwardness is the process of infinitizing the finite, of freeing the self from the purely finite realm of **Sittlichkeit**. This again does not mean that Kierkegaard subscribes to a notion of the self that interprets the infinite as something that totally divorces it from daily dealings with others. It suggests, rather, that the human being, in the process of becoming self-reflective, comes to understand the given actuality (the finite) from a more subjectively enlightened point of view. Consequently, the individual who has acquired this new level of certitude

begins to act more decisively and responsibly. Inwardness, for Kierkegaard, is involved and responsible action in the world:

> The most concrete content that consciousness can have is conscious-
> ness of itself, of the individual himself—not the pure self-conscious-
> ness, but the self-consciousness that is so concrete that no author, not
> even one with the greatest power of description, has ever been able to
> describe a single such self-consciousness, although every single human
> being is such a one. This self-consciousness is not contemplation, for
> he who believes this has not understood himself, because he sees that
> meanwhile he himself is in the process of becoming and consequently
> cannot be something completed for contemplation. This self-con-
> sciousness, therefore, is *action*, and this *action* is in turn inwardness,
> and whenever inwardness does not correspond to this consciousness,
> there is a form of the demonic as soon as the absence of inwardness
> expresses itself as anxiety about its acquisition. (CA, 143; my em-
> phasis)

If silence is inwardness, therefore, we can conclude that it is a
prerequisite for the development of a wholly responsible, committed, and engaged subject whose relationship to the world has been
enhanced as a consequence of the expansion of (ethical) reflection
and its translation into action. Silence, for Kierkegaard, connotes a
disposition in which the responsible self relates to the other, neither
at the level of pure externality nor at the level of the mundane alone,
but from the perspective of heightened ethical awareness that the
teleological suspension engenders. This suggests that for a passionate
understanding to be cultivated, there must be an ideal distance between individuals; that is, the more a life is commensurable with the
given actuality, "the more the conversation will tend to become a
trivial rattling and name-dropping" (TA, 99), and the less one will
come to a concrete and active understanding of oneself and others.
Silence, in this context, may thus be construed as a positively ironic
mode of dialogue in which interlocutors communicate on the basis
of a mutual passionate understanding and concentration. This "inward orientation of silence is the condition for cultured conversation," while chattering, as "the caricaturing externalization of
inwardness, is uncultured" (TA, 99). Kierkegaard remarks on ironic
silence as follows: "'To be silent' means while reflecting to be able to
speak, that is, about everything else imaginable, for otherwise it is
conspicuous and suspicious for someone to be silent, and then it is
not exactly silence, not complete silence" (JP 3983, vol. 4, p. 99).

For Kierkegaard, the difference between Socrates and Abraham as ethical exemplars lies in the fact that whereas Socrates admonished the self to become negatively free, Abraham's actions represent the way an individual can transform that negative freedom into a positive liberty. This, of course, should not be confused with positive freedom in the Hegelian sense; rather, by resigning from the world or the given actuality, Abraham reenacts the Socratic move but, unlike Socrates, follows this with the move of faith, or the affirmation of the actual from a passionately inward perspective. Abraham, therefore, personifies the ethic of responsibility in that he transforms the negative freedom realized in the suspension of the ethical into a positive experience of responding to the call of the other. In challenging the notion that the law is the manifestation of the divine design on earth, he begins to question his own motivations. What he is sacrificing, as a consequence, is his dependency on any morality that is strictly rule-based or which functions merely to preserve the existing order. Abraham recognizes that Socratic irony is not enough to ensure the successful return to the concrete lived experience of the individual after the movement of resignation. His use of positive irony in the moment of crisis suggests that his silence is not a refusal to engage the ethical authorities in dialogue, but rather a means of ensuring that relationships are made more concrete and enduring. Abraham's silence is "essential speaking." Although he communicates with all in the universal, he maintains an ideal distance from his partners in communication. Risking responsibility as a knight of faith requires a teleological suspension of the "assimilationist" ethic of *Sittlichkeit* and an affirmation of a radically responsible ethic that resolves in concrete practical and responsible action.

4

Repetition and Selfhood

IN THIS CHAPTER I will analyze in some detail Kierkegaard's related theories of repetition (*Gjentagelsen*)[1] and selfhood. The category of

---

[1] This category will be of fundamental significance when I discuss the Kierkegaard-Derrida relationship in chapter 6. An extensive catalogue of secondary literature is devoted either in full or in part to Kierkegaard's category of repetition. The following titles are deserving of particular attention: Harold Bloom, ed., *Kierkegaard* (New York: Chelsea House, 1989); John D. Caputo, "Hermeneutics and the Recovery of Man," in *Hermeneutics and Modern Philosophy*, ed. Brice R. Wachtarhauser (Albany: SUNY Press, 1986), 416–45, *Radical Hermeneutics: Repetition, Deconstruction, and the Hermeneutic Project*, and "Kierkegaard, Heidegger, and the Foundering of Metaphysics," in *International Kierkegaard Commentary*, vol. 6, *"Fear and Trembling" and "Repetition,"* ed. Perkins, 201–24; Edward Casey, "Imagination and Repetition in Literature," *Yale French Studies* 52 (1975): 250–66; André Clair, "Médiation et répétion: Le lieu de la dialectique kierkegaardienne," *Revue des Sciences philosophiques et théologiques* 59 (1975): 38–78, and *Pseudonymie et Paradoxe: Le Pensée Dialectique de Kierkegaard* (Paris: J. Vrin, 1976); Connell, *To Be One Thing*; Stephen Crites, "'The Blissful Security of the Moment': Recollection, Repetition, and Eternal Recurrence," in *International Kierkegaard Commentary*, vol. 6, *"Fear and Trembling" and "Repetition,"* ed. Perkins, 225–46; Cutting, "Levels of Interpersonal Relationships," 73–86, and "The Possibility of Being-with-Others for Kierkegaard's Individual" (Ph.D. diss., University of New Mexico, 1976); Gilles Deleuze, *Difference and Repetition* (Bath: Athlone Press, 1994); Janet Mason Ellerby, "Repetition and Redemption" (Ph.D. diss., University of Washington, 1989); Elrod, *Being and Existence*; Ferguson, *Melancholy and the Critique of Modernity*; Gouwens, *Kierkegaard's Dialectic of the Imagination*, 141–275, "Understanding, Imagination, and Irony in Kierkegaard's Repetition," in *International Kierkegaard Commentary*, vol. 6, *"Fear and Trembling" and "Repetition,"* ed. Perkins, 283–308, and *Kierkegaard as Religious Thinker* (Cambridge: Cambridge University Press, 1996); Victor Guarda, *Die Wiederholung: Analysen zur Grundstruktur menschlicher Existenz im Verständnis Søren Kierkegaard* (Konigstein/Ts.: Forum Academicum in der Verlagsgruppe, 1980); Lacan, *Four Fundamental Concepts of Psycho-Analysis*, 17–64; Vincent B. Leitch, *Deconstructive Criticism: An Advanced Introduction* (London: Hutchinson, 1983), 60–87; Louis Mackey, *Points of View: Readings of Kierkegaard* (Tallahassee: Florida State University Press, 1986); Henry Earl McLane, "Kierkegaard's Use of the Category of Repetition: An Attempt to Discern the Structure and Unity of His Thought" (Ph.D. diss., Yale University, 1961); Roger Poole, *Kierkegaard: The Indirect Communication* (Charlottesville: University Press of Virginia, 1993); Paul Ricoeur, "Religion, Atheism, and Faith," trans. Charles Freilich, in Ricoeur, *The Conflict of Interpretations: Essays in Hermeneutics*, ed. Don Ihde (Evanston: Northwestern University Press, 1974), 440–67; Ronald Schleifer, "Irony,

repetition is fundamental for anyone aspiring to make sense of Kierkegaard's authorship as a whole, in that it provides a coherence to the multifarious and often disparate techniques this thinker employs. More importantly, however, Kierkegaard contends that it is through the "movement" of repetition that the individual acquires a sense of oneself as a being with the capacity to exercise passionate responsibility; that is, the transition from objective disinterestedness to passionate ethical subjectivity requires an education in repetition. In relation to the broader aims of this work, I will argue that repetition is central for the realization of the community of ethically oriented selves, the establishment of which, I maintain, was Kierkegaard's primary vocation.

REPETITION: A CLIMACEAN DEFINITION

Gjentagelsen literally means a "taking again." It connotes, as Johannes Climacus says, "rebirth" (*Gjenfødelsen*),[2] or in the spiritual sense, a "second coming":

> This matter of being born—is it thinkable? Well, why not? But who is supposed to think it—one who is born or who is not born? The latter, of course, is unreasonable and cannot occur to anyone, for this notion certainly cannot occur to one who is born. When one who is born thinks of himself as born, he of course is thinking of this transition from "not to be" to "to be." The situation must be the same with rebirth. Or is the matter made more difficult by this—that the non-being preceding the rebirth has more being than the non-being that precedes birth? But who, then, is supposed to think this? It must of course be one who is reborn, for it would be unreasonable to think

Identity, and Repetition," *Substance* 25 (1980): 44–54, Ronald Schleifer and R. Markley, *Kierkegaard and Literature: Irony, Repetition, and Criticism* (Norman: University of Oklahoma Press, 1984); Calvin O. Schragg, *Philosophical Papers: Betwixt and Between* (Albany: SUNY Press, 1977); Lorenzo C. Simpson, *Technology, Time, and the Conversations of Modernity* (New York: Routledge, 1995), 63–135; George Stack, "Kierkegaard and the Phenomenology of Repetition," *Journal of Existentialism* 7 (1966–67): 111–25, *Kierkegaard's Existential Ethics* (University: University of Alabama Press, 1977), and "Repetition in Kierkegaard and Freud," *Personalist* 58 (1977): 249–61; M. C. Taylor, *Kierkegaard's Pseudonymous Authorship*; Henri-Bernard Vergote, *Sens et répétition: Essai sur l'ironie kierkegaardienne* (Orante: Éditions du cerf, 1982); Walsh, *Living Poetically*.

² See M. C. Taylor, *Kierkegaard's Pseudonymous Authorship*, 330.

that one who is not reborn should do it, and would it not be ludicrous
if this were to occur to one who is not reborn? (PF, 20)

The individual who is reborn, according to Climacus, is not someone
who comes into existence for the first time, but someone who has a
history, who lives and resides as all other individuals do in the concrete milieu of everyday affairs. The difference is, however, that this
individual has "taken up" the past, has come to a more comprehensive understanding of it by having performed a critical diagnosis of
his or her relationship to the world in which he or she is embedded.
We could say that repetition is the process of rethinking the past
from the point of view of the future. This requires for its effectuation
the form of engaged and passionate double reflection that I have
argued the ethical exemplars, Socrates and Abraham, epitomize in
their confrontations with the established order. Both advocate that
the individual, who heretofore has been living a life of pure immediacy and externality, migrate inward, or become "incommensurable"
with the given actuality that deifies itself at the expense of freedom
and truth. Such acts of personal responsibility lead to a passionate
intensification of subjectivity. Vigilius Haufniensis, pseudonymous
author of *The Concept of Anxiety,* defines subjectivity as "certitude
and inwardness" (CA, 141), both of which "can be attained only by
and in action" (CA, 138). The realization of subjectivity, for this
writer, requires a type of "meaningful action," what he calls "earnestness": "Inwardness, certitude, is earnestness" (CA, 151). Constantin Constantius concurs with this assessment when he says:
"Repetition—that is actuality and the earnestness of existence. The
person who wills repetition is mature in earnestness" (R, 133). Repetition is, therefore, "not a mere 'repetition of the same,' abandoning
itself wholly to the past,"[3] but "the acquired originality of disposition" (CA, 149). It is "originality" of action.

In the context of Constantius's text, *Repetition: A Venture in Experimenting Psychology* (1843), one is furnished with the first sustained reflection on the nature of the category. The pseudonym
opens his discourse by explaining how significant repetition is for
those engaged in the study of modern philosophy:

Say what you will, this question will play a very important role in modern philosophy, for *repetition* is a crucial expression for what "recollec-

---

[3] Simpson, *Conversations of Modernity,* 57.

tion" was to the Greeks. Just as they taught that all knowing is a recollecting, modern philosophy will teach that life is a repetition. . . . Repetition and recollection are the same movement, except in opposite directions, for what is recollected has been, is repeated backward, whereas genuine repetition is recollected forward. Repetition, therefore, if it is possible, makes a person happy, whereas recollection makes him unhappy. (R, 131)

Kierkegaard, as highlighted in the previous chapter, had much respect for Greek philosophy, especially in the guise of Socrates. However, he ultimately rejects the Greek paradigm in favor of a Christian model. He makes this quite apparent in his posthumously published *The Point of View for My Work As an Author:*

I for my part tranquilly adhere to Socrates. It is true, he was not a Christian; that I know, and yet I am thoroughly convinced that he has become one. But he was a dialectician, he conceived everything in terms of reflection. And the question which concerns us here is a purely dialectical one, it is the question of the use of reflection in Christendom. We are reckoning here with two qualitatively different magnitudes, but in a formal sense I can very well call Socrates my teacher—whereas I have only believed, and only believe, in one, the Lord Jesus Christ. (POV, 41)

In his attack on Greek recollection, Kierkegaard singles out Platonic speculation (and its Hegelian counterpart) as the corrupting force of the age. Although he looks to Socrates as moral guide and teacher, he nonetheless subjects the Socratic thesis—that all knowledge is recollection—to severe scrutiny. Kierkegaard is here making a critical distinction between Socrates, Plato's mouthpiece, and the individual who ironically took issue with the given actuality. Johannes Climacus explains:

By holding Socrates to the thesis that all knowing is recollecting, one turns him into a speculative philosopher instead of what he was, an existing thinker who understood existing as the essential. The thesis that all knowing is a recollecting belongs to speculative thought, and recollecting is immanence. . . . To emphasize existence, which contains within it the qualification of inwardness, is the Socratic, whereas the Platonic is to pursue recollection and immanence. (CUP, 206)

By elucidating the distinctions between Plato and Socrates in this manner, Climacus demonstrates that existence (subjectivity, inwardness) is opposed to the Platonic immanentist theory of knowledge, which specifies that truth is located in the individual's soul. According to Plato, the soul is an immortal entity that knows and sees all things. Only by coming to know the soul, therefore, can a knowledge of the truth be realized.

Plato's discussion of recollection as the way the individual can grasp the truth is staged primarily in the *Meno*.[4] The dialogue commences with Plato asking, "How far does truth admit of being learned?" In response, Meno asks: "How on earth are you going to set up something you don't know as the object of your search?" (80d5).[5] How, that is, can the learner come to a knowledge of the truth if he or she has no awareness of what truth is to begin with? A learner, according to Meno, must have some identifiable object in any form of inquiry. Meno's paradox is, however, based on the mistaken belief that truth is something located outside the human soul and not contained within the soul itself. For Plato, however, the answer to Meno's problem is that truth is accessible only through the process of self-knowledge, which is equivalent to a knowledge of the soul, since the soul has acquired a knowledge of all things, both heavenly and earthly, through past experience. What each subject must do to gain a comprehensive sense of this truth is to surmount one's forgetfulness, which comes from having been thrown into a world of sensory illusion. It is the priority of all beings to deflect attention from this ephemeral realm in order to remember (*anamnesis*) what the soul has previously learned. Recollection is thus the act of calling forth truth that is immanently preserved in the soul.

We can now discern why Constantius perceives recollection to be a "repetition backwards": the individual who is striving to realize truth need only recollect what the soul has learned in the past. Truth, therefore, is a recollection of what has already been. Repetition, however, is a movement in which there is a "recollection forward," or to use an expression made popular by Gadamer, a *fusion* of the past with the future. It requires, therefore, not merely a passive reflection on what has been, but as Lorenzo Simpson suggests, "an applicative

---

[4] Plato, *Meno*, trans. W. K. C. Guthrie, in Plato, *Collected Dialogues*, ed. Edith Hamilton and Huntington Cairns (Princeton: Princeton University Press, 1978), 353–84.

[5] Ibid., 363.

recollection oriented toward future action."[6] As such, repetition demands a form of personal "transcendence" whereby the learner appeals to some higher ideal, other than the *logos* of recollection, in the quest to gain an understanding of the truth.

In his attempt to counter the Platonic theory of recollection as the "metaphysical" view of life, Kierkegaard, through the use of Johannes Climacus, reconstructs the original problematic introduced in *Meno*. *Philosophical Fragments* opens with what the pseudonym calls a "thought project," or an imaginary investigation, in which he reconsiders Meno's question, "Can the truth be learned?":

> Insofar as the truth is to be learned, it of course must be assumed not to be—consequently, because it is to be learned, it is sought. Here we encounter the difficulty that Socrates calls attention to in the *Meno* as a "pugnacious proposition": a person cannot possibly seek what he knows, and, just as impossibly, he cannot seek what he does not know, for what he knows he cannot seek, since he knows it, and what he does not know he cannot seek, because, after all, he does not even know what he is supposed to seek. (PF, 9)

As we have seen, Socrates rebuts his interlocutor by invoking the notion of recollection. The truth, according to this account, is contained within the soul of the individual. Socrates, as a historical agent, is only an occasion for the truth to be comprehended; he is but a midwife whose importance as a teacher is of no consequence once the learner comes to know the self in recollection. That is, because the soul is the divine element in the human being, and because self-knowledge is therefore "God-knowledge," "the fact that I have learned [the truth] from Socrates or from Prodicus . . . can concern me only historically" (PF, 12). In fact, because truth is recalled rather than learned, the moment of my coming into contact with Prodicus or Socrates cannot be regarded as having any effect on one's "eternal happiness," for this I had been in possession of from the dawn of time. Once the individual discovers that this is the case, "the temporal point of departure" loses all its significance.

Climacus's reflection on the role of the teacher in the Platonic account of recollection underscores the primacy given to the eternal at the expense of the historical. However, Climacus does not hold

---

[6] Simpson, *Conversations of Modernity*, 57.

the view that truth can be possessed by an existing individual in any immanent sense.[7] If, for Kierkegaard, "the coiled-springs of life-relationships" are to be made more resilient, all individuals must make a concerted effort to relate to the "idea." This involves, in accordance with our observations on the nature of repetition, a personal transcendence (suspension) of one's immediate situation ("given actuality") with the objective of reclaiming that same world from the ethical point of view. Becoming passionate about the self in this way requires, as in the case of Abraham, that the individual teleologically suspend his or her place in the ethical, *qua* universal, sphere of existence. This implies that in a "spiritual trial," when the agent sacrifices the immediate world (what Anti-Climacus calls "the secular human mentality"), he or she does so with a view to realizing a "higher" goal, a more profound ideal. The impetus for such resolved and committed action comes from outside, challenging as it does the methods of justification employed by the state or the "established order"; that is, the truly responsible individual strives to become self-reflective by attempting to learn what the essential nature of the "idea" is.

According to Johannes Climacus, the point in time when the individual comes to recognize that truth is a process of gradual and painstaking becoming, and not something that has been perennially present to the learner in his or her soul, is the "moment *in time*" that "must have such decisive significance that for no moment will I be able to forget it." This is so because in that moment, the eternal truth (in contradistinction to relative and probable truths) "came into existence [*blev til*]" (PF, 13). Otherwise stated, the pursuit of truth in this moment becomes a significant ideal for the particular existing individual. The historical point of departure for Climacus thus does indeed have importance for the learner.

Climacus reconstructs Meno's paradox to prove the efficacy of this latter claim. He contends that if the historical moment is to have significance, it must be demonstrated that at no time before the learner came into possession of the truth was the truth present to him or her, "not even in the form of ignorance." The learner, that

---

[7] See Evans's exceptional reading of *Philosophical Fragments* in *Passionate Reason*, especially chapter 3, "Constructing an Alternative to the Socratic View of 'The Truth.'"

is, must be considered to have no knowledge of the truth whatsoever; he or she "has to be defined as being outside the truth" (PF, 13).

The argument in the *Fragments* turns at this point to the role of "the teacher" in the truth process.[8] Unlike in the Platonic paradigm, the teacher cannot merely be the "occasion" for the learner's recollection of the truth, but must bring to the learner's attention that he or she is in a state of "untruth." However, the learner must have the "condition" for learning and understanding the truth, for if the learner "were himself the condition for understanding the truth, then he merely needs to recollect, because the condition for understanding the truth is like being able to ask about it—the condition and the question contain the condition and the answer. (If this is not the case, then the moment is to be understood only Socratically)" (PF, 14). If the learner was not in possession of the condition, the teacher would be incapable of making the learner reflect on his or her untruth.

The presence of "the condition," therefore, is that upon which "all instruction depends." Climacus concludes that if this is the case, then the teacher is not responsible for giving the learner the condition, and that this "must be done by the god himself" (PF, 15).[9] But this begs the response: if it is the god himself who is responsible for giving the individual the condition for the realization that he or she is in untruth, then surely the individual has been in possession of the truth for all eternity, and the teacher is only the occasion for this realization. The upshot of this is that "the moment" when the eternal truth comes into existence once more loses its "decisive significance." Climacus responds to this seeming contradiction in his argument as follows:

> Now, inasmuch as the learner exists [*er til*], he is indeed created, and, accordingly, God must have given him the condition for understanding the truth . . . but insofar as the moment is to have decisive significance (and if this is not assumed, then we do in fact remain in the Socratic), he must lack the condition, consequently be deprived of it.

---

[8] See Hugh C. Pyper, "The Lesson of Eternity: Christ as Teacher in Kierkegaard and Hegel," in *The International Kierkegaard Commentary*, vol. 7, "*Philosophical Fragments*" *and "Johannes Climacus*," ed. Robert L. Perkins (Macon: Mercer University Press, 1994), 129–45.

[9] I will analyze the precise nature of the Kierkegaardian god as the highest ethical prototype in chapter 5.

This cannot be due to an act of god (for this is a contradiction) or to an accident (for it is a contradiction that something inferior would be able to vanquish something superior); it must therefore have been due to himself. (PF, 15)

Climacus posits the belief that if the historical moment is to retain its significance, the learner must lack the condition by having forfeited it him- or herself. It is god as teacher, therefore, who is the occasion for reminding the individual that he or she is in a state of untruth "through his or her own fault." The state of being in untruth, which is brought about by the learner, is what Climacus calls "sin."

The sinful condition is one in which the individual considers him- or herself capable of acquiring a comprehension of the truth without any external assistance. If, indeed, such assistance is required it is considered only as the occasion for the recollection of immanent truth, as in the Socratic paradigm. Climacus, however, has set himself the task of trying to prove that learning the truth requires the assistance of a teacher who can create the conditions for its acquisition, not merely as an occasion, but with decisive significance. Hence, as a result of the learner's having lost his or her liberty by sacrificing the condition, the pseudonym asks what one should call a teacher who endeavors to reclaim this condition and the truth for the sinful individual: "Let us call him a *savior*, for he does indeed save the learner from unfreedom, saves him from himself. Let us call him a *deliverer*, for he does indeed deliver the person who had imprisoned himself, and no one is so dreadfully imprisoned, and no captivity is so impossible to break out of as that in which the individual holds himself captive!" (PF, 17). Climacus contends that the teacher who delivers the learner from his or her own captivity (untruth) will never be forgotten; the "blissful security" the savior brings to the life of the despairing individual ensures that the god will not "disappear Socratically," for the moment of deliverance, when truth is revealed to the individual, is "unique," decisive, and "filled with the eternal." It is also, however, momentary and passing: it occurs in "the twinkling of an eye," and yet it is *the fullness of time*" (PF, 18).

Having demonstrated that the Socratic response to Meno is not in itself sufficient, Kierkegaard, with the introduction of what he considers a necessary condition for the realization of truth—the teacher as God and savior—has opened the way for a discussion of the centrality of repetition as the means by which the learner sustains the relationship with the teacher in time, thus ensuring that he or she never again succumbs to the despair of sinfulness. It will be recalled that repetition *is* inwardness, certitude and understanding, and originality of action. It is therefore the means by which the individual becomes self-reflective or, to appropriate the words of Johannes de Silentio once again, "passionately concentrated." I have been arguing that this is what is demanded of the subject if he or she is intent on satisfying the requirements intended to bring about comprehensive community alliances. In line with the analysis proffered in chapter 1, it may now be concluded that "the idea" or guiding ethical ideal Kierkegaard encourages his reader to passionately reflect on is just this notion of the teacher as deliverer. The object of becoming self-reflective is to transform one's existence by actualizing this "idea" in one's own life. This means that the learner must make the acquisition of truth, as in the case of Abraham, his or her highest *telos*. All relative ends, which are considered "the highest" by those with the "purely human mentality" or those in absolute externality, must be suspended:

> Even a relative *telos* partially transforms a person's existence. But since existence in our speculative nineteenth century has unfortunately been changed into a thinking about everything possible, we even more rarely see an energetic existence oriented just to a relative *telos*. To will to amass money energetically already transforms a human life, to say nothing of the absolute *telos*, willing in the highest sense. All relative willing is distinguished by willing something for something else, but the highest *telos* must be willed for its own sake. (CUP, 393–94)

We have seen how Climacus interprets repetition (*Gjentagelsen*) as a rebirth (*Gjenfødelsen*)—not, however, in the sense of a coming into existence for the first time, but in terms of being born again. This is based on his contention that when the learner receives the truth and the condition, he or she does not become a human being, for he or she "already was that." What he is suggesting, rather, is that through the transformation of existence, which occurs the moment the individual is delivered from untruth by receiving the condition from the redeemer, the world is actualized to an extent never before experienced in the life of the individual, since he or she was dispassionate and disinterested in the nature of truth. Climacus says that "he becomes a person of a different quality or, as we can also call it, a *new* person" (PF, 18). This suggests a form of "conversion" in which the learner becomes conscious that heretofore he or she was in untruth. With this realization the individual suspends, or resigns from "his former state"—the sinful condition—but in such a way that he or she feels a certain remorse for having taken so long to become conscious of his or her inauthenticity. Such "repentance" is indicative of the "spiritual trial" that must be endured when the learner opts to exemplify the responsible and earnest life through critical and engaged double reflection. For rebirth in the Kierke-gaardian sense signifies a loss of the immediate self who is at home in the external world; that is, to realize a self in the manner advo-cated requires the learner to "deny" or "forget" what he or she con-sidered to be truth while in the condition of sin. The "moment" when one becomes conscious, through instruction from the teacher, that culpability for the loss of the condition rests with oneself is the point at which the individual adopts a critical distance from what was hitherto believed to be actuality, that is, in Derrida's words, "ar-tifactuality." This, of course, constitutes the transformation of exter-nality to inwardness: one dies to, or denies, the world of immediacy in which one's highest ethical *telos* is to become fully commensura-ble with the established order, with the aim of transforming one's existence according to the demands of the guiding "idea," which we have now ascertained is God.

The denial of the external self, therefore, involves a type of suffer-ing, in that the individual must tear him- or herself away from the given actuality while in pursuit of truth. Abraham's spiritual trial epitomizes the fear and trembling indicative of this passionate ac-tion. His rebirth to the world upon sacrificing the universal is fraught with the anxiety generated by having to surrender what was most essential to him before the suspension of the ethical was enacted. However, the suffering that accompanies the transformation of exis-tence is not caused by having to withdraw from the external world, but from having to remain within the world and yet hold fast to a guiding *telos* that is incommensurable with that of the universal. "Religious inwardness," or what Kierkegaard calls the truly ethical point of view, is such a "rebirth" to actuality:

The meaning of the religious suffering is dying to immediacy; its actuality is its essential continuance, but it belongs to inwardness and must not express itself externally (the monastic movement). When we take the religious person, the knight of hidden inwardness, and place him in the existence-medium, a contradiction will appear as he relates himself to the world around him, and he himself must become aware of this. The contradiction does not consist in his being different from everyone else . . . but the contradiction is that he, with all this inwardness hidden within him, with this pregnancy of suffering and benediction in his inner being, looks just like all the others—and inwardness is indeed hidden simply by his looking exactly like others. (CUP, 499)

So far I have been arguing that Kierkegaard's category of repetition, as developed by Johannes Climacus in *Philosophical Fragments,* takes the form of a reconsideration of Meno's paradox. In his deliberations as to how an individual comes to possess the truth, this thinker discounts the immanentist notion of recollection held by Plato's Socrates. Specifying that the individual must be brought from alienation, or "sin," to authenticity, the pseudonym argues that truth can be realized only with the assistance of a teacher, which he terms "the God." The God, we learned, is the unconditioned ideal that can save the individual from the estranging power of leveling and the apathy of abstract disinterested reflection. In so doing, it acts as a catalyst for the learner to become self-conscious, or to be born once more to the world. In other words, the God gives new life to the individual by providing the condition for him or her to become passionately concentrated. As such, the self acquires a new level of understanding, which in turn allows him or her to communicate at a more intense and responsible level with the other.

At this point I wish to further extrapolate many of the arguments Climacus has put forward in his defense of the assertion that truth is not recollected but requires a repetition in one's life of the essential qualities that the God exemplifies as the highest ethical paradigm. My aim in so doing is to further compound the claim that, for Kierkegaard, God is the guiding ethical idea that acts as a cohesive force between individuals. I will undertake this by developing a systematic analysis of the nature of the "self" throughout the authorship. I have underscored how a fundamental knowledge of the self is the most basic requirement for any individual wishing to take up the ethical point of view. It is therefore necessary to examine more closely the Kierkegaardian notion of self-consciousness, for this will ultimately allow me to undertake a thorough examination of the category of repetition as a central motif in Kierkegaard's descriptions of the various stages of personal development.

A Kierkegaardian Definition of Selfhood

In chapter 3 we drew the vital distinction that each one of Kierkegaard's pseudonyms makes between the "human being" and the "self." In that context, I made use of Anti-Climacus's pivotal definition: "a human being is a synthesis of the infinite and the finite, of the temporal and the eternal, of freedom and necessity" (SUD, 13). To recall, a synthesis, being "a relation between two," is still not a self. A self, rather, is an "established relation," or "a relation that relates itself to itself and in relating itself to itself relates itself to another" (SUD, 13–14). In saying that the human being is composed of the above-mentioned sets of categories, Anti-Climacus is suggesting that there is both a physical and a psychical dimension to its constitution; that is, there is in each human being a finite, temporal, and necessary component (the physical) that relates to the infinite, eternal, and free element (the psychical). Freedom from this purely human state necessitates, however, the individual's purposeful determination to actualize the unbounded possibilities its infinite and eternal dimensions present for contemplation and consideration. In other words, only when the individual relates its possible modes of being-in-the-world to what it is by necessity can a "self" emerge.

Being responsible in the Kierkegaardian sense is thus a matter of redefining oneself, or of seeing oneself not in terms of one's social roles alone, but as an individual who has the potential to transform his or her life according to certain guiding ethical ideals. As I have argued, such a process involves penetrating the illusions of "public" life by adopting a critical disposition in relation to what the human being is considered objectively and simply. Becoming self-conscious, therefore, is the most fundamental requirement Kierkegaardian ethics makes upon the individual.

The pseudonyms consider such a broadening of the scope of consciousness the necessary antidote to the malaise of modernity: passive reflection and leveling. Earlier we saw how engaged, critical reflection and understanding is demanded of the individual if this inauthentic condition is to be replaced by genuine dialogue between self ånd other. Given these considerations, I want to analyze in some detail at this juncture what Johannes Climacus has described as the state of untruth, sin, as developed in the context of Anti-Climacus's reflections on the notion of the self in *The Sickness unto Death*. In so doing, I will probe further into the nature of double reflection as an intensified form of subjective understanding. My central claim will be that faith is what makes possible an understanding of truth after the merely human form of understanding breaks down and gives way to self-knowledge.

Anti-Climacus states that the self is an established relationship. That is, self-knowledge can be gleaned once the human being comes to the realization that responsible agency is possible only after there is an acknowledgment that truth cannot be attained immanently but only through an act of transcendence, a repetition of one's initial coming into existence. This depends, according to the pseudonym, on the God-figure's providing the condition for man to be saved from sin. The God as ideal or *telos* is, therefore, what precipitates what Vigilius Haufniensis has termed "originality of action" in the life of the human being. When individuals, however, do believe that truth is something to be conceived immanently, the self is considered to be in "despair." The despairing individual is one who believes that he or she has the capacity to come into possession of the truth without having recourse to the God as ethical prototype and ideal. Such an individual takes for granted that because the human being is by necessity constituted as a synthesis of the temporal and the eternal, he or she can gain access to eternity without the assistance of the savior. The earnestness of repetition is, however, the fact that the individual can be given new life, or can repeat (take again) the life of immediacy or exteriority from the perspective of inwardness. As I have argued, the life of the individual does not ostensibly change when such inwardness is cultivated. Rather, one's orientation toward the given actuality is what is modified. Becoming subjective thus is not a process of withdrawal from the established order, but a method of bringing to fruition a more just and ethical society in which all participants have the capacity to relate to one another as selves.

For this type of essential equality to be realized between the

human being and the unconditioned ideal, and in order that the
(subjective) truth generated by repetition can gain a foothold in the
lives of individuals, despair must be surmounted. It is important,
however, not to interpret despair as a feature of the ontological constitution of the human being. It is rather a possibility that lies in the
synthesis:

> Despair is the misrelation in the relation of a synthesis that relates
> itself to itself. But the synthesis is not the misrelation; it is merely the
> possibility, or in the synthesis lies the possibility of the misrelation. If
> the synthesis were the misrelation, then despair would not exist at all,
> then despair would be something that lies in human nature as such.
> That is, it would not be despair; it would be something that happens
> to a man, something he suffers, like a disease to which he succumbs,
> or like death, which is everyone's fate. (SUD, 15–16)

Despair is engendered by the individual, upon whom "rests the responsibility for all despair at every moment of its existence" (SUD,
16). By refusing to accept the condition that the God provides in
order that truth be realized, a misrelation in the synthesis is formed;
that is, the human being fails to become self-reflective by relating
itself to itself in the manner prescribed. The pseudonym refers to
this malady as "the sickness unto death"—not death in the physical
sense, but the death of the "purely human" self. Repetition, as a
process of being born anew to the world, can only come into effect
after such a death, or a crucifixion of human understanding, has
taken place. Despair is, however, a limited power, and ill equipped
to withstand the all-pervasive force of the eternal, or the God, in the
life of the individual:

> A person in despair despairingly wills to be himself. But if he despair-
> ingly wills to be himself, he certainly does not want to be rid of him-
> self. Well, so it seems, but upon closer examination it is clear that the
> contradiction is the same. The self that he despairingly wants to be is
> a self that he is not (for to will to be a self that he is in truth is the
> very opposite of despair), that is, he wants to tear his self away from
> the power that established it. In spite of all his despair, however, he
> cannot manage to do it; in spite of all his despairing efforts, that power
> is the stronger and forces him to be the self he does not want to be.
> (SUD, 20)

Having described how an individual comes into despair, Anti-Climacus turns to delineating despair's various forms. What is vital to

take cognizance of at this juncture, according to the author, is how decisive a role consciousness plays in determining the type of despair a particular individual is suffering at any given moment. For as Anti-Climacus explains: "Generally speaking, consciousness—that is, self-consciousness—is decisive with regard to the self" (SUD, 29). Before proceeding to an examination of the numerous types of despair the pseudonym lists, we will turn our attention to Kierkegaard's more systematic comments on the nature of consciousness and time, remarks that will serve to elucidate further the nature of repetition.

TIME AND THE SELF

In his didactic account of the nature of anxiety, Vigilius Haufniensis undertakes an analysis of the self with a view to describing its temporal dynamic. In this context, the pseudonym defines the self as "a synthesis of the temporal and the eternal" (CA, 85). This synthesis, unlike those discussed thus far, involves only two factors; that is, it seems that there is no "third factor," the synthesizing force Anti-Climacus calls "spirit." Spirit, to repeat, is a doubly reflected consciousness, or a form of self-awareness that Kierkegaard calls "subjective knowledge." Once the self has drawn itself out of the purely human and objective point of view by relating itself to itself, or by rethinking the past (what one is necessarily) in terms of futural possibilities, spirit emerges. But, as stated, Haufniensis does not perceive the synthesis of the temporal and the eternal to have this spiritual dimension. He presents his problem in the following terms:

> Man, then, is a synthesis of psyche and body, but he is also a synthesis of the temporal and the eternal. . . . As for the latter synthesis, it is immediately striking that it is formed differently from the former. In the former, the two factors are psyche and body, and spirit is the third, yet in such a way that one can speak of a synthesis only when spirit is posited. The latter synthesis has only two factors, the temporal and the eternal. Where is the third factor? And if there is no third factor, there really is no synthesis, for a synthesis that is a contradiction cannot be completed as a synthesis without a third factor, because the fact that the synthesis is a contradiction asserts that it is not. What, then, is the temporal? (CA, 85)

In order to give a satisfactory response to this question, the pseudonym initiates a critique of what Mark Taylor calls "spatialized
time."[10] For Haufniensis, if time is considered "an infinite succession," it will also be thought in terms of "the present, the past, and
the future." Such a distinction is, however, the product of "the relation of time to eternity and through the reflection of eternity in
time," and is not, as those advocates of spatialized time believe,
"implicit in time itself" (CA, 85). Haufniensis contends that the
division of present, past, and future could only make sense if a definite present—what he terms "a foothold" in the infinite succession
of time—could be secured. However, because "every moment, as
well as the sum of the moments, is a process (a passing by), no
moment is a present, and accordingly there is in time neither present, nor past, nor future" (CA, 85). If one mistakenly concludes that
the division between past, present, and future is actually *in* time, it
is because time is being **represented** through the use of a spatial metaphor in which "infinite succession comes to a halt" (CA, 85). The
idea behind this belief is that when time is considered from the
perspective of the philosopher or the objective thinker, it is explica-
ble only by way of certain representational techniques. Taylor sheds
much light on this rather complex notion:

> It is from the movement of an object through space that one derives
> the concepts of before and after. The space that the object has tra-
> versed is the "before," the past, and the space yet to be traversed is
> the "after," the future. If the observer thinks that he can count the
> movements of the object, he arrives at the "now," the present. Under-
> stood according to the model of an object moving through space, time
> is a line composed of an infinite series of points. The points represent
> the successive presents that divide the past from the future.[11]

For Haufniensis, the spatial and representational models inevitably
lead one to incorrectly consider time as an "infinite, contentless
nothing" (CA, 86).

To further his explanation and analysis, Haufniensis turns at this
point to a category of immense significance: "the moment" (*Øiblik-
ket*).[12] In the context of analyzing how God gives the human being

---

[10] M. C. Taylor, *Kierkegaard's Pseudonymous Authorship*, 81.

[11] Ibid., 83.

[12] See CA, 49–50, 80–91, 103, 105, 110, 117–18. Much of Climacus's argument
in *Philosophical Fragments* revolves around this notion.

the condition to be born to the world anew in an act of personal transcendence, Climacus notes in *Philosophical Fragments* that it is in the "moment" that such a rebirth takes place. In countering the notion of recollection set forth by Plato's Socrates, this pseudonym informs his reader how it is necessary for God to enter the temporal realm with a view to saving man. This, he concludes, might seem absurd and offensive to those whose thought categories are purely objective in nature. For those, however, who are prepared to sacrifice, or die to, the given actuality so that, through passionate concentration on the guiding ethical idea, they might become one with the God in love, all offense is annulled. The alienated life of the objective individual is thus transformed and renewed—in Kierkegaard's terms, *repeated*—through the encounter with the savior. To become self-conscious through repetition in this way suggests that the individual has comprehended the fact that the immanent process of recollection, as a means of reaching truth, is essentially bogus. As Anti-Climacus reminds us: "Not until a self as this specific single individual is conscious of existing before God, not until then is it the infinite self" (SUD, 80).

It is in the *moment,* therefore, that this confrontation between the God and the single individual takes place. As truth cannot be recollected, the encounter with the eternal takes place in time. It is important to note here again that the cultivation of inwardness that guarantees the individual liberation from the bondage of sin, or untruth, is not a flight from time, but something that occurs while the learner is firmly situated in his or her historical milieu. Inwardness is not to be confused with subjective interiority, but can be considered the way in which the passionate self strengthens dialogue and harmony with his or her neighbors. Rather than being thought of as withdrawal, inwardness should at all times be considered as "indirection," in the sense of indirect communication, or the means by which genuine dialogue is realized.

With this in mind, Haufniensis attempts a definition of "the moment":

> Thus understood, the moment is not properly an atom of time but an atom of eternity. It is the first reflection of eternity in time, its first attempt, as it were, at stopping time. For this reason, Greek culture did not comprehend the moment, and even if it had comprehended

the atom of eternity, it did not comprehend that it was the moment, did not define it with a forward direction but with a backward direction. Because for Greek culture the atom of eternity was essentially eternity, neither time nor eternity received what was properly its due. (CA, 88)

For the Greeks, the moment had no significance. This was because they had a qualitatively different notion of eternity than that espoused by Christianity. While the Greek conception claimed that knowledge of the self is a means of acquiring a direct and immediate knowledge of truth in recollection, the radical form of Christianity championed by the pseudonyms maintains that truth is something the individual must strive after. This is why the God-figure is a necessary component in the learner's advancement toward a realization of truth; the God-man (a synthesis of the temporal and the eternal) becomes for the individual the new criterion against which he or she evaluates all currently held values and beliefs. I will consider the reason for Kierkegaard's choice of such a figure—or at least the ethical motivation that persuaded him to consider the God-man as the antidote to the ills (both social and personal) of the age—more comprehensively in chapter 5. For now it is sufficient to note that to become self-conscious, and thus to grasp at truth, requires for Kierkegaard that eternity (*qua* God-man) be continually reflected in time.

Haufniensis is thus led to conclude that "the synthesis of the temporal and the eternal is not another synthesis but is the expression for the first synthesis, according to which man is a synthesis of psyche and body that is sustained by spirit" (CA, 88). This means in essence that the synthesis of the temporal and the eternal, in which the moment is posited, is the very condition for all other syntheses. For without the moment as an atom of eternity, all possibility is lost to man. In other words, the God-man, who comes into time to save the learner from the guilt of sin (or in more secular terms, to save the individual from the dominant ideology that the immediate despairing self conflates with reality) is the truth that sets him or her free.

To clarify what is at stake here, Haufniensis introduces "the concept of *temporality*." Unlike the temporal realm, which may be described as time divorced from eternity, or as time defined by one who "is in time and is only of time" (CA, 86), *temporality* denotes the point at which eternity is intersected by time, and time is pervaded by eternity. Such a division, contends the pseudonym, is not a representation of time, but the manner in which time should be thought by existing individuals: "Only with the moment does history begin. . . . The moment is that ambiguity in which time and eternity touch each other, and with this the concept of *temporality* is posited, whereby time constantly intersects eternity and eternity constantly pervades time. As a result the above-mentioned division acquires its significance: the present time, the past time, and the future time" (CA, 89).

The future, however, as both Haufniensis and Johannes Climacus argue, "in a certain sense signifies more than the present and the past, because in a certain sense the future is the whole of which the past is a part, and the future can in a certain sense signify the whole" (CA, 89). The idea that an openness to the future permits individuals to transcend the "given actuality," with the aim of coming to a more comprehensive understanding of "who" they are, or of retrieving the past from the standpoint of the future, lies at the heart of the Kierkegaardian project. For the future "is the incognito in which the eternal, even though it is incommensurable with time, nevertheless preserves its association with time" (CA, 89); that is, the future contains the possibility for each individual to choose to relate to the idea of the eternal while in time.

On this reading, the eternal is that which serves to save the individual from time as infinite succession, or from the notion of time favored by the Greeks; because the Greeks maintained that truth is to be found in the preexistence of the soul, the future was without relevance for them. Indeed, Kierkegaard's Christian concept of repetition, "by which eternity is entered forwards," is the opposite of the Hellenic notion of recollection, which teaches that "the eternal lies behind as the past that can only be entered backwards" (CA, 90). For the Christian, however, the future is an opening onto a greater horizon in which the eternal breaks in upon the stream of daily affairs. To become conscious of the self's capacity to touch the eternal in time is to recognize that "the moment" holds the key to salvation.

If Kierkegaard has the Greeks in mind when he criticizes the theory of recollection, he is equally concerned about the effects of the Hegelian theory of the same name. As highlighted in the discussion of Climacus's restaging of the *Meno* dialogue, recollection is a meta-physical movement that attempts to halt the flow of time. For advocates of the theory of recollection, the temporal realm is somewhat inferior to the celestial world of forms or ideas, wherein truth resides. For Kierkegaard, in contradistinction, truth is not something static, immutable, or eternally identifiable, but something one must strive after. Truth, that is, is not an unchanging, atemporal *eidos,* but something that we, as "poor existing individuals" bound inextricably to the temporal flux, are constantly chasing and seeking. We might say that there is no pure access to truth *qua* truth, no transcendental standpoint from which an existing individual can access truth. As temporal beings, we are thrown into situations, into what Kierke-gaard, in relation to Socrates' ironic challenge to the established order, calls the "given actuality." It is up to us, according to Con-stantius, if we are to become self-conscious, to bring forth actual-ity—as the necessary feature of the self-synthesis—in new and original ways through the process of repetition: "When the Greeks said that all knowing is recollecting, they said that all existence, which is, has been; when one says that life is a repetition, one says: actuality which has been, now comes into existence" (R, 149). To establish an identity requires that the individual make sense of the social context into which he or she has been thrown. This can only be achieved, according to Constantius, by bringing such actuality into existence time after time. By the expression "bringing into exis-tence," Kierkegaard means a continual process of producing afresh what has been simply given through birth. More concretely ex-pressed, repetition implies bringing to new life what has become established through tradition. For Kierkegaard, thus, identity, self-identity, is not simply given, but is something to be generated through the novelty of repetition.

In turning his attention to the Hegelian notion of mediation, Kierkegaard aims to develop a critique of a "modern-day" form of Greek recollection. We get some sense of his misgivings in a passage from *Repetition,* which is worth quoting in full:

> But I must constantly repeat that I say all this in connection with repetition. Repetition is the new category that will be discovered. If one knows anything of modern philosophy and is not entirely ignorant of Greek philosophy, one will readily see that this category precisely

explains the relation between the Eleatics and Heraclitus, and that repetition proper is what has mistakenly been called mediation. It is incredible how much flurry has been made in the Hegelian philosophy over mediation and how much foolish talk has enjoyed honor and glory under this rubric. One should rather seek to think through mediation and then give a little credit to the Greeks. The Greek explanation of the theory of being and nothing, the explanation of "the moment," "non-being," etc. trumps Hegel. "Mediation" is a foreign word; "repetition" is a good Danish word, and I congratulate the Danish language on a philosophical term. (R, 148–49)

For Constantius, mediation attempts to still time; it endeavors to reduce differences between individuals and things so that a reductive form of identity is generated. It could be said—and here I appropriate the language of *Two Ages* once more—that for Kierkegaard mediation levels the distinctions that are vital for securing genuine relationships between individuals. What distinguishes the Greek version of recollection from its modern-day speculative counterpart is that the Greeks, as Constantius reminds us, either followed the Eleatic principle of non-change or "produced an honest Aristotelian account of it"[13] in the form of *kinesis,* which insists on the centrality of motion and change. Speculation, however, tends to talk of movement and change while at the same time attempting to negate them. This is what all of the pseudonyms find so offensive about Hegel's dialectical metaphysic: by emphasizing the idea of subjective becoming in opposition to the traditional substantial model that talked of change as a product of necessity, Hegel opened a new dawn for philosophy. However, in formulating a teleological dynamic, he cheated the forces of time and change. The future in this model is not an open-ended horizon of possibility, but another phase in *Geist*'s evolution toward absolute fulfillment. In the words of one Kierkegaardian commentator:

> Hegel made a show of embracing time and *kinesis* even while subverting them to his own purposes. Hegelian time is not authentic, radical, Christian temporality, in which everything hinges on the "instant" ["moment"], the decision. It is a time which is not exposed to flux and contingency but precisely insulated from their effects. It is a time made safe by eternity, underwritten by reason, regulated by

---

[13] Caputo, *Radical Hermeneutics,* 17.

necessity. . . . Hegelian time lacks what is truly proper to time: contingency, freedom, exposure to the future.[14]

Whereas Kierkegaard underscores his belief that the future is loaded with unpredictability and contingency, the Hegelian alternative specifies the dialectical regularity in world history. Kierkegaard, that is, places "decision" (either/or) at the heart of responsible action because of his commitment to the belief that there is no overarching scheme to which individuals can turn in times of crisis. This is why Johannes de Silentio never tires of reminding those who would take up a knighthood of faith in order to join Abraham on Mount Moriah that decision without recourse to universal standards of goodness is a "moment" of madness.[15]

Johannes Climacus reflects on these matters in his chapter on "Becoming Subjective" in the *Concluding Unscientific Postscript*. In this context, he juxtaposes the notion of the immanent and teleological nature of Hegelian "world history" with his own idea of ethical individuality. According to the pseudonym, Hegel comes unstuck when he takes it for granted that world history has an ethical dimension intrinsic to it. World history, in Climacus's reading of Hegel, is a complete abstraction in that it provides an account of the human race without reference to any particular individual. The "human race" is thus an idea conceived purely *in abstracto.* As with his critique of Hegel's social ethics, Kierkegaard is arguing here for a notion of the ethical that does not take the form of a universal creed or categorical imperative, or one that has its source in the natural law or the laws of the state (*qua* established order). For him, as for Climacus, the ethical "is predicated on individuality and to such a degree that each individual actually and essentially comprehends the ethical only in himself" (CUP, 155). Otherwise expressed, world history is structured in accordance with metaphysical laws and categories such as "cause and effect, ground and consequent." As a result, the *telos* that is immanent in world history is construed speculatively and metaphysically:

Insofar as the individuals participate in the history of the human race by their deeds, the observer does not see these deeds as traced back to

---

[14] Ibid., 18.

[15] I will return in some detail to this issue in chapter 6 while considering the nature of Kierkegaard's "postmodern" notion of community.

the individuals and to the ethical but sees them as traced away from the individuals and to the totality. Ethically, what makes the individual's own is the intention, but this is precisely what is not included in world history, for here it is the world-historical intention that matters. World-historically, I see the effect; ethically, I see the intention. But when I ethically see the intention and understand the ethical, I also see that every effect is infinitely indifferent, that what the effect was is a matter of indifference, but then of course I do not see the world-historical. (CUP, 155)

While world history looks to the effect of actions in order to ascertain whether they are in keeping with the absolute *telos*, the truly ethical individual has no such concern; for such an individual, subject to contingency as he or she is, the result of action is unforeseeable. We could say here that Kierkegaard's emphasis on decision and intention in ethical matters is a way of elucidating how we, as existing individuals, have no metaphysical supports to depend on when it comes to acting practically; that is, Kierkegaard's radicalization of what it means to be ethical stems from his conviction that we have no way of predicting what form the outcome of our actions will actually take. This is not to suggest that the probable consequences of action should not play a role in determining just how one ought to act in any given circumstance. To the contrary, I interpret Kierkegaard to be asserting here that because there can be no recourse to a "divine design" or a "world-historical process" with a predetermined teleological structure that would explain the effects of action as satisfying certain dialectical criteria, the individual must be extra vigilant and conscientious in making ethical decisions. For if it is the *intention* behind any action that counts, the individual who acts accordingly must be prepared to take personal responsibility for the ramifications of his or her actions. Such is what causes the madness in the moment of decision. When Climacus says that "every effect is infinitely indifferent," he is implying that the effects of action cannot be preprogrammed or accurately gauged in advance. In the constant flow of existence, the individual is bound up in a concatenation of events and practices, all of which are subject to the whim of contingency, that inexorable tide of chance happenings and occurrences over which one has no control. However, due to the individual's capacity to perform repetition, or originality of action, the ethical subject can constantly strive to approximate a certain guiding goal, principle, or, in Kierkegaard's language, "idea." Although one can never guarantee that the idea in mind will be actualized, there is a possibility that in repetition it will someday be brought to fruition. This is why Constantius says that repetition "has the blissful security of the moment" (R, 132).

The Hegelian version of "recollection" is, therefore, more anathema to Kierkegaard than that proclaimed by the Greeks. Giving the impression that movement is an essential dimension of one's philosophical scheme while concomitantly seeking a way into eternity via the back door where movement will be stilled—for him this is just another metaphysical ruse to evade the responsibilities presented by existence. Indeed, it is the claim that time is in some sense "logical" (e.g., world-historical process) or that logic produces motion or change that draws the most scathing and ironic response from Kierkegaard:

> In logic, no movement must *come about*, for logic is, and whatever is logical only *is*. This impotence of the logical consists in the transition of logic into becoming, where existence [*Tilværelse*] and actuality come forth. So when logic becomes deeply absorbed in the concretion of the categories, that which was from the beginning is ever the same. Every movement, if for the moment one wishes to use this expression, is an immanent movement, which in a profound sense is no movement at all. One can easily convince oneself of this by considering that the concept of movement is itself a transcendence that has no place in logic. (CA, 13–14)

Repetition, in contradistinction, keeps the individual moored to time, to the implacable stream of motion and change; it is the process of becoming free, both from the dubious certainty provided by metaphysics and from the illusions of the given actuality, the established order, and the present age. In producing identity, repetition brings forth a self (spirit) that has come to the understanding that the laws of speculative logic can never govern existence. Such an understanding (what we have called throughout this work "passionate concentration," "understanding *in concreto*," or "double reflection") is what sets the existing individual free:

> When movement is allowed in relation to repetition in the sphere of freedom, then the development becomes different from the logical development in that the *transition becomes* [*vorder*]. In logic, transi-

tion is movement's silence, whereas in the sphere of freedom it becomes. Thus, in logic, when possibility, by means of the immanence
of thought, has determined itself as actuality, one only disturbs the
silent self-inclosure of the logical process by talking about movement
and transition. In the sphere of freedom, however, possibility remains
and actuality emerges as a transcendence. (R, 309–10)

When in logic one talks of possibility becoming actual, nothing new
disturbs the dialectical harmony that speculation has generated; the
past always contains the seed of what is to come. The future can in
a certain sense be foretold. In repetition, however, what becomes,
what is actualized, transcends entirely the category of possibility.
Possibility (*posse*), in other words, is incapable of projecting with
accuracy what will emerge in actuality. Hence the sphere of actuality
transcends the circumscribing nature of the logic of idealism. As
John Caputo poignantly remarks: "There is always a 'remainder' no
matter how much is subtracted from the individual by the taxing
business of everyday existence."[16]

Johannes Climacus takes up many of these themes in his famous
"Interlude" in *Philosophical Fragments* (72–88). It is in this context
that the pseudonym poses the vexed question of whether the past is
more necessary than the future, or "has the possible, by having become actual, become more necessary than it was?" Along with Constantius, Climacus takes the view that "the change of coming into
existence is the transition from possibility to actuality," or from non-
being to being. This begs the question, therefore, as to whether the
"necessary" can come into existence, given that it is "always related
to itself and is related to itself in the same way" (PF, 74). The pseudonym answers by stating that coming into existence constitutes the
experience of "suffering [*Liden*]," and the necessary is incapable of
suffering:

> Coming into existence is a change, but since the necessary is always
> related to itself and is related to itself in the same way, it cannot be
> changed at all. All coming into existence is a *suffering* [*Liden*], and
> the necessary cannot suffer, cannot suffer the suffering of actuality—
> namely, that the possible . . . turns out to be nothing the moment it
> becomes actual, for possibility is *annihilated* by actuality. Precisely by
> coming into existence, everything that comes into existence demon-

---

[16] Caputo, *Radical Hermeneutics*, 21.

strates that it is not necessary, for the only thing that cannot come
into existence is the necessary, because the necessary *is*. (PF, 74)

Repetition, as a genuine movement in time, does not have the comfort of immanentist speculative movements, whose aim it is to negate time. Repetition, as a process of becoming self-conscious, has
always to do with the actual, which transcends the sphere of possibility. In fact, producing a self in time requires the annihilation of possibility. This is not to suggest that the possible does not play a
significant part in such a production, but only that becoming passionate about possibility implies a recognition by the individual that
this sphere is merely a propaedeutic to existential decision that, in
turn, resolves in actuality. As a being in time, struggling with the
flux, the individual is subject to contingency and dispersal. Such an
individual, it could be said, is never *present* to itself, can never
achieve full self-transparency. The future dislocates the present from
itself, disturbs and disrupts the stream of consciousness. Hence there
is nothing necessary about the identity of the person. It has no world-
historical *telos* it can immanently realize, nor is it the simple unfolding of a determinate pattern. As one who attempts to establish an
essential equality with the eternal in the moment, the individual *is*
not. Rather, repetition points the individual toward a future full of
possibilities—none of which, however, can be actualized in full.

Repetition, the process of being born to the world as a responsible
and vigilant self through the intervention of God (I will return to
this central feature of repetition below), "occurs in freedom, not by
way of necessity," for "nothing coming into existence comes into
existence by way of a ground, but everything by way of a cause" (PF,
75). The "cause" Climacus adverts to here is what he calls "a freely
acting cause," and the idea behind this notion emanates from the
belief that God *freely* chose to create the world, and in so doing
became its freely acting cause. Caputo, in his general analysis of
repetition in **Radical Hermeneutics**, explains: "The very being of the
world is contingent inasmuch as it originates in a free act of divine
creation, and everything that happens in the world happens contingently. Not even the laws of nature give evidence of pure necessity
since the phenomena which these laws govern might never have ex-
isted and since the laws themselves could be altered by the divine

freedom. The Christian world is free; the Greek world is necessi-
tarian."[17]

Climacus is lending support here to Haufniensis's elaboration of
temporality as the intersection of time by eternity. The existing individual, in annihilating possibility through responsible choice and decision in the moment, exposes the past to the contingency of what
is to come, what cannot be anticipated. Climacus takes pains to
point out that the past was itself brought into existence through
such a freely acting cause; that is, the past can in no sense be thought
of as being "necessary," for it could have been otherwise had the
winds of contingency blown in another direction. The upshot of this
is that "the past has indeed come into existence" and is thus a form
of actualized possibility. It came into existence through a change
that was freely enacted in the "instant" of passionate choice by a
temporally bound existing individual. If this was not the case, according to the pseudonym, time would have no significance. Everything would be the product of necessity:

> The future has not occurred as yet, but it is not, because of that, less
> necessary than the past, inasmuch as the past did not become neces-
> sary by having occurred, but, on the contrary, by having occurred, it
> demonstrated that it was not necessary. If the past had become neces-
> sary, the opposite conclusion could not be drawn with respect to the
> future, but on the contrary it would follow that the future would also
> be necessary. If necessity could supervene at one single point, then we
> could no longer speak of the past and the future. To want to predict
> the future (prophesy) and to want to understand the necessity of the
> past are altogether identical, and only the prevailing fashion makes
> the one seem more plausible than the other to a particular generation.
> (PF, 77)

The existing individual is, therefore, temporally situated and, as
such, is not subject to the laws of necessity. All historical becoming
is governed by a certain "illusiveness" (*Svigagtighed*) in that "it cannot be sensed directly and immediately" (PF, 81). Here Climacus
seems to be intimating that because the historical is the process of
individuals bringing things into existence, and because coming into
existence implies the actualization of possibility in the instant of

---

[17] Ibid., 18.

decision, the state of affairs that results will not necessarily corre-
spond to the intentions of those who have willed them. In keeping
with his hypothesis, the pseudonym maintains that in the process of
historical becoming the outcome of action can never be guaranteed,
but rather is always a product of contingency. The results of action
inevitably transcend the intentions formulated in possibility. Hence
the historical confounds those who seek direct intuitive apprehension of the past and the future or those who claim to have detected
a linear historical progression of the Hegelian kind: "Immediate sen-
sation and immediate cognition cannot deceive. This alone indicates
that the historical cannot become the object of sense perception or
of immediate cognition, because the historical has in itself that very
illusiveness that is the illusiveness of coming into existence"
(PF, 81).

Because of the contingent nature of historical events, the individual is unable to have recourse to "apprehension" or "knowledge" of
the past in order to gauge what might happen at some future point.
According to Climacus, however, "belief" (*Tro*) is required if we are
to make any sense of historical becoming. The individual who believes, that is, does not presuppose that what he or she sees or knows
in any immediately given apprehension is indubitable, but rather
affirms that what is believed did at one time or another "come into
existence." This, of course, suggests that in belief the individual is
alert to the fact that the past did not evolve necessarily, that the
outcome of actions and events could not have been determined absolutely.[18]

To believe, therefore, is to attest to the fact that, as existing individuals, we are not inextricably bound to the past, that it can be
rethought and re-created through originality of action—what we
have been calling "repetition." For belief, as Constantius argues, is
"an act of freedom, an expression of the will" (PF, 83). As such, if
freedom and will resolve in something new, or if they bring forth an
actual state of affairs that in some way transcends the possible that
precedes it, then belief, rather than knowledge, is the activity that
produces identity.

---

[18] See the interpretations of many of these themes in both Evans, *Passionate Reason*, and Robert C. Roberts, *Faith, Reason, and History: Rethinking Kierkegaard's
"Philosophical Fragments"* (Macon: Mercer University Press, 1986).

Belief and Faith

Before proceeding with a detailed analysis of the two categories, belief and faith, I want to tease out the distinction between the two forms of necessity mentioned in the preceding sections of this chapter. To recall, Anti-Climacus asserts that the self is composed of both a possible and a necessary component. However, in the course of the foregoing argument on the Kierkegaardian notion of time, we saw how Johannes Climacus denies the possibility that the past can in any sense be determined as a *necessary* feature of experience. This seeming contradiction calls for clarification.

The form of necessity Anti-Climacus is insisting on as an integral feature of the self refers to the ineluctable situatedness of the individual in history and in time, something speculative metaphysics cannot negate. As stated in chapter 1, for Kierkegaard there is no neutral ground outside history that can objectively adjudicate between competing notions of truth.[19] This is a further reason why he affirms that "subjectivity is truth": as "poor existing individuals" we are able neither to extricate ourselves from time nor to recollect eternity (in either Plato's or Hegel's sense) while we are immersed in the inexorable historical flow. The subjective point of view is thus the only one from which we can posit what we believe the truth to be.

The objection could be raised at this stage that Kierkegaard is advocating just another form of relativism or perspectivalism. According to this argument, his invocation of God is a move he must make if he is to avoid such charges. However, Kierkegaard is by no means opposed to what we call "truth" or "reason." If anything, his authorship stands as a testimony to the ability reason and truth possess to rejuvenate themselves. What he does attempt to oppose and counter, however, is the traditional notion of truth that many previous metaphysical schemes relied upon. While he denies that the Platonic, enlightened, and idealistic forms of reason can serve to engender genuine self-awareness, Kierkegaard is far from renouncing reason in the broadest sense. Objecting to the claims the tradition has made on behalf of a certain type of reason does not necessarily imply that one is an irrationalist, or indeed that one is seeking to

---

[19] This notion will be integral to my assessment of Kierkegaard's postmodernism below.

delimit reason's potential for grounding truth.[20] It does suggest, however—and this is the position I contend Kierkegaard holds—that reason ("double reflection" and "passionate concentration" amount to such rejuvenated reason) has a greater capacity and potential than has been hitherto assumed in the history of philosophy. What form such "double reflection" or reason takes will be the subject of some deliberation below.

When Johannes Climacus argues against the idea that the past is more necessary than the future, he is not contradicting the view taken by his more "religious" fellow author, Anti-Climacus. This is so because Johannes is emphasizing the contention that although what we are thrown into from birth—one's actuality *qua* history and time—is an inescapable (necessary) feature of "who" we are, the events that constitute this history did not come to be **necessarily**. In other words, there is no immanent teleological dynamic at work, no necessary development that generated the events of the past. To be in time and history means that one is subject to contingency; nothing happens, as Kierkegaard says time and again, "as a matter of course." Rather, because states of affairs are brought into **existence** by **existing** individuals who are temporally bound, they could very well have turned out otherwise. To transcend the given actuality requires exposing the established order's fraudulent claim that there is a certain necessity governing the evolution of history, that there is a divine utopia, or indeed that the state is the realization of such a utopia. Such deification of truth, reason, and order reveals an ignorance (sin) of the very nature of existence. Only through faith and belief, through the movement of repetition, can despair of this fundamental kind be surmounted. As Constantius remarks, only in repetition can "metaphysics come to grief" (R, 149).

Having dealt with the distinction between the two notions of necessity formulated in the texts of Climacus and Anti-Climacus, I am now in a position to analyze two of the most complex categories in Kierkegaard's thought: belief and faith. Before examining the Kierkegaardian theory of time and the temporal in the previous section, I briefly defined what Anti-Climacus describes as "a misrelationship in the self": despair. There are various forms of despair, or various

---

[20] I am suggesting here that through double reflection, or passionate subjective knowledge, reason realizes its full potential.

types of misrelations the self can suffer. At a most general level, despair can be defined as "sin" in the sense given to it by Climacus in *Philosophical Fragments*: the loss of the condition that one must have if a knowledge of truth is to be acquired. For this pseudonym, sin, or the purely human point of view, can be overcome through the intervention of a savior, which for Kierkegaard means the figure of Jesus Christ. Truth, therefore, is not merely given, and neither can it be recollected immanently; instead, it requires an active transformation in the individual—the movement of repetition.

In more specific terms, despair prevents the individual from breaking free of the leveled age of passive reflection (metaphysics). This is equivalent to saying that in sin the individual is unaware that he or she has the potential to become free, to become a self. For as Anti-Climacus reminds his reader, "the self is freedom" (SUD, 29). In reference once again to Kierkegaard's analysis of time, we could add that the sinful attitude or consciousness delimits the self's capacity to make the transition from possibility to actuality in which novelty emerges.

In *The Sickness unto Death*, Anti-Climacus undertakes a quite specific analysis of despair "only with regard to the constituents of the synthesis": finitude/infinitude, temporal/eternal, freedom/necessity. Each relation has the potential to relate itself to itself, which Anti-Climacus once more calls "freedom." As I outlined in chapter 1, when Kierkegaard talks of the relation relating itself to itself, he is simply implying that the existing individual has the potential to call into question the efficacy of the prevailing political, religious, ethical, and philosophical codes governing reality; that is, to be a self in Kierkegaard's terms is to fulfill one's ability to rethink the given or the actual with the aim of freeing oneself from inherited prejudice. Here we can see once more why he believes this to be an ethical gesture: to be responsible requires that one be attentive and vigilant to what is other than the self, to what lies outside the manifold of immediate experience. To appropriate the language of earlier chapters, becoming ethical and responsible means adopting a critical disposition in relation to the given order with the objective of identifying who the establishment has excluded in seeking to preserve and maintain itself. This requires that one cultivate a sensitivity toward those who have been cast to the margins, those who are without a voice and sometimes without a name—the type of people, in other words, favored by the Christ-figure. Such, as I argued above, is what teleologically suspending the ethical in the name of a certain religious spirit is about—seeking justice for the least among us. As such, Kierkegaard set the tone for what we have come to know as "postmetaphysical ethics." His concern was to keep open every ethical scheme, every paradigm that sought to preserve the dominant ethos. Repetition is precisely what keeps us alert to the voices of those "poor existing individuals" who have been crushed in the name of "law and order."

The following quote from *The Sickness unto Death* highlights how Kierkegaard's related notions of time and the self are intimately bound up with his highly charged ethical and political concerns:

> The self is the conscious synthesis of infinitude and finitude that re-lates itself to itself, whose task is to become itself, which can be done only through the relationship to God. To become oneself is to become concrete. But to become concrete is neither to become finite nor to become infinite, for that which is to become concrete is indeed a syn-thesis. Consequently, the progress of the becoming must be an infi-nite moving away from itself in the infinitizing of the self, and an infinite coming back to itself in the finitizing process. But if the self does not come back to itself, it is in despair, whether it knows it or not. Yet every moment that the self exists, it is in a process of becom-ing, for the self in potentiality does not actually exist, is simply that which ought to come into existence. Insofar, then, as the self does not become itself, it is not itself; but not to be itself is precisely despair. (SUD, 29–30)

Anti-Climacus, it is clear from this passage, supports Climacus's con-tention that truth for subjective individuals can be achieved only through a relationship to God. God, to recall, is the teacher who issues a summons to man to transcend the given actuality by sus-pending belief in the metaphysical idea of truth as something to be recollected immanently. In so doing, man is born to the world anew. Otherwise stated, the individual repeats the given through originality of action so as to engender something novel and transcendent.

Anti-Climacus contends that to teleologically suspend one's rela-tionship to the established order, or indeed to cultivate subjectivity and inwardness through repetition, is not a matter of fleeing respon-sibility or relinquishing one's social and communal ties; rather, "to become oneself is to become *concrete*" (my emphasis). Subjective concretion is achieved through a synthesis of the finite (the past) and infinite constituents of the individual; the subject is a being-between (*inter-esse*). So the process is not one of surrendering one-self to the infinite with the aim of satisfying the demands of a form of subjectivity founded on isolated interiority. If, in order to become a self, the individual must move away from itself in an infinitizing process, it also must come *"back to itself* in the finitizing process" (my emphasis). In short, the infinitizing process seeks to repeat, or recontextualize, the individual's finite experience. As such, the self continually oscillates between past and future, or opens the past to the future in the instant (moment) of responsible decision.

To be responsible, or to be passionately engaged at an ethical level, demands thus that one take cognizance of the fact that the past is not more necessary than the future. That is, when one comes to acknowledge that the past is neither the manifestation of a divine design nor the product of an immanent teleological dynamic, but rather a concatenation of historical contingencies, one is set free from the debilitating condition that is founded on the belief that what one has formerly affirmed as being "ethical" might in fact be simply a mere adherence to conventional mores that are maintained in order to preserve the given actuality. This is not to suggest that Kierkegaard is advocating a radical postmodern position in which the past is erased entirely. He is not holding to a position that denies the inescapability of the past—that is, the individual's historical embed-dedness—but to one that is sensitive to the fact that the past can be rethought or revised by way of the individual's capacity to imagine otherwise. The individual is claimed by the past but is in no way bound totally to that past. The imagination, as the faculty *instar omnium,* keeps alive the possibility of change (SUD, 31).

To be truly responsible, for Kierkegaard, is to affirm the possibility of imagining otherwise, of calling into question what has been tradi-tionally celebrated as truth, reason, ethics, and community with a view to making each of these structures own up to its contingent configuration. To lack the infinite, or the capacity to envision situa-tions otherwise, is to adhere to what Anti-Climacus calls a purely "secular view," one asserting that the established order (which comes into being from a general conflation of the past with a divine plan) is the concrete manifestation of truth. Anti-Climacus is obliquely gesturing in the direction of Climacus and Constantius

here in that he holds to the distinction they draw between the purely
human (secular) point of view and the point of view of the self. He
too believes that the individual can be born again, or otherwise
stated, he considers repetition as a movement forward in which what
has been can be given new life. By holding firm to the finite, the
traditional demarcations that separated one individual from the
other are compounded and the past is rigidified:

> As a matter of fact, in the world there is interest only in intellectual or
> esthetic limitation or in the indifferent (in which there is the greatest
> interest in the world), for the secular mentality is nothing more or less
> than the attribution of infinite worth to the indifferent. The secular
> view always clings tightly to the difference between man and man and
> naturally does not have any understanding of the one thing needful
> (for to have it is spirituality), and thus has no understanding of the
> reductionism and narrowness involved in having lost oneself, not by
> being volatilized in the infinite, but by being completely finitized, by
> becoming a number instead of a self, just one more man, just one
> more repetition of this everlasting *Einerlei* [one and the same].
> (SUD, 33)

For Anti-Climacus, despairing individuals hold firm to the finite
largely because they have been tricked by "the others." By "the others" I believe the pseudonym means those who have preceded the
self, those whose interests are served by maintaining the current
order, or those who deify the prevailing orthodoxy: "Surrounded by
hordes of men, absorbed in all sorts of secular matters, more and
more shrewd about the ways of the world—such a person forgets
himself, forgets his name, divinely understood, does not dare to believe in himself, finds it too hazardous to be himself and far easier
and safer to be like the others, to become a copy, a number, a mass
man" (SUD, 33–34). The one suffering such despair acquires "an
increasing capacity for going along superbly in business and social
life, indeed, for making a great success in the world" (SUD, 34). But
this success is merely counterfeit. It is won by holding firm to the
immediate life, the essence of which is to preserve the status quo at
the expense of a genuinely responsible ethic that is indefatigably
committed to opening up this given actuality to new possibilities.
This would, according to Anti-Climacus, require "risk." Perhaps in
the manner of Socrates, Abraham, and Jesus Christ it might demand
a transgression or a contravention of the law. Such is what "ventur-

ing" in the Kierkegaardian sense implies: losing one's life in order to obtain life anew; teleologically suspending the ethical in the form of unconditional sacrifice so that justice might be done; walking among the lepers so that the victim's voice can be heard. Such "venturing" does not guarantee that life's security can be maintained; in actualizing possibilities, the individual is never assured that what is projected will come to pass—actuality can either fall short of, or exceed, possibility. This is the opposite of believing that one's actions are governed necessarily by a linear historical teleology, or that they are stages in the ever-evolving life of *Geist*. The future for the pseudonyms is open-ended, incalculable, and unprogrammable. Not to venture is not to gain:

> The world considers it dangerous to venture in this way—and why? Because it is possible to lose. Not to venture is prudent. And yet, precisely by not venturing it is so terribly easy to lose what would be hard to lose, however much one lost by risking, and in any case never this way, so easily, so completely, as if it were nothing at all—namely, oneself. If I have ventured wrongly, well, then life helps me by punishing me. But if I have not ventured at all, who helps me then? (SUD, 34)

If Anti-Climacus emphasizes the function and role of imagination in his analysis of despair as defined by finitude/infinitude, he determines whether the synthesis of possibility/necessity is authentic or in despair by observing whether the self has cultivated faith and belief. Being composed of a necessary dimension, the self is factically bound. As such, it is somewhat hindered from actualizing many of the possibilities that occur to it through the faculty of imagination. If the individual, however, does not transform possibility into necessity, the self is lost by fantastically reflecting itself out of existence.

The pseudonym's discussion of necessity's despair (i.e., a lack of possibility) is the context in which he introduces the categories of belief and faith. In chapter 3, I briefly considered the category of faith in terms of Johannes de Silentio's portrayal of Abraham's sacrifice. At this point, however, it is important to tease out the implications of this vital notion for Kierkegaard's theory as a whole, given that it is centrally bound up with the question of responsibility as defined thus far. The main objective in so doing is to argue in favor of faith as the highest passion of the "poor existing individual," or the most versatile form of understanding that individual can generate.

I have maintained that faith for Kierkegaard is not a blind, irrational leap into an unknown abyss, but rather the movement by which "speculative reason," in its traditional "metaphysical" mode, gives way to a more liberated form of reason—what Caputo calls a "post-metaphysical rationality," and what Kierkegaard refers to as "double reflection"—that ceaselessly strives to put itself in question. Following Derrida and Caputo, I want to say that if an ethics of genuine responsibility is to be founded, the movement of faith—as an activity that undermines the securities of a complacent religiosity based on the pretensions of speculative reason—needs to be experienced. As Derrida says, "Responsibility and faith go together, however paradoxical that might seem to some, and both should, in the same movement, exceed mastery and knowledge."[21]

Anti-Climacus asserts that to lack faith and belief is to lack possibility; the despair of a purely necessary being is that he or she has no possibility that can be actualized in the moment of responsible decision. Nothing, that is, can be brought to life in repetition. In necessity, the despairing individual continually affirms the existing order. To imagine it otherwise would be an offense to the purely human and secular mentality that wants to deify the establishment. The passion for what, following both Johannes de Silentio and Derrida, I will call "the impossible," or what cannot be teleologically predetermined by the speculative dialectician, is, however, "the very formula for losing the [human] understanding." It is what makes us fear and tremble for the security the given actuality guarantees. Understanding, according to the pseudonym, gives way to faith and belief. Faith, on this telling, is an affirmation of the future as that through which possibility emerges to be actualized in the moment; it is the belief that time is not an immanent process, but a series of instants in which the individual succeeds in rethinking the past from the point of view of the future. The movement of faith involves an acknowledgment by the individual that the past can be repeated through exposure to a future ripe with possibility: "This is the good health of faith that resolves contradictions. The contradiction here is that, humanly speaking, downfall [of the understanding] is certain, but that there is possibility nonetheless. Good health generally means the ability to resolve contradictions. . . . To lack possibility

---

[21] Derrida, *The Gift of Death*, 6.

means either that everything has become necessary for a person or that everything has become trivial" (SUD, 40). Necessity's despair, according to Anti-Climacus, is usually the condition suffered by "the determinist," "the fatalist," and, as remarked in chapter 1, those with a "philistine-bourgeois mentality":

> Fatalism and determinism lack possibility for the relaxing and mitigating, for the tempering of necessity, and thus lack possibility as mitigation. The philistine-bourgeois mentality thinks that it controls possibility, that it has tricked this prodigious elasticity into the trap or madhouse of probability, thinks that it holds it prisoner; it leads possibility around imprisoned in the cage of probability, exhibits it, imagines itself to be the master, does not perceive that precisely thereby it has imprisoned itself in the thralldom of spiritlessness and is the most wretched of all. (SUD, 41–42)

As explained above, the past is not necessary in that it has "come into existence." For Kierkegaard, coming into existence suggests that the object of apprehension came to be through a series of contingent events; even though the individual sees an object in immediate apprehension, he or she is without the capacity to state with absolute certainty *how* that thing came into existence. In attempting to refute the world-historical immanentist theory of becoming, Kierkegaard emphasizes the need for belief in all epistemological matters; that is, as existing individuals we have no way of saying with certainty that something has come into existence necessarily, or as a result of the dialectical unfolding of nature, as is Hegel's wont. Rather, "belief is not a knowledge but an act of freedom, an expression of will" (PF, 83). As such, the believer has no knowledge or direct intuitive understanding of things in their fullness. What appears for apprehension is the product of the actualization of possibility by existing beings, which, ..s we have been arguing, is entirely subject to contingency. To believe, therefore, is to affirm what exceeds direct conscious awareness; as Derrida might say, believing constitutes an affirmation of the other's alterity:

> Thus at no moment does the past become necessary, no more than it was necessary when it came into existence or appeared necessary to the contemporary who believed it—that is, believed that it had come into existence. Belief and coming into existence correspond to each other and involve the annulled qualifications of being, the past and

the future, and the present only insofar as it is regarded under the annulled qualification of being as that which has come into existence. (PF, 86)

The point Climacus is making here is pivotal: through belief and faith the individual is able to rethink the past, or in strictly Kierke-gaardian terms, is able to relate the (necessary, actual) self to itself (possible, infinite) in the moment. Otherwise stated, as the past has come into existence, it can be repeated through originality of ac-tion—what Kierkegaard calls the movement of passionate inward-ness, in which the self reflects critically upon the prevailing political and ethical codes and norms. This is so because the past, once it has come into existence, does not become a closed book. Let us say that the contexts of which the past is composed are undelimitable, or are always open to revision in a positive sense:

> The possibility from which emerged the possible that became the ac-tual always accompanies that which came into existence and remains with the past, even though centuries lie between. As soon as one who comes later repeats that it has come into existence (which he does by believing it), he repeats its possibility, regardless of whether there may or may not be more specific conceptions of this possibility. (PF, 86)

Faith, therefore, is the process in which the self relates itself to itself, or the means by which the subjective individual affirms that what it has interpreted itself essentially and necessarily to be hitherto is in fact open to revision. Johannes de Silentio confirms this view in *Fear and Trembling* when he says that

> the highest passion in a person is faith, and here no generation begins at any other point than where the previous one did. Each generation begins all over again; the next generation advances no further than the previous one, that is, if that one was faithful to the task and did not leave it high and dry. That it should be fatiguing is, of course, something that one generation cannot say, for the generation does indeed have the task and has nothing to do with the fact that the previous generation had the same task, unless this particular genera-tion, or the individuals in it, presumptuously assumes the place that belongs to the spirit who rules the world and who has the patience not to become weary. (FT, 122)

Each generation, according to Kierkegaard, has the task of putting its most hallowed truths and values in question. Faith is the category through which the passionate individual (or the generation) approaches this task of creating itself anew. If a particular generation passively accepted the efficacy of the beliefs and practices of a previous generation, then it might have objective, disinterested knowledge of facts, but it would not have subjective truth or a passionate engagement with truth. The truths and values of one generation are always open to revision by succeeding generations. Alternatively stated, what the current generation holds to be the truth can be "repeated" by those yet to come. Like repetition, "faith" is the watchword in every ethical and metaphysical view. It is the means by which one affirms that the past has "come into existence" and can, therefore, only be believed and not known with certainty. It is an affirmation of a future yet to come, one that exceeds the mastery of the universal order, in that it has yet to be spoken of, framed in language, or documented. Kierkegaard is at pains throughout the authorship to stress how we, as "poor existing individuals," should not be concerned with the "results" of the actions of our forebears.

To exist is to become a self through the actualization of possibilities in the moment of decision. Actuality, however, always exceeds possibility. Faith, as one's highest passion, is an affirmation of what exceeds possibility, what breaks into time unexpectedly, or what causes the established order to fear and tremble. Kierkegaard compares the life of an individual and a generation to an artist's sketch or design that prefigures the eventual production; the plan inevitably falls short of the work itself, due to its being outside the work (*hors d'oeuvre*) or coming before the event. The analogy highlights the fact that a life in time can never predict what the actualization of possibility will bring into existence:

> When an artist sketches a plan, the design of a work, however accurate the sketch is, there is always something indefinite. Not until the work is finished, not until then can one say: Now there is not the slightest indefiniteness, not of a single line, not of a single point. Thus there is only one sketch that is completely definite, and that is the work itself, but this of course means that no sketch is or can be completely and unconditionally definite. (WL, 104)

To risk and to venture in faith, finally, is to believe that what has come into existence, or indeed what will come into existence, cannot be "known" in a purely speculative or objective manner. Subjective truth is an affirmation of what exceeds speculative mastery, or the totalizing tendencies of the law and the state.

At various point throughout this discussion I have stated that if the individual is to be saved from sin, or if the individual is to be given the condition for the attainment of truth, he or she must come into contact with the God as highest ethical exemplar. Through this association, the individual is born to the world a second time. I have called the process of coming into (subjective) truth "repetition." Repetition, that is, is not a process of escaping time or of entering eternity through the back door, but how the individual who is situated and embedded in time comes to consolidate a relationship with the eternal that preserves his or her association with time through the moment of passionate decision. The point to be emphasized here is that if the individual is to take up the ethical point of view, he or she must, according to Kierkegaard, establish a relationship with God *in time*. The Kierkegaardian subject, in becoming a self or in sacrificing the human point of view, does not withdraw into a state of pure objectless interiority. To do so would be to safeguard itself from the contingencies of time, something to which Kierkegaard could never subscribe. Inwardness, as Haufniensis has suggested, is understanding *in concreto*, which can be achieved only through originality of action, or repetition. Self-knowledge, for Kierkegaard, corresponds to such understanding. Rather than being irrational as a result of critiquing objective reason and knowledge, self-knowledge, faith, and belief liberate reason from its speculative shackles. In so doing, reason (double reflection, subjective knowledge) is given greater scope to challenge the efficacy of its metaphysical caricatures. The point is that the "poor existing individual," in becoming self-aware, does not abandon time or reason, but comes to the realization that the paradox of existence is that eternity does uphold a relationship to time. This does not, however, suggest that the individual and God become one. It does suggest, however, that in faith the self can be saved from despair while continuing to exist in the world.

5

The God-Man As Unconditioned Ethical Prototype

In this chapter I will examine in detail the notion of God that Kierkegaard develops throughout his authorship. My objective is to analyze the precise nature of what he determines as the guiding ethical principle, or what he calls in *Two Ages* "the idea." The importance of this notion lies in the fact that God, as the object of faith and love (in the Kierkegaardian sense of Christian love as self-denial), binds together individuals who have become self-conscious in the manner described, in the form of a radical Christian community existence. The final chapter will go some way toward an extrapolation of this Kierkegaardian community ideal. For the moment, however, I will, in the light of my analysis in chapter 4, provide a description and definition of the God-figure from those texts that are essentially preoccupied with this theme—most notably, *The Sickness unto Death* and *Practice in Christianity*. In this context I will argue that the God-man for Kierkegaard supersedes Socrates and Abraham as ethical prototypes. This in turn will permit me to defend Kierkegaard further against those who claim that the teleological suspension of the ethical opens the way for fundamentalism, genocide, and immorality. For I will argue that the Kierkegaardian God is a radically Christian God who seeks perpetually to undermine the established order in favor of those whose voices are never heard in a universal sense. This will lend support to my earlier contention that the Abraham story is for Kierkegaard a metaphor for what is required of each individual if genuine ethical responsibility is to be engendered, not a call for murder on Moriah.

GOD AS ETHICAL GOAL AND CRITERION

We have seen how Anti-Climacus in *The Sickness unto Death* considers faith and belief the antidotes to necessity's despair, which is to lack possibility. In this text, the pseudonym compares such despair to being dumb: "If losing oneself in possibility may be compared with a child's utterance of vowel sounds, then lacking possibility would be the same as being dumb. The necessary is like pure consonants, but to express them there must be possibility. If this is lacking, if a human existence is brought to the point where it lacks possibility, then it is in despair and in despair every moment it lacks possibility" (SUD, 37). For Anti-Climacus, possibility is equatable with language; that is, possibility suggests that the individual is in possession of imagination and reflection, both of which are indicative of linguistic competence. This theory is spelled out in more detail in *De Omnibus Dubitandum Est*, where Johannes Climacus, in a discussion of what it means to doubt, asks how a being can become self-conscious. Consciousness, he maintains, is the mediation of reality and ideality. Reality corresponds to the immediate world, the world in which everything is true because there is no mind to think that it is not; that is, "reality" for the pseudonym is pure givenness. Ideality, however, corresponds to language. Consciousness implies, according to Climacus, that the individual cancels immediacy through his or her use of language. As I will suggest more forcibly below, Climacus, in a style that resonates with Derrida's, denies that the self can have unmediated access to what is other, whether it be a thing or, indeed, another mind. For once the subject speaks, immediate access to the other is blocked off: "Immediacy is reality; language is ideality; consciousness is contradiction [*Modsigelse*]. The moment I make a statement about reality, contradiction is present, for what I say is ideality" (DODE, 168). Because selves are linguistically embedded, pure, unmediated consciousness is impossible.

Through the mediation of ideality and reality, possibility emerges. Reality by itself cannot reflect; ideality, likewise, cannot idealize when it has nothing before it. It is therefore through the collision—or mediation in consciousness—of the ideal and the real that possibility and repetition can come into play. To be conscious thus implies that through the passion of imagination what appears to be real and steadfast is in fact haunted by possibility.

Repetition, as I have argued, should not be thought of as a continual repetition of the same, but rather as originality of action, in which the self resigns from the established order with the objective of affirming what cannot be circumscribed by this order, in that it is a possibility yet to be actualized or "to come."[1] Repetition, that is, does not threaten the established order or signal its downfall; it seeks only to keep such structures open, to prevent them from deifying their most sacred tenets and values. Kierkegaard's objective in the authorship is not to generate a passive withdrawal from the life into which one has been thrown, but to show how the anxiety of the temporal life cannot be avoided by any existing individual. Hence he does not wish that the individual renounce his or her responsibilities to the given actuality, but only that one should avoid becoming complacent about the facts of existence by hanging onto the securities the state guarantees. This is why both Socrates and Abraham remain within the life of the community while attempting to demonstrate how the establishment has turned ethics into a mere rule-following procedure. Repetition, being the watchword in every ethical view, and that which brings metaphysics to grief, is thus the process of being both inside and outside the law, inside and outside the state, inside and outside (objective) truth. Kierkegaard never denies that one is inextricably bound to a social, political, ethical, and religious context. What he does dispute, however, is that such contexts should be guarded from critique and change.

In the context of his critique of the immediate and entirely unre-flective life of the aesthete in the second volume of *Either/Or,* the pseudonym Judge Wilhelm concurs with this reading of repetition when he denies that by choosing the ethical one must renounce entirely the aesthetic. Otherwise stated, what is repeated in the transition from one stage of consciousness to the next is what has been. Repetition endeavors to "bring to life again" the given actuality by

---

[1] To preempt what I intend to argue in the final chapter, let me quote a recent comment by John Caputo, who defines deconstruction in these most obvious Kierkegaardian terms:

"If one day someone were to put a microphone in my face and ask me . . . whether I could put deconstruction in a nutshell, I would reverently bow my head, or maybe I would fold my hands and look unctuously to heaven, or maybe I would spread my arms facing the palms of my hands heavenward (for better reception), in any case, whatever posture I would assume, I would invoke the ancient Hebrew word:

Amen

Of which I would then offer a modern (or postmodern?) translation:

Viens, oui, oui."

Deconstruction in a Nutshell: A Conversation with Jacques Derrida, edited and with a commentary by John D. Caputo (New York: Fordham University Press, 1997), 201–2.

freeing it from its inherent prejudices and by opening it up to a future full of possibility:

> And yet nevertheless there is here a question of a choice, yea, of an absolute choice, for only by choosing absolutely can one choose the ethical. By the absolute choice the ethical is posited, but from this it does not follow by any means that the aesthetical is excluded. In the ethical the personality is concentrated in itself, so the aesthetical is absolutely excluded or is excluded as the absolute, but relatively it is still left. In choosing itself the personality chooses itself ethically and excludes absolutely the aesthetical, but since he chooses himself and since he does not become another being by choosing himself but becomes himself, the whole of the aesthetical comes back again in its relativity. (E/O, 2:181–82)

Climacus makes a similar point when he remarks:

> If that fallacy discussed above could remain, that ideality and reality in all naiveté communicated with one another, consciousness would never emerge, for consciousness emerges precisely through the collision, just as it presupposes the collision. Immediately there is no collision, but mediately it is present. As soon as the question of a repetition arises, the collision is present, for only a repetition of what has been before is conceivable. . . . When ideality and reality touch each other, then repetition occurs. (DODE, 171)

For Kierkegaard, language is essential in order to open up the given actuality to a limitless future, one that cannot be calculated in advance due to its being wholly subject to contingency. Identity, therefore, is not something static, or indeed something essential, but rather the result of an active process of self-questioning in which the subject keeps history and time alive. As Constantin Constantius informs us, eternity must be entered in a forward-moving fashion; one cannot simply run out the back door of existence by recollecting (*anamnesis*) eternity in its fullness.

We saw in the previous chapter how, for Anti-Climacus, the despair of finitude is to lack infinitude, while the despair of necessity is to lack possibility. Such a misrelationship implies that the self is not conscious of itself as a being subject to time and contingency. However, at this stage of existence each individual is conscious of him- of herself as a particular being with a social role, one who defines oneself only in terms of the position he or she holds in community.

Recalling Kierkegaard's description of the present age, we can say that this individual lacks passion—the passion of irony, self-sacrifice, and responsibility. Having only a "human" or "natural" point of view, rather than self-knowledge, the individual comes to understand "who" he or she is in terms of the past alone, believing that the past is the product of necessity. As a member of the established order, one's responsibility is to the state, its laws, and its institutions. Here there is no critical engagement or passionate double reflection with the prevailing ethical and political paradigms that mark one state off from the next, and indeed one individual from the other. This form of identity that unites individuals on the basis of their common allegiance to the universal has, according to Kierkegaard, not only leveled the singularity of each particular existing individual but also annulled the possibility of possibility. That is, the experience of fear and trembling—the anxiety that defines the process of self-questioning, of critically analyzing one's inherited beliefs and practices, and of cultivating a genuine sense of social and ethical responsibility—is replaced by smug complacency at both the ethical and more general philosophical levels.

Such is what we have been calling, following Anti-Climacus, "despair." To lack possibility is to lack an openness to the future, an openness to the other that unsettles and disturbs the leveled order of passive reflection (objective knowledge). As explained above, the self, in relating itself to itself, does not extricate itself from tradition or its past. Repetition, as a form of auto-critique, brings new life to the past by exposing it to the undelimitable future. To be in despair, however, means that one is not prepared to venture in this way or to take the risk that possibility demands. Anti-Climacus calls this "inclosing reserve" [*Indesluttethed*] (SUD, 63), an expression intended to suggest a form of dumbness or silence cultivated by one who lacks possibility.

In the previous chapter I discussed Climacus's refutation of the Platonic theory of knowledge as enunciated in the **Meno**. There the emphasis was on how the individual comes into possession of the truth. In those pages, Climacus argues for an essential equality to be generated between the self and God if the alienation of sin is to be surmounted; that is, having lost the condition to realize the truth through the process of recollection in either its Platonic or Hegelian forms, the individual, if he or she is to gain release from his or her self-enclosed past, must "resign" from the purely human order. This does not signal a flight from actuality into unlimited possibility or into a direct, unmediated relationship with God, but is rather the process of taking up a critical standpoint in relation to the given order while acting in accordance with the requirements of the guiding ethical "idea." Only after each individual has been empowered to make such an act of resignation can the coiled springs of life-relationships be made flexible once more. Kierkegaard's notions of resignation and faith are the means by which the self relates to this idea. I have already spelled out how Kierkegaard undermines objective knowledge or traditional philosophical rational paradigms in favor of subjective knowledge or double reflection (what he calls "ethico-religious knowledge").[2] In its more developed form, as we saw in the previous chapter, such double reflection becomes faith. In order to show how resignation, as a teleological suspension of the ethical, leads to faith, in which the individual relocates him- or herself within the ethical sphere with a heightened sense of genuine responsibility (repetition), it is important to consider to what extent the individual should relate him- or herself to God as the "idea," and on what basis this relationship should be founded.

For Climacus, to acquire possession of the truth one must be born to the world a second time. This can only happen by eradicating necessity's despair—by becoming passionate about the possible. Achieving this requires an acknowledgment by the individual that the past is not more necessary than the future, but that it is possibility made actual through the concerted decisions of those who came before. This implies that the established order, or the universal, is always open to revision and change. Being passionate in this way suggests an awareness by the self that one can be saved from the despair of pure necessity. Because, as Climacus has argued, we cannot *know* (objectively/speculatively) what has come into existence, but only *believe* that it has come into existence, we are prevented from ever having *direct* knowledge of the past. There is, as Johannes de Silentio assumes, a "residual incommensurability" involved in all acts of apprehension. Such is what this pseudonym calls "the impossible," or that which unexpectedly comes into existence after the possible has been actualized in the "moment" of decision: "Every-

---

[2] See chapter 1.

one shall be remembered, but everyone became great in proportion to his *expectancy*. One became great by expecting the possible, another by expecting the eternal; but he who expected the impossible became the greatest of all" (FT, 16). The aim of my final chapter will be to argue that it is precisely in this affirmation of *the* impossible that Kierkegaard and Derrida come closest to one another as thinkers committed to an ethics of responsibility. For now, however, it is sufficient to say that, for Kierkegaard, the impossible is that which exceeds speculative and objective comprehension and circumscription.

As "poor existing individuals," we are all subject to contingency, chance, and time. This means that selves have no teleological dynamic driving them forward toward a predetermined *telos*, or pure self-fulfillment. According to Anti-Climacus, such an idea is bound to offend those who hold steadfastly to the objective point of view or those whose interests are best served by the maintenance of the established order. For to believe "is the very formula for losing the understanding" (SUD, 38), an understanding that holds firmly to the human point of view, or the purely objective understanding. For despair to be overcome, and for essential (subjective) truth to be possessed, there must be a denial of this "human" self. That is, one must die to the purely necessary self (externality) in order to effect a synthesis that relates itself to itself (inwardness). In the act of repetition, the individual keeps the past (the necessary self) open to the future as the bearer of the impossible, or what exceeds the teleological horizon. Human understanding gives way, that is, to subjective knowledge, the cultivation of which ensures that the self ceases to see itself only in terms of its past history and its social roles. The self in repetition, the one who has risked the responsibility of resignation, does not deny its necessary dimension, for as we now know, Kierkegaard insists on the ineluctability of time and finitude. Such a self is, however, both inside and outside the established order, in that one does not attempt to overcome the self one has become, but endeavors only to keep the possibility of change alive. The self is outside the order to the extent that it sees the need for appropriating a higher ethical ideal than that of the state itself, or indeed its laws. This is why for Constantius "repetition is the watchword [*Løsnet*] in every ethical view" (R, 149), since it keeps all ethical schemes and paradigms open to revision, forcing them to radically question the efficacy of their principles for generating a responsible ethic motivated by concern for the other.

To hold the human point of view, recalling Climacus's argument in *Philosophical Fragments*, is to be in sin. In order to escape this condition, it is necessary that the individual be "reborn" to the world anew. This rebirth occurs, according to Climacus, in the moment when the learner becomes one with God in "the form of a servant" (PF, 31–34). Thus, to relate oneself to the "idea" (in Kierkegaard's sense) is to relate oneself to God in the lowliest of forms. In other words, there can be no consciousness that one is in sin, or of how one may be saved, except through the intercession of the God as servant in time. For the truth is something to be learned, not to be speculatively memorized (*Aufhebung*). Only by way of the intervention of God can the individual be liberated from the clutches of tradition (universality, established order, given actuality) and reborn in repetition: "In the consciousness of sin, the individual becomes aware of himself in his difference from the universally human, which in itself is only an awareness of what it means to exist *qua* human being. Since the relation to that historical event (the god in time) conditions the consciousness of sin, there could not have been the consciousness of sin during all the time before this historical event occurred" (CUP, 584). Because the God has come into existence, he provides the condition of possibility. Alternatively expressed, the God makes real the possibility of the self's relating itself to itself in passionate concentration, with the aim of transforming the past through critical reflection resolving in effective decision: "The believer has the infallible antidote for despair—possibility—because for God everything is possible at every moment" (SUD, 39–40).

If the criterion for becoming a self is simply man or the state, the individual will be incapable of fulfilling his or her highest potential as a responsible being. However, if the self identifies God as the highest ethical criterion, one can affirm his or her allegiance to the state without confusing what it means to be truly ethical with the mere observance of one's social duties. In much the same spirit as de Silentio's treatment of these issues in *Fear and Trembling*, Anti-Climacus reflects on the transformation that is engendered once the self decides to relativize one's duties to the state in favor of affirming the God-figure as one's highest ethical goal and criterion:

THE GOD-MAN AS UNCONDITIONED ETHICAL PROTOTYPE 123

The child who previously has had only his parents as a criterion becomes a self as an adult by getting the state as a criterion, but what
an infinite accent falls on the self by having God as the criterion! The
criterion for the self is always: that directly before which it is a self,
but this in turn is the definition of "criterion." Just as only entities of
the same kind can be added, so everything is qualitatively that by
which it is measured, and that which is its qualitative criterion
[Maalestok] is ethically its goal [Maal]; the criterion and goal are what
define something, what it is. (SUD, 79)

If, as Anti-Climacus claims, the self becomes a self by virtue of being
before God, then to sin, or to be in despair, is to hold steadfast to
lesser criteria; that is, the most accentuated form of despair is to
obdurately cling to purely human criteria while being conscious that
God is the highest of all ethical standards:

Despair is intensified in relation to the consciousness of the self, but
the self is intensified in relation to the criterion of the self, infinitely
when God is the criterion. In fact, the greater the conception of God,
the more self there is; the more self, the greater the conception of
God. Not until a self as this specific single individual is conscious of
existing before God, not until then is it the infinite self and this self
sins before God. (SUD, 80)

According to the pseudonym, to hold to one's necessary (purely
human) dimension with the aim of conserving the old order, without
realizing that the past does not constitute a phase in the world-historical process or in *Geist*'s dialectical divine design, but is the product of a series of moments in which situations come into existence
through contingent factors, is to sustain the alienation of inclosing
reserve. Only through faith can the despairing individual realize redemption and affirm God as the supreme ethical ideal.

Anti-Climacus's definition of faith is central to any appreciation
of the God-figure as the standard of radical responsibility in the work
of Kierkegaard: "faith is: that the self in being itself and in willing to
be itself rests *transparently* in God" (SUD, 82; my emphasis). To rest
transparently in God is the aim of any self that wills to be itself.
However, to be oneself demands that the self relate itself to itself.
This simply means that in sacrificing the purely human self, or in
dying to the world of given actuality, the self affirms that it has the
possibility of becoming otherwise. For to be reborn, or to be born to

the world a second time in repetition (just as Abraham received the universal back in the form of Isaac), requires that one suspend one's universal certainties and affirm what cannot be inclosed or established in the present. The faculty of imagination opens the self up to what is incommensurable in this way.

The case of de Silentio's Abraham is worth revisiting here as a model of this type of self- sacrifice. Abraham resigns from the universal by adopting a critical distance from the dominant political and ethical codes that subdue authentic responsibility. In so doing, he passionately affirms what could not have been preprogrammed or calculated in advance by any teleological scheme, what would have been impossible for mediation to make sense of. This is the passionate concentration faith requires: in saying "yes" to what confounds speculative reason, the knight of faith keeps the establishment open to what it has excluded while securing its own identity. Repetition, unlike recollection, does not seek to compound a given identity, does not endeavor to divinize the given state of affairs by showing how it is a stage in the passage to eternity. Repetition does not attempt to cheat existence or time, but is a temporal movement through and through.

Recall at this point how Climacus emphasizes the role of the teacher in all matters appertaining to the acquisition of truth: Socrates, unlike the God in time, is prevented from bringing the learner to new life because of his belief that the truth is something to be recollected. The truth in this circumstance is something that is *known* by the individual, in that he or she possesses it prior to Socrates' intervention. The latter is merely the occasion for an awakening to truth once more. Consequently, those who have recollected the truth with Socrates' help were not actually given the truth by *him*, since they possessed it all the while. For these reasons, Socrates, at least according to Climacus, is not to be owed anything by those whom he assisted:

> The person who understands Socrates best understands specifically that he owes Socrates nothing, which is what Socrates prefers, and to be able to prefer this is beautiful. The person who thinks that he is so very indebted to Socrates can be quite sure that Socrates gladly exempts him from paying, since Socrates certainly would be dismayed to learn that he had given the person concerned any working capital whatsoever to exploit in this way. But if the whole structure is not

Socratic—and this is what we are assuming—then the follower owes the teacher *everything* (which one cannot possibly owe to Socrates, since, after all, as he himself says, he was not capable of *giving birth*), and this relation cannot be expressed by talking extravagantly and trumpeting from the housetops but only in the happy passion which we call faith, the object of which is the paradox—but the paradox specifically unites the contradictories, is the eternalizing of the historical and the historicizing of the eternal. (PF, 61)

For Climacus, purely human knowledge is insufficient for coming to terms with the fact that the eternal enters time in the form of a servant, with the objective of providing the condition for realizing truth. Such knowledge "is either knowledge of the eternal, which excludes the temporal and the historical as inconsequential, or it is purely historical knowledge" (PF, 62). In the case of repetition, however, because the teacher is responsible for bringing the learner into truth by providing him or her with the condition for relating oneself to oneself, the learner is eternally indebted to him. For if the God had not intervened, the existing individual would have perpetually remained in alienation and ignorance. To have faith, therefore, is to subjectively engage with the person of the teacher, not simply as occasion, but as the criterion for the attainment of truth:

> Now if we assume that the structure is as we have assumed (and unless we do, we go back to Socrates), namely, that the teacher himself provides the learner with the condition, then the object of faith becomes not the *teaching* but the *teacher*, for the essence of the Socratic is that the learner, because he himself is the truth and has the condition, can thrust the teacher away. Indeed, assisting people to be able to do this constituted the Socratic art and heroism. Faith, then, must constantly cling firmly to the teacher. (PF, 62)

The teacher is thus the object of faith; what he teaches can indeed be learned objectively, but he himself cannot be *known* as such.

The kernel of Climacus's argument here is that the despairing individual needs the God-figure to acquire the condition for becoming a self. This is the contradiction that lies at the heart of faith: if the individual received the condition from any source other than God, it would not be *the* condition. However, if the condition is to be received at all, the learner must be capable of *identifying* it as *the* condition. Hence, if the God is to put the learner in possession of the condition, "he must be man" (PF, 62). This is the absolute paradox around which Kierkegaard's thought revolves: if the God-figure is to be considered as the highest ethical criterion and goal, and if the learner is to attain the condition for realizing this ethical standard in his or her life, then the God must appear in a human form in order to be recognized. We must suppose that the God, by appearing in human form, "came into existence," or that the eternal entered time in the "moment." As I have made clear above, however, there can be no *immediate* knowledge of what has come into existence. The best we can do is believe that it has come into existence, that it came into existence through the actualization of possibility, or through freedom:

> Every time the believer makes this fact the object of faith, makes it historical for himself, he repeats the dialectical qualifications of coming into existence. No matter how many millennia have passed by, no matter how many consequences that fact elicited in its train, it does not therefore become more necessary (and, viewed definitively, the consequences themselves are only relatively necessary, inasmuch as they rest in that freely acting cause), to say nothing of the most inverted notion of all, that it should become necessary because of its consequences, since consequences as a rule have their basis in something else and do not give the basis for that. No matter how many preparations for that fact, no matter how many hints and symptoms of its coming a contemporary or a predecessor saw, that fact was not necessary when it came into existence—that is, that fact is no more necessary as future than it is necessary as past. (PF, 88)

The God-figure is an object of faith, or belief "in an eminent sense," to invoke Climacus's expression. The learner, that is, must believe that such a figure can provide the condition for releasing him or her from inclosing reserve. It is with the aid of this highest of all ethical exemplars that the individual comes to learn that being responsible and earnest, rather than merely conflating a dutiful observance of the law with genuine ethical behavior, demands that there be a teleological suspension of the established ethical order. There can be no comfort, as suggested in chapter 3, for one prepared to relate oneself (possible self) to oneself (past, established order, given actuality) in this way. Having no recourse to universal standards, the individual who decides to look to God in the form of a servant as a guiding ethical principle must do so in fear and trembling, or with a good dose of anxiety. Having suspended certitude in the finite ethical criteria that serve only to maintain the order of the state, Kierkegaard's learner endeavors to become educated, in faith, in the extraordinary, in what is absurd to merely human comprehension:

> In order that an individual may thus be educated absolutely and infinitely by the possibility, he must be honest toward possibility and have faith. By faith I understand here what Hegel somewhere in his way correctly calls the inner certainty that anticipates infinity. When the discoveries of possibility are honestly administered, possibility will discover all the finitudes, but it will idealize them in the form of infinity and in anxiety overwhelm the individual until he again overcomes them in the anticipation of faith. (CA, 157)

Practicing Christianity

Kierkegaard's theory of faith is the bedrock of what I have been calling his theory of community existence. Although he considers it each individual's obligation to become a responsible self, this does not preclude his advancing an argument for a social theory based on an ethics of radical responsibility. If Socrates and Abraham exemplify the tensions involved in challenging the established order from the ironic standpoint, Jesus Christ ("idea," "teacher," "servant"), as the ultimate ethical prototype, signifies the highest ideal for all existing beings. In developing further the arguments of the *Fragments*, Anti-Climacus attempts to demonstrate, in a practical sense, how one can actually rest transparently in God; that is, the pseudonym endeavors to train the reader how to achieve what Climacus calls an "essential equality"[3] with the God-figure.

It might seem, as some commentators tend to charge, that the overtly Christian dimension of Kierkegaard's oeuvre denies him any credible philosophical legitimacy. I wish to challenge such assumptions, however, by arguing that it is precisely in the radical Christianity he promotes that one can identify the truly remarkable

---

[3] "Essentially equality" for Climacus means a "likeness" or essential similarity. One should not get the impression that by appropriating this phrase he believes that the qualitative distinction between man and God can be broken down. God is always the ideal, but one to be imitated nonetheless.

philosophical contribution Kierkegaard has bequeathed to the contemporary milieu.

Reason, Faith, and Religion

In continually underscoring the fundamental significance of the category of repetition so far in this work, I have sought to elucidate the general manner in which Kierkegaard proceeds with his critical enterprise. For in being the "watchword in every ethical view," as well as that "upon which metaphysics comes to grief," repetition serves as the thorn in the flesh of any inflexible metaphysical scheme or any ethical paradigm that reduces the singularity of individuals to the whole or to the system. This is not to suggest, however, that Kierkegaard seeks to go beyond metaphysics or ethics; repetition enables the individual to take again what has already been, but from a more passionate point of view. That is, the individual, in resigning from the given actuality, or in teleologically suspending the dominant ethical-cum-political paradigm, aims only to critically evaluate the efficacy of its norms, those that have hitherto regulated his or her relationship to others and to the state. In so doing, the individual does not suspend his or her community alliances in favor of a secluded, hermetic subjectivity, but is reborn in faith to the world anew. That is, to rethink or reevaluate one's relationship to one's community, society, or state does not entail a complete divorce from the situation in which one is embedded. It suggests rather that one relativizes what was once central as a guiding principle in favor of a higher ideal that engenders a greater degree of ethical, social, and personal harmony. Hence the dominant metaphysical and ethical schemes are retained (repeated), but in the process they are kept open to change and continual correction.

This is why Kierkegaard looks to figures who have traditionally been on the margins of philosophy *as such*; figures like Socrates and Abraham, who have transgressed the letter of the law in the name of truth and responsibility. In challenging the universalist assumptions of the prevailing orthodoxies, both of these marginal men have emphasized the belief that to be ethical—indeed, to be genuinely philosophical—requires that the individual sacrifice one's security in the established order. Their contention rests on the belief that there are no certainties in existence, no metaphysical or ethical guardrails underpinned by strong transcendental foundations. Furthermore, they stress that all establishments are the products of contingency and that the finite is the only "order" of the day.

To relate to oneself in this way, or to become conscious of oneself as a "poor existing individual," demands a more concrete understanding, or what we have called, following de Silentio, "passionate concentration." For identity is a matter of becoming self-*conscious*, of reflecting on *who* one is. That is, Kierkegaard does not specify that rational reflection must be dispensed with, but he does contend that disinterested objective reflection should be overcome in favor of self-knowledge or reflection.

In a recent treatment of related issues, John Caputo argues in favor of a notion of "interested reflection" or "double reflection" similar in constitution to that advanced by Kierkegaard. In the spirit of Climacus's unrelenting gibes at Hegel's systematic portrait of reason (*Geist*), Caputo writes:

> We have draped reason with institutional authority. We have made it a *princeps*, an *arché*/king, not only by turning it into a rigorous technique and fixed method but by giving it political authority, by creating a rationality-caste, a guild of specialists and professional practitioners of reason. The original Enlightenment idea of reason—as a protest against entrenched authority—has so withered away that what nowadays calls itself reason is the latest and most dangerous authority of all. What we call reason today is a central power tightly circled by bands of military, technical, and industrial authorities which together make up the administered society.[4]

For Caputo—and in saying this he helps us understand much about Kierkegaard—reason has lost its vocation as an emancipatory power. Through its institutionalization, reason has become redundant as the faculty *instar omnium*; it has surrendered its capacity to imagine things otherwise than as they initially appear. As models of dissent, Socrates and Abraham represent a threat to the institution in its metaphysical or ethical manifestation. In heralding the cause of singularity, or in lending support to what is ground under by such institutionalization, both of Kierkegaard's prototypes row against the prevailing rational tide. Consequently, they are considered no more than irrationalists and immoralists:

---

[4] Caputo, *Radical Hermeneutics*, 234.

Kant spoke of "pure" reason and the "autonomy" of reason. But that is a dangerous abstraction, for reason is always already embedded in systems of power. To a great extent what "reason" means is a function of the system of power which is currently in place, and what is irrational is what is out of power. Indeed, it is the essence of the power which institutionalized reason exerts that it is able to define what is out of power as "irrational." . . . One enlists the authority of the institution in the service of one's own ideas. And those who dissent have to show that they are not against reason or the country—that they are not mad or traitorous—when they are only against the ideas which currently prevail.[5]

Caputo urges a loosening up of reason by calling for its liberation from the grips of all institutional circumscription. Like Kierkegaard, however, he does not want to abandon institutions completely. This is why he too emphasizes the need for repetition in the sense of radical transformation, rather than wholesale dissolution or destruction. For the aim here is to make one's traditionally held truths more pliable by revealing how such formations are the products, not of necessity, but of contingency. In other words, Caputo holds to the belief that responsibility demands that we be both inside and outside the traditional metaphysical, political, and ethical frameworks into which we are thrown and through which we acquire an identity. To conclude that the traditional Enlightenment notion of reason is now defunct does not mean that one has given up on reason entirely. For Caputo, it signals that reason has once again been put into play in all its joyful fullness:

We are not in the position of having either to make the leap out of reason into another sphere or to remain confined within it. The idea is to emancipate those who live within reason's sphere of influence, to introduce liberal reforms into its laws, to reinsert the play which informs even calculative thought. . . . If things are as we say, in flux, in undecidable drift and slippage, and if reason is to respond to things, to keep up a correspondence with them (according even to the most classical demand of the metaphysics of truth), reason must play it loose, be capable of unexpected moves, of paradigm switches, of following up unorthodox suggestions. The most reasonable view of reason denies that you can write a handbook about the way reason works.[6]

[5] Ibid., 229.
[6] Ibid., 228.

As we saw in chapter 1, Kierkegaard's theory of repetition strives to debunk the myth that metaphysics functions according to some form of disinterested reason. For Kierkegaard, truth can never be capitalized or universalized. To say that truth is subjectivity should not alarm those who fear a dissipation into relativism, for in expressing such a thing Kierkegaard wants to say that "truth," "metaphysics," and "reason" are the contrivance of those already situated in a particular time and place. The Kierkegaardian objective is to make reason "interested," in the sense in which Climacus and Constantius use this word: *"inter-esse"* or "being between." As Caputo says, reason is "always already betwixt and between—*inter-esse*—this interest or that"—it plays no specific game, but it can be used in different ways by a number of competing interests.

These points are given further credence by Merold Westphal, who remarks that Kierkegaard recognizes "that human reason is a social enterprise and, as such, historically conditioned."[7] According to this commentator, institutionalized reason is synonymous with what I have been calling, following Kierkegaard, "purely human knowledge," as opposed to "self-knowledge." Because it is "historically conditioned," human reason is a limited form of speculation that seeks to perpetuate the sinfulness of the race. I interpret "sinfulness" to mean the misrelationship the self suffers while being ignorant of the saving power of the God-figure, or the one who gives the learner new life upon disturbing the established order. It is only after the individual has sacrificed this purely human dimension, however, only after one has died to pure immediacy and necessity through the affirmation of possibility (or indeed impossibility), that one can be born to the world anew. "Interested" reflection or subjective knowledge, therefore, can be equated with faith, in that once reason is disestablished it seeks to affirm what lies beyond the purview of any particular belief system or conceptual paradigm (see CUP, 189–251).

Faith, as the process whereby the self relates itself to itself, is not by any standard a blind irrational movement. Rather, I contend, following Caputo and Westphal, that it is reason's true vocation to be faithful. In recognizing that all historical formations (state, given actuality, etc.) are the products of contingency, the individual affirms their susceptibility to change and mutability. Such an affirma-

---

[7] Westphal, *Kierkegaard's Critique*, 22.

tion is founded on the hope that accommodation can now be made with what the established order excludes with the intention of safeguarding its own identity.

Now, for Kierkegaard, as for the two commentators just cited, religion is generally the most productive means by which the established order protects itself against the offensive threat that faith poses; that is, institutionalized religion acts as the legitimizing force for many of the principles that sustain the establishment. As Westphal observes:

> . . . Kierkegaard is sensitive to the sociology of knowledge. He knows that social groups make themselves legitimate through the propagation of belief systems in which the established order is justified. He also knows that religions are usually the most effective institutions in the practice of "world-building" and "world maintaining" function. He recognizes (and this is crucial) the degree to which this process determines what is to count as Reason in any given context.[8]

In this context, reason is not a liberating faculty, but merely the means by which individuals come to identify "the authority of the established order, thereby participating in its self-deification."[9] If there is to be religion motivated by a radical ethics of responsibility, one that is not in the service of orthodoxy, then it must come in the form of a threat to the establishment. It must be, to appropriate an expression used frequently by Jacques Derrida and John Caputo, "a religion without religion," or a form of religious practice that does not tie one essentially to a particular religion associated with a particular people or culture. Such a religion without religion demands faith; that is, rather than being merely in the service of institutionalized reason, this radical religion endeavors to push reason back on its own resources by giving it independence from its speculative stereotype. Consequently, reason or objective reflection is given new life (repetition) by being transformed into engaged and passionate subjective reflection, resolving in concrete action. It becomes passionate about the future, for it knows that, as Constantius tirelessly reminds his reader, eternity can only be entered in a forward-moving fashion.

As I have suggested in these reflections on repetition, the Christ-

---

[8] Ibid., 23.
[9] Ibid.

figure exemplifies to the highest degree the way in which religion of this kind can pose a problem for the established order, or for any world-historical formation that cannot own up to its own contingent foundations. Jesus Christ, according to Kierkegaard, offends in a manner similar to both Socrates and Abraham in that he seeks to prevent the good and the true from becoming fossilized in established customs and rituals. In a particularly incisive passage, Westphal makes clear what is at issue here:

> It becomes necessary to say that "faith is against the understanding" because "faith is on the other side of death," the death that dies to immediacy, selfishness, and worldliness. This is to say that the offense of contemporaneity with Christ means not just that the socially sanctioned reasonableness of belief is rendered questionable, but also that the socially sanctioned rightness of behavior is rendered suspect. Like Socrates, Christ was executed as an infidel because he refused to recognize the established order as the criterion of virtue and goodness. In this sense Christ was an offense even without claiming godhead. He showed "what 'the truth' had to suffer in every generation and what it must always suffer" by not retreating from the collision between piety and the established order.[10]

The God-man, that is, shows the way to all learners by becoming a witness to the truth. It is through him that each individual can receive the condition of faith. This requires, however, that one become contemporaneous with the God-figure, one who suffered in the name of justice.

Kierkegaard's God-figure is not the (patriarchal) God of the Old Testament, the God of Abraham, or indeed the "absolutely other" of Levinas. He is the God of *Practice in Christianity*, the living God whose call to sacrifice amounts to giving up all worldly possessions for the welfare of all those denied a privileged position in the established order. God here is not represented as he is in traditional metaphysical or scholastic accounts, where the emphasis is on how his existence can be rationally proved. Rather, the distinction between faith and reason collapses as we come to realize that to have faith in such a God is a process of disclosing reason's true vocation as a power that turns on novelty, dissent, and originality. By representing God in this way, Kierkegaard became the first philosopher to break with

---

[10] Ibid., 24.

the assumption that "Christian philosophy must in fact abstract from the historical figure of Jesus"[11] with his life, his sayings, and his singularity. Hence, to practice Christianity is to take the side of those whose lives the Christ-figure championed, those who do not feature prominently in the established order, and those whose singularity has been crushed by universality. This form of "religion"—for this is what Kierkegaard calls the "religious stage of existence"—affirms that the Christ-figure who so offended the Pharisaical order has entered time in the "moment" of faith. To be religious in this sense means to have a belief that one can be reborn (repetition) as a result of the intervention of a singular individual who has come into existence claiming to be God. Repetition, unlike recollection, cannot mediate such a spectacle. This, according to Kierkegaard, is the cold truth of repetition.

For Kierkegaard, thus, religion is anything but institutionalization, for faith is disestablished reason, reason that no longer serves the interests of the prevailing order. This form of radicalized religion is neither a way of escaping or evading history or time nor a means of withdrawing from the needs of the moment so as to take up a privileged place in eternity, but rather the manner in which we say "yes" to the life we live here and now. Religion, on this account, is an ethics of vigilance, earnestness, and responsibility, since it has as its guiding example and idea the figure of one who stood firm against the powers that be in the name of justice. Because it is not socially sanctioned or legitimated, and because it favors those who are out of favor with the establishment, Kierkegaard's radical religion is deemed absurd, mad, and offensive.

The Historical Christ As Unconditioned Ethical Prototype

I have argued that faith, for Kierkegaard, constitutes an act of relating oneself to oneself by which one rests transparently in God or in the power that creates the self. It is important to interpret this, not in the sense of physical creation, but as *spiritual* creation. Kierkegaard's God-figure represents the means by which we come to challenge our preconceived notions of personal, ethical, and political

---

[11] John D. Caputo, "Metanoetics: Elements of a Postmodern Christian Philosophy" (forthcoming), 7.

identity; by making this figure our guiding principle, we are exposed to what the established order conceals from view, what threatens our traditional self-certainties. This does not, however, signal destruction, for faith is an affirmation of life, an affirmation of new life, an affirmation of what exceeds the horizon of the given actuality.

The question of precisely how one comes to receive the condition of faith is the theme of Anti-Climacus's reflections in *Practice in Christianity.* The pseudonym, with the aim of rehearsing in more practical terms the ideas put forth in *The Sickness unto Death,* begins by stating that "contemporaneity is the condition of faith, and, more sharply defined, it is faith" (PC, 9). Faith thus means coming into contemporaneity with the unconditioned ethical prototype, Jesus Christ. Otherwise stated, it is through the God-man that one can ultimately be set free.

The highest of all prototypes for Kierkegaard is not Father Abraham; neither is it the figure of Socrates, who demands that we die to the material life with the aim of nourishing the soul; it is, however, an individual notable only for his simplicity and purity of heart, one who does not come in glory, but in the form of one of the establishment's outsiders. Such an individual seeks not to overthrow the state or the present order of things; he endeavors, rather, to make the state responsible by *responding* to those who do not hold high office, or those who are shown no mercy by the law. In short, to be religious in Anti-Climacus's sense requires that one speak *against* those who cause suffering and misery, and *for* those whom the body politic has denied a voice. This is why Kierkegaardian religion can be interpreted as a politics of exodus, a politics of the vanquished and dispossessed.

Kierkegaard's Jesus-figure is thus an offense to those who have a vested interest in maintaining prevailing belief systems. He stands outside the law and contravenes its most sacred tenets, not with the objective of spilling blood or of transcending the world of illusion for a world of heavenly forms, but in the name of those who have no legal status or standing. He teleologically suspends the ethical (*Sittlichkeit*) to respond to a higher calling, not from a God without form, but from "the poor and wretched." To respond to the other in this way requires that we go beyond the usual forms of charitable exercises that are fully sanctioned by the powers that be; the ethical injunction is to welcome those with whom we have nothing in common, those who are symbols of our worst fears. To them we should say—if we aspire, that is, to be genuinely responsible: "Come here to me, all you who labor and are burdened, and I will give you rest!" (PC, 23). No individual is a foreigner to one who can say this with conviction.

Such an ethics of responsibility demands, therefore, excessive generosity and hospitality; it requires that one die to the purely finite and necessary dimensions of the self in order to welcome the other:

> It will not do, when one is living in abundance oneself or at least in joy and gladness, to reside together in a house and live together in a common life and in daily association with the poor and wretched, with those who labor and are burdened. In order to invite them to come to one in this way, one must oneself live in the very same manner, poor as the poorest, poorly regarded as the lowly man among the people, experienced in life's sorrow and anguish, sharing the very same condition as those one invites to come to one, those who labor and are burdened. (PC, 13)

Living contemporaneously with the God-figure requires, according to Kierkegaard, that one make no particular place one's home; it commands that one roam like Abraham, the wandering Jew, in no set direction. For the outcasts and the marginalized are not a specific feature of any particular generation, age, or community. They are perennially with us in various manifestations and forms. We are, therefore, called to have compassion and fellow feeling with the types whom Jesus, the God-man, associated with, those who have no kingdom or earthly resting place—in short, those who have no home and who are not associated with any particular sect or tribe.

This ethics of compassion and mercy that Anti-Climacus sets out induces in those who contemplate it the most horrifying fear and trembling. For it requires that one become politically subversive, that one stand on the margins with those who have no role to play in the formal functions of the state or community. According to the pseudonym, this is no merely *human* compassion, but a *divine* compassion. It functions according to a totally unconditioned criterion, one which demands that the individual sacrifice all relative criteria:

> The unconditioned, everything that provides the criterion of unconditionality, is *eo ipso* the sacrifice. For people are willing enough to prac-

tice compassion and self-denial, willing enough to seek after wisdom etc., but they want to determine the criterion themselves, that it shall be to *a certain degree*. They do not wish to do away with all these glorious virtues; on the contrary, they want—at a cheap price—to have as comfortably as possible the appearance of and the reputation for practicing them. Therefore, as soon as the true divine compassion appears in the world it is unconditionally the sacrifice. It comes out of compassion for people and it is people who trample it down. . . . The point is, it is urgent for the world to preserve the appearance of being compassionate; this now makes the divine compassion into an untruth—ergo the divine compassion must go. (PC, 60)

The unconditioned criterion is an offense to human sensibility and an absurdity to the secular mentality. Rarely, therefore, is it appropriated as a guiding ethical ideal or principle. Few are willing to risk such a degree of responsibility, knowing as they do the level of suffering that sacrifice of this kind engenders.

The historical figure of Christ, he who led a life of poverty and penury, he whose associates were the lepers and the lame, the prostitutes and paralytics, is for Kierkegaard the ideal. He is a symbol of liberation and new life, not in the sense of taking people out of the world and into eternity, but by championing the cause of those who have been ground under by the system or the world-historical process. In exposing the established order to its other in this way, the Christ, through his actions and his sayings, shows just how contingent all historical formations are; that is, by standing with the lowest he demonstrated that states, communities, societies, and in fact all social institutions are founded on an exclusionary gesture. In so doing, he bore testimony to the fact that if we seek equality and justice, then all such institutions should be open to transformation and change until such a time as they can accommodate the destitute and the outcasts. Such is the responsibility of those who count themselves among the truly ethical and compassionate.

From this analysis we can see why Climacus termed repetition a form of "rebirth": to be born to the world anew through the saving power of God in servant form is to liberate oneself from the despair of the age (sin) by having faith in the absurd and the paradoxical, or more simply put, by affirming what is anathema and alien to the established order. It is, as Constantius remarks, a forward-moving process in which the individual has hope in a future to come, in

something that is not set to unfold teleologically. Such hope is motivated by a passion for the impossible, for what cannot be objectively
anticipated. As such, it is a hope that one day injustice might be
overcome. This is the hope of faith, the hope that is bound up with
affirming the Christ as ethical paradigm and prototype.

Anti-Climacus follows Climacus in claiming that for the learner
the teacher is everything, not merely an occasion for the recollection
of truth. The emphasis is not, therefore, placed on the Christ of
history, but on the historical Christ, that is, on the actual *life* of the
Jesus-figure. For to come to know of Jesus Christ from official history
is to avoid the offense of standing in the midst of a figure clad in
rags while claiming to be God. For the pseudonym, the only genuine
possibility of becoming contemporaneous with this figure is to treat
him as one who has "come into existence." Accordingly, one does
not come to *know* him *as such;* he is simply an object of faith and a
sign of offense and impropriety. Otherwise put: if to have faith is to
rest transparently in God, then it requires that one stand with the
God in servant form and with all those for whom he had divine
compassion. Such is the radical sacrifice required of those for whom
religion becomes a priority: it enjoins one to stand alongside those
who suffer and are demeaned in the name of the good and the true
as defined by the rational order.

The marvel that history is at a loss to explain is that this particular
human being was in fact God, that one so unlike the Messiah (in
that he did not come in glory) was in fact the Messiah: "It is true
that we all look forward to an expected one, but that it is God in
person who is to come is not the expectation of any rational person,
and every religious person shudders at the blasphemy of which this
person is guilty" (PC, 46). If the expected one had lived up to general expectations, he would have surely come to pledge his support
for the established order and the elected people, that particular community for whom he supposedly had a particular fondness. But he
did not come in glory; he came rather in abasement, in the least-
expected form. In so doing, he did not take the side of any one
people, but of all those who are unlikely ever to be considered "the
elect": "So [it is] the lowly, destitute man with twelve poor disciples
from the commonest class of people, for a long time an object of
curiosity but later in the company only of sinners, tax collectors,
lepers, and madmen, because merely to let oneself be helped by him

meant to risk one's honor, life and goods, in any case exclusion from the synagogue" (PC, 37). The established order, in being unable to make any credible sense of the God-man, in finding it paradoxical that he should want to reject the sacred pieties of the given actuality, is drawn to contend that he is simply mad, irrational, and an outlaw. To take the side of those who have been vanquished in the name of the law, or to walk with those whose needs are not protected by the law, is the quickest way to come to grief in an environment that determines the law as the manifestation of God's divine design on earth:

> Divine compassion, however, the unlimited recklessness in concerning oneself only with the suffering, not in the least with oneself, and of unconditionally recklessly concerning oneself with each sufferer— people can interpret this only as a kind of madness over which we are not sure whether we should laugh or cry. Even if there had not been any other obstacle for the inviter, this alone would have been sufficient for him to come to grief in the world. (PC, 58)

What must be asked at this point, therefore, is how one can actually become contemporaneous with the God in lowly form; how, that is, can we, as learners, stand with him and risk the responsibility of having divine compassion for what John Caputo calls the "cast of outsiders," or "the nobodies, the nullities, the nothings"?[12] Otherwise expressed, how exactly can each individual challenge the established order, the present age, the world-historical process, or the given actuality through the movement of faith? The response proffered by Anti-Climacus begins by once more emphasizing the category of offense. For one cannot become faithful, cannot take the God-man to be the unconditional ethical principle, unless one has first been offended by an individual human being in a state of degradation announcing that he is God. If one construes "the whole thing altogether historically, of beginning with letting him be dead" (PC, 107), then one can avoid being offended; that is, if our focus is deflected from *this* human being here and now standing before me to the figure in the founding story of the Christian movement, which is transmitted in a secondhand fashion through history, we can then come to know more about him and his motives. Furthermore, be-

---

[12] Ibid., 12.

cause he is considered the founder of what has since become an established order—Christendom—it is convenient for most so-called Christians, according to Anti-Climacus, to judge the God-man by the *results* of his life, rather than by his actual life as a "poor existing human being" in his singularity. But to have the *life* of Jesus as one's ideal, prototype, or paradigm—this is the ethical demand Christian responsibility imposes upon the individual. It is a matter of actualizing, through responsible decision, the possibility of doing the impossible, of becoming like the historical figure of Christ who gave comfort to the wretched and the miserable. Such an ethics of responsibility is naturally offensive and scandalous to those who have internalized the belief system of the establishment. To *admire* the Christ in his "loftiness," or as world history portrays him, while forgetting entirely his "lowliness" is to render him knowable merely in an objective or speculative sense. For Anti-Climacus, however, the obligation imposed upon each individual by repetition is that one *imitate* the Christ, as the lowly champion of all sufferers.[13] In so doing, one keeps alive religion's vocation as a defiant and liberating gesture:

> Does not Christian teaching about ethics and obligation, Christianity's requirement to die to the world, to surrender the earthly, its requirement of self-denial, does not this contain enough requirements—if they were to be obeyed—to produce the danger of actuality that makes manifest the difference between an admirer and an imitator, makes it manifest precisely in this way, that the imitator has his life in these dangers and the admirer personally remains detached although they both are nevertheless united in acknowledging in words the truth of Christianity? Thus the difference still remains. The admirer will make no sacrifices, renounce nothing, give up nothing earthly, will not transform his life, will not be what is admired. . . . The imitator, however, aspires to be what is admired. (PC, 252)

In so doing, the "imitator *is* or strives *to be* what he admires"; in other words, one must "become just as poor, despised, insulted, mocked, and if possible even a little more" (PC, 241). Such are the requirements of what Kierkegaard calls the *imitatio Christi.*

---

[13] For an argument that takes much the same line as my own, see Gouwens, *Kierkegaard as Religious Thinker*, chapter 6; see also Joseph O'Leary, *Religious Pluralism and Christian Truth* (Edinburgh: Edinburgh University Press, 1996), especially the final chapter, "The Empty Christ," 205–58.

By becoming one with the despised, the Christ-figure revealed himself in an **indirect** way; that is, as an individual human being without any distinguishing godly marks, he could only communicate his true essence obliquely. The notion of indirect communication is of vital significance in any assessment of the work of Kierkegaard. In the context of Anti-Climacus's discussion of the unconditional ethical paradigm, however, it takes on immense relevance when one endeavors to observe how the pseudonym proposes that one become an imitator in the highest sense, or how one comes to identify the God-man as the object of faith. The God-man, according to the pseudonym, is a sign, "a sign of contradiction," in that he is unrecognizable as *God*. Consequently, because the communicator of the message does not reveal himself directly, his communication is indirect:

> If someone says directly: I am God; the Father and I are one, this is direct communication. But if the person who says it, the communicator, is the individual human being, an individual human being just like the others, then this communication is not quite entirely direct, because it is not entirely direct that an individual human being should be God—whereas what he says is entirely direct. Because of the communicator the communication contains a contradiction, it becomes indirect communication; it confronts you with a choice: whether you will believe him or not. (PC, 134)

The object of indirect communication is to effect in the learner a dialectical "reduplication"; that is, the aim of the subjective communicator is to bring the individual with whom he or she is communicating to the point where that person undergoes a personal metamorphosis through responsible choice or decision. Subjective (indirect) communication encourages the learner to become self-reflective, or as Anti-Climacus would say, to relate oneself to oneself in passionate concentration, what he calls in *Practice in Christianity* "double reflection" (PC, 133).

In the case of the God-man, the objective is to provide the necessary condition in order for the individual to have faith in the teacher. As we have seen, faith's form of responsibility demands that one imitate the God-man in his lowliness, which in turn requires that the individual cultivate divine compassion for the cast of outsiders. Such is the ethical criterion Kierkegaard recommends that all human beings appropriate. In so doing, one answers the appeal from those whose singularity crumbles in the face of oppressive universality. By appearing in the form of the poor and worthless, the God-man testified (indirectly) to the fact that faith can never reassure. Faith is inwardness in that it is motivated, as Johannes de Silentio says, by a passion for the impossible, or for the inbreaking of the eternal into time, which occurs only in the moment; that is, the faithful individual can never know for certain that the Christ-figure is God. If he had come in glory or in loftiness, the future would have shut down, and the poor would have always remained with us. By appearing incognito, however, he keeps the hope of justice alive. In other words, through repetition, or dialectical redoubling, the individual is brought to new life by imitating what is most offensive and threatening to the establishment, or by taking the side of those with whom one can least identify. This is why, according to Anti-Climacus, offense and repulsion are the preconditions for coming to faith:

> The contradiction is to require of a person that he make the greatest possible sacrifice, dedicate his whole life to being sacrificed—and why? Well, there is no "why"; so it is indeed lunacy, says the understanding. There is no "why," because there is an infinite "why." But wherever the understanding comes to a standstill in this way, there is the possibility of offense. If there is to be any triumphant breakthrough, there must be faith, for faith is a new life. (PC, 120)

Faith, or religion, on Kierkegaard's terms, can thus be defined as a gesture toward singularity. By taking the Christ-figure as the ideal paradigm to be imitated by each individual, he presents a pragmatic way to deal with the plagues besetting the modern age, those contemporary ills among which can be counted massification, leveling, ideology, and most especially, social discrimination. Kierkegaard's antipathy to organized Christianity, or Christendom, stems from his belief that the genuine ethical message the Christ-figure brought through his deeds and actions has been occluded by the powers that be as a means of self-preservation and self-deification. To practice Christianity, however, requires that one affirm what is out of power, what the law looks at with suspicion, and what offends and repulses our most sacred beliefs and mores. In other words, to have faith in the God-man requires standing with him in lowliness and suffering for the truth as he did. Such is the passion of inwardness, the passion for what exceeds all forms of institutionalized reason, the passion for social justice. By championing the cause of the singular over the universal, the God-man offended both the state and the prevailing religious order. His aim in so doing was not to precipitate social unrest and disharmony but to inspire fear and trembling before God, or in the name of those whom God most profoundly represented. Responsibility is a matter, according to Kierkegaard, of deciding in fear and trembling whether one will affirm the God-man—whether, that is, one will have faith and believe in him in his lowliness, or whether one will hold fast to the securities of Christendom or the state.

6

A Politics of the Émigré

IN THIS FINAL CHAPTER I will demonstrate how Kierkegaard's ethics of responsibility can act as the foundation for a radical conception of social relations. In the opening chapters I suggested that Kierkegaard's attack on the Hegelian notion of *Sittlichkeit* was motivated by a desire to surmount leveling so as to establish a form of social cohesion in which the "coiled springs" of life-relationships are made more resilient. Now I will argue that Kierkegaard's development of a passionate form of responsibility, one in which the God-man is the ideal to be imitated and followed, is a means by which the idea of community is not jettisoned but rather rethought in an original and dramatic way.

To fully appreciate the social dimension of Kierkegaard's work, it is important to attend to the *post*modern strain that figures so prominently in his oeuvre. Indeed, there is nothing new or original in making the case for Kierkegaard as a postmodern thinker or as a precursor to deconstruction. Over the last decade, numerous writers have shown just how concrete such an affiliation actually is. Commentators such as Louis Mackey and Martin Matustík have convincingly demonstrated that Kierkegaard has as much status as Nietzsche as a progenitor of many strains of contemporary European thought.[1] For these and many similar critics, Kierkegaard's strategies of indirect communication, pseudonymity, and irony—along with the more contentious motifs of the teleological suspension of the ethical, the crisis and madness generated by ethical decision, the passion for the other, and the inexorable defense of the "poor existing individual" whose singularity is always under threat from assimilationist pro-

---

[1] See Mackey, *Points of View*; Matustík, *Postnational Identity*. See also Michael Weston, *Kierkegaard and Modern Continental Philosophy: An Introduction* (London: Routledge, 1994), which attempts to situate Kierkegaard in relation to such thinkers as Nietzsche, Heidegger, Wittgenstein, Derrida, and Levinas. As we shall see, however, the work of John D. Caputo provides the most convincing argument in favor of treating Kierkegaard as one of the major forerunners of many contemporary trends.

grams (I am thinking here especially of Hegelian dialectics and established Christianity)—are employed to optimum effect most radically
in the work of Jacques Derrida. As I showed in chapter 1 with reference to Kierkegaard's indictment of "public opinion" and the press,
the Kierkegaardian strain in Derrida's work has revealed itself most
especially in Derrida's later texts, but it can also be detected in many
of the early texts—even, I would argue, as early as many of the essays
from the 1960s collected and published in *L'écriture et la différance*
(1967). It is, however, in Derrida's most recent publications that we
can see how palpable Kierkegaard's influence is. It is my working
hypothesis that Derrida's readings of Kierkegaard in these texts, or
his oblique invocations of the latter throughout his authorship, contribute much to the debate surrounding Kierkegaard as a social philosopher and to our understanding of him as a thinker of radical
heteronomy and responsibility. Otherwise expressed, I will argue
that Derrida's insights supply us with the means to make a credible
case for Kierkegaard's inclusion in mainstream ethical and political
philosophy today. Through a reading of some of Derrida's recent
pronouncements, especially his most overtly Kierkegaardian treatment, "Donner la mort" (1992), I will give substance to the claim
that at the heart of Kierkegaard's enterprise is a theory of community
that calls for serious appraisal.

I do not, however, want to obfuscate the most obvious difference
that exists between Kierkegaard and Derrida: Kierkegaard is a Christian philosopher and Derrida is not. While I do believe that their
philosophies are driven by essentially the same ethical impulse, I am
less prepared to fully conflate both. Nevertheless, I am convinced
that the radical form of Christian ethics Kierkegaard develops has
many parallels with the "ethics" advanced by deconstruction.

Such convergences have been the primary focus of many of John
Caputo's works. His location of a Christian/Kierkegaardian strain in
postmodernism is adequate proof that the form of Christianity put
forward by Kierkegaard need not alienate those who hold trenchantly
to deconstruction's ostensibly secular tendencies.[2] In part 2 of this
chapter, therefore, I will argue that Caputo's application of Derridean postmodernism to his very Kierkegaardian Christianity enables

---

[2] See especially Caputo's *The Prayers and Tears of Jacques Derrida* (Bloomington:
Indiana University Press, 1997).

us to answer the vexed question as to whether or not Kierkegaard is simply a Christian philosopher for a Christian people or one whose ethical and social theories can find use among all denominations. Caputo's notion that the "kingdom of God" is here and now, present at hand—a loosely knit kingdom of mortals bound only by a common concern to see "justice"[3] done—goes a step further than Derrida in making the case for Kierkegaard's legitimacy as a philosopher who is not only marked by his obsession to beat back the tide of Hegelianism but also has much to teach contemporary readers.

In conclusion, I will suggest that even though Derrida and Caputo have gone to great lengths to help us reach an understanding of Kierkegaard that could not have been realized without the emergence of deconstruction, there is much in Kierkegaard that neither of these exponents has yet tapped. That is, although Derrida's and Caputo's readings of Kierkegaard afford us immense insights, they have failed to take cognizance of the theory of community that is the natural outgrowth of Kierkegaard's ethics of responsibility, a theory to be found mostly in his much-neglected *Works of Love*.

PART 1: THE END OF THE BOOK

Kierkegaard As Postmodernist

Recent years have seen a steady proliferation of critical commentaries whose most pervasive and guiding conviction has been to extrapolate the deconstructive dimension of Kierkegaard's thought. The theorist most responsible for initially giving substance to what seemed a most dubious alliance was Mark C. Taylor, a commentator who took the first tentative steps toward consolidating what has now become known as "the Kierkegaard-Derrida relationship."[4] By emphasizing their common distrust of Hegelianism as something that favors the needs of the universal rather than the singular, Taylor prepared the way for many sensible and insightful readings and reappraisals of Derrida as a thinker eminently faithful to a tradition which, up to that point at least, he had been accused of undermining and in some cases destroying. Taylor's approach also provided a new

---

[3] I shall discuss in some detail the meaning of "postmodern justice" below.
[4] See M. C. Taylor, *Deconstructing Theology*.

impetus to Kierkegaard studies, which at that time were seriously running the risk of turning Kierkegaard into a thinker who had absolutely nothing to offer those attempting to make sense of a rapidly emerging postmodern world.

In his much-acclaimed and highly controversial *Altarity* (1987),[5] Taylor gave substance to his belief that Kierkegaard was a major forerunner of deconstruction and the thinker with whom Derrida had a most oblique yet concrete relationship. Derrida, on this reading, is perhaps Kierkegaard's closest ally from a panoply of thinkers ranging from Heidegger to Levinas, all of whom Taylor treated as philosophers devoted to the Kierkegaardian challenge of retrieving singularity from Hegel's dialectical web. In Derrida, according to Taylor, there is a restaging of Abraham's nomadic perambulations, his transgression of the prevailing order, and his use of positive irony to free himself from the universality of the law, all of which are fundamental Kierkegaardian motifs. It is, however, in his discussion of the use both authors make of literature as a means of countering the "culture of the book" that Taylor comes into his own. By highlighting their commitment to textuality and their rethinking of the notion of authorship, Taylor precipitated a rich debate in which Kierkegaard was exhumed from the vaults, brushed down, and given a new credence—not only among hermeneutic and deconstructive philosophers, but also amid the ranks of a new breed of literary theorists and theologians.

Nevertheless, not all of the ramifications of Taylor's project have proved to be of positive value. The benefits of attempting to "contemporize" Kierkegaard by aligning him with Derrida et al. are, as we shall see, manifold. However, the problems become poignantly manifest when Taylor writes in an idiom that is, in the main, inaccessible to a large majority of uninitiated Kierkegaard and general philosophy readers. Taylor's Derrida is the Derrida of "From Restricted to General Economy: An Hegelianism without Reserve," an early essay in which he undertakes a reading of Georges Bataille's *L'experience intérieure* (1943).[6] He is not the Derrida of "Violence and Metaphysics" (1964),[7] nor is he too concerned with the problems of

---

[5] M. C. Taylor, *Altarity*.

[6] See Jacques Derrida, *Writing and Difference*, trans. Alan Bass (London: Routledge, 1978), 251–77.

[7] Ibid., 79–153.

La voix et le phénomène (1967)[8] or with the questions of justice and responsibility, for which he has become so noted over the past ten years. The upshot of this is that Taylor's Derrida plays into the hands of those detractors (John Searle, Barry Smith, and Ruth Marcus, to name only the most prominent) who claim that deconstruction is not only philosophically ineffective but also ethically and politically dangerous.[9] The fact that Derrida and Kierkegaard do have something worthwhile to say at the ethical and political level is thus undermined by a project that fails to readily translate what appear to many as lessons in wanton obscurantism.

The reaction to Taylor's project—and to those that he and others have inspired and influenced—among mainstream Kierkegaardian commentators has been no less muted. In recent years one notable dissenting commentator has emerged who has as her guiding priority the aim of making Kierkegaard independent of Derrida and his fold. The thinker in question is Sylvia Walsh, whose *Living Poetically* (1994) has become a latter-day landmark of Kierkegaardian scholarship. Walsh can indeed be commended for having undertaken a systematic study of the Kierkegaardian corpus in a clear and accessible manner, and one whose general thesis is original and appealing. However, the subtext of *Living Poetically* takes the form of Walsh's rejection of the thesis that Derrida is the most Kierkegaardian of our contemporary philosophical minds, on the grounds that he is unconcerned with the basic questions of ethics, existence, and singularity. However, in reacting to what might be broadly called the "Taylor school of thought"—that is, being so concerned with stemming the postmodern tide that appears to have engulfed Kierkegaard—Walsh fails to locate the obvious Kierkegaardian impulse of Derrida's work. If Taylor can be criticized for not having sufficiently teased out the way in which reading Kierkegaard from Derrida's point of view can enable one to identify in Kierkegaard's project a radical ethics of responsibility and a particularly postmodern notion of community, and for having lost sight of certain fundamental tenets central to both projects as a consequence of having conceded too much to wordplay and a certain "Derrida-speak," Walsh is no less to blame

---

[8] Jacques Derrida, *Speech and Phenomena, and Other Essays on Husserl's Theory of Signs*, trans. David B. Allison (Evanston: Northwestern University Press, 1973).

[9] See Derrida, *Points*, 399–421.

for not having explored the striking similarities that exist between Kierkegaard and Derrida (especially the later Derrida). That is, since Taylor's work has succeeded in teaching us that the force and depth of Kierkegaard's contribution is enough to warrant his inclusion in contemporary debate, Kierkegaard's legacy can best be served by claiming for him a status equal in measure to that held by Nietzsche for many decades now.

Although Walsh goes a good way toward ensuring that Kierkegaard is acknowledged as a thinker who can be appealed to in our contemporary situation, she does little to convince those at the forefront of mainstream ethical and political philosophy that this nineteenth-century figure can stand as a viable alternative to many of the opposed and competing paradigms that have claimed the allegiance of so many. Although there is enough in Kierkegaard to persuade the reader that he can hold his own against such paradigms, it is more than a useful exercise to analyze his texts from a Derridean perspective, since much of what Derrida does in his later work is to push certain Kierkegaardian themes and ideas to the limit—without doing an irreparable violence to them in the process. Taylor never succeeded in adequately showing how this takes place. Walsh is likewise unable to defend such a thesis because her Derrida is at another, yet no less extreme, level just as unrecognizable as Taylor's.

For Walsh, Kierkegaard's work revolves around the notion of what it means to "live poetically." Like the German romantics, Kierkegaard considers the poetic an intrinsic feature of the existential condition of the individual. Unlike the romantics, however, he does not believe one should endeavor to construct the self "through experimentation and play with an infinity of possibilities"; that is, according to Walsh, the romantics had a vision of the self that was aesthetic through and through, ironic in the most extreme sense, and "destructive, rather than constructive."[10] While adhering to the basic principles of romanticism—that is, that the self has a strong aesthetic component or dimension—Kierkegaard considers it necessary to transform this purely aesthetic mode in order to cultivate a more genuine and responsible self, one that actualizes its potential by attuning itself in a radically ethical and religious mode. However, in a similar manner to the Hegelian systematic, the aesthetic dimension

---

[10] Walsh, *Living Poetically*, 2.

of the personality is not negated but retained in a modified form. This suggests that the self does not divorce itself from the world in which it is embedded, but rather becomes more passionately engaged with the world and with those with whom it is shared— especially those who are out of favor with the ruling orthodoxy, whether religious or secular—through the cultivation of double reflection and faith. As Kierkegaard remarks in the posthumously published *Point of View for My Work As an Author*: "The religious is present from the beginning. Conversely, the aesthetic is present again at the last moment" (POV, 12). According to Kierkegaard, and this is the guiding theme of Walsh's work, this form of radical responsibility emphasizes the centrality of the imagination, as the faculty *instar omnium*, for the realization of selfhood. This is not, however, to be confused with the romantic variant, in that Kierkegaardian imagination is not a means of escape from factical situatedness, but the capacity by which the individual is permitted to transform the established order or the given actuality in new and original ways. This, of course, is what we have come to know as "repetition." Hence, the aesthetic becomes productive in a concrete sense for Kierkegaard, while for the romantics it allows for unbounded Promethean self-creation which denies that the individual is ineluctably rooted in time and history. Walsh, from the very outset of her study, elucidates this distinction between Kierkegaard and the romantics:

> "Living poetically" is an intriguing phrase that Kierkegaard first uses in his early writings to characterize what he regards as an attempt by the German romantic poets to construct their personal lives in the same manner as they create works of art. Through the exercise of a boundless artistic freedom, he claims, they seek to construct their self-identities through experimentation and play with an infinity of possibilities concocted by the imagination and tried out in a variety of roles and personal experiences with others. . . . He thus rejects it in favor of an alternative understanding of living poetically construed in an ethical and religious framework. Unlike its Romantic counterpart, this mode of living poetically is one that affirms both possibility and actuality, a sense of our historical situatedness and finite limitations as well as freedom, and the construction of human personality through a process of self-development, rather than self-creation, in relation to the infinite or divine.[11]

---

[11] Ibid.

Walsh's portrayal of Kierkegaard's rejection of the prevailing mood of romanticism in favor of a form of ethico-religious poetics is apposite and timely. For too long it has been considered a given that Kierkegaard's poetic devices and his stress on the importance of the imagination were ancillary to the purely religious dimension of his work. In pursuing this particular line of argument, Walsh convincingly argues that fundamental to Kierkegaard's primary commitment is a sense of how vital the aesthetic feature of personality is to a fully realized existence.

As I have noted, Walsh does not confine herself to a purely formal exegesis of the imagination or the broader regions of the aesthetic throughout the Kierkegaardian corpus. She extends the purview of this analysis at the end of her study by asking what it would take to live poetically in the present age. Walsh is concerned with debunking the view that Kierkegaard represents an extreme form of individualism, one that can be fulfilled only through an abdication of social commitment and responsibility. She contends that many of the ills that plagued nineteenth-century Denmark were not specific to that time alone but perennially precipitate human misery and despair. Consequently, Kierkegaard's analysis can be interpreted not only as a particular response to particular circumstances, but one that could be applied with the same measure of effect and force today. With this view I am in total agreement. This is why both Walsh and I consider it an obligation to situate Kierkegaard in the contemporary debate, hoping that his insights might thereby receive the attention and recognition they deserve. Walsh argues:

> As we have seen, Kierkegaard's thought was developed to a large extent in response to, and as a critique of, the prevailing literary, philosophical, social, and religious movements of his own time. . . . I have noted how Kierkegaard both directly and indirectly subjects these movements to criticism, revealing the ironic negativity, isolation, anxiety and despair, lack of passion, aimless becoming and bourgeois aestheticism he believed to be characteristic of his age. To a considerable extent, and perhaps in some instances to an even greater degree, these same conditions may be said to characterize the twentieth century as well. I cannot at this point enter into a full-scale analysis of these tendencies in the present age, but I do want to call attention to a cluster of issues that, in my view, contain some important implications for the project of living poetically in the present age. These is-

sues have to do with the emerging attitude toward self-identity, gender differences, and the relation to the other in the recent movement that calls itself "postmodernism" or "deconstruction."[12]

It is with the closing lines of this statement that the differences between my project and Walsh's come sharply into focus: whereas she believes that postmodernism and deconstruction have many of the same features as the movements against which Kierkegaard railed, I want to argue that deconstruction in particular gives us a means of rethinking and reinventing Kierkegaard in such a way that his work can become even more relevant for us today. If Taylor's postmodern Kierkegaard has little to teach us at an ethical, social, or even political level as a result of an overreliance on Derridean form rather than content, Walsh, in an attempt to exorcise the latter, creates a Kierkegaard who would also find it difficult to recommend himself to a contemporary public. Walsh's apparent failure to take more than a cursory glance at the Kierkegaardian strategies appropriated by Derrida severely curtails and delimits her capacity to set forth guidelines as to how it might be possible to live poetically with others in the present age. I will give substance to these contentions below. Presently, however, I wish to attend to Walsh's argument more closely.

For Walsh, Kierkegaard's thought "constitutes in some fundamental ways a critique of postmodernism as well as of the Hegelian and early German romantic philosophies of the modern era." Her more precise target, however, is deconstruction, which, she argues, "bears a close resemblance to the early German romantic mode of living poetically, as characterized by Kierkegaard, in the assertion of an endless process of experimentation and play with a multiplicity of interpretations and roles in language, or writing."[13] Deconstruction, which is conflated with postmodernism in this context (a charge I will dispute below), is interpreted by Walsh as a mode of thought that commits all the worst crimes of romanticism, since it promotes unregulated aesthetic free play and unlimited self-creation. As such, it does not represent "the beginning of a new era of thought," but rather the culmination of the worst excesses of a movement the young Kierkegaard sought to undermine.

---

[12] Ibid., 244–45.
[13] Ibid., 245.

With the intention of putting "some substance into these contentions," Walsh provides for her reader an account of "the program of deconstruction."[14] Her most basic claim here is that deconstruction is equivalent to what Kierkegaard called "negative irony," a form of irony I touched on briefly in chapter 3. In that discussion I was keen to stress that Kierkegaard, in reaction to Hegel's critique of irony—not only its romantic variation, but irony in all its manifestations—opts ultimately for a notion of positive irony, exemplified most especially in the figure of Abraham. Here irony is treated as a prerequisite for the cultivation of an ethical disposition that is radically responsive to the call of the other. Kierkegaard sees positive irony as a means of attaining inwardness, or self-knowledge and understanding. It is my belief that Derrida is far from being an exponent of negative irony (i.e., romantic irony), but a thinker who possesses all the attributes of the positive ironist in the strong Kierkegaardian sense of this expression.

For Walsh, however, deconstruction signifies the acme of romanticism; Derrida's work is "an endless process of textual dismantling and reinscription that seeks to undermine and displace established forms of literary and philosophical interpretation based on a metaphysics of presence or revelation of truth, calling into question by this practice the very notions of truth and fixed meaning."[15] Walsh's Derrida takes delight in breaking down, at the expense of value, all "established hierarchical oppositions in texts," thus opening up a whole gamut of interpretations, none of which can claim the status of truth. Because deconstruction is even more "thoroughgoing than previous forms of romantic irony," claims Walsh, it can not only be blamed for bringing the established order, *qua* actuality, to its knees, but it can also be charged with having jettisoned "any underlying foundation or reality of that which appears."[16] Despite not having quoted a single line from Derrida in support of her thesis, and without having listed one book by the same author in her bibliography, Walsh concludes her discussion of Derrida's contribution with the following reflection:

> Deconstruction thus rejects the notion of any final, unified or closed system of truth or self-identity that may be attained in thought or

---

[14] Ibid., 247.
[15] Ibid.
[16] Ibid., 248.

imagination, substituting instead the epistemological principle of un-decidability concerning the truth or falsity of anything. To inscribe this displacement, postmodern writers resort literarily to word play, parody, mime, preface writing, collage, and other techniques of writing to dislodge and negate the possibility of coming to or disclosing some original or definitive truth in a text or thesis.[17]

It is true, as Walsh goes on to claim, that Kierkegaard would oppose any mode of thought that privileged the aesthetic over an ethics of responsibility, or indeed over his particular form of politically subversive religion. And if that is what one believes deconstruction is guilty of perpetrating, then Kierkegaard is by no means a deconstructionist *avant la lettre*. But it is precisely this caricature of both Derrida and deconstruction afforded by Walsh that I am contesting here. As I will argue below, Derrida is just as opposed as Kierkegaard to any form of reckless aestheticism. Indeed, Derrida, like Kierkegaard, chooses at times to make use of "word play, parody, mime, preface writing, collage," but only as a means of challenging the pretensions of any institution or tradition (academic or otherwise) that purports to be in possession of "the Truth." Both authors, however, do not consider such (literary) techniques ends in themselves, but rather ironic methods to jolt the reader into becoming earnest and responsible.

This is what Taylor seems to overlook in his most recent work on Kierkegaard and Derrida. Taylor's initial insights on the close links that exist between the two were most prescient, but his manner of teasing out the similarities in the approach adopted by each thinker has given rise to the type of concerns raised by Walsh. This, in my belief, does nothing for either Kierkegaardian or Derridean scholarship, or indeed for those of us who find it a worthy intellectual enterprise to draw out the parallels between these philosophers.

In her effort to rescue Kierkegaard from a movement she believes to be even more extreme than German romanticism, Walsh directly identifies Taylor as the source of her worry. For her, Kierkegaard's notion of the self has a "given structure," while "postmodernism rejects the notion of any determinate, proper, or ultimate self-identity, opting instead for a philosophy of difference that privileges the concept of 'the other' over the concept of the self."[18] This is a highly

---

[17] Ibid., 248–49.
[18] Ibid., 249.

contentious statement, both in what it says of Kierkegaard and in the particular variant of postmodernism Walsh rejects most stridently—deconstruction. If Walsh is claiming by this that Kierkegaard holds to a notion of the self that takes a teleological or a dialectical form, in the spirit of Hegel, then she is surely mistaken. Of course, Kierkegaard borrowed much from Hegel's theory of identity, but it was precisely in his determination to show that the self does not have any determinate form *as such* that he developed his own notion of personal development based on choice, responsibility, and faith. I suggest, however, that Walsh subscribes to the view that Kierkegaard's theory of the self is one with an originally given structure so as to demonstrate that Taylor's Derrida (whom she conflates with the actual Derrida) bears no resemblance to Kierkegaard either in form or content. She says:

> Just as there is no "correct" interpretation of a text in postmodernism, there is no true or originally given structure that constitutes the self either; rather, the subject, or subjectivity, is regarded as constituted temporally in relation to otherness, or that which it is not, but the force of desire, which signals a gap or lack of self-identity, so that the "I" is constantly deferred. Instead of becoming a self or adopting the project of self-identity, therefore, one postmodernist writer suggests that we think of ourselves as "personae," ironically donning masks to preserve nonidentity as we play various roles as actors on the stage of life. Insofar as any concept of self-identity is operative in postmodern "serpentine wandering," as Mark C. Taylor characterizes the movement, it is one that remains open, undefined, and experimental, as in German romanticism.[19]

The "postmodernist writer" to whom Walsh refers is John Caputo, and in the accompanying footnote she writes that his suggestion ("that we think of ourselves as 'personae,' ironically donning masks to preserve nonidentity as we play various roles in life") "sounds familiarly like the playacting of the romantic ironist as characterized by Kierkegaard in *The Concept of Irony* and artistically portrayed in the first volume of *Either/Or*."[20] This characterization of Caputo is founded on an observation that is taken totally out of context. In fact, Caputo (in these pages from *Radical Hermeneutics*) is coming

---

[19] Ibid., 250.
[20] Ibid., 12.

as close as any commentator has to a realistic discussion of how Kierkegaard might be applied (without doing him the injustice of an outrageous hermeneutic violence) to the social and ethical crises that we in the modern world must daily contend with. Furthermore, it is true that Caputo is a "postmodernist" writer, but one who surely cannot be reconciled with the description of that trend proffered by Walsh. His brand of postmodernism strives not to jettison truth or the tradition, but to make them own up to their own insecurities. This, I wish to emphasize, was exactly the same type of modus operandi that Kierkegaard employed. I shall return to this later in the chapter. Suffice it to say for now, however, that Walsh's conflation of postmodernism with deconstruction and her failure to discriminate between various strands of postmodernism lead her into the trap of confusing projects that, although they might both be attempting to rethink Kierkegaard in original and novel ways, have at bottom entirely distinct influences and objectives. Caputo's Kierkegaard bears scant resemblance to Taylor's, even though both of these writers are working on the assumption that Derrida's attempt to push to the limit many Kierkegaardian themes might actually assist us in gleaning a greater understanding of Kierkegaard's work and in making him a central participant in current philosophical debates.

Let us say at this stage, therefore, that the consequences of both the Taylor and Walsh approaches to the Kierkegaardian strains in Derrida's thought have not ultimately served the best interests of that body of thinkers committed to either deconstruction or Kierkegaard. If Taylor has sold Kierkegaard and Derrida short through an overemphasis on form and by not teasing out to a sufficient degree the implications for ethics of the Kierkegaardian/Derridean transgressive gestures, Walsh, in her effort to rid Kierkegaardian scholarship of a Derrida whom no serious exponent of the latter's work would recognize, has delimited her potential to realize her stated objective of ensuring that Kierkegaard take his place as a serious partner in contemporary philosophical dialogue. Walsh's attempt to show how one can "live poetically in the present age" is commendable in theory, but it fails to work here because of the author's refusal to allow Kierkegaard any association with Derrida, Caputo, or any other serious postmodernist. Through a closer reading of Derrida's works, Walsh might have succeeded in discriminating between, on the one hand, deconstruction and postmodernism, and on the other,

Derrida and that version of Derrida made popular by commentators like Taylor.

As I will show in the following pages, deconstruction, far from being just another version of German romanticism, something for which Kierkegaard had indeed much contempt, is a richly Kierkegaardian way of thinking and philosophizing for those attempting to cope with the demands of the present age. The particular brand of Derridean deconstruction promoted by Caputo, one deeply cognizant of the (Kierkegaardian) Judeo-Christian strains of Derrida's work, is the most convincing form in which this debate has so far been framed. Finally, I wish to conclude by making a case for the idea that what the deconstructive readings of Kierkegaard have thus far ignored is perhaps the most postmodern note chiming in the Kierkegaardian corpus: the notion of neighborly love developed in *Works of Love*, a text that teases out many of the implications of the thesis set forth in **Practice in Christianity**.

Derrida's Recovery of the Sign

Since the late 1980s there has been a sustained attempt by many commentators, myself included, to defend Kierkegaard not only as a vigilant ethicist willing to stand out on a limb in support of the singularity of the existing individual, but also as a social and political thinker whose response to the crises of his time has an enduring appeal, not least for those of us searching for a way forward today. Our reading of Kierkegaard from this perspective has been helped and influenced by a concomitant reading of the work of Jacques Derrida. Unlike the two authors discussed in the previous section, Taylor and Walsh, I do not consider it propitious, on the one hand, to interpret Kierkegaard as a thinker who compares favorably with Taylor's Derrida; nor do I feel drawn to the opinion, enunciated most dramatically by Walsh, that there is nothing gained by associating Kierkegaard with Derrida, since to do so would require adopting the indefensible stance of claiming that Kierkegaard was an exponent of German romanticism. What I want to argue here is that there is a more fundamental point of contact between these two thinkers than Taylor, Walsh, or indeed many others allow for. In reading Kierkegaard and Derrida side by side, one is drawn inevitably to conclude that there is a guiding impulse common to both sets of texts, an impulse driven by a passionate concern to find a means of engendering social equality based on an ethics of responsibility. Hence what I want to demonstrate at this juncture is that Derrida, far from being yet another example of unbridled romanticism, is as responsibly committed as the Kierkegaard I have argued in favor of in this book.

Before the publication in 1992 of "Donner la mort" (*The Gift of Death*), Derrida had not treated the work of Kierkegaard in any sustained fashion. The latter had appeared for many years to be Derrida's silent interlocutor, an elusive figure who haunted the pages of some of Derrida's most important texts, but one with whom the latter had only an oblique relationship. More recently, however, the spirit and the letter of much of Derrida's output are indeed strikingly Kierkegaardian. Like Taylor, I am not convinced that this overtly "Kierkegaardian turn" signals any kind of new departure. Indeed, their works are, on the whole, motivated by similar deeply held convictions, not the least of which is a driving passion to make a case for the singularity of the "poor existing individual" in the face of systematic and totalizing forms of control. It is my belief, in other words, that since its inception deconstruction has been driven by a profoundly Kierkegaardian ethical commitment, in that it has consistently sought to focus attention on the marginalized and the dispossessed, what in recent years has become known simply as "the other." Deconstruction's response to the call of the other, I am suggesting, reveals an ethics of responsibility that owes much to the proto-ethics I have identified in the pseudonymous authorship.

In showing how Derrida's early work revealed many implicit Kierkegaardian characteristics and features, my objective is to indicate how the culmination of Derrida's Kierkegaardianism in the last decade or so allows the reader to extrapolate a (deconstructive) theory of community from Kierkegaard's corpus. Otherwise expressed, reading Kierkegaard from the perspective of the later Derrida opens up a way in which we can make more concrete the assertion that Kierkegaard's ethics of responsibility is the foundation upon which he forms his idea of community. This is not to suggest that it is a prerequisite to read Derrida in order to identify the social dimension of Kierkegaard's thought. What indeed it does suggest, however, is that to look at Kierkegaard through a Derridean lens provides us with a means of making more sense of Kierkegaard's social ideals and of making a more credible case for the Kierkegaardian thesis in main-stream contemporary debate.

The most pervasive voice speaking through the Derridean and Kierkegaardian texts is that of Hegel. Both thinkers are engaged in a subtle critique of Hegelian dialectics that aims at disclosing the cracks and fissures that perforate the system. That said, both authors admit to owing a great debt to Hegel: I noted in chapter 2 how crucial an understanding of Hegel's philosophy, especially his social ethics, is for an understanding of Kierkegaard's development, not only as the original thinker of the question of responsibility, but also for his social philosophy. Derrida too never shies away from express-ing his admiration for Hegel. In his first experimental work, *Glas* (1974), he begins by asking:

> What, after all, of the remain(s), today, for us, here, now, of a Hegel?
>
> For us, here, now: from now on that is what one will not have been able to think without him.
>
> For us, here, now: these words are citations, already, always, we have learned that from him.[21]

Likewise, we might call Johannes Climacus's *Concluding Unscientific Postscript* a long meditation on Hegel, revealing at one and the same time the mastery and yet the pathos of one so convinced of the ethical merits of speculative idealism. That is, Kierkegaard and Der-rida, believing as they do in the requirements of singularity, do not try to situate themselves outside the system, for this in turn would only affirm the system. They do, however, locate themselves in the interstices between the universal and the particular moments or phases of conscious development in an effort to demonstrate how the assimilation of the particular by the universal is an unethical gesture, despite Hegel's best intentions. If viewed from this perspec-tive, the Kierkegaardian lineage in Derrida's thought is revealed with greater perspicuity.

If Kierkegaard is opposed to any notion of time that allows the individual to evade the responsibilities of existence or to be swept along by the tide of any grand metaphysical scheme, such as Hegel's "world-historical process," Derrida is no less so. The latter, contrary

---

[21] Jacques Derrida, *Glas*, trans. John P. Leavey, Jr., and Richard Rand (Lincoln: University of Nebraska Press, 1986), 1.

to the readings of Walsh et al., is as committed to the idea of a historically embedded subject as is his forebear, Kierkegaard. Furthermore, both of these thinkers look to what they call "repetition" as a way of halting the seemingly inexorable advance of *Geist's* teleological impulse. Theirs, I want to argue, is a gentle deconstruction of the Hegelian notion of the self, one that does not endeavor to destroy the self per se, but merely to "resituate" it. Considered from this point of view, these authors' seemingly diverse approaches are seen to converge at a number of crucial junctures. In line with the argument developed in preceding chapters, in which I suggested that Kierkegaard's ethics of responsibility is motivated by a call from the other, from the "most wretched," deconstruction too, I am convinced, is an openness to the heteronomous, to that which disturbs the Hegelian dialectic whose beginning is presupposed in its end. Derrida says this quite clearly when he remarks that "deconstruction is not an enclosure in nothingness, but an openness towards the other."[22] The consequence of this for the "self" or the "subject" is anything but nihilistic in the Nietzschean or romantic sense. Such an approach seeks to make the subject more ethically aware and socially engaged, in that the subject does not aspire to be anything more than what it is—in the words of Kierkegaard, "a poor existing individual." In countering claims to the contrary, Derrida might just as well be Kierkegaard when he remarks:

> I have never said that the subject should be dispensed with. Only that it should be deconstructed. To deconstruct the subject does not mean to deny its existence. There are subjects, "operations" or "effects" (*effets*) of subjectivity. This is an incontrovertible fact. To acknowledge this does not mean, however, that the subject is what it *says* it is. The subject is not some meta- linguistic substance or identity, some pure *cogito* of self-presence; it is always inscribed in language. My work does not, therefore, destroy the subject; it simply tries to resituate it.[23]

Derrida's theory of repetition is the key to understanding the raison d'être of deconstruction. Like the Kierkegaardian variation, Der-

---

[22] Jacques Derrida, "Deconstruction and the Other," in *Dialogues with Contemporary Continental Thinkers: The Phenomenological Heritage*, ed. Richard Kearney (Manchester: Manchester University Press, 1984), 124.

[23] Ibid., 125.

ridean repetition endeavors to challenge the metaphysical tendency to structure experience teleologically. Alternatively, it could be said that repetition of this kind emphasizes the contingency of every philosophical, ethical, political, juridical, and topographical formation, demonstrating as a consequence how ill-conceived those theories are that construe any particular formation as the necessary coming to fruition of a determined *telos* or utopia. Repetition, that is, tries to reveal the inconsistencies it takes to be inherent in the great philosophical metanarratives from Greece to the present. It is, however, from the perspective of Derrida's riposte to Hegel that we can best glean how repetition functions and how it is for this thinker, as well as for Kierkegaard, the necessary condition for a genuine ethics of responsibility.

As with Kierkegaard, Derrida's career has been marked by an unflagging aspiration to read Hegel otherwise. He too is concerned by the teleological force by which *Geist* is propelled toward a full and absolute recollection of itself, surmounting in the process all difference and otherness. At the same time, however, Derrida is not convinced that an outright rejection of the Hegelian paradigm should be sought. He contends, rather, that the Hegelian critic must situate him- or herself within the dialectical fabric of the systematic framework so as to play on the weak spot of the speculative *Encyclopaedia*. For Derrida, Kierkegaard hit the mark when he sought to expose the notion of recollection (*Aufhebung*) as a task that is just too difficult for existing individuals; being situated in time or in the daily flow of events, individuals are incapable of coming to any atemporal or ahistorical standpoint. All experience is mediated through language or signs, or what Derrida will call "*écriture.*" It is just at the point where Hegel attempts to reduce the significance of language or, in the case of his treatment of religion, symbolization (*Vorstellung*) that Derrida's stylus tip will begin to flow.

While Hegel announces the overcoming of contradiction between two terms through mediation, in which both give way to a third term, Derrida discounts such logic of identity amid difference in favor what he calls neologistically *différance*. Derrida explains in a 1971 interview why the notion of *différance* is not simply Hegelian "difference":

> Since it is still a question of elucidating the relationship to Hegel—a difficult labor, which for the most part remains before us, and which

in a certain way is interminable, at least if one wishes to execute it rigorously and minutely—I have attempted to distinguish *différance* (whose *a* marks, among other things, its productive and conflictual characteristics) from Hegelian difference, and have done so precisely at the point at which Hegel, in the greater *Logic*, determines difference as contradiction only in order to resolve it, to interiorize it, to lift it up (according to the syllogistic process of speculative dialectics) into the self-presence of an onto-theological synthesis. *Différance* ... must sign the point at which one breaks with the system of *Aufhebung* and with speculative dialectics. Since this conflictuality of *différance*— which can be called contradiction only if one demarcates it by means of a long work on Hegel's concept of contradiction—can never be totally resolved, it marks its effects in what I call the text in general, in a text which is not reduced to a book or a library, and which can never be governed by a referent in the classical sense, that is, by a thing or by a transcendental signified that would regulate its movement.[24]

This quote highlights the impressive subtlety and obliquity of Derrida's critique of Hegelian dialectics. *Différance* cannot simply be reconciled with its dialectical opposite through the power of negation; that is, the other cannot simply become one with the same, cannot become present to consciousness in any apodictic or pure sense. *Différance* divides consciousness against itself, in that it signifies that the other is always already embedded in a linguistic context, is always the effect of a signifying play that cannot be stilled or subdued.

In systematically elucidating this notion of *différance* before the Société Française de Philosophie in 1968, Derrida once more attempts to explain the "a" of his neologism in reference to the Hegelian project. In so doing, he refers to the fact that the sign for Hegel, *qua Vorstellung*, is that which preserves for memory the original intuition of what is other and alien to consciousness. In order for reason to fully assimilate such intuitions, however, the physicality of the sign must be negated while its spirit is interiorized (*Erinnerung*). It is not coincidental, therefore, that in the third part of the *Encyclopaedia of the Philosophical Sciences*, entitled *The Philosophy of Mind*,[25] Hegel compares the sign to a pyramid that is both a sign of

---

[24] Jacques Derrida, *Positions*, trans. Alan Bass (Chicago: University of Chicago Press, 1981), 44–45.

[25] G. W. F. Hegel, *The Philosophy of Mind*, trans. W. Wallace and A. V. Miller (Oxford: Clarendon Press, 1971), 179–223. See also my treatment of these issues in both "Murder on Moriah" and "Playing on the Pyramid."

presence and a sign of death; that is, the sign signifies death (the intuition is no longer full) and life (it contains the spirit of the intuition). The sign, therefore, is comparable to the "a" of *différance*, which houses both the living and the dead:

> Now it happens, I would say in effect, that this graphic difference (*a* instead of *e*), this marked difference between two apparently vocal notations, between two vowels, remains purely graphic: it is read, or it is written, but it cannot be heard. It cannot be apprehended in speech, and we will see why it also passes the order of apprehension in general. It is offered by a mute mark, by a tacit monument, I would even say by a pyramid, thinking not only of the form of the letter when it is printed as a capital, but also of the text in Hegel's *Encyclopaedia* in which the body of the sign is compared to the Egyptian Pyramid.[26]

The tomblike "A," which cannot be spoken, signifies that difference is never merely the simple other of the same. Difference for Hegel is always coimplicated with its opposite, since it is a particular moment in the dialectical becoming of the self. By supplementing the "e" with the "a," however, Derrida suggests that the graphic mark, or the sign, cannot be mediated by speculative reason to the point that it is fully negated.

Rather than privileging resurrection or recollection (*Aufhebung*), both Kierkegaard and Derrida emphasize death, in the sense of an irretrievable loss of full self-certainty. If Hegel's logic requires that the other—the singular or the particular—be negated for the sake of *Geist*'s retrieval of itself from the alien and objective sphere, Derrida and Kierkegaard insist that the other is absolutely other (*tout autre*). The other, that is, signals the death of full self-plenitude in that the singularity of the other naturally evades the speculative grasp of *Geist*. We could say that the other is both present and absent: like the Kierkegaardian God-man, the other is incognito; as with Abraham, it is residually incommensurate with the given actuality: "The *a* of *différance*, thus, is not heard; it remains silent, secret and discreet as a tomb: *oikésis*. And thereby let us anticipate the delineation of a site, the familial residence and tomb of the proper in which is produced, by *différance*, the *economy of death*."[27] As the translator of

---

[26] Jacques Derrida, "Différance," in *Margins of Philosophy*, trans. Alan Bass (New York: Harvester Wheatsheaf, 1982), 3–4.

[27] Ibid., 4.

"Différance" notes: " 'Tomb' in Greek is *oikésis,* which is akin to the Greek *oikos*—house—from which the word 'economy' derives (*oikos*—house—and *nemein*—to manage)."[28] This observation is highly significant: in his *Lectures on the Philosophy of Religion,* Hegel interprets the tomb as the site of the coming to be of the Holy Family, or the dialectical emergence of the Holy Trinity.[29] It is the place, therefore, out of which God overcomes his estrangement from himself in the Resurrection. Out of death comes life, or in exchange for death, eternal life is granted. The tomb for Hegel is thus a place of commerce in which death is the legal tender in an economy of the same.

For Derrida, however, the tomb signals the death of the Holy Family, the rupturing of the dialectical circle of exchange. For as a sign that eludes phonetic utterance, the tomb symbolizes the irrecoverability of lost presence. The sign, being a necessary moment in *Geist*'s dialectical trajectory, cannot simply be negated but must be taken up (*Aufhebung*) by consciousness. According to Derrida, however, the sign at this point cannot be dispensed with. Instead, it continues to haunt in spectral form. The trace of the other, that is, forever divides consciousness against itself.

Derrida's *différance* is not directed or governed, therefore, by any extralinguistic signified such as *Geist.* The power of the sign is undelimitable. This does not mean that for Derrida there is no such thing as reference, but only that referents can never be perceived in any raw or decontextualized state. Otherwise stated, according to the logic of deconstruction, there can never be pure, uninterpreted facts. To be placed in a context means that one is at the receiving end of an entire history of events whose movement has not been logically determined. Having no necessity or hidden dynamic, this flow of events is not the working out of any divine design. The subject's history, thus, being an unregulated stream of singular events that has been traced in memory through graphic inscription, is not something reason can make present to itself. Reason, according to Derrida, can-

---

[28] Ibid., translator's note no. 2.

[29] G. W. F. Hegel, *Lectures on the Philosophy of Religion: The Lectures of 1827* (1-vol. ed.), ed. Peter C. Hodgson, trans. R. F. Brown et al. (Berkeley: University of California Press, 1988). For an argument similar to my own see Kevin Hart, *The Trespass of the Sign: Deconstruction, Theology, and Philosophy,* 2nd ed. (New York: Fordham University Press, 2000).

not relieve the written trace—cannot, that is, rehabilitate the life of which the trace is but a simulacrum. The trace, being a mark of presence in absence, testifies to the self's unavoidable failure to become one with itself. The trace, in other words, signals that speculative memory (*Erinnerung*) cannot disentangle the real from the sign; they are two sides of the same coin.

Différance, consequently, does not have any linear structure; it does not have a genealogy, as the notion of "difference" does in Hegel's *Encyclopaedia*. Hence, *différance* announces that there is no beginning and no end to history, signification, or the temporal flow of events:

> There is nowhere to begin to trace the sheaf or the graphics of différance. For what is put into question is precisely the quest for a rightful beginning, an absolute point of departure, a principal responsibility. The problematic of writing is opened by putting into question the value *arkhé*. What I will propose here will not be elaborated simply as a philosophical discourse, operating according to principles, postulates, axioms or definitions, and proceeding along the discursive lines of a linear order of reasons.[30]

The sign, that is, is not something added to the thing itself, something that permits reason's reappropriation of some original presence or some beginning. Signs, as Saussure argued, acquire an identity by virtue of being related to other signs, not by virtue of being the sign of some "thing" outside the signifying process.[31] Signs, that is, are chosen by the community of speakers arbitrarily and have no natural relation to anything outside "in the world." The sign, however, is the totality of two components: the signifier and the signified. Derrida defines the signified as "the concept, the ideal meaning," while the signifier "is what Saussure calls the 'image,' the psychical imprint of a material, physical—for example, acoustical—phenomenon."[32] As a concept, the signified, being part of a sign that is arbitrarily chosen and which can be identified as the sign it is only in relation to other signs, "is inscribed in a chain or in a system within which it refers to the other, to other concepts, by means of the systematic play of

---

[30] Derrida, "Différance," 7.
[31] See Ferdinand de Saussure, *Course in General Linguistics*, trans. Roy Harris (London: Duckworth, 1983).
[32] Derrida, "Différance," 10.

differences."[33] This "play of differences" that allows for the identity of each concept (signified) is the possibility of any conceptualization whatsoever, for it is in and through a concept's difference from other concepts that it becomes the concept it is, not by being the mental correlation of an unmediated referent. This play, according to Derrida, provides "the possibility of conceptuality, of a conceptual process and system in general." The play, which is neither the concept nor the word (signifier/acoustic substance) but the possibility of both, is the nearest Derrida comes to describing the "nature" (if such a thing were possible) of *différance:*

> What is written as *différance,* then, will be the playing movement that "produces"—by means of something that is not simply an activity—these differences, these effects of difference. This does not mean that the *différance* that produces differences is somehow before them, in a simple and unmodified—in-different—present. *Différance* is the non-full, non-simple, structured and differentiating origin of differences. Thus, the name "origin" no longer suits it.[34]

Différance, we can therefore say, is nothing (no-thing) in and of itself, but is the structural possibility of concepts, institutions, programs (ethical, philosophical and political), and so forth, coming into operation.

According to our analysis, what appears to be "present" to consciousness at any particular time can never be fully present; because a concept is the concept it is because it exists in relation to other concepts in the textual chain, there is always the trace of concepts that have preceded it and of those that it in turn will produce. Presence, once again, is the effect of what is absent (non-present). All conceptual formations are haunted by the other that differentiates "every being" from itself both spatially and temporally. Derrida calls this play of signification that constitutes what appears as a being present "archi-writing, archi-trace, or *différance.*"[35] The trace, in other words, counts for Derrida as the most fundamental condition of experience; the recovery of origins, which inspires and motivates Hegelian recollection, is precisely what Kierkegaard and Derrida oppose on the basis of their joint conviction that the temporal flux

---

[33] Ibid.
[34] Ibid., 11.
[35] Ibid., 13.

cannot be stilled. According to Constantin Constantius, recollecting backward in an attempt to retrieve an absolute beginning is what causes the greatest degree of unhappiness for the existing individual. The trace, however, signifies that a complete recovery of origins is impossible, that the system of signification always predates any attempt by the conscious subject to become one with itself through the dialectic of *Aufhebung*.

As with Kierkegaard, Derrida is here attempting to demonstrate that any teleological scheme that anticipates a future that amounts solely to a recovery of lost origins is founded on an exclusionary gesture; that is, if the programmable order proceeds toward a predetermined *telos*, it must exclude that which has the capacity to threaten or undermine its fulfillment. In the case of Hegel, the entire order of signification needs to be negated if *Geist*'s intention to comprehensively rationalize all objective exteriority is to be brought to fruition. For Derrida, however, it is precisely this "order" that, while sounding the death knell of absolute presence, affirms life, or what Kierkegaard calls "existence."

Kierkegaard's "Deconstructive" Method

If Derrida strives to undermine the Hegelian claim to absolute knowledge by demonstrating how it is structurally impossible to bypass the sign, or what Hegel calls in his treatment of religious consciousness *Vorstellung*, Kierkegaard aspires to impede the world-historical process, or *Geist*'s teleological advance toward pure abstract thought, by arguing that the "sign" of contradiction, the God-man, cannot be speculatively mediated. Although Derrida does not appropriate Kierkegaard's "ideal"—the God-man—as an ethical prototype, I will argue that because Kierkegaard's notion of God is such a deconstructed notion, one with practical ethical and political significance, it finds a suitable analogue in Derrida's ideal of justice beyond law. To realize this aim, I will first turn my attention to Derrida and Kierkegaard's strikingly similar theories of repetition as a means of opposing Hegelian recollection. I will commence this inquiry by focusing on the ideas of communication, intentionality, and literature, which are central to both critical enterprises.

In my earlier evaluation of Kierkegaard's radical ethics of responsibility, I contended that the related categories of irony and faith, rather than being forms of irrationality that have little to do with the serious question of ethics, play a pivotal role in the formation of responsibility. Faith, at least in its Kierkegaardian variation, is crucial in the formation of positive irony or inwardness, defined throughout this work as the individual's cultivation of a critical distance from the dominant philosophical, ethical, and political codes governing reality. Otherwise expressed, faith, being a hope in and affirmation of what exceeds the purview of the established order and the given actuality, requires a teleological suspension of the ethical, *qua* established juridical and ethical program, with the aim of engendering a more concrete and genuinely ethical relationship with the other. This, I suggested, requires the "double reflection" of repetition, in which the individual overcomes the leveled order of abstract reflection (that state in which the self takes it for granted that popularly held truths and values are *the* truth) through a process of critical reasoning in which one tests the veracity of what was formerly held to be truth in both an epistemological and ethical sense. To exist implies that the individual is historically situated, thus subject to contingency, time, and chance. In typically Kierkegaardian language, the self is in an inexorable state of becoming. The upshot of the Climacean idea that truth is subjectivity is that truth does not have any transcendental or objective basis, but is something whose functioning is predicated upon the existence of flesh-and-blood human beings who are subject to this endless tide of becoming. Hence, for Kierkegaard, truth is not the expression of the divine design of *Geist*, for such a thing "is a metaphysical *telos*" only. His concern is with "individual intention," not with the objective intention of the world-historical process. To quote once more a crucial passage from *Concluding Unscientific Postscript*:

> Insofar as the individuals participate in the history of the human race by their deeds, the observer does not see these deeds as traced back to the individuals and to the ethical but sees them as traced away from the individuals and to the totality. Ethically, what makes the deed the individual's own is the intention, but this is precisely what is not included in world-history, for here it is the world-historical intention that matters. World-historically, I see the effect; ethically I see the intention. (CUP, 155)

To exist means, in philosophical terms, that one is caught up inextricably in a concatenation of beliefs and truths, none of which can claim an absolute status. Each existing individual is at the receiving end of an entire network of truths, all of which have their own histories. Kierkegaard and Derrida primarily contest the assumption that there is a single, overarching history of truth, such as that which lies at the heart of Hegel's notion of the world-historical. Situated in the midst of the flux of time, we are unable to construct a grand narrative of truth, since this would require the capacity to take up an ahistorical vantage point, something existence does not permit. Truth, therefore, has no teleological necessity to it; each individual affirms the beliefs of his or her own historical context, but because these beliefs are the product of contingency and not necessity, they can be modified or repeated as the occasion demands.

Such productive repetition requires a reason beyond instrumental and institutionalized reason—not one that is in the service of some teleologically determined order of knowledge, but rather one which affirms that all philosophical, ethical, and political formations are trembling configurations that, having come into existence, are not just the latest manifestation of *Geist*. Such "reason beyond reason," or double reflection, challenges the established order of truth by pressing against its own limits in order to expose the given actuality to an unprogrammed future. The horizon of absolute knowledge, or of full presence, gives way to a faith that is not non-knowledge *as such,* but a type of knowing that is always attentive to the fact that the present order is haunted from within by the trace of the other, and under threat from without by a future that cannot be calculated in advance. Existence, that is, provides no metaphysical guardrails to lend stability to any contingent formation.

For Johannes de Silentio, having faith requires that one become positively ironic. We saw above how irony for Kierkegaard is more than just a literary technique; in its positive sense, it is a way to disestablish the prevailing order (ethical and political)—not directly, but in a subtle and oblique way. For Kierkegaard, ironists—in this case Socrates, Abraham, and Jesus Christ—cannot speak directly, since to communicate directly would be to communicate in the language of the universal. Irony, however, calls for indirect communication, or at least an acknowledgment that for effective communication to be realized it must take an indirect form. The ironist adopts this strategy because he or she sees the need to communicate with the other from the point of view of subjectivity; if something is communicated directly, or if it is believed that the speaker's intention can be directly picked up by the listener, then the communication is simply objective and the content of the communication has no significance for the recipient: as objective knowledge, it has no essential bearing on the actual life of the individual. Subjectively communicating with the other, however, requires that the speaker recognize that the receiver has the ability to interpret the message from a particular perspective, and that the message in the hands of the other can take on new and original significance. The ironist is thus one who is both inside and outside the state or the present order: inside to the degree that he or she challenges from within, and outside due to his or her being sensitive to the fact that the given actuality is not the product of teleological progress and thus should be always cognizant of its own limitations.

Although Kierkegaard and Derrida are both considered ironists par excellence,[36] few attribute any great ethical and political import to their ironic method. I want to argue that understanding Kierkegaard and Derrida from an ethical and political point of view depends upon appreciating the specific nature of irony employed by both thinkers, for it is through an understanding of irony as indirect communication that we can acquire an insight into how proximate to one another the individual theories of repetition are.

In the section in *Of Grammatology* entitled "The End of the Book and the Beginning of Writing,"[37] Derrida explains that the book signifies closure in that, like Hegel's system, it has a beginning, middle, and end. As such, it is an expression of what the tradition held to be "good writing": devoid of the parasitic and divinely motivated. As a divine totality, the book sought to repress the disseminative play of writing, in that writing in its "bad" form represented transgression and a loss of purity and origin. In response, Derrida argues that Hegel's book, being the archetypal logocentric gesture, is both dismissive of and yet dependent on writing and signification. Hegel, that is, affirms difference in a way that none of his philosophical predecessors succeeded in doing, but only to ultimately reduce it to the status of the same. It has been Derrida's vocation, and indeed Kierkegaard's

---

[36] See Richard Rorty, *Contingency, Irony, and Solidarity* (Cambridge: Cambridge University Press, 1989), 122–37.

[37] Jacques Derrida, *Of Grammatology*, trans. Gayatri Chakravorty Spivak (Baltimore: Johns Hopkins University Press, 1974), 6–26.

too, to show that writing (*différance*) is irrepressible, that it cannot be contained or mediated by reason, *qua Geist*. If Kierkegaard sounds the alarm in the name of ethics and singularity, Derrida's work acts as a counter-chime. Both authors want to situate themselves on the margins of the book so as to give a voice to those who have not succeeded in making it into the book. In other words, Kierkegaard and Derrida take up the cause of the marginalized, of those who are not at home in the system (Abraham, perhaps), those whom we might call the dispossessed. They endeavor to make a claim for those who have been excluded by the totality, those who are without a voice and a *presence*.

Although Derrida has from the very outset of his intellectual itinerary attempted to demonstrate how Hegel's book is haunted from within by *différance*, it was Kierkegaard who first took Hegel to task on this account. Kierkegaard's entire authorship seeks to undermine and destabilize the notion that the book is a direct communication from some divine source. This is why he does not consider himself a writer of books, but simply a "supplementary clerk," one who has a passion for fragments, postscripts, dialectical lyrics, and simple prefaces. In his "Preface" to *Fear and Trembling,* de Silentio makes the following observation:

> The present author is by no means a philosopher. He has not understood the system, whether there is one, whether it is completed; it is already enough for his weak head to ponder what a prodigious head everyone must have these days when everyone has such a prodigious idea. Even if someone were able to transpose the whole content of faith into conceptual form, it does not follow that he has comprehended faith, comprehended how he entered into it or how it entered into him. The present author is by no means a philosopher. He is *poetice et eleganter* [in a poetic and refined way] a supplementary clerk who neither writes the system nor gives promises of the system, who neither exhausts himself on the system nor binds himself to the system. He writes because to him it is a luxury that is all the more pleasant and apparent the fewer there are who buy and read what he writes. (FT, 7)

Kierkegaard, that is, goes to extreme lengths to rescue writing from the systematic procedure of bookbinding. The exercise of bookbinding is nothing less than hilarious, which is why one of Kierkegaard's pseudonyms is named "Hilarious Bookbinder." For writing is an exercise that exposes an author to a reader, who in turn interprets the work from a particular point of view, which is why Kierkegaard ironically published posthumously (after the death of the author!) a "point of view" for his work as an author. Bookbinding, for Kierkegaard, is a frantic attempt by those who want to maintain the law, or to preserve the totality, to keep the margins solid. They feel compelled to prevent nothing from slipping outside the work (*hors texte*).

In response to the those who seek "to transpose the whole content of faith into conceptual form," Hilarious Bookbinder writes, for the amusement of his reader, a "truthful history of the book" (SLW, 3). In this little fragment, the pseudonym reports that "several years ago" a Mr. Literatus left some manuscripts with Hilarious for the purpose of having them bound. Being in no hurry, Mr. Literatus imposed no time restrictions on the bookbinder, and the manuscripts remained in the latter's possession for more than three months, during which time Mr. Literatus died, "and his heirs, who were abroad, received the books through the probate court" (SLW, 3). Believing the matter closed after having been reimbursed for his labor, Hilarious suddenly came upon "a small package of handwritten papers," which, after some speculation, both he and his wife were forced to conclude belonged to the late Mr. Literatus. As so much time had elapsed, and because no one had laid claim to the papers, the bookbinder "stitched them together in a colored paper folder so that they would not lie around and clutter up the shop" (SLW, 4). However, he did utilize the "book" every so often: he used it to educate his children in the art of reading aloud, and encouraged them to copy pages from it so as to imitate "the beautiful letters and flourishes" in the art of "penmanship."

Shortly thereafter, a "normal-school graduate and candidate in philosophy" became teacher to one of the bookbinder's sons. On seeing the stitched-up papers, he asked to borrow the "book." Hilarious offered to make him a present of it, "but he was too honorable . . . so he borrowed it." After returning the writings to the bookbinder, the tutor exclaimed: "You presumably were unaware of what a glorious gift and donation providence has allotted to your household in this book you so casually wanted to give away. If it comes into the right hands, a book such as this is worth its weight in gold" (SLW, 5). Hilarious concludes his history of the book with the following reflection: "So it had come to pass as the good normal-school graduate and candidate in philosophy advised me . . . that my service was greater because it was not one book I would publish but several books, probably by several authors. In other words, my learned friend assumes that there must have been a fraternity, a society, or an association of which that literatus had been the head or president and therefore had preserved the papers" (SLW, 6). The significance of this vignette for understanding Kierkegaard's work should not be underestimated: to attempt to circumscribe a text within a binding and then to append a signature to this book amounts to a claim by the author that he or she has control over the destiny of the text, that no textual "play" or reinterpretation of the text's content is permissible.

For both Kierkegaard and Derrida, Hegel is such a bookbinder; his *Encyclopaedia* mirrors reason's totalizing impetus in that it narrates, as if from an atemporal or ahistorical vantage point, the progress of *Geist* as it seeks to identify with the other as a mark of the same. I noted at the beginning of this work how Hegel's *Philosophy of Right* equates being ethical with mere observance of the law, and that those who take a critical distance from the law in order to meet the demands of a radical responsibility are considered at best alienated from the established order, and at worst evil. Such a text claims to tell the story of the law as if there were a single law that had an identifiable origin and a projected end. The hilarity of this bookbinding, or totalizing, becomes apparent when it is considered that in making the claim for "good writing" (a writing that is the mark of the divine or *Geist*) it is assumed that what is alien to the structure of the book—that is, the play of signification—can either be mastered in the service of the bookbinder or simply reduced to the order of the same.

Throughout this analysis I have shown how Derrida attempts to confound the spirit of bookbinding through his notion of *différance*, or by contending that identity (which is a totalizing gesture) is a product of the differential relations between signs. This, to reiterate, suggests that identity is never pure, never self-contained, but rather that which ineluctably contains the mark of the other. In other words, there are forces, such as language and tradition, that preexist the individual—forces that claim the individual and color his or her conception of what is true and what is good. Such "unconscious" forces, being irreducible to reason, are incapable of being subsumed or sublated into a speculative totality. They are "present" to consciousness only in the form of a graphic mark or trace, or what the tradition has considered nothing more than "bad writing."[38] The moral of Hilarious Bookbinder's preface is that existing individuals, being subject to time, history, and contingency, can never lay claim to a truth of truths, can never master, contain, or subdue the textual forces that precede reflection. Otherwise stated, the author can never claim full authority over what he or she says, does, or writes; the book is always lacking, never finished, always in the process of becoming. This is why the bookbinder has to assume, after receiving for a second time the papers of Mr. Literatus, that there is more than one voice speaking through the pages of the text, that they amount not only to one book, but many books by several authors. Any attempt to still the textual forces at play or to enclose the other in the order of the same signifies a denial by the author, or the bookbinder, of the fact that all books, and indeed all signatures, contain the possibility of being reinterpreted. As the products of existing beings who are in the constant process of becoming, texts have, like their authors, uncertain futures. They can be "repeated" in the Kierkegaardian and, as we shall see, Derridean sense of that word.

In a highly ironic tone, Climacus directly foreshadows Derrida's 1972 study "Outwork"[39] when, in the *Postscript,* he applies to Hegel's *Phenomenology* the findings of Hilarious Bookbinder: "It would then become a question of the importance of the Hegelian phenomenology for the system, whether it is an introduction, whether it is in turn incorporated in the system; further, whether Hegel may not even have the amazing merit of having written not only the system but two or even three systems, which always takes a matchless systematic head, and which nevertheless seems to be the case, since the system is completed more than once etc." (CUP, 117). The question for Climacus is whether the *Phenomenology,* which came before the logical *Encyclopaedia,* was merely a preface to the latter or whether it was contained within the system. The intimation here is that, like the lost papers of Mr. Literatus, Hegel's *Phenomenology* overruns the binding process and thus undermines the entire dialectical project.

Both Kierkegaard and Derrida thus challenge the metaphysical

---

[38] Ibid., 17–18.
[39] See Jacques Derrida, *Dissemination,* trans. Barbara Johnson (London: Athlone Press, 1981), 1–59.

bias in favor of the book (as an immanent teleology that unfolds systematically toward an anticipatable end) by emphasizing the errant nature of writing, involving individual readers and writers who are factically bound and who are subject to an inexorable tide of events, none of which can be fully determined in advance. A book about existing beings, both thinkers assert, must be written by an existing being, and one who is just as susceptible to the flux of events as the book's reader. For Kierkegaard—and this also holds true for Derrida, as we shall see below—God is the only being who can have a view from nowhere, or who can legitimately be said to have the ability to write a book on existence. Climacus, who writes in fragments and delights in writing after the end of the book, or in postscripts, develops this point in the following style:

> A system of existence [*Tilværelsens System*] cannot be given. Is there, then, not such a system? That is not at all the case. Neither is this implied in what has been said. Existence itself is a system—for God, but it cannot be a system for any existing [*existerende*] spirit. System and conclusiveness correspond to each other, but existence is the very opposite. Abstractly viewed, system and existence cannot be thought conjointly, because in order to think existence, systematic thought must think it as annulled and consequently not as existing. Existence is the spacing that holds apart; the systematic is the conclusiveness that combines. (CUP, 118)

Existence, that is, is only finished after the death of the existing subject, and it is not the job of existing beings to ascertain what lies thereafter. It is, therefore, impossible for one who is still subject to the temporal tide of factical events to draw conclusions about existence as if he or she—a particular individual with a proper name living at a certain time and place—had the ability to haul the self out of existence. This is why Constantin Constantius and Vigilius Haufniensis insist that eternity can only be entered in a forward-moving fashion; to contend that eternity can be recollected in time—or what amounts to the same thing, that one can write a systematic account of existence from an eternal standpoint in which all linguistic and contextual features of existence have been nullified—is the wont of metaphysicians who hold stubbornly to the belief that through "productive memory" one can slip out the back door of a life regulated by time:

Who is supposed to write or finish such a system? Surely a human being, unless we are to resume the peculiar talk about a human being's becoming speculative thought, a subject-object. Consequently, a human being—and surely a living, that is, an existing, human being. . . . But if he is a human being, then he is indeed existing. Now, all in all, there are two ways for an existing individual: either he can do everything to forget that he is existing and thereby manage to become comic . . . because existence possesses the remarkable quality that an existing person exists whether he wants to or not; or he can direct all his attention to his existing. It is from this side that an objection must first be made to modern speculative thought, that it is not a false presupposition but a comic presupposition, occasioned by its having forgotten in a kind of world-historical absentmindedness what it means to be a human being, not what it means to be human in general, for even speculators might be swayed to consider that sort of thing, but what it means that we, you and I and he, are human beings, each one on his own. (CUP, 120)

For Climacus, to exist means to be responsible, to be ethical in the radical sense I have given to this word throughout this work. The most significant feature of the pseudonym's critique of the culture of the book and of the speculative method employed by Hegel is the fact that although, as he says, the system has a place for the ethical, *qua* theory of rights, it denies a place to a critical ethics that takes the side of the "poor existing individual" over and against the established order or the state. In the system, which presupposes that existence has finished, the law is universally applied (we must remember here how in *Fear and Trembling*, de Silentio equates the law, the ethical—*qua Sittlichkeit*—and the universal). To observe the law is to guarantee one's rights as a free citizen within the state. However, the law, as (according to Hegel) the manifestation of the divine design on earth, does not accommodate the requirements of singularity or of existing beings. It fails to make provision for singular situations that require a loosening up of the law in the name of a greater justice. This was precisely the critique Anti-Climacus used against the deification of reason or the state by the given actuality: unless it is recalled that all institutions originate in and through the impulse of existing human beings, and unless it is further remembered that such institutions are there to serve those same existing beings, then singularity will be ground under by the weight of the system.

To be genuinely ethical, for Climacus, demands that the individual hold fast to the basic principle of existence: humans are beings who constantly strive, in that we are incapable of making our way out of the temporal flow of life. As such, the institutions that we have founded must also be subject to change. If it is not conceded that the law can and should be teleologically suspended in favor of the demands of social justice, subjectivity and singularity are simply, to recall what Kierkegaard says in *The Present Age*, leveled. They are relegated simply to a paragraph in the system:

> In committee deliberations, it is quite all right to include a dissenting vote, but a system that has a dissenting vote as a paragraph within it is a queer monstrosity. No wonder, then, that the system survives. It proudly ignores objections; and if it comes across a particular objection that appears to draw a little attention, the systematic entrepreneurs proceed to have a copyist make a copy of the objection, which is thereupon recorded in the system, and with the bookbinding the system is finished. (CUP, 123)

The notion of a radical ethics of responsibility is thus inextricably bound up with the question of communication in the thought of Kierkegaard and Derrida. Both authors are deeply cognizant of the fact that they are existing beings writing for, or communicating with, existing beings. Consequently, they both find the idea of bookbinding a comic process. Their writings are designed to give the reader a sense of his or her particularity or singularity. Because each author has nothing more to offer than a particular point of view, in that neither one has access to pure, unmediated truth, they both write so as to keep the reader alert to his or her mortality and finitude. This is why Kierkegaard addresses his "dear reader," and why Derrida continually emphasizes the importance of personal "style" in the production of works.

Owing to their common conviction that there must be an end to the book and a beginning to writing, both Kierkegaard and Derrida opt for a form of indirect communication over the direct discourse of systematic philosophy. Neither is prepared to surrender his singularity to take up the ahistorical vantage point of idealistic metaphysics; that is, the aim of these works is not to usher the reader out of existence, but to make the reader aware that he or she is in a constant state of becoming, and that the future, because it is unknown, holds out the possibility for both personal and institutional change. Writing, which has no end as such but comes in the form of post-scripts, fragments, and lyrics, all of which transgress the margins of the book, does not have a teleological direction. Its course, rather, is indirect because it is subject to multifarious contingent factors. Communication between two existing individuals, contextually bound as each one is, is never transparent or pure. Such considerations will help us make sense below of the pseudonymous strategies employed by Kierkegaard while also lending an insight into why Derrida places so much emphasis on the function and role of the "signature" throughout his work.

Communication and Repetition

Derrida, no less than Kierkegaard, is concerned to deconstruct the book in the name of writing. His attention is focused on what cannot be contained within the system, on what breaks its margins or is simply granted a paragraph in the *Encyclopaedia*. He calls our attention to the fact that we cannot escape our factical situatedness, that the other cannot ultimately be reduced to the status of the same, but is something, by virtue of its singular situation, that appeals for affirmation. In a manner reminiscent of Climacus's discussion of the hilarity of the bookbinding process in the *Postscript*, Derrida in *Circumfession* (1991) strives to undermine the pretension of drawing up a system for existing beings. This text could easily stand as a sequel to Kierkegaard's posthumously published *Point of View for My Work As an Author*, in that it is co-written by Geoffrey Bennington, who attempts to write a definitive intellectual biography of Derrida in standard book form, while Derrida writes "in a sort of internal margin, between Geoffrey Bennington's book and work in preparation," "fifty-nine periods and periphrases" that challenge and exceed Bennington's systematic overview. A short, unsigned introduction spells out the significance of this exercise:

> The guiding idea of the exposition comes from computers: G.B. [Bennington] would have liked to systematize J.D.'s [Derrida] thought to the point of turning it into an interactive program which, in spite of its difficulty, would in principle be accessible to any user. As what is at stake in J.D.'s work is to show how any such system must remain essentially open, this undertaking was doomed to failure from the

start, and the interest it may have consists in the test, and the proof, of that failure. In order to demonstrate the ineluctable necessity of the failure, our contract stipulated that J.D., having read G.B.'s text, would write something escaping the proposed systematization, surprising it.[40]

Whether it be the book or, indeed, the computer program, one existing individual's effort to write of another will always prove futile, for it is precisely by virtue of the fact that both individuals are existing—and thus temporally and historically situated—that they can indeed escape being pinned down by the established (metaphysical or social) order. Derrida, like de Silentio, wants to deconstruct the horizon of absolute knowledge, of the programmable; he does not seek the possible, for the possible is anticipatable and can therefore be written into the system, but he has a driving passion for the future as something that can always disrupt the given actuality and the prevailing order.

Like Constantius and Climacus, Derrida is passionate about what eludes the bookbinder, what cannot be directly communicated by the programmer, Bennington, or what cannot be spoken about by the speculative philosopher, Hegel. Derrida, that is, holds out for "the impossible" (that which exceeds the order of the same) and that which, like the papers of Mr. Literatus, surprises and shocks the powers that be upon entering the system. De Silentio, let us recall, was, long before Derrida, the first to signal that what the age requires is a passion for the impossible: "One became great by expecting the possible, another by expecting the eternal; but he who expected the impossible became the greatest of all" (FT, 16). Such is, as I asserted above, the nature of genuine faith: a hope in and affirmation of what exceeds speculative mastery. This is why, moreover, Anti-Climacus defines faith as the process whereby the single individual relates oneself to oneself, or wills to be oneself. The self one wills to be, of course, is one that challenges the established order by emphasizing the primacy of existence and becoming. Such faith, as hope and affirmation, might contest the value of speculative reason, but it is far from contesting the value of reason per se. For reason to face its limits, which it does in faith, does not mean that it must simply

---

[40] Geoffrey Bennington and Jacques Derrida, *Jacques Derrida* (Chicago: University of Chicago Press, 1993), 1.

abdicate; rather, it attempts to reason otherwise, thinking the unthought of the institutionalized form of reason in so doing. Reason, that is, becomes (as Derrida would put it) "inventive": it tries to accommodate (without reducing to the same) the other (*différance*) that systematic reason tried to make present by giving it a paragraph in the *Encyclopaedia*. Derrida has "never loved anything but the impossible."[41] His is a faith no less certain than de Silentio's.

Derrida's love for the impossible and his deconstruction of the book in the name of *différance* have their common origin in a 1971 essay entitled "Signature, Event, Context."[42] Here he follows Kierkegaard by placing at the forefront of his philosophical considerations the role of communication. As I have stressed, communication is problematized when the play of signification cannot be stilled and when it is realized that direct authorial intention is undermined by such features as existence, temporality, and textuality. Derrida begins his analysis by asking if "the word *communication* corresponds to a concept that is unique, univocal, rigorously controllable, and transmittable": "One must first of all ask oneself whether or not the word or signifier 'communication' communicates a determinate content, an identifiable meaning, or a describable value. However, even to articulate and to propose this question I have had to anticipate the meaning of the word *communication:* I have been constrained to predetermine communication as a vehicle, a means of transport or transitional medium of a *meaning,* and moreover of a unified meaning."[43] For Derrida, however, such a "predetermined" meaning of the word "communication" is wholly restrictive and does not take into account the fact that this word "designates nonsemantic movements as well."[44] Communication, that is, should not be thought of solely as a "transmission of meaning" in the literal sense; one cannot undertake a study of communication without also considering the related concepts of "context" and "writing." "Writing" should be interpreted here as "inscription" in the broadest possible

[41] Ibid., *Circumfession* (Periphrase 1), 3.

[42] Jacques Derrida, "Signature, Event, Context," in *Margins of Philosophy,* 307–30; reprinted in Jacques Derrida, *Limited INC* (Evanston: Northwestern University Press, 1988), 1–23. I will quote from the from the essay as it appears in *Limited INC.*

[43] Derrida, *Limited INC,* 1.

[44] Ibid.

sense. While vocal communication between two interlocutors is limited to the particular context in which the discourse is taking place,
writing "in the same time and in the same space, would be capable
of relaxing those limits and of opening the same field to a very much
larger scope."[45] As we have seen, writing constitutes a system of signifiers whose free play cannot be stilled by any metaphysical urge to
bypass the sign (Hegel) in order to obtain full self-presence. The
sign, therefore, "presupposes a certain absence" in that, as a trace of
the other, it evades the grasp of speculative consciousness. Recalling
once more the "pyramid" analogy, the sign ("A") is the site of both
presence and death. As such, the written sign is not merely "an (ontological) modification of presence" but contains within itself the
possibility of being reinscribed in a context alien to and other than
that of its original inscription.

Derrida's contention here is based on his belief that "a written
sign is proffered in the absence of the receiver." This absence, however, should not be construed simply as a "distant presence," but
"must be capable of being carried to a certain absoluteness of absence if the structure of writing, assuming that writing exists, is to
constitute itself."[46] The implication here is that if written communication is to function as *written* communication, it must, as Derrida
says, "remain readable despite the absolute disappearance of any receiver." In other words, after the end of the book (*qua* teleological
systematization), writing, as the product of contextually bound existing individuals, cannot be contained or programmed; that is, writing does not cease to function as writing once the addressee (*telos*)
of the message disappears:

> In order for my "written communication" to retain its function as
> writing, i.e., its readability, it must remain readable despite the abso-
> lute disappearance of any receiver, determined in general. My commu-
> nication must be repeatable—iterable—in the absolute absence of the
> receiver or of any empirically determinable collectivity of receivers.
> Such iterability (*iter*, again, probably comes from *itara*, *other* in San-
> skrit, and everything that follows can be read as a working out of the
> logic that ties repetition to alterity) structures the mark of writing
> itself, no matter what particular type of writing is involved (whether

---

[45] Ibid., 3.
[46] Ibid., 7.

pictographical, hieroglyphic, ideographic, phonetic, alphabetic, to cite
the old categories). A writing that is not structurally readable—
iterable—beyond the death of the addressee would not be writing.[47]

Writing—or any instituted graph, mark, or trace—can be repeated
after the death of the author or after the demise of the bookbinder;
writing, one might say, is structurally capable of exceeding the particular context in which it was initially framed.

The possibility of what Derrida calls "iteration" or "repetition"
ensures that contexts are kept open, that the text breaks free of all
attempts to enclose it within the margins of a totality. Derrida's theory of repetition is analogous to Kierkegaard's notion not only in the
letter, but in spirit also. Repetition is related to alterity, as Derrida
remarks, because it brings to life once more the instituted trace by
opening it up to something new that was not anticipated in the
system. Repetition, as originality of action, opens the text to an unanticipatable future that has no set direction or projected course.
Writing, in other words, emanating from existing beings who are
temporally and historically situated, is not guided toward its destination by *Geist* or by some godlike intention. To invoke the spirit of
Kierkegaard, we could say that because existing beings are in a constant process of becoming, they are unable to retrieve truth through
the process of recollection; the thesis that truth is subjectivity suggests that truth is not directly communicated to those factically embedded, but must be sought through an endless process of repetition
in which the past is continually exposed to a future exceeding the
site of the same. If iteration or repetition were not a feature of the
communicative process in this way, tradition would have no way of
sustaining itself. For a tradition to function it must be possible for it
to be maintained after the death of its founders. This implies that
for a tradition to survive it is necessary for those who continue to
exist after the death of the original addresser and addressee to "repeat" what has been with the objective of opening it up to a future
that cannot be determined in advance. This is precisely what Abraham undertakes in de Silentio's narrative: he exposes the given actu-

---

[47] Ibid. It is helpful to contrast Derrida's position on the role of communication
with that adopted by the hermeneutic strain in contemporary French philosophy.
For a stimulating example of such work, see Leonard Lawlor, *Imagination and
Chance: The Difference between the Thought of Ricoeur and Derrida* (Albany: SUNY
Press, 1992).

ality, or the established order (universal, *Sittlichkeit*), to the other as a future that keeps open the possibility of change and revision. If a tradition (ethical, juridical, political, philosophical), as an archive of instituted traces, is not capable of being repeated anew, it would simply die. This is why, for de Silentio, the age requires faith rather than (speculative) knowledge, an openness to the other rather than systematic closure. Derrida follows both the pseudonym and Abraham when he comments in his exchange with John Searle:

> But often while analyzing a certain ethicity inscribed in language—and this ethicity is a metaphysics (there is nothing pejorative in defining it as such)—they [speech-act theorists] reproduce, under the guise of describing it in its ideal purity, the given ethical conditions of a *given* ethics. They exclude, ignore, relegate to the margins other conditions no less essential to ethics in general, whether of *this given* ethics or of *another*, or of a law that would not answer to Western concepts of ethics, right, or politics. Such conditions, which may be anethical with respect to any given ethics, are not therefore anti-ethical in general. They can even open or recall the opening of another ethics, another right, another "declaration of rights," transformation of constitutions, etc. It is such conditions which interest me when I write of iterability and of all that is tied to this quasi concept in a discourse and in other texts. . . . The ethical-legal-political implications of all these gestures would be easy enough to show.[48]

Iteration or repetition, therefore, is for Derrida, as for Constantius, "the watchword in every ethical view," and that which is responsible for bringing "metaphysics to grief." Its operation challenges the presumption that the given actuality, the established order, or the universal realm of the ethical makes on its own behalf as the guardian of a given ethics, such as *Sittlichkeit*. Repetition, that is, undermines what Derrida calls an "intentionalist teleology," which aims at a direct, uncontaminated form of communication of objective ideas from one tradition to the next, or simply from speaker to listener.

For Derrida, as for Kierkegaard, being always aware that communication is not a matter of *Geist* communicating with itself but of existing beings communicating with other existing beings, what is communicated can never contain the "pure plenitude" of the speak-

---

[48] Derrida, "Signature, Event, Context," 122.

er's intention. If such plenitude were ever realized—if, in other words, *Geist* ever became absolute, its *telos* having been brought to fruition—life, according to Derrida, would simply come to an end. In a similar manner to Climacus's reflections on the dangers of book-binding for existing beings, Derrida asserts that if one could shut the system down, as is Hegel's wont, time would also shut down. To exist implies that one has a future, but if the future has been determined by *Geist*, existence is no more:

> I would say not simply that "intention doesn't necessarily imply pure plenitude," but that it necessarily can and should *not* attain the pleni-tude towards which it nonetheless inevitably tends. Plenitude is its *telos*, but the *structure* of this *telos* is such that if it is attained, it as well as intention both disappear, are paralyzed, immobilized, or die. The relation to the *telos* is therefore necessarily dual, divided, split. What is understood as *telos* must therefore be rethought. And it is precisely to the extent that this relation to *telos* is also intricate, com-plex, split, that there is movement, life, language, intention, etc. Plen-itude is the end (the goal) but were it attained, it would be the end (death).[49]

For Derrida, although repetition is existing beings' capacity to bring to life again what is sedimented in tradition, or indeed what is communicated through the trace, it cannot recover this in full. What is repeated, given that it is inscribed and encoded in cultural mem-ory, always bears traces (*différance*) of an other that denies itself to consciousness. Through repetition, one can say, we can access what has been transmitted from the tradition in which each individual is embedded, but only in a partial sense. This does not mean, however, that there can be no effective communication as such, but rather that because the system is threatened from within by an other that it cannot systematize, and by an other from without whose arrival cannot be planned for (what Derrida calls the *"arrivant"*), direct communication (book communication) must give way to indirect communication (written communication):

> What in this context I call iterability is at once that which tends to attain plenitude and that which bars access to it. Through the possi-bility of repeating every mark as the same it makes way for an idealiza-tion that seems to deliver the full presence of ideal objects (not

---

[49] Ibid., 128–29.

present in the mode of sense perception and beyond all immediate
deictics), but this repeatability itself ensures that the full presence of
a singularity thus repeated comports in itself the reference to something else, thus rending the full presence that it nevertheless announces. This is why iteration is not simply repetition.[50]

When Derrida remarks at the end of this passage that "iteration is
not simply repetition," he is suggesting that iteration is not simply
duplication or repetition of the same; repetition as originality is the
type of (Kierkegaardian) repetition Derrida favors.

If it is the case that what is given in actuality contains a trace of
the other, as Derrida contends, then the established order cannot
claim to be the material manifestation of *Geist*'s divine design, in
that it is an effect of "written" communication. More simply, this
suggests that all ethical, philosophical, and political institutions and
contexts, as historical and contingent formations, can be repeated
and reiterated. Accordingly, the founder(s) of such institutions cannot will that they be preserved in their original unity and integrity,
for as Derrida stresses, "a context is never a gesture that is neutral,
innocent, transparent, disinterested."[51] The construction of a context is always a political gesture in that "it implies, insofar as it involves a determination, a certain type of non-"natural" relationship
to others."[52] Being non-natural, contexts (ethical, philosophical, political, etc.) are "never secured or simple, there is an indefinite opening of every context, an essential nontotalization" at work.[53] It is
precisely this non-natural dimension of each and every context that
allows for the possibility that contexts will be repeated:

> The proof that I have not "put . . . the stability of interpretative con-
> texts radically in question" is that I incessantly recall, as I did a short
> while ago, that I take into account and believe that it is necessary to
> account for this stability, as well as for all the norms, rules, contractual
> possibilities, that depend upon it. But what does it mean to account
> for a stability? On the one hand, it does not necessarily mean to
> choose or accept or try to conserve the stability for its own sake, no
> matter what the cost; it is not tantamount to being "conservative."
> And on the other hand, to account for a certain stability (by essence

---

[50] Ibid., 129.
[51] Ibid., 131.
[52] Ibid., 136.
[53] Ibid., 137.

always provisional and finite) is precisely not to speak of eternity or of absolute solidity; it is to take into account a historicity, a nonnaturalness, of ethics, of politics, of institutionality, etc. If recalling this is to put radically into question the stability of contexts, then, yes, I do that. I say that there is no stability that is absolute, eternal, intangible, natural, etc. But that is implied in the very concept of stability. A stability is not an immutability; it is by definition always destabilizable.[54]

Contexts, that is, are "only relatively firm, neither absolutely solid [fermeté] nor entirely closed [fermeture]." They are founded on an exclusionary gesture, in that to determine a context implies that one is attempting to still the play of the (traced) other that is an inherent feature of its composition. For Derrida, repetition is precisely that which keeps a context from becoming overdetermined; in other words, it is because contexts are effects of **différance** that they cannot shut down or become established totalities. Contexts can, and must, be subject to the most critical rereadings and reevaluations; it is the responsibility of each individual, according to Derrida, to undertake a deconstructive reading of one's tradition, repeating what is worthy in its legacy while teleologically suspending the hierarchical and totalizing features predominating therein, the aims of which are to keep the context stable, secure, and uncontaminated. Such a "double reading," or what Derrida calls "double writing" in his afterword to Limited INC (we will see how close this notion is to Kierkegaard's "double reflection," which I have already introduced in relation to the "Kierkegaardian God" above but which is rooted more firmly in the former's theory of indirect communication), is the strategy required for genuine repetition to be effected:

> [Double writing] designates a sort of irreducible divisibility, "quasi-transcendental," as I have said elsewhere, of "deconstructive" writing. It must inevitably partition itself along two sides of a limit and continue (up to a certain point) to respect the rules of that which it deconstructs or of which it exposes the deconstructibility. Hence, it always makes this dual gesture, apparently contradictory, which consists in accepting, within certain limits—that is to say, in never entirely accepting—the givenness of a context, its closedness and its stubbornness [sa fermeture et sa fermeté].[55]

---

[54] Ibid., 151.
[55] Ibid., 152.

For Derrida, repetition as double writing means, on the one hand, affirming (repeating) what is retainable within a tradition, while on the other hand it means maintaining a level of critical debate among all its participants with the objective of keeping the context from freezing over or shutting down. It is a process of being both inside and outside the tradition, of keeping a vigilant guard over what the tradition excludes in the name of what it determines as sacred. Like Socrates, Abraham, and Jesus Christ (Kierkegaard's ethical exemplars), the deconstructionist engages in a constant process of self-questioning by "not entirely accepting the givenness of a context," knowing as he or she does that such a formation is non-natural, and is furthermore the product of a non-natural contract between existing individuals. The established order, when subjected to double writing, is exposed to its own historicity and to its utterly contingent composition.

Repetition and Invention

At this juncture I wish to return to the question of the book as a model of systematization and to the question of writing as that which transgresses the totality, for it is on this point that one can best appreciate how the Kierkegaardian and Derridean approaches converge. The book, as Kierkegaard explains, is the result of an existing individual's attempt to evade time, mortality, and finitude; it is a testimony to the dialectician's objective to proclaim that he or she has a view from nowhere and that the system, which he or she has activated, is on target to reach its destination. Hegel's *Encyclopaedia* represents for Kierkegaard, as for Derrida, the dangers inherent in teleological programming and long-term speculative planning, signaling as it does the immanent closure of all contexts.

For Kierkegaard and Derrida, however, all programs have a history in that they are established by existing individuals who are situated in time. To sign a text, therefore, allows one to consider this book from a historical perspective, that is, from the perspective of the particular author in question. Such is the nature of what Derrida terms "the proper name," or the name of the singular individual who has lived an irreplaceable life, coming as he or she does at the end of a unique configuration of events. Like the nature of writing in general, according to Derrida, the name continues to function even in the event of the death of the named individual. That is, the name of the author continues to leave its mark even though the author (*qua* existing individual) has ceased to be. Like all institutions and contexts, the author is an institution with a history, one that is as vulnerable as any other to the effects of repetition. As Kierkegaard has taught us in relation to the comedy involved in bookbinding, the author's direct intention cannot be perpetuated *via* the book, for the gesture of signing a text implies that the work is the product of an existing individual and is therefore a very particular form of expression that cannot be guaranteed to reach its intended destination. As Geoffrey Bennington argues, "So we shall say that even while I am alive, my name marks my death. It already bears the death of its bearer. It is already the name of the dead person, the anticipated memory of a departure. The mark which identifies me, which makes me me rather than anyone else, depropriates me immediately by announcing my death, separating me a priori from the same self it constitutes or secures."[56] In other words, the signature of an author "is always accompanied de jure by the mark of a place and a date."[57] An author's signature, we could say, is supposed to guarantee for legal reasons that the work on which the signature is printed, and not signed firsthand, is an original and self-contained work. However, as we have seen in the case of Derrida's subverting of Bennington's system and Kierkegaard's anecdotal analysis of the problems involved in determining who the author of any text is, the signature can never be used as a means of tracing the original intentions behind the work. This is because the author, as an existing individual who holds particular beliefs that are effects of *différance,* has no predetermined thesis as such. That is, the work can never be programmed in advance of its being written, for writing is not a process that unfolds according to any teleological scheme, but rather takes time, is irregular, and is merely the final phase in a whole concatenation of events including research, drafting, rewriting, correcting, and so forth. Writing, like existence itself, is subject to the "law" of temporality.

Derrida and Kierkegaard both draw attention to the fact that Hegel wrote his preface after the system was complete. In so doing,

[56] Bennington and Derrida, *Jacques Derrida,* 149.
[57] Ibid., 150.

Hegel showed, despite himself, that the book, like all institutions, contexts, and programs, cannot contain writing. The preface (Kierkegaard wrote a book simply entitled *Prefaces!*), as a precis to the system, endeavors to bind the text and hold it together in a unified totality. The crowning gesture of such a device is the signature of the author, which is usually placed at the end of the preface, along with the date and place of inscription. In signing thus, the author claims to have drawn all the disparate strands of his or her work together under one name. The book is at this moment perceived to be finished, complete, and ready for binding.

The signature, however, does not guarantee the stability of the system or the program: it presupposes the inevitability of repetition, in that for the book to function as a book the signature must be reproducible. If the book is to survive, that is, it must be reproduced *en masse*. In broader terms, for an institution to become stabilized it must be affirmed repeatedly. If such were not the case, it would simply be impossible for anything to take root and acquire an identity.

Like all writing, however, the book does continue to exist after the death of the author, since it communicates indirectly with those who outlive him or her. This it does by virtue of repetition as reduplication, but also by virtue of repetition as double writing, or iteration. On this note Derrida poses the following question:

> Does the absolute singularity of signature as event ever occur? Are there signatures?
>
> Yes, of course, every day. Effects of signature are the most common thing in the world. But the condition of possibility of those effects is simultaneously, once again, the condition of their impossibility, of the impossibility of their rigorous purity. In order to function, that is, to be readable, a signature must have a repeatable, iterable, imitable form; it must be able to be detached from the present and singular intention of its production. It is its sameness which, by corrupting its identity and its singularity, divides its seal [*sceau*].[58]

The signature, according to Derrida, must by its very nature be repeatable. Iteration ensures that the signature is kept alive, but in so doing it also divorces the author from his or her communication. It could be said here that the law of repetition disestablishes the

---

[58] Derrida, "Signature, Event, Context," 20.

author, *qua* programmer and systematizer. By opening up the book to be read by the other, the author leaves him- or herself open to double writing, in which the reader "countersigns" the work from a perspective unknown to the author. The reader, that is, affirms the institution merely by reading the work. At the same time, however, the reader does more than simply reproduce the author's signature: he or she "signs" it from his or her unique and singular perspective. The upshot of this process is that while the reader keeps the author's name in circulation, he or she simultaneously opens up that name, or the authorial institution, to a different or other reading that frees it from the original context of composition.

As with Kierkegaard's theory of repetition, which states that the dominant political, philosophical, and ethical codes governing reality are not jettisoned in repetition, or in a teleological suspension, but revitalized from a more ethically concerned perspective (hence Constantin's belief that repetition is the watchword in every ethical view), repetition for Derrida is also not something that threatens to destroy contexts, institutions, or traditions. Derridean repetition, to the contrary, seeks to open the established order to the possibility of something not taken account of in its constitution—something, that is, which makes the institutional order tremble. Repetition makes way for what the system cannot account for, for something wholly alien to the program. The system, or what Kierkegaard might refer to as "institutional reason," is "offended" by this "other" beyond the given context ("actuality" in Kierkegaard's idiom) that appears paradoxical to it.

Repetition in this sense is "double affirmation": the reader affirms the author in the act of reading, while at the same time affirming the text's potential to be read otherwise, or to be read "out of context." In this respect, repetition is the act of teleologically suspending the given context with the aim of taking it up again from the point of view of the other. Contexts, being porous and permeable, are always under threat from what is to come, from what cannot be mediated by the calculable order of the same. To read the book otherwise, or to countersign the book, is one such way for the other to disrupt authorial hegemony. For in so doing, the responsible reader not only affirms the prevailing institution (by saying "yes" to it) but also alerts it to its own untenability as something that can

protect itself from the other, the different, the foreign, or the heterogeneous.

Kierkegaard calls this point of disruption or suspension the "moment." As I explained above, for Kierkegaard the future cannot be
accounted for by the dialectician, but is rather "the incognito" in
that it exceeds the purview of consciousness. Nothing, that is, can
be determined absolutely about the future: it defies speculation and
is therefore not of the order of the known (CA, 89). Faith, as hope
in and affirmation of the incoming of the unprogrammable (what
Kierkegaard calls the "eternal"), is required to keep existing individuals on the lookout for the impossible, or for the unanticipatable
countersignature.

Derrida's revelations about his life and work in *Circumfession* seek
to demonstrate to the systematizer, in this case Bennington, how
futile it is for any author to assert his or her authority over a text
simply by the act of signing. In this instance, the author is not only
once more testifying to the fact that the nature of temporal existence is inimical to the bookbinding process, but also to the fact that
it is no less difficult for each author to undertake a self-portrait, as if
repetition and *différance* are features of experience that do not apply
to the experience the self has of itself. If the Hegelian notion of
selfhood can be metaphorically illustrated in the form of a circle that
presupposes its end in its beginning, signifying in so doing that the
other, which is alien to the self, can be drawn in and reduced to
the status of the same, both Derrida and Kierkegaard rethink this
metaphor as a circle with a "broken middle," one that is "out of
joint." The circle, as symbol of the system, is prevented from reflecting back on itself by virtue of what Derrida calls a certain *destiner-
rance*.

In opposition to the idea that the self can overcome alienation by
identifying the other as a mark of presence, Derrida stresses the absence inherent in every seeming plenitude. This absence, which the
"a" of *différance* signifies, prevents an author from directly commun-
ing with the other as if full, systematic comprehension between author and reader were possible; in other words, repetition undermines
the author's will to hear him- or herself speak by opening his or her
communication up to an other whose destination remains unknown.

While we may affirm that what Derrida is doing when he seeks to
surprise Bennington—and what Kierkegaard is hoping to achieve

when he employs pseudonyms to compose anti-systematic, anti-absolutist, and anti-dialectical fragments and postscripts—is a mark of their uncircumscribable singularities as "poor existing individuals," we must also agree that such particular "inventions" cannot ensure that the authors in question will be protected from the law of iteration. Indeed, the point they are making through the use of such gestures and techniques is precisely that selfhood, whether it be Hegel's, Kierkegaard's, or Derrida's, is a product of repetition, and as such is in need of constant reinvention. This means keeping it open not simply to the possible, but to the impossible, as that which surprises, shocks, and unsettles all contexts and programs. As Derrida argues in his essay "Psyche: Invention of the Other":

> For the other is not the possible. So it would be necessary to say that the only possible invention would be the invention of the impossible. But an invention of the impossible is impossible, the other would say. Indeed. But it is the only possible invention: an invention has to declare itself to be the invention of that which did not appear to be possible; otherwise it only makes explicit a program of possibilities within the economy of the same.
>
> It is in this paradoxical predicament that a deconstruction gets underway. Our current tiredness results from the invention of the same and from the possible, from the invention that is always possible. It is not against it but beyond it that we are trying to reinvent invention itself, another invention, or rather an invention of the other that would come, through the economy of the same, indeed while miming or repeating it . . . to offer a place for the other, to let the other come.[59]

"The impossible," being incognito, heralds a future in which the order of (speculative) knowledge gives way to a time of faith, or a time in which the self affirms unconditionally "a responsibility that transcends this or that determination of a given context."[60]

The other to come—the other that disturbs and unsettles the established order, the given actuality, and the Hegelian circle of exchange—is that for whom both Kierkegaard and Derrida have a relentless passion. More simply stated, and in line with our assessment of the Kierkegaardian God-man in the preceding chapter, the

---

[59] Jacques Derrida, "Psyche: Invention of the Other," in *Acts of Literature*, ed. Derek Attridge (New York: Routledge, 1992), 341. Originally published in Jacques Derrida, *Psyché: Inventions de l'autre* (Paris: Galilée, 1987).

[60] Derrida, "Afterword," *Limited INC*, 152.

other for Kierkegaard—the "ideal"—is that which continually puts the self in question; simply by being other, it ruptures all forms of self-security. Genuine responsibility for Kierkegaard takes the form of an opposition to the pervasive tendency of the present age to deify reason (an abstract, objective form of disinterested reflection) and the state by affirming or responding to the appeal from the other as one who has no place to call his or her own in the established milieu.

The Christ-figure, as Kierkegaard's highest ethical ideal, not only represents the paradoxical instance of embodied divinity but is also a symbol for the "most wretched," or for those who are on the margins of the state. When we are enjoined by Kierkegaard to enact the *imitatio Christi*, we are called to teleologically suspend the current order (since it is exclusionary) with the aim of rethinking our identity so as to include those whom we consider alien, other, or foreign. Such self-questioning should not take the form of theoretical reflection (or "knowledge" in Hegel's sense), but of faith or double reflection. For to stand with the most wretched is an action that "offends" institutional reason, or indeed confounds speculation, in that the Christ-figure for Kierkegaard is incognito (like the knight of faith, he cannot be "known" as such). Otherwise stated, since the Christ-figure is, as Anti-Climacus says, "a *sign* of contradiction," he is never present to consciousness, but present only in his absence. Like the "a" of *différance*, which impedes the march of *Geist* toward full reconciliation with itself, Kierkegaard's ethical ideal evades being absorbed in full by the dynamic of the dialectic.

The poor, the outcasts, the lepers and the lame—all those on whose behalf the God-man spoke most eloquently—are incommensurable with the established order. Like the God-man, their time is not now, not the present, but always to come. This explains why the "most wretched" represent the ideal in practical terms for Kierkegaard: there will always be those who have no place in the system, those whom the speculative program simply does not accommodate, those who will be forever alien, marginalized, and other. Teleologically suspending the ethical order is a means of responding to the call of these others with the aim of opening up what Derrida would call the context, so as to welcome in the stranger while preserving his or her difference. Such is the nature of repetition: rethinking what has been from the point of view of what is to come, what must come if a genuinely ethical response is to be engendered.

So far I have argued that the means by which both Kierkegaard and Derrida oppose systematization are strikingly similar. I will expand on these claims at this juncture by asking just how congruous their equally controversial and provocative theories of ethical responsibility actually are, and if such theories are sufficient to act as a basis for genuine community existence. In so doing, I will demonstrate that Kierkegaard not only anticipates Derrida in method and technique, but that he also foreshadows some of the most seemingly innovative and original contributions that deconstruction has made in recent years.

PART 2: A POSTMODERN CHRISTIAN ETHIC

The Gift

The opening to the other, which both Kierkegaard and Derrida celebrate through their significantly similar theories of repetition, is discussed more specifically in Derrida's writings in terms of what he calls "the gift." The gift has played a central role in the evolution of Derrida's intellectual formation since he first introduced it in relation to his deconstructive reading of Hegelian *Sittlichkeit* in *Glas* (1974). It is perhaps Derrida's most Kierkegaardian gesture, due to its being inextricably related to the themes of repetition and invention that are bound up with the Kierkegaardian/Derridean critique of Hegelian systematization. By the time Derrida published both *Donner le temps* (*Given Time*) in 1991 and "Donner la mort" (*The Gift of Death*) a year later, it had become evident not only that Kierkegaard's influence had grown but also that his traces could be located on nearly every page of both texts.

The gift is an economic symbol, or in more Hegelian terms, it is caught up in a circular economy. The motif of the circle, as a symbol of the self's dialectical odyssey from estrangement to full self-security, is the key to understanding what is at issue in these texts. In keeping with our reflections throughout, let us think of the circle in terms of "the book" that presupposes its end in its beginning and which totalizes what is other and alien by ordering them systematically. Now, such a speculative circular movement (bookbinding) is precisely what both Kierkegaard and Derrida have called into question through their plea on behalf of the "poor existing individual" who cannot evade the contingency of history and time. The gift can be characterized in terms of its economic value as something that is presented by someone (a self) to an other; that is, the gift is given by a donor and is accepted in an economy of exchange by a donee. According to Derrida, however, a pure gift can never be presented; once a gift is presented by one individual to the other, an obligation is imposed on the donee to reciprocate the generosity of the donor by returning to the donor a gift that exceeds in value the original offering. In such an economy of exchange, the Hegelian dialectic of sameness amid difference is at work: while the self gives to the other, he or she does so with the prospect of receiving back in kind, or recouping his or her loss. The end, therefore, is presupposed in the beginning, and vice versa. That is, the self can "recollect" what it has lost in the original act of giving through an economic payback from the other. The other is thus in debt to the self.

Derrida points out that the word "economy" has its etymological roots in "law" as "*nomos*," and in "home" as "*oikos*." We saw above how the Hegelian self strives to mediate what is foreign with the aim of reducing this otherness to sameness so as to become one with itself. The self, in other words, desires to surmount alienation with the projected long-term gain of coming home to itself. Such is the law of the circular economics at work here; the foreign must ultimately submit to the law of the same:

> The figure of the circle is obviously at the center, if that can be still said of a circle. It stands at the center of any problematic of *oikonomia*, as it does of any economic field: circular exchange, circulation of goods, products, monetary signs or merchandise. . . . This motif of circulation can lead one to think that the law of economy is the— circular—return to the point of departure, to the origin, also to the home. So one would have to follow the odyssean structure of the economic narrative. *Oikonomia* would always follow the path of Ulysses. . . . The being-next-to-self of the Idea in Absolute Knowledge would be odyssean in this sense, that of an economy and a nostalgia, a "homesickness," a provisional exile longing for reappropriation.[61]

As with "good writing," which keeps the book intact and the authorial institution upright, the circular economy of exchange keeps the

---

[61] Jacques Derrida, *Given Time: I. Counterfeit Money*, trans. Peggy Kamuf (Chicago: University of Chicago Press, 1992), 6–7.

self present, or next to itself; in the system of exchange, the self can anticipate the nature of a deferred gain, and it can program the system so as to ensure that a full and equal measure will return to the self after any form of excessive expenditure. Like the book, therefore, the circular economy is teleologically structured.

For Derrida, however, when one offers a gift to someone, the gift *as such* is annulled. For a gift to be a gift, it must be given without the prospect of return; it must, that is, break the circle of reappropriation. However, once the donee receives a gift, it can no longer be said to be a gift, for as soon as one accepts the gift it is already caught up in the economy of exchange. It seems, therefore, that there can be no such thing as a pure gift, for once one gives, an obligation is automatically placed on the other to return:

> But is not the gift, if there is any, also that which interrupts economy? That which, in suspending economic calculation, no longer gives rise to exchange? That which opens the circle so as to defy reciprocity or symmetry, the common measure, and so as to turn aside the return in view of the no-return? If there is gift, the *given* of the gift (*that which* one gives, *that which* is given, the gift as given thing or as act of donation) must not come back to the giving. . . . It must not circulate, it must not be exchanged, it must not in any case be exhausted, as a gift, by the process of exchange, by the movement of circulation of the circle in the form of return to the point of departure . . . it must *keep* a relation of foreignness to the circle, a relation without relation of familiar foreignness.[62]

The aporia is evident: for an economy to be generated, there must be a process of giving and receiving gifts; that is, the gift must be presupposed in any economy, and yet once it is drawn into an economy the gift ceases to be a gift. The gift, otherwise stated, must maintain or keep "a relation of foreignness to the circle." There must, that is, be no intention to give, for in desiring or intending to give to the other, "a constituted subject, which can also be collective—for example, a group, a community, a nation, a clan, a tribe—in any case, a subject identical to itself and conscious of its identity," seeks only "to constitute its own unity and, precisely, to get its own identity recognized so that that identity comes back to it, so that it can reappropriate its identity: as its property."[63] Thus

---

[62] Ibid., 7.
[63] Ibid., 10–11.

the gift should not appear *as such* to the beneficiary if this relation of foreignness or otherness is to be maintained.

We have seen how both Kierkegaard and Derrida advocate an opening up to "the impossible" as a means of breaking free of the limits arbitrarily imposed by the bookbinder or the systematizer. In arguing for repetition and iteration, both thinkers attempt to undermine the claims of speculation by emphasizing that the written communication of an existing individual continues to exist after the disappearance of both the sender and the receiver; that is, semantically structured contexts (an example of which is the book) are not natural totalities and are thus always vulnerable to repetition. Contexts do not follow any teleological course, since they are the products of contingency. A context, therefore, never shuts down in the manner of a system; as the result of non-natural associations between existing individuals who are time-bound, contexts open onto an unprogrammable future, a future that is, as Kierkegaard tells us, incognito. Affirming what is always to come, we have learned, is to have faith in "the impossible" (what cannot be preprogrammed), or opening the way to let the other come. For in saying "yes" to the other in this way, one is maintaining a relation to what is foreign to the circle. The gift, because it is always to come, or is yet to be "invented," is incognito: it exceeds the purview of speculative reason while answering the call of faith or doubly reflected reason. The gift, that is, keeps the circle of time flowing by forever withdrawing. The gift, Constantius might say, keeps hope alive.

It must not be assumed, however, that the gift occupies some space of absolute exteriority or that it has no relation whatsoever to we who are ineluctably situated within economy. For while the gift, as the other to come (the impossible), cannot be known in any speculative sense, our desire for it keeps us longing and striving. It could be said, in relation to Derrida's broader concerns, that the gift is the affirmation of the possibility of the other (whom I do not know *as such* in that he or she could very easily countersign the text after my death) to recontextualize and reiterate:

> It is a matter—desire beyond desire—of responding faithfully but also as rigorously as possible both to the injunction or the order of the *gift* ("give" ["*donne*"]) as well as to the injunction or the order of meaning (presence, science, knowledge): *Know* still what giving *wants to say,*

> *know how to give*, know what you want and want to say when you give, know what you intend to give, know how the gift annuls itself, commit yourself [*engage-toi*] even if commitment is the destruction of the gift by the gift, give economy its chance.[64]

While the gift is not directly phenomenalizable, in that it is never present, it is, however, that which keeps desire (for the other) burning.

While Hegel makes desire central to the functioning of the dialectic, it is ultimately subdued and sated once the self has completed its Odyssean trajectory homeward. Kierkegaard's ethics of responsibility, on the other hand, functions according to repetition, which takes the form of a constant striving to keep the established order from deifying itself to such an extent that it loses sight of the "poor existing individual." In other words, the "poor existing individual" is that for the sake of which the fear and trembling precipitated by the act of teleologically suspending the ethical is endured: one *desires* to transgress the law of the same, or the economic circle of reappropriation ("the universal" in both Hegel's and Kierkegaard's lexicon), in the name of the other whose time has yet to come, or who has yet to be made to feel at home in the system. Such excessive generosity, offensive as it is to those who are safeguarded by the system, and an absurdity to the "knights of good conscience," is exemplified by the one who sacrifices being-next-to-self. This is not blind faith, but an affirmation of what is foreign to the system, or to institutionalized reason. Inwardness requires that, like Abraham, one dissent from the universal consensus and take the side of what those who constitute the universal would find it impossible to affirm. This is why Derrida believes that we must begin "by the impossible": in opening up to the other through the generous act of self-denial or sacrifice, the self must be aware that he or she cannot nullify his or her place in a tradition—we are always already situated in a context. The suggestion is, rather, that we must be vigilantly alert to the call of the other, both from within the tradition (the other *traced* in memory) and from the other to come. The other to come (the impossible *qua* gift), therefore, is what draws the self out of the circle of sameness by inspiring one to adopt a critical stance in relation to the established order. Double writing (repetition/iteration), which

---

[64] Ibid., 30.

takes the form of this teleological suspension, must "reinvent" the
other by pushing up against the limits of the given actuality in a
manner reminiscent of Abraham and the God-man. Such is how the
responsible self keeps "a relation of foreignness to the circle" while
remaining caught within the circle:

> If the figure of the circle is essential to economics, the gift must re-
> main *aneconomic*. Not that it remains foreign to the circle, but that it
> must *keep* a relation of foreignness to the circle, a relation without
> relation of familiar foreignness. It is perhaps in this sense that the gift
> is the impossible.
>
> Not impossible but *the* impossible. The very figure of the impossi-
> ble. It announces itself, gives itself to be thought as the impossible. It
> is proposed that we begin by this.[65]

John Caputo succinctly sums up what is at issue here when, in a
recent commentary on a roundtable held with Derrida, he says:

> Derrida thus points to a double injunctive, which is a bit of a double
> bind (that's a surprise), *both* to give *and* to do commerce, to love God
> and mammon. He is saying at one and the same time: (1) *Give*, but
> remember how the gift limits itself. Because there never *is* a gift (*don*),
> the gift is *the* impossible that we all desire; because it annuls itself the
> instant it would come to be, if it ever does, the gift is what we most
> want to make present. The gift is our passion and our longing, what
> we desire, what drives us mad with desire, and what drives us on. That
> means that we must keep watch over our gifts, which should be ways
> of exceeding and surpassing ourselves, emptying and divesting our-
> selves, lest they turn into something less than they (already) are, bits
> of self-aggrandizing selfishness meant to show the other what we can
> do, self-serving "presents" (*présents*, *cadeaux*) belonging to the sensi-
> ble, rational circle of time in which we are not giving to the other but
> making an exhibit of ourselves.[66]

As writers, neither Kierkegaard nor Derrida aspires, like the systematic bookbinder, to contain within artificially constructed borders the effects of his work. Writing, as Derrida tries to prove to
Bennington and Kierkegaard to his "dear reader," is the product of a
multitude of forces that are transmitted via the trace, forces that
cannot be stilled by the phenomenalizing intent of the speculative

---

[65] Ibid., 7.
[66] Caputo, *Deconstruction in a Nutshell*, 147.

theoretician. As merely an existing individual, neither author can inoculate his texts from repetition; they are both inside particular traditions (inside the circle)—this is what determines them as singular—and yet they open themselves up to what each tradition cannot take account of in its long-term economic planning. They give not to receive or to reappropriate (or to simply draw the reader into the circle of the same), but to let the other come. For both of these authors aspire to awaken in the reader of the text an urge to counter-sign from his or her particular point of view; they aim, that is, to indirectly communicate the fact that all totalities are themselves the product of repetition, that all institutions and formations (ethical, philosophical, political, theological) are contingently configured, hence revisable. They show that death (self-denial) is an intrinsic dimension of life (self-becoming), and that without acts of excessive generosity, in which we open up to the other by keeping a relation of foreignness to the circle, tradition itself would die.

The Gift of Death

Up to this point I have been highlighting how similar the anti-sys-tematic and anti-Hegelian approaches adopted by Kierkegaard and Derrida are. In so doing, I have argued that an appreciation of the latter's notion of the gift is necessary for understanding the ethical and political implications of each thinker's theories of authorship, communication, repetition, and singularity. I will now advance this analysis by focusing on Derrida's direct treatment of Kierkegaard in The Gift of Death, with the objective of establishing just how con-gruous Kierkegaard's ethics of responsibility is with Derrida's most recent pronouncements.

Derrida's direct confrontation with Kierkegaard, although a long time coming, should not have been unexpected. As early 1964, in his first essay devoted to the work of Levinas, "Violence and Metaphys-ics," Derrida says of Kierkegaard:

> Let us add, in order to do him *justice*, that Kierkegaard had a sense of the relationship to the irreducibility of the totally-other, not in the egoistic and esthetic here and now, but in the religious beyond of the concept, in the direction of a certain Abraham. And did he not, in turn—for we must let the other speak—see in Ethics, as a moment of Category and Law, the forgetting, in anonymity, of the subjectivity of

religion? From his point of view, the ethical moment is Hegelianism itself, and he says so explicitly. Which does not prevent him from reaffirming ethics in repetition, and from reproaching Hegel for not having constituted a morality.[67]

Even at this early stage of his career, Derrida had come to appreciate how, through the concept of repetition, Kierkegaard had deconstructed Hegelian ethics (*Sittlichkeit*) with the aim of affirming justice beyond the law. In other words, *The Gift of Death* should not be seen as a new turn in Derrida's thought, but merely the context in which he brings to fruition many themes he had treated obliquely since 1964.

In line with the argument in this work, Derrida's portrait of Kierkegaard in *The Gift of Death* is guided by the impulse of Johannes de Silentio's *Fear and Trembling*, a text Derrida considers pivotal for anyone wishing to understand his particular strain of postmodern ethics:

> The trembling of *Fear and Trembling*, is, or so it seems, the very experience of sacrifice. Not, first of all, in the Hebraic sense of the term, *korban*, which refers more to an approach or a "coming close to," and which has been wrongly translated as "sacrifice," but in the sense that sacrifice supposes the putting to death of the unique in terms of its being unique, irreplaceable, and most precious. It also therefore refers to the impossibility of substitution, the unsubstitutible; and then also to the substitution of an animal for man; and finally, especially this, by means of this impossible substitution itself, it refers to what links the sacred to sacrifice and sacrifice to secrecy.[68]

What is so original in Derrida's treatment of this text is the emphasis he places on "secrecy," a category bound up with the related notions of "residual incommensurability," "irony," and "singularity" in the Kierkegaardian oeuvre. For Derrida, Kierkegaard's Abraham does not *choose* to keep the secret of God's injunction from his family; Abraham responds to the call of the other to sacrifice the unique one, his son Isaac, without *knowing* the "ultimate rhyme and reason" behind his actions. "He is sworn to secrecy," says Derrida, "because he is in secret."[69] Abraham, as we have seen, does speak, but he speaks "in

---

[67] Derrida, "Violence and Metaphysics," in *Writing and Difference*, 111.
[68] Derrida, *The Gift of Death*, 58.
[69] Ibid., 59.

tongues," or responds indirectly and with a touch of irony. In order to teleologically suspend the ethical order (*qua Sittlichkeit*), he must avoid using the language of systematization; in other words, Abraham disengages from the structures of *Sittlichkeit* by communicating "in order not to say anything about the essential thing that he must keep secret."[70] For these reasons, Abraham, Kierkegaard's Abraham, is radically responsible. In opening up to the other, in sacrificing what is most precious to him—that is, his beloved son, whose singularity is unsubstitutable—Abraham dies to himself as ethical subject in order to respond to that which exceeds the order of the same. This other (the impossible, the unanticipatable) remains "a secret" to the extent that it cannot be known *as such*, cannot be reduced to a phase in *Geist*'s dialectical unfolding toward absolute truth. In pushing against the limits of standard generosity to welcome the other—what Kierkegaard calls the process of "self-denial"— Abraham says "yes" to what comes after "the book" has been concluded; he affirms, that is, the singularity of the other, whose advent shocks, surprises, and unsettles.

Abraham is both inside and outside the universal: inside to the extent that his beliefs and practices have been determined by the universal order, and outside due to his being aware that the established order must be suspended in the name of what it excludes. Otherwise expressed, Abraham is alert to the logic of the gift as that which disrupts the circle of reappropriation. His secret takes the form of a call from the other, the other which, due to the non-natural nature of contexts, has yet to be "invented."

Derrida, therefore, is no less committed than Kierkegaard to the moral of the story of Abraham's sacrifice of the universal ethical sphere. He too interprets the ethical moment as Hegelianism itself, which does not, in turn, "prevent him from reaffirming ethics in repetition." For, along with Kierkegaard, Derrida sees in this narrative a lesson in "the concept of duty and absolute responsibility":

> The moral of the fable would be morality itself, at the point where morality brings into play the gift of the death that is so given. The absolutes of duty and of responsibility presume that one denounce, refute, and transcend, at the same time, all duty, all responsibility, and every human law. It calls for a betrayal of everything that mani-

---

[70] Ibid.

fests itself in general, the very order and essence of manifestation; namely, the essence itself, the essence in general to the extent that it is inseparable from presence and from manifestation. Absolute duty demands that one behave in an irresponsible manner (by means of treachery and betrayal), while still recognizing, confirming, and reaffirming the very thing one sacrifices, namely, the order of human ethics and responsibility. In a word, ethics must be sacrificed in the name of duty.[71]

In seeming agreement with the notion of responsibility I have attributed to Kierkegaard throughout this work, Derrida asserts that genuine responsibility does not amount simply to an observance of one's obligation under the law, or to fulfilling one's duty in accordance with the formulations of traditional deontological paradigms. The type of responsibility both Kierkegaard and Derrida espouse would undoubtedly "offend" the proponents of such schemes. Being absolutely dutiful, for these thinkers, requires both a suspension of the law as *Geist's* divine design and a countersigning of the ethical treatises that have dominated ethical reflection in the Western metaphysical tradition. This explains why both writers also insist that in the act of absolute duty one does not withdraw into some interior space, for to do so would be an attempt to annul one's factical situatedness and responsibilities. Rather, one is obliged, through repetition or reiteration, to rethink such traditional paradigms while in the midst of existence. That is, repetition, being the watchword in every ethical view, seeks not to destroy the law and ethics, for one is always already "before the law," inside it as it were; it endeavors, however, on the basis that they are historically determined formations, to open them up to diverse readings and interpretations. For Kierkegaard and Derrida, the books of Western ethics, no less than any legal or political constitution, must submit to the requirements of singularity. To respond to the call of the singular, to put singularity before universality, is the manner in which ethics can be reaffirmed in repetition.

Responding to the requirements of singularity, however, entails, according to Derrida, the madness of a double bind: when I respond to the call of the other, when I press against the limits of economy in order to give a gift of death (when, in other words, I sacrifice

---

[71] Ibid., 66–67.

myself for the good of the other), I sacrifice all those "other others," as Derrida calls them, to whom I owe fidelity. In tending to the needs of the singular, that is, I rescind my duty to all my other fellows in the sphere of the universal:

> As soon as I enter into a relation with the other, with the gaze, look, request, love, command, or call of the other, I know that I can respond only by sacrificing ethics, that is, by sacrificing whatever obliges me to also respond, in the same way, in the same instant, to all the others. I offer a gift of death, I betray, I don't need to raise my knife over my son on Mount Moriah for that. Day and night, at every instant, on all the Mount Moriahs of this world, I am doing that, raising my knife over what I love and must love, over those to whom I owe absolute fidelity, incommensurably.[72]

Caring for the singular requires each individual, in the moment of madness, to break free of the circle of exchange in which one is bound to all other others at a universal level. According to both Kierkegaard and Derrida, the decision to respond to the incoming of the other is a madness in that it requires a sacrifice of inestimable proportions. The gift of death "would be a gift," says Derrida, "only at the instant when the paradoxical instant (in the sense in which Kierkegaard says of the paradoxical instant of decision that it is madness) tears time apart."[73] That is, the present time is torn apart in the instant, or "moment," when the individual turns to the future as the time of the impossible and the gift. In the case of Abraham, "God" is the name of the absolute other who calls from beyond the circle of reappropriation or the sphere of the universal; "God," that is, demands that Abraham sacrifice what he loves most in the world, his son, in the name of a singular obligation beyond the law. "God," in other words, is the name, as Kierkegaard suggests in *The Concept of Anxiety,* for a future that is incognito, what he calls the "eternal," which preserves its relation to time in the paradoxical "moment" of decision. Abraham ruptures the circle of time so as to respond to God, while being incapable at the same time of extricating himself totally from the circle. Otherwise expressed, Abraham cannot free himself totally from the universal; even as he is raising the knife over Isaac's head, he remains obligated, bound both to the ethical and to God:

---

[72] Ibid., 68.
[73] Derrida, *Given Time,* 9.

In order to assume his absolute responsibility with respect to absolute duty, to put his faith in God to work, or to the test, he must also in reality remain a hateful murderer, for he consents to put to death. In both general and abstract terms, the absoluteness of duty, of responsibility, and of obligation certainly demands that one transgress ethical duty, although in betraying it one belongs to it and at the same time recognizes it. The contradiction and the paradox must be endured *in the instant itself*. The two duties must contradict one another, one must subordinate (incorporate, repress) the other. Abraham must assume absolute responsibility for sacrificing his son by sacrificing ethics, but in order for there to be a sacrifice, the ethical must retain all its value; the love for his son must remain intact, and the order of human duty must continue to insist on its rights.[74]

Abraham does not "know" what the outcome of his decision to respond to the singular call of the other, whose "unpronounceable" name is "God," will be. Deciding to affirm what cannot be calculated by any speculative program or teleology implies a certain degree of "nonknowledge," as Derrida calls it, in that the ramifications of a truly responsible decision can never be known before the fact. The time of the singular is always "out of joint" and nonmanifest; "it remains irreducible to presence or to presentation, it demands a temporality of the instant without ever constituting a present."[75] Its time is a secret time. From this Derrida draws the following conclusion:

If God is completely other, the figure or the name of the wholly other, then every other (one) is every (bit) other. *Tout autre est tout autre.* . . . [This] implies that God, as the wholly other, is to be found everywhere there is something of the wholly other. And since each of us, everyone else, each other is infinitely other in its absolute singularity, inaccessible, solitary, transcendent, nonmanifest, originarily nonpresent to my ego . . . then what can be said about Abraham's relation to God can be said about my relation without relation to every other (one) as every (bit) other [*tout autre comme tout autre*], in particular my relation to my neighbor or my loved ones who are as inaccessible to me, as secret and transcendent as Jahweh. Every other (in the sense of each other) is every bit other (absolutely other).[76]

This is not to suggest that Derrida believes that the otherness of the other "is" God; rather, it implies that the name "God" is adequate

---

[74] Derrida, *The Gift of Death*, 66.
[75] Ibid., 65.
[76] Ibid., 78.

to stand for what Caputo calls "the absolute secret which is nestled within the heart of each individual."[77] While this appears to have the general structural features of religion, it does not take the form of any particular religion as such.

We can best appreciate the significance of what is at issue here by analyzing what Derrida proceeds to say in *The Gift of Death* concerning Kierkegaard's relationship to Levinas. For in making some vital distinctions between Kierkegaard and Levinas, Derrida makes it possible for us to appreciate what Kierkegaard can offer at a social and political level more fully than we could have had he not extrapolated these differences. For if the themes of sacrifice, responsibility, and the secret can be shown to be central to what Derrida has to say about his other recent concerns, such as democracy and justice, then it is possible to argue that Kierkegaard's concerns are not far removed.

Derrida, Kierkegaard, Levinas

In the introduction I highlighted some salient distinctions between Kierkegaard and Levinas as a means of rebutting the latter's charge that Kierkegaard's is a "violent" philosophy, one that sacrifices the ethical relation to the other in the name of solitary egoism. While dealing with many of the same themes in *The Gift of Death*, Derrida argues that Levinas's critique of Kierkegaard, in which Levinas calls into question Kierkegaard's demarcation of the ethical from the religious, needs to be assessed with finer precision. Derrida contends that when Levinas rebukes Kierkegaard for prioritizing religion at the expense of ethics, he fails to appreciate that Kierkegaard's "religious stage" signals a reaffirmation of ethics in repetition. That is, Levinas, in Derrida's account, misses the proto-ethical dimension of Kierkegaard's radicalized Christianity. Furthermore, because Levinas, as Derrida remarks, "also wants to distinguish between the infinite alterity of God and the 'same' infinite alterity of every human, or of the other in general, then he cannot be said to be saying something different from Kierkegaard."[78] Otherwise expressed, if Levinas charges Kierkegaard with having emphasized the religious over the

---

[77] Caputo, "Instants, Secrets, and Singularities," 222.
[78] Derrida, *The Gift of Death*, 84.

ethical, Levinas is no less guilty for having made indistinguishable the "infinite alterity of god and that of every human."[79] In the final analysis, Levinas's ethics appears to have the same guiding impulse as Kierkegaard's religion:

> Even in its critique of Kierkegaard concerning ethics and generality Levinas's thinking stays within the game—the play of difference and analogy—between the face of God and the face of my neighbor, between the infinitely other as God and the infinitely other as another human. . . . [Levinas] cannot therefore distinguish so conveniently between the ethical and the religious. But for his part, in taking into account absolute singularity, that is, the absolute alterity obtaining in relations between one human and another, Levinas is no longer able to distinguish between the infinite alterity of God and that of every human. His ethics is already a religious one. In the two cases [Levinas's and Kierkegaard's] the border between the ethical and the religious becomes more than problematic, as do all attendant discourses.[80]

Now *The Gift of Death* makes clear that in Derrida's own work "the border between the ethical and the religious becomes more than problematic." Derrida's thinking is driven by a Kierkegaardian spirit to the extent that it " 'repeats' the possibility of religion without religion" by permitting "a discourse to be developed without reference to religion as institutional dogma," or a "genealogy of thinking concerning the possibility and essence of the religious that doesn't amount to an article of faith."[81] As I have noted, "God" signifies for Derrida the secret, the secret of what confounds the anticipation of full self-certainty. This is why Derrida is closer to Kierkegaard than he is to Levinas. For Kierkegaard's God is one who identifies with the singularity of existing beings, with those who have no safeguards under the law, and with those whose welfare is not guaranteed by ethics—those, in other words, who are foreign to the established order because they are unable to become fully disclosed in the manner that Hegelian *Sittlichkeit* demands. This is why Kierkegaard's religion should also be considered a religion without (institutionalized, established) religion.

---

[79] Ibid.
[80] Ibid., 83–84.
[81] Ibid., 49.

If observed from the point of view of each author's critique of Hegelianism, the differences between Kierkegaard and Derrida on the one hand and Levinas on the other become even more apparent and pronounced. While it may be argued, as it has been recently by Mark Taylor and Merold Westphal, among others,[82] that from this perspective the Kierkegaardian and Levinasian projects converge at many crucial junctures, the fundamental distinctions should not be overlooked. Indeed, while it is true that such predominant themes as "the Other," "the singular," and the notion of "communication," worked out in *Otherwise Than Being or Beyond Essence*,[83] have a distinctly Kierkegaardian ring to them, it is not correct to argue that for these reasons Kierkegaard and Levinas should be thought of as fellow travelers. It can be seen quite clearly why this is the case by returning briefly to Derrida's confrontation with Levinas in "Violence and Metaphysics."[84] In this text Derrida attempts to correct Levinas's reading of Husserl and Hegel, and in so doing he inadvertently demonstrates how similar he and Kierkegaard are on the questions of "the Other," "the singular," and so forth. While it is quite straightforward to see why Derrida privileges the Kierkegaardian strategy over that employed by Levinas from a reading of *The Gift of Death* alone, "Violence and Metaphysics" gives greater substance to my claim that Derrida is more Kierkegaardian at heart than he is Levinasian.

Ostensibly, Levinas's objection to Hegelian phenomenology in *Totality and Infinity* is similar in tone to that developed by both Kierkegaard and Derrida in their respective corpuses:

> Hegelian phenomenology, where self-consciousness is the distinguishing of what is not distinct, expresses the universality of the same identifying itself in the alterity of objects thought and despite the opposition of self to self. "I distinguish myself from myself; and

---

[82] See Mark C. Taylor, "Infinity," in *Altarity*, 185–216; Merold Westphal, "The Transparent Shadow: Kierkegaard and Levinas in Dialogue," in Matuštík and Westphal, *Kierkegaard in Post/Modernity*, 265–81.

[83] Emmanuel Levinas, *Otherwise Than Being or Beyond Essence*, trans. Alphonso Lingis (The Hague: Martinus Nijhoff, 1981).

[84] For a comprehensive guide to the Levinas-Derrida relationship, see Simon Critchley, *The Ethics of Deconstruction: Derrida and Levinas* (Oxford: Blackwell, 1992). See also my "The Politics of Exodus: 'Hospitality' in Derrida, Kierkegaard, and Levinas," in *The International Kierkegaard Commentary*, vol. 16, "Works of Love," ed. Robert L. Perkins (Macon: Mercer University Press, 1999), 167–92.

therein I am immediately aware that this factor distinguished from me is not distinguished. I, the selfsame being, thrust away from myself; but this which is distinguished, which is set up as unlike me, is immediately on its being distinguished no distinction for me." The difference is not a difference; the I, as other, is not an "other." . . . The I that repels the self, lived as repugnance, the I riveted to itself, lived as ennui, are modes of self-consciousness and rest on the unrendable identity of the I and the self.[85]

Once again, according to Levinas, the "I" as singular being is thought of as a mere moment in the dialectic of the same; in other words, the otherness of the other, the other's "alterity" (what Kierkegaard calls "residual incommensurability," and Derrida, "*différance*"), is ultimately subsumed in **Geist**'s drive to become fully reconciled with itself. Levinas considers Hegel to be promoting "the concreteness of egoism," or a desire that is motivated by a will to make the other "my" alter ego. The way to escape such narcissistic egoism, according to Levinas, is through an affirmation of the other as "absolutely Other," as "the Stranger who disturbs the being at home with oneself [*le chez soi*]."[86] The Other (*l'autrui*), as absolutely Other, emerges in and through the ethical relationship I have with the other in what Levinas terms the "face-to-face" encounter. Of this he says:

A relation whose terms do not form a totality can hence be produced within the general economy of being only as proceeding from the I to the other, as a *face to face*, as delineating a distance in depth—that of conversation, of goodness, of desire—irreducible to the distance the synthetic activity of the understanding establishes between the diverse terms, other with respect to one another, that lend themselves to its synoptic operation. The I is not a contingent formation by which the same and the other, as logical determinations of being, can in addition be reflected within a thought.[87]

In the face-to-face encounter, the self does not determine the nature of the other in terms of commonality or analogy, but in terms of its absolute dissimilarity, its irreducible and infinite transcendence.

[85] Emmanuel Levinas, *Totality and Infinity: An Essay on Exteriority*, trans. Alphonso Lingis (Pittsburgh: Duquesne University Press, 1969), 36–37.
[86] Ibid., 39.
[87] Ibid.

This signals the truly ethical moment between the self and the other
that Hegel never took account of:

> Ethical subjectivity dispenses with the idealizing subjectivity of ontol-
> ogy which reduces everything to itself. The ethical "I" is subjectivity
> precisely in so far as it kneels before the other, sacrificing its own
> liberty to the more primordial call of the other. For me, the freedom
> of the subject is not the highest or primary value. The heteronomy of
> our response to the human other, or to God as the absolutely Other,
> precedes the autonomy of our subjective freedom. As soon as I ac-
> knowledge that it is "I" who am responsible, I accept that my freedom
> is anteceded by an obligation to the other.[88]

Such a notion of responsibility, which takes the form of a response
to the other who "precedes the autonomy of our subjective freedom," would not be alien to the notions of responsibility developed
by both Kierkegaard and Derrida; indeed, much of what Levinas
writes on the primordial call issued by the other has inspired and
influenced not only Derrida, but a host of contemporary thinkers.
Derrida's objection, therefore, is not aimed at the main thrust of
Levinas's work.

Derrida does see a problem, however, in Levinas's contention that
the other is somehow *totally* asymmetrical, *totally* different, or *absolutely* exterior. In a discussion of Husserl's "Fifth Cartesian Meditation" and its relationship to Levinas's thought, Derrida launches a
critique of this Levinasian thesis.[89] His argument centers around

---

[88] Emmanuel Levinas, "Ethics of the Infinite," in Kearney, *Dialogues with Contemporary Continental Thinkers*, 63.

[89] For those who might consider it unusual to speak of Kierkegaard and Husserl
in the same context, it is worthwhile to observe the manner in which Caputo deftly
draws these ostensibly dissimilar thinkers together by way of the concept of repetition in *Radical Hermeneutics*. Maurice Nathanson, however, provides the most convincing evidence that Husserl and Kierkegaard have something in common. Upon
stating that "it should be clear to any reader of Kierkegaard and Husserl that their
views of reason involve divergent conceptions of the nature of man," Nathanson
reports the following: "That such divergence did not keep Husserl from appreciating
Kierkegaard is attested to by Lev Shestov, who writes: 'Learning that I had never
read Kierkegaard, Husserl began not to ask but to demand—with enigmatic insistence—that I acquaint myself with the works of the Danish thinker. How was it
that a man whose whole life had been a celebration of reason should have led me
to Kierkegaard's hymn to the absurd?' " Maurice Nathanson, *Edmund Husserl: Philosopher of Infinite Tasks* (Evanston: Northwestern University Press, 1973), 166 n.
20.

Levinas's claim that Husserl's notion of "analogical appresentation" ends up reducing the other to the same; that is, Levinas contends that when Husserl argues in favor of analogical appresentation as the way the other as other becomes present to my ego, he ignores the other's undelimitable transcendence. For as Derrida remarks, "to make the other an alter ego, Levinas says frequently, is to neutralize its absolute alterity."[90]

In this context, Derrida's defense of Husserl contra Levinas is significant in that it strikes a blow, albeit subtle, at the heart of the Levinasian project, one that, it might be argued, Levinas struggled all his life to recover from. Derrida neatly synthesizes the core of his disagreement in the following paragraph:

> [Husserl] is concerned with describing how the other *as other*, in its irreducible alterity, is presented to me. Is presented to me . . . as originary nonpresence. It is the other as other which is the ego's phenomenon: the phenomenon of a certain non-phenomenality which is irreducible for the ego as ego in general (the eidos ego). For it is impossible to encounter the alter ego (in the very form of the encounter described by Levinas), impossible to respect it in experience and in language, if this other, in its alterity, does not *appear* for an ego (in general). One could neither speak, nor have any sense of the totally other, if there was not a phenomenon of the totally other, or evidence of the totally other as such. No one more than Husserl has been sensitive to the singular and irreducible style of this evidence, and to the original non-phenomenalization indicated within it.[91]

In appearing to the ego phenomenologically, the other is not, for Husserl, reducible to the same; for in the very act of appearing, the other, *qua* alter ego, shows itself to be somewhat "non-phenomenalizable." To be totally other, simply stated, requires that the other be somewhat **known** to the ego, for if the other were not similar (analogical) to the ego, the ego would simply have no way of identifying it *as* other. The upshot of Derrida's argument is that what is absolutely other is only absolutely other because we **experience** it as such. "To make the other an alter ego," therefore, far from "neutralizing its absolute alterity," allows its alterity to be affirmed. Derrida continues:

---

[90] Derrida, "Violence and Metaphysics," 123.
[91] Ibid.

The necessary reference to analogical appresentation, far from signify-ing an analogical and assimilatory reduction of the other to the same, confirms and respects separation, the unsurpassable necessity of (non-obedieative) mediation. If I did not approach the other by way of analogical appresentation, if I attained to the other immediately and originally, silently, in communion with the other's own experience, the other would cease to be the other. Contrary to appearances, the theme of appresentative transposition translates the recognition of the radical separation of the absolute origins, the relationship of absolved absolutes and nonviolent respect for the secret: the opposite of victori-ous assimilation.[92]

The reference to "the secret" at the end of this passage is im-mensely significant. As early as 1964, Derrida, contrary to the claims made by those who dispute the presence of an inherent ethical di-mension to his thought, was already focusing on the notion of in-commensurable singularity, which has become such a feature of so much of his recent work. This particular reference signifies that in-commensurability (the otherness of the other, the secret) cannot be affirmed unless the ego is related to the other; it is only as a result of recognizing sameness that we can say "yes" to otherness and separa-tion. As if to preempt himself by thirty years, Derrida writes of the other as "the stranger" (following Levinas in this) whose singularity is irreducible to full objective scrutiny, but who must be *recognized* as stranger for this to be ascertained:

The stranger is infinitely other because by his essence no enrichment of his profile can give me the subjective face of his experience *from his perspective*, such as he has lived it. Never will his experience be given to me originally, like everything which is *mir eigenes*, which is *proper* to me. This transcendence of the nonproper no longer is that of the entirety, always inaccessible on the basis of always partial at-tempts: transcendence of *Infinity*, not of *Totality*.[93]

Husserl, according to Derrida, legitimates his use of the term "to-tally other" by virtue of the fact that he acknowledges "an inten-tional modification of the ego" through analogical appresentation. Levinas, on the other hand, refuses to entertain such a modification. To do such a thing "would be a violent and totalitarian act for him."

---

[92] Ibid., 124.
[93] Ibid.

Consequently, assesses Derrida, Levinas "deprives himself of the very foundation and possibility of his own language"; that is, "What authorizes him to say 'infinitely other' if the infinitely other does not appear as such in the zone he calls the same?"[94] This question calls Levinas to account for his belief that the otherness of the other is in some sense infinite, that it is always already outside or exterior to the order of the same.

The alter ego, argues Derrida, is somewhat the same, in that it is an ego, and yet it is other by virtue of the fact that it too can say "ego" or "I." The other (alter), in saying "ego," separates itself from all other egos in the same space:

> The egoity of the other permits him to say "ego" as I do; and this is why he is Other, and not a stone, or a being without speech *in my real economy*. This is why, if you will, he is a face, can speak to me, understand me, and eventually command me. Dissymmetry itself would be impossible without this symmetry, which is not of the world, and which, having no real aspect, imposes no limit upon alterity and dissymmetry—makes them possible, on the contrary. This dissymmetry is an *economy* in a new sense; a sense which would probably be intolerable to Levinas.[95]

Derrida is here expressing what he has not ceased to enunciate in many different ways and forms since this early confrontation with Levinas, and most especially in his treatment of the gift: we are always already caught inside a tradition or a dialectical economy; we are, that is, claimed by forces, such as language and the law, that precede us and determine our beliefs and practices. For Derrida there can be no escape from the circle or economy of exchange; we can push against its limits—"tear time apart," as he puts it—but we are incapable of going outside it into some absolutely exterior site. In Derrida's language, we can strive after the gift, but once the gift is presented it is simultaneously annulled. Derrida could very well be asking Levinas in this context, as he asks his reader in *Given Time*, to "give economy a chance." For it is only in being with the other that we can recognize the other as other, as one whose singularity is irreducible to my phenomenological gaze (*différance*). This is why I have insisted throughout this work on the need to appreciate the

---

[94] Ibid., 125.
[95] Ibid., 125–26.

importance of Hegel for both Kierkegaard and Derrida. While it is obvious that both authors reject the teleological impetus of the Hegelian logic and dialectic as a bookbinding system, each nevertheless recognizes how right, up to a point, Hegel was:

> Despite the logical absurdity of this formulation, this economy is the transcendental symmetry of two empirical asymmetries. The other, for me, is an ego which I know to be in relation to me as an other. Where have these two movements been better described than in *The Phenomenology of Mind*? The movement of transcendence toward the other, as invoked by Levinas, would have no meaning if it did not bear within it, as one of its essential meanings, that in my ipseity I know myself to be other for the other.[96]

We are always in the midst of the flow of existence, which amounts to saying that we are embedded in determined contexts with others. Hegel's genius lay in showing how identity is formed in and through mutual recognition between conscious beings in such contexts. Individuals, that is, come to a knowledge of themselves only by recognizing themselves as the other of other individuals. Hegel and Husserl, therefore, while always in need of deconstruction for their respective tendencies toward absolute knowledge/closure and pure eidetics, are two fundamental sources of the specifically Derridean approach to the question of the other. We can see how clearly Derrida appreciates this in one of his most anti-Levinasian statements concerning the nature of "narcissism":

> There is not narcissism and non-narcissism; there are narcissisms that are more or less comprehensive, generous, open, extended. What is called non-narcissism is in general but the economy of a much more welcoming, hospitable narcissism, one that is much more open to the experience of the other as other. I believe that without a movement of narcissistic reappropriation, the relation to the other would be absolutely destroyed, it would be destroyed in advance. The relation to the other—even if it remains asymmetrical, open, without possible appropriation—must trace a movement of reappropriation in the image of oneself for love to be possible, for example.[97]

In highlighting the differences between Derrida and Levinas, I wish is to demonstrate why it is a mistake to think of the Kierke-

---

[96] Ibid., 126.
[97] Derrida, "There Is No *One* Narcissism," in *Points*, 199.

gaardian project in Levinasian terms. Kierkegaard anticipates Derrida's critique of Levinas by following a line of reflection which argues that the "wholly other" is not "*absolutely* other" in Levinas's sense, but is the otherness that becomes apparent in and through the dialectic of ego and alter ego. The individual, that is, comes to know that the other is irreducibly incommensurable with the order of the same, or comes to the realization that there is something secret or nonmanifest about the other, not because the other is "*infinitely* other," but because the alter ego's experience of the world is different from the ego's for the simple reason that they say "I" from two distinct perspectives. When Derrida speaks of the need for narcissisms he is merely reiterating this point. Unless I can identify myself to a certain degree in the other, how can I come to love that other? There can indeed be non-narcissism in moments of self-abandon and sacrifice. Such is what occurs in the case of Abraham. But this does not mean that Abraham escapes the economy of exchange and reappropriation totally; in saying "yes" to the other, he welcomes the foreign in an instant of madness. This is the point at which the circle ruptures and the circular time of the dialectic slips out of joint. Abraham does, however, return to the economy once he goes through the ordeal of the double bind. He is both inside and outside the law (economic and legal)—he is never exterior to it in any absolute sense. He is, in other words, both inside and outside ethics, at once bound not only by the ethical demand placed upon him by the universal but also by the obligation he has to the singular other whose time is always disjointed, never circular. Abraham, we might say, is conscious of the fact that once the gift of death is presented to the other, it is automatically annulled.

The upshot of this detour into the Derrida-Levinas debate is that while many parallels announce themselves between Kierkegaard/Derrida and Levinas, there is ultimately a divergence of thought that is so profound that it must be stressed and taken account of in any attempt to situate these authors within a common context and conversation. In so doing, the originality of both the Kierkegaardian and Derridean approaches becomes all the more evident. Kierkegaard and Derrida could never subscribe to a notion of God as that which is *totally* heterogeneous to the circle of exchange or totally other; on the other hand, neither could they affirm the Hegelian God, who is totally time-bound and subjectivized. "God," for both these thinkers, appears and yet does not appear, is manifest and yet nonmanifest. In Kierkegaard's language, God is a *"sign* of contradiction": he appears as one who takes the side of the most wretched, while at the same time being incognito. He is at once both in time, in the form of a "poor existing individual," and outside the temporal horizon as that which, in the instant of madness, breaks up the circular economy. This is why, in the act of repetition, in that moment when, through double reflection or faith, we affirm what is beyond the purview of established (institutionalized) speculative reason, "metaphysics comes to grief."

But for Levinas, the Other, as *absolutely* different, is still caught within a metaphysical bind. Strictly speaking, the Other is "beyond" both the physical and the political. I am using "the political" here in the sense Derrida gives to it in *Limited INC* when he remarks that the determination of each context is a political act in that "it implies, insofar as it involves a determination, a certain type of non—'natural' relationship to others."[98] Levinas's "Other" or "Infinite," that is, precedes all such political totalities. Such a conclusion is founded on his assumption that the ethical precedes the political. But both Kierkegaard and Derrida are sensitive to the fact that we are always already inside the "present age" or the given actuality, that what one calls the ethical order must be reclaimed once the madness of the teleological suspension of the law has passed. We are, in other words, bound to the ethical order while simultaneously being alert to the call of what is repressed and oppressed by it. Responsibility means responding to the call of one's tradition, one's political totality, while concurrently responding to what is outside or excluded by that tradition. This is the way the God-man and Abraham both personify the type of hypervigilance espoused by Kierkegaard and Derrida. Caputo explains:

> The Levinasian gesture that requires deconstruction, even demythologization, is to reify this infinity, to make it a metaphysical being—which Levinas then cannot call Being and will not call a mere fiction. The Levinasian gesture is like the Heideggerian to just this extent: that it attributes actuality or reality to what it valorizes, that it claims this infinity is real, *ad literam, ad infinitum.* But in Derrida, the quasi infinity of undeconstructible justice is neither Being nor otherwise

---

[98] Derrida, *Limited INC*, 136.

than Being; the excess is not the excess of being but the excess of a linguistic performance, an excess within the operations made possible and impossible by *différance*, in response to the singularity lying on the edge of *différance*. In Derrida, infinity means a hyperbolic responsiveness and responsibility, a hyperbolic sensitivity.[99]

Responding Justly

In their similar responses to the needs of the singular other, both Kierkegaard and Derrida displays a strongly political and social dimension. In their attempts to keep the established order—as a political totality in which each individual is ineluctably situated—responsive to the call of the other, they activate what Derrida refers to as "the politics of exodus, of the emigré."[100] Such a politics acquires its impulse from the Abrahamic strategy of teleologically suspending the ethical, as the juridical sphere, with the aim of welcoming the other whose needs are not tended to by the law, those who, like the gift, exceed the circular (Hegelian) economy of exchange. Abraham, as de Silentio remarks, is an emigrant from the sphere of the universal. He takes leave of his ethical sensibility, or his duty as a participant in the daily affairs of the state, in order to affirm what is incommensurable with the given actuality. In so doing, he pushes up against the borders of the circle in the hope that he might identify a small perforation through which the other may come. Like all nomadic wanderers, he does not *know* where exactly he is supposed to be going or where his home is.

More specifically, Kierkegaard and Derrida are not merely cognizant of the ethical implications of the Abrahamic story. They are equally alert to its political implications, because for them genuine responsibility is as much a political gesture as an ethical one. This is why Derrida interprets Abraham's radical responsiveness as a will to see justice done. For Derrida, as for Kierkegaard, the law, as that which guarantees the autonomy of the universal or the state, is, like any text, the product of a play of signifiers or the result of non-natural relationships formed between individuals. When Hegel asserts, therefore, that the law is the material manifestation of *Geist*'s

---

[99] John D. Caputo, "Hyperbolic Justice: Mythologizing Differently with Derrida and Levinas," in *Demythologizing Heidegger*, 200.
[100] Derrida, "Deconstruction and the Other," 120.

divine design, he is, for these thinkers, overlooking the fact that as
an instance of "writing," the law is revisable, repeatable, and reiter-
able. The origin of the law, therefore, is to a certain degree "mystical" due to its being the effect of a differential play. Laws, as Derrida
asserts, have no grounds or foundations as such:

> Since the origin of authority, the foundation or ground, the position
> of the law can't by definition rest on anything but themselves, they
> are themselves a violence without ground. Which is not to say that
> they are in themselves unjust, in the sense of "illegal." They are
> neither legal nor illegal in their founding moment. They exceed the
> opposition between founded and unfounded, or between any founda-
> tionalism or anti-foundationalism. Even if the success of performa-
> tives that found law or right (for example, and this is more than an
> example, of a state as guarantor of a right) presupposes earlier condi-
> tions and conventions (for example in the national or international
> arena), the same "mystical" limit will reappear at the supposed origin
> of said conditions, rules or conventions, and at the origin of their dom-
> inant interpretation.[101]

As Climacus reminds us, "faith is a *happy* passion." The fact that
Abraham deconstructs the order of the calculable—or the time of
systematic bookbinding, in which the conclusion is foreseen or anticipated as the final stage in the teleological scheme—should not
come as bad news. Faith, as a passion for the impossible, for what
exceeds the horizon of absolute knowledge, is not bad news, but
good news that should indeed make us happy. "We may even see in
[the fact that law is deconstructible]," according to Derrida, "a
stroke of luck for politics, for all historical progress."[102] Hence the
teleological suspension of the ethical, in which the knight of faith
makes way for the incoming of the other, is good news for both
politics and historical progress, in that it implies that historical becoming is not stilled once the end of the world history is announced
by Hegel.

As I have argued, however, the individual can never be totally outside the political or established order: although Abraham could not
speak any universal language, he nevertheless had to speak and act

---

[101] Jacques Derrida, "Force of Law: 'The Mystical Foundation of Authority,'"
trans. Mary Quaintance, *Cardoza Law Review* 11 (1990): 943.

[102] Ibid., 944–45.

within the ethical sphere. If becoming responsible simply amounted to withdrawing from all social intercourse and severing all personal and political bonds, as some have claimed both Kierkegaard and Derrida suggest we do, it would not be a spiritual trial. Abraham's deconstruction of the law is a madness precisely because he must remain within the jurisdiction of the law while simultaneously answering the call of the other outside the law. The teleological suspension of the law thus takes place on the margins, somewhere between the law and what is to come—on the rim of the circle of exchange, so to speak.

Responding to the singular call of the other, affirming "the impossible," is for Kierkegaard what we might call a "hyper-ethical" sacrifice, or as Vigilius Haufniensis calls it, a "second ethics." In Derrida's lexicon, "second ethics" is equal to "justice."[103] By defining justice as "an experience of the impossible,"[104] Derrida rebuts those who would accuse him, and indeed Kierkegaard, of advocating a dangerous formalism; that is, there are those who argue that responding to the call of the other amounts to irresponsibility, in that "the other" we "must" affirm could very easily be any individual or group that has been marginalized, including those who cause suffering. By emphasizing deconstruction's passion for justice, however, Derrida proves himself to be affirming victims rather than the victimizers. The voice of the other, the voice of God that calls Abraham in both the Kierkegaardian and Derridean readings of this story, should not, therefore, be confused with "the call" that fundamentalists speak of when they come to account for and to justify their misdeeds. As we

---

[103] In recent years there has been a proliferation of texts dealing with Derrida's contentious notion of justice, the best of which are the following: Geoffrey Bennington, *Legislations: The Politics of Deconstruction* (London: Verso, 1994); Caputo, *Against Ethics*, "Hyperbolic Justice," "Commentary" in *Deconstruction in a Nutshell*, and *Prayers and Tears*; Drucilla Cornell, "The Violence of the Masquerade: Law Dressed Up as Justice," in *Working Through Derrida*, ed. Gary B. Madison (Evanston: Northwestern University Press, 1993), 77–93, and her excellent *Philosophy at the Limit* (New York: Routledge, 1992); Richard Kearney, *Poetics of Modernity* (Atlantic Highlands, N.J.: Humanities Press, 1995). For critical responses to the ethical dimension of Derrida's thought, see Richard J. Bernstein, *The New Constellation: The Ethical-Political Horizons of Modernity/Postmodernity* (Oxford: Polity Press, 1991), and "An Allegory of Modernity/Postmodernity: Habermas and Derrida," in Madison, *Working Through Derrida*, 204–29; Hilary Putnam, *Renewing Philosophy* (Cambridge: Harvard University Press, 1992), 108–33.
[104] Derrida, "Force of Law," 947.

saw in the previous chapter, Kierkegaard also considers identifying with the lowest, the victims, the "most wretched," as the most responsible way of challenging the established order. In answering the call, we respond, therefore, to the lowliest, whose singularity (hidden and secret) has been crushed by the law and who are urgently in need of some justice.

Justice is an experience of "the impossible" because it affirms that which disrupts the circular order of the same, of what surprises and shocks the systematic author. We could say that justice is the time of the singular or the "poor existing individual," a time that is out of joint with the teleological course of world history. Responding to those who call for justice requires, for both Kierkegaard and Derrida, a judgment, or as seen in the preceding analyses of both *Given Time* and *The Gift of Death,* a genuine decision (an either/or) that seeks to generate a state of affairs in which the other is made welcome in the prevailing economy. In this case, it is not a matter of applying a law or an ethical program, for this in no way amounts to a decision of the Kierkegaardian and Derridean kind; the law, that is, must be suspended when we attend to the welfare of the singular. This is so because to make an appeal for justice requires taking the side of those whose welfare is not protected under the law. To invoke *The Gift of Death* once again, the ethical order must be sacrificed in the moment of responsible decision, and yet—and herein lies the double bind—the law and the ethical sphere cannot be suspended for longer than the time it takes to make a decision. Derrida argues:

> I think that there is no justice without this experience, however impossible it may be, of aporia. Justice is an experience of the impossible. A will, a desire, a demand for justice whose structure wouldn't be an experience of aporia would have no chance to be what it is, namely a call for justice. Every time that something comes to pass or turns out well, every time that we placidly apply a good rule to a particular case, to a correctly subsumed example, according to a determinant judgment, we can be sure that the law (*droit*) may find itself accounted for, but certainly not justice. Law (*droit*) is not justice. Law is the element of calculation, and it is just that there be law, but justice is incalculable, it requires us to calculate with the incalculable; and aporetic experiences are the experiences, as improbable as they are necessary, of justice, that is to say of moments in which the decision between just and unjust is never insured by a rule.[105]

---

[105] Ibid.

For Derrida, as for Kierkegaard, there must be laws and legal institutions to protect right and freedom. Once again, Abraham pushes
against the limits of the circle in order *to give* more than the law
requires, but he does not, like Levinas, seek to break free of the
circle. All he can say in response to the injunction is *"me voici!"*
("here I stand!") in the midst of existence. His aim, therefore, is not
to break the law, but to loosen it up slightly so that the voice of the
singular might be heard. To act on behalf of the singular individual
is to offend, as Kierkegaard has argued, speculative consciousness,
for such an action seeks not the assurances of a rule or a law, but the
groundlessness of Abrahamic faith. Faith itself is the madness of
acting without calculation. For both thinkers, justice and responsibility demand such an experience of aporia.

Derrida and Kierkegaard both consider the freedom of an individual to be central to any ethics of responsibility. Recall that Anti-
Climacus argues that the passionate self, the self that relates itself
to itself in double reflection or repetition, "is freedom." In order,
that is, for the self to make ethical judgments, one must have the
ability to choose between various options, or between conflicting
judgments. In Abraham's case, there was no "reason" as such for
him to make the decision he did; he could very easily have chosen
not to respond to the call of the other. According to Derrida, however, Abraham's action was just, for in the moment of decision when
he emigrated from the universal sphere of right and law, he made a
judgment that was not merely the application of a law or a rule, but
one in which he sought freely to suspend (*épokhè*) the law in the
name of singularity. Abraham, that is, recognized that the law does
not derive from nature, but is a contingently configured formation
that is forever susceptible to reinterpretation and repetition. He recognized, moreover, that answering the call of singularity does not
entail a dissolution of the law, but rather its "reinvention." If the law
is to be just, if it is to guarantee freedom and right, it must undergo
constant revision in response to those singular situations for which
the law has made no provision. Derrida describes what the repetition
of law entails:

> In short, for a decision to be just and responsible, it must, in its proper
> moment if there is one, be both regulated and without regulation: it
> must conserve the law and also destroy it or suspend it enough to

have to reinvent it in each case, rejustify it, at least reinvent it in the reaffirmation and the new and free confirmation of its principle. Each case is other, each decision is different and requires an absolutely unique interpretation, which no existing, coded rule can or ought to guarantee absolutely.[106]

For a decision to be responsible and genuine—in other words, for it to be just—the individual must respond to the obligation the law places on him or her while responding at the same time to "the always heterogeneous and unique singularity of the unsubsumable example."[107] If one did not have to judge, as Abraham did, between one's obligation to the state or the universal order and one's obligation to the singular situation, a decision would not have been a responsible decision. Undecidability is thus the most fundamental requirement in the decision-making procedure. For in any decision worthy of its name, we have no way of knowing what the precise ramifications of the decision will be. In Hegel's teleological scheme of ethics, each action has a purpose in the general drive toward self-knowledge. But in the ethics of responsibility endorsed by both Kierkegaard and Derrida, there is no such horizon toward which we are moving. All we can do is have faith, or believe that in the moment of decision we are acting in the best interests of justice and singularity:

> This "idea of justice" seems to me to be irreducible in its affirmative character, in its demand of gift without exchange, without circulation, without recognition or gratitude, without economic circularity, without calculation and without rules, without reason and without rationality. And so we can recognize in it, indeed accuse, identify a madness. And perhaps another sort of mystique. And deconstruction is mad about this kind of justice. Mad about this desire for justice.[108]

The desire for justice demands that decisions be made, not confidently, but in a moment of madness. Undecidability is not, therefore, as the charge suggests, "indecision," but a decision made without the support or application of a program, one that endeavors to privilege singularity over universality.

According to Derrida, political and ethical decisions are urgently

---

[106] Ibid., 961.
[107] Ibid., 963.
[108] Ibid., 965.

demanded; a truly just decision "cannot furnish itself with infinite information and the unlimited knowledge of conditions, rules or hypothetical imperatives that could justify it."[109] Derrida is not suggesting here that decisions should be made without deliberation—he is not, that is, supporting a form of unbridled decisionism. No, both Kierkegaard and Derrida recognize the importance of reflection; we saw, for example, how in the course of Kierkegaard's assessment of the "present age" he stresses that "reflection is not the evil, but the state of reflection, stagnation in reflection, is the abuse and the corruption that occasion retrogression by transforming the prerequisites into evasions" (PA, 96). "Double reflection," or engaged critical reflection that results in firm resolution, is the form that Kierkegaard recommends we practice. Derrida likewise is committed to ethico-political deliberation once it is recognized that it must be followed urgently by "the moment of decision, *as such*." For justice does not wait; it cannot wait:

> To be direct, simple and brief, let us say this: a just decision is always required immediately, "right away." It cannot furnish itself with infinite information and the unlimited knowledge of conditions, rules or hypothetical imperatives that could justify it. And even if it did have all that at its disposal, even if it did give itself the time, all the time and all the necessary facts about the matter, the moment of *decision, as such*, always remains a finite moment of urgency and precipitation, since it must not be the consequence or the effect of this theoretical or historical knowledge, of this reflection or this deliberation, since it always marks the interruption of the juridico- or ethico- or politico-cognitive deliberation that precedes it, that must precede it. The instant of decision is a madness says Kierkegaard. This is particularly true of the instant of the just decision that must rend time and defy dialectics.[110]

Justice, like the gift, is *the* impossible. It is what we madly desire, and yet it is impossible to realize *as such*. Justice can never be "presented," it will never make a pure gift of itself, in that once it is appropriated in the instant of responsible decision it translates into law, and law, as we have seen, is not justice. Derrida is keen to point out that when he talks of this "idea of justice," he has no specific

---

[109] Ibid., 967.
[110] Ibid.

"idea" as such in his mind. Justice, to reiterate, is neither a *telos* nor a horizon that will become manifest in its fullness at some specific time in the future. Rather, it remains extraneous to the economy of exchange, for no particular context is just all the way down. Justice, thus, is always "to come."

We can say, therefore, that to desire justice is to desire what the law excludes or represses; because every situation that demands justice is singular and unique, justice has no single, unique form. This is why it is always to come, in that there will always be individual demands for justice. And for Derrida, the political space is where such a cry for justice can always be heard:

> Politicization, for example, is interminable even if it cannot and should not ever be total. To keep this from becoming a truism or a triviality, we must recognize in it the following consequence: each advance in politicization obliges one to reconsider, and so to reinterpret the very foundations of law such as they had previously been calculated or delimited. This was true for example in the Declaration of the Rights of Man, in the abolition of slavery, in all the emancipatory battles that remain and will have to remain in progress, everywhere in the world, for men and for women.[111]

Abraham is caught between the law and justice; his is a passion for the singular, for the one whose time is not of the present or the given actuality. Justice calls to him to resign, in the moment of a mad decision, from the universal order so as to respond to the claim the outsider places on him. Abraham's is a politics of exodus, a politics of liberation in which the marginalized and subservient are released from the bondage of political and legal institutions that have lost their sense of fair play and justice. Abraham's faith, his hope in and affirmation of what is to come—which of course requires a good deal of imagination (the faculty *instar omnium*) and double reflection—has, we may conclude, weighty political significance.

Democracy and Community

The way to understand and appreciate how Derrida's notion of what he calls a "democracy to come" relates to Kierkegaard's social and political thinking is to analyze the place of the category of "love"

---

[111] Ibid., 971.

in their respective discourses. I will argue that Derrida's themes of "hospitality" and "generosity," which underpin his theory of democracy, are closely related to what Kierkegaard sought to describe under the heading of "Christian love." Before moving on to such an analysis, however, I will look briefly at the nature of the relationship between the Derridean themes of justice and democracy. This will enable us to ascertain precisely how an Abrahamic politics of exodus can have practical political force.

Derrida's "Jew-Greek" notion of a "democracy to come" is guided by an Abrahamic scruple to secure justice for the émigré, the outsider, and the stranger, for those whose time is never circular but always out of joint. Derrida, like Kierkegaard, considers Abraham's spiritual trial as a political gesture that must be repeated time and again if a genuine ethics of responsibility is to be enacted. In a number of recent works, Derrida has set his mind to elaborating how this Abrahamic politics of exodus lies at the heart of his ideas of democracy, hospitality, and community.

In his controversial *Specters of Marx* (1993), Derrida begins with an "exordium," a technique borrowed no doubt from de Silentio's *Fear and Trembling*. Therein the author informs us that he is "getting ready to speak about ghosts, inheritance, and generations, generations of ghosts, which is to say about certain *others* who are not present, nor presently living, either to us, in us, or outside us, it is in the name of *justice*."[112] Derrida, that is, wishes once more to address the question of justice, as something that is not yet, whose time is not of the present, for such a time is only that of "laws and rights." The time of justice is the time of those who have long since passed (*revenants*) and those whose time is still to come (*arrivants*). Derrida is pledging himself in this context to a "politics of memory, of inheritance, and of generation":

> No justice . . . seems possible or thinkable without the principle of some *responsibility*, beyond all living present, within that which disjoins the living present, before the ghosts of those who are not yet born or who are already dead, be they victims of wars, political or other kinds of violence, nationalist, racist, colonialist, sexist, or other kinds of exterminations, victims of the oppressions of capitalist imperialism

---

[112] Jacques Derrida, *Specters of Marx: The State of the Debt, the Work of Mourning, and the New International*, trans. Peggy Kamuf (New York: Routledge, 1994), xix.

or any other forms of totalitarianism. Without this *non-contemporaneity with itself of the living present*, without that which secretly unhinges it, without this responsibility and this respect for justice concerning those who *are not there*, of those who are no longer or who are not yet *present and living*, what sense would there be to ask the question "where?" "where tomorrow?" "whither?"[113]

Derrida makes a plea here for the victims of suffering, for those who have long since passed and for those who are yet to arrive. To seek justice, he argues, is to stand on the side of the victim. Let us recall how both Kierkegaard and Derrida have always been alert to the voices of those who are non-contemporaneous. Both these thinkers consistently undermine the hubris of systematic bookbinders who seek to still time by containing existence and "bad writing" within a program or a speculative *Encyclopaedia*. For both, however, all particular contexts are undelimitable; they remain open in spite of the best efforts of those whose aim it is to totalize and circumscribe. Such "non-contemporaneity with itself of the living present" is what keeps the context open to the call of those who are strangers to the system, those "poor existing individuals" and singular others. Theirs is a future time, one that is not teleologically programmed or circular. Theirs is not the time of the possible, but of the impossible.

To break free of the world-historical process, to push against the borders of the circular economy of dialectics, as both Abraham and the God-man do, is to have respect for those who are not yet there, for the stranger and the foreigner. One should strive in this instance to sacrifice the self in the name of the other, to give up being at home with oneself in order to let the other be. This is a gift that the self presents to the singular other; it requires that the self surrender all it properly owns within the realm of *Sittlichkeit*.

As I have suggested, however, neither Derrida nor Kierkegaard is opposed to tradition or to communal bonds; indeed, for these thinkers there can be nothing outside of political contexts. What they do oppose is the propensity of communities and political totalities to establish rigid borders that maintain a culture of closure toward the other. We saw how both Anti-Climacus and de Silentio struggle against the deification of both the state and speculative or objective reason, and how Derrida from the very outset of his career has chal-

---

[113] Ibid.

lenged the established order in the name of the dispossessed and the exiled. In this way they keep a check on hegemonies of all forms. The politics of exodus, therefore, does not aim toward either absolute unity or diversity; it seeks rather to keep existing formations or contexts on the lookout for singularities. Abraham, remember, teleologically suspends the ethical only long enough for the requirements of singularity to be attended to. Derrida's remark in a recent roundtable discussion of these matters crystallizes what is at stake here:

> I do not think we have to choose between unity and multiplicity. Of course, deconstruction—that has been its strategy up to now—insisted not on multiplicity for itself but on heterogeneity, the difference, the disassociation, which is absolutely necessary for the relationship to the other. The privilege granted to unity, to totality, to organic ensembles, to community as a homogenized whole—this is a danger for responsibility, for decision, for ethics, for politics. That is why I insisted on what prevents unity from closing upon itself, from being closed up. This is not only a matter of description, of saying that this is the way it is. It is a matter of accounting for the possibility of responsibility, of a decision, of ethical commitments. To understand this, you have to pay attention to what I would call singularity.[114]

For Derrida, as we know, singularity "is not simple unity or multiplicity": identity is always the effect of *différance,* or as Kierkegaard would say, identity is something that, in the process of relating itself to itself, relates itself to another. Identity for both these thinkers does not presuppose autonomy, but implies that the self is ineluctably related to the other (both past and future). There can be responsibility and ethical commitments only when this alterity is affirmed as that which is non-contemporaneous with the present time of the self. In other words, justice amounts to expanding the borders in order to welcome the foreigner. Such is what is meant, therefore, when it is suggested that the self should sacrifice being at home with itself (self-presence) so as to let the other come:

> There is no culture or cultural identity without this difference *with itself.* A strange and slightly violent syntax: "with itself" [*avec soi*] also means "at home (with itself)" [*chez soi*]. . . . In this case, self-differ-

---

[114] Jacques Derrida, "The Villanova Roundtable," in Caputo, *Deconstruction in a Nutshell,* 13.

ence, difference to itself [*différance à soi*], that which differs and diverges from itself, of itself, would also be the *difference (from) with
itself* [*différance (d') avec soi*], a difference at once internal and irreducible to the "at home (with itself)" [*chez soi*].[115]

Such an opening toward the time of the victim, the stranger, and
the foreigner requires that we "change destinations," that we jettison the notion of a teleologically structured identity and go "beyond
our heading."[116] With this metaphor Derrida is suggesting that for
justice and democracy to come, we must move beyond the supposed
course of Greco-European time toward "the heading of the other,"
which is "perhaps the first condition of an identity or identification
that is not an egocentrism destructive of oneself and the other."[117]
Like de Silentio's Abraham, who heads off in an unknown direction,
rupturing the circle of reappropriation as he goes, the one who takes
the new heading must push against the limits of the border in order
to offer unbounded generosity and hospitality to those who have no
paragraph in the system. This is how one "relates oneself to oneself,"
or the way in which identity is subjected to rigorous appraisal. Genuine responsibility demands that we open our borders in order to affirm the other whose unanticipatable entry unsettles self-security,
while concomitantly maintaining some sense of identity: this is the
aporia, or the double bind facing those who wish to seek justice in
the madness of a teleological suspension:

> Neither monopoly nor dispersion, therefore. This is, of course an apo-
> ria, and we must not hide it from ourselves. I will even venture to say
> that ethics, politics, and responsibility, *if there are any*, will only ever
> have begun with the experience and experiment of the aporia. . . . The
> condition of possibility of this thing called responsibility is a certain
> *experience and experiment of the possibility of the impossible: the testing
> of the aporia* from which one may invent the only *possible invention,
> the impossible invention*.[118]

For Derrida, therefore, a community based on the politics of exodus would not be homogeneous or totalizing. His hope is for a "com-

[115] Derrida, *The Other Heading*, 9–10.
[116] Ibid., 15.
[117] Ibid.
[118] Ibid., 41.

munity without community,"[119] or a community that is open to the other who calls for mercy. Because some individual or group will always be excluded from "our" community, Derrida's "*open* 'quasi'-community" is always to come. "It has an essential relation to the singularity of the event, of that which is coming but (therefore) 'has not happened.' "[120] Justice and democracy are what victims both past and present pray and hope for; each victim, that is, begs for an act of excessive generosity, for a gift that will tear the circular walls of *Sittlichkeit* apart. The response to such appeals is in each case different because injustice and exclusion take many forms. This is why responsibility requires an "impossible invention." Because we can never anticipate the incoming of a singular call for justice, there must be a moment of undecidability in which we try to invent an adequate response to meet the demands of the other issuing from a particular situation. But this can only last an instant, for justice and mercy cannot wait. Such an open community whose identity is always in question is indeed an "anarchic kingdom," one that is perpetually undergoing the most dramatic metamorphoses. Caputo explains:

> The community to come calls us from the future, alerting us to the walls that communities—European, American, and Chinese, Christian, Jewish and Islamic, here as everywhere, today as always, communities as such, by their very structure as community—throw up against the foreigner. The community to come calls up a certain generosity, calls for a gift of a "community without unity," at "loose ends," and invokes another, more flattering idea of community, as com-*munus*, with munificence and extravagance, in a community *without* community, as an identity which begs to differ with itself.
> Community. Hospitality. Welcome to the Other. Justice.[121]

A *Community of Neighbors*

Having outlined the various features of Derrida's notion of a democracy to come, I wish to complete this discussion by analyzing closely how all this relates to Kierkegaard's ethics of responsibility. As I said

---

[119] I are borrowing this phrase from John Caputo. See *Deconstruction in a Nutshell*, 106–25.

[120] Derrida, *Points*, 351.

[121] Caputo, *Deconstruction in a Nutshell*, 124.

above, the way to understand and appreciate how Derrida's notion of a community without community relates to Kierkegaard's social and political thinking is to analyze the place the category of "love" occupies in their respective discourses. Let us see why this is so.

While the theme of love is an abiding preoccupation for Kierkegaard, its role in Derrida's work is not so easily discernible. Apart from his discussion in *Glas* of Hegel's treatment of love in "The Spirit of Christianity and Its Fate," it is dealt with only sporadically.[122] Sparse as they might be, however, Derrida's allusions to love are of immense significance. The following comment from a 1982 interview with Christian Descamps underscores the relevance of love for any attempted deconstruction: "Deconstruction as such is reducible to neither a method nor an analysis (the reduction to simple elements); it gives beyond critical decision itself. This is why it is not negative, even though it has often been interpreted as such despite all sorts of warnings. For me it always accompanies an affirmative exigency, I would even say that it never proceeds without love."[123] To affirm the other, whose singular call for justice disrupts the economy of the same, is to love. Love in this context cannot be conflated, therefore, with a desire for recognition by the other, but takes the form of what Derrida calls a "renunciation" of one's self (*qua* presence) "which somehow surrenders to the impossible," or to the other-than-self. Unlike Hegel, who asserts that "ethical life, love, means precisely the giving up of particularity, of particular personality, and its extension to universality,"[124] Derrida considers love a way of transgressing the universal for the sake of the particular, or of teleologically suspending the ethical in the name of an other who is irreducible to the "we" of *Sittlichkeit*.

What is most notable, however, about Derrida's reflection on love is that he speaks of it in terms of a "letting be," that is, a form of *Gelassenheit* in the spirit of Eckhart and Heidegger.[125] To love only the same is not genuine love for Derrida, for even those with the hardest hearts love their own; to love, rather, is to release the other

---

[122] Derrida, *Glas*, 1–77. See also Caputo, *Prayers and Tears*.

[123] Derrida, "The Almost Nothing of the Unpresentable," in *Points*, 83.

[124] Hegel, *Lectures on the Philosophy of Religion: The Lectures of 1827* (1-vol. ed.), 427–28.

[125] A definitive study of the Eckhart-Heidegger connection is John D. Caputo, *The Mystical Element in Heidegger's Thought* (Athens: Ohio University Press, 1978).

from dialectical enclosure and circumscription, to let, in other words, the other come:

> As you describe this *Gelassenheit*, [one is] careful not to talk about love. . . . But why not recognize there love itself, that is, this infinite renunciation which somehow *surrenders to the impossible* [*se rend à l'impossible*]? To surrender to the other, and this is the impossible, would amount to giving oneself over in going toward the other, to coming toward the other but without crossing the threshold, and to respecting, to loving even the invisibility that keeps the other inaccessible. To surrendering one's weapons [*rendre les armes*]. . . . To give oneself up [*se rendre*] and to surrender one's weapons [*rendre les armes*] without defeat, without memory or plan of war: so that this renunciation not be another ruse of seduction or an added stratagem of jealousy.[126]

Derrida is calling here for a loosening up of the family scene, of the borders that divide "us" from "them," and for a laying down of defensive weapons. *Gelassenheit* means a love without jealousy, a love, that is, for every other, and not just for those with whom one has common cause. *Gelassenheit* is a giving without exchange and a generosity that exceeds demand. For Derrida, it signifies most especially a form of openness to the other that is motivated by a "belief in the worthiness of us all to be included in the [open quasi-] community."[127] To love the other is to respond to his or her appeal for justice and for democracy.

Now, while Kierkegaard does not talk of love in terms of *Gelassenheit*, his idea of "Christian love," developed and articulated in *Works of Love* (1847), comes close in many respects to this notion.[128] Kierkegaard's "Christian love," that is, also takes the form of a sur-

---

[126] Jacques Derrida, "Sauf le nom (Post-Scriptum)," in *On the Name*, trans. John Leavey, Jr. (Stanford: Stanford University Press, 1995), 74.

[127] Caputo, *Radical Hermeneutics*, 266.

[128] For more on the pivotal theme of love in the work of Kierkegaard see Martin Andic, "Confidence as a Work of Love," in *Kierkegaard on Art and Communication*, ed. George Pattison (New York: St. Martin's Press, 1992), 160–85; Elrod, *Kierkegaard and Christendom*, 164–92; Gouwens's fine discussion of these matters in *Kierkegaard as Religious Thinker*, 186–232; Louise Carroll Keeley, "Subjectivity and World in *Works of Love*," in Connell and Evans, *Kierkegaard's Vision of Community*, 96–108; Kirmmse, *Kierkegaard in Golden Age Denmark*, 306–28; Michael Plekon, "Kierkegaard the Theologian: The Roots of His Theology in *Works of Love*," in Connell and Evans, *Kierkegaard's Vision of Community*, 2–17; Walsh, *Living Poetically*, 243–66.

rendering to the impossible, or a sacrificing of one's self (*donner la mort*) *qua* ethical subject for the love of the one who is ground under by the law. Let us see how this is so.

Kierkegaard makes a vital distinction at many junctures throughout his authorship between what he terms "erotic love" (*Elskov*) and "Christian love" (*Kjerlighed*). Associated closely with erotic love is the classical virtue of "friendship," which takes the form of "passionate preferential love" (WL, 53). In other words, both erotic love and friendship, because they are shown only to those with whom we prefer to be associated, are types of "self-love," or prejudicial love: "Just as self-love selfishly embraces this one and only *self* that makes it self-love, so also erotic love's passionate preference selfishly encircles this one and only beloved, and friendship's passionate preference encircles this one and only friend. For this reason the beloved and the friend are called remarkably and profoundly, to be sure, the *other self*, the *other* I" (WL, 53). As in Hegel's reduction of the particular to the universal, or the "I" to the "we," the self that desires only itself sees the other not *as* other but as the same. The other is simply the "other I," the alter ego, the medium through which the self becomes identical with itself. In somewhat broader terms, loving of this kind leads to a cultivation of colonies "of the same in a culture of identity which gathers itself to itself in common defense against the other."[129] In such a culture, the walls of *Sittlichkeit* stand firm, are unshakable, and act as a protective device against the stranger and foreigner. Unlike Abraham, who sacrifices the universal so as to respond to the demand made by the wholly other, the self-lover gives of him- or herself only to receive in equal measure. Such love is not an excessive act of generosity toward the other, but an economic gesture of the most restricted kind: "When the lover or friend is able to love only this one single person in the whole world (which is a delight to the poet's ears), there is an enormous self-willfulness in this enormous devotion, and in his impetuous, unlimited devotion the lover is actually relating himself to himself in self-love" (WL, 55).

The way to break free of the circumscribing grip of self-love, according to Kierkegaard, is to cultivate "Christian love," or what we have been referring to as "self-denial." Otherwise stated, Christian

---

[129] Caputo, *Deconstruction in a Nutshell*, 115.

love endeavors to break the spell of self-love by introducing the concept of the "neighbor" (*Næste*). Kierkegaard defines the neighbor as one "who is nearer to you than anyone else, yet not in the sense of preferential love, since to love someone who in the sense of preferential love is nearer than anyone else is self-love" (WL, 21). "The neighbor," rather, "is what thinkers call 'the other,' " which means in effect that the neighbor is not anyone in particular, not one toward whom we show a particular predilection or personal preference—for "do not the pagans also do the same?"—but "all people" (WL, 21). Rather than construing the other in terms of one's own self, the one who practices self-denial loves the other simply as other. The neighbor is "self-denial's middle term that steps in between self-love's *I* and *I*, but also between erotic love's and friendship's *I* and the *other I*" (WL, 54). Unlike friendship and erotic love, both of which serve to cut the individual "off from everyone else" in that the friends or lovers "actually do become one self," love for the neighbor does not result in a dialectical union between self and other in which difference is negated; instead, it preserves each individual's singularity and alterity.

According to Kierkegaard, "God" is the decisive factor in neighborly love. For Kierkegaard, God is man's highest ethical criterion, the "offensive" prototype each individual is called upon to imitate. The individual who stands in contemporaneity with the God-man does not discriminate between the others with whom he or she comes in contact, for the God-man came not to take the side of any "chosen" or "elect" people, but of all peoples irrespective of political or religious affiliation. To love God, therefore—to imitate him or to accept him as the ideal—means that "you also love the neighbor and in the neighbor every human being." Christian love, therefore, does not discriminate on the basis of mere earthly distinctions. In fact, such love generates genuine equality between all: "**Love for the neighbor is therefore the eternal equality in loving,** but the eternal equality is the opposite of preference. This needs no elaborate development. Equality is simply not to make distinctions, and eternal equality is unconditionally not to make the slightest distinction. Preference, on the other hand, is to make distinctions; passionate preference is unqualifiedly to make distinctions" (WL, 58). This, of course, is not to suggest that Kierkegaard considers it essential that all differences between individuals should be nullified in neighborly love; he is not, that is, proposing a softer form of Hegelianism. For if this were the case he would be promoting the very form of "leveling" he is seeking to surmount. Kierkegaard's objective, rather, is to specify that singularity is best safeguarded in the context of a loosely bound kingdom of neighbors (near-dwellers). In such a kingdom, one denies one's self by letting the other be, which in turn engenders *genuine* equality between the self and the other: "In being king, beggar, rich man, poor man, male, female, etc., we are not like each other—therein we are indeed different. But in being the neighbor we are all unconditionally like each other. Dissimilarity is temporality's method of confusing that marks every human being differently, but the neighbor is eternity's mark—on every human being" (WL, 89). Christian love is "without why," a *Gelassenheit* that takes the form, as Derrida says, of a "coming toward the other but without crossing the threshold, and to respecting, to loving even the invisibility that keeps the other inaccessible." It is "a love without jealousy that would allow the other to be."[130] For Kierkegaard, in like manner, if love is to be released from "the sickness of jealousy," it must undergo "the change of eternity by becoming duty" (WL, 35).

Kierkegaard is arguing here for a notion of duty that, if observed, generates individual freedom and autonomy; that is, according to Kierkegaard, neither erotic love nor friendship can resolve in genuine freedom, for both are dependent forms of love. It must be stated, however, that such "duty" does not take the form of a moral imperative, but is more like an appeal or a call from the other, every other with whom we come into contact. It is only by letting the other go in self-denial (Christian love) that both the self and the other can acquire independence.

According to Kierkegaard, Christian love is the true "fulfilling of the Law."[131] I have argued that the community to come "calls up a certain generosity," or an excessive display of hospitality in which we respond to those pleas for justice and mercy that come from the other. Kierkegaard's belief that works of love fulfill the law is far from being at variance with this notion. For him, "the Law is the skeleton,

---

[130] Derrida, "Sauf le nom," 74.

[131] As we shall see, "to fulfill the law" in Kierkegaard's sense does not mean to act dispassionately in accordance with the dictates of universal law. It suggests rather a Derridean gesture of making the law responsive to those whose welfare it has failed to secure.

the bony structure, the dehydrated husk," while "love is the fullness," in that "it truly fulfills the law and more" (JP, 3:2403; WL,
408). Self-denial, or neighborly love, is a process of lifting the law,
suspending it momentarily for the sake of the "poor existing individual" who has been ground under by its universal dictates. In a manner reminiscent of Derrida, Kierkegaard speaks of the law as
"somewhat indefinite," a pale shadow of "what is to come." To make
an ethical judgment merely by applying the law is to turn the self, as
Derrida says, into a "calculating machine"; it is to become deaf to
the demands for justice that require, not application, but "suspension" (teleological). The law must be suspended in the instant of
genuine decision, in the instant of madness, for what is required
is not (objective, speculative) knowledge, but faith, for a genuine
judgment is one that proceeds "without calculation and without
rules, without reason and without rationality."[132] Kierkegaard anticipates this central feature of Derrida's thinking when he argues:

> The relation of love to the Law is here like the relation of faith to
> understanding. The understanding counts and counts, calculates and
> calculates, but it never arrives at the certainty that faith possesses. . . .
> Similarly, when the Law has set, as it were, all its provisions on a
> person and hunted him weary because there is a provision everywhere,
> and yet every provision, even the most definite, still has the indefi-
> niteness that it can become even more definite . . . then a person is
> taught to understand that there must be something else that is the
> fulfilling of the Law. (WL, 105)

According to Kierkegaard, "a human being always groans under the
Law" in that "he sees only requirements" and "he meets only the
rigorousness that in its infinitude can continually become more rigorous" (WL, 105). "The Law," simply stated, is "the very opposite
of life"; it "is like death." However, neither Kierkegaard nor Derrida
considers it possible to dissolve the law. What they do call for is a
"reinvention" or a "repetition" of the law, with the aim of making it
more responsive to the idiosyncratic demands of each particular
event. Kierkegaard considers this the way to bring the law to life
anew (repetition).

If the law "takes" or "requires," love "gives"; it is gift beyond
exchange, a giving up or a surrendering to the other in a manner

---

[132] Derrida, "Force of Law," 965.

reminiscent of the God-man. Love tears the Hegelian circle of reappropriation apart by seeing every other as neighbor, as a singular
other who desires mercy. This is why Kierkegaard states that "Christianity teaches that love is a relationship between: a person—God—a
person, that the God is the middle term," and that "to love God is
to love oneself truly; to help another person to love God is to love
another person; to be helped by another person to love God is to be
loved" (WL, 107). For to hold the Christ-figure as one's highest
ethical exemplar requires that the individual show love and mercy to
all, especially the "most wretched" and despised. Such Christian
love is magnanimous to a fault, affirming the hidden singularity and
residual incommensurability of every other; it teaches that "the
Christian must, if it is required, be able to hate father and mother
and sister and the beloved" (WL, 108); that is, the Christian must
emigrate (politics of émigré) from the sphere of the universal in
order to disrupt the "family scene" (*qua Sittlichkeit*). Caputo comes
close to Kierkegaard on this issue:

> You get nowhere in the kingdom by being well born, well bred and
> well to do. You get nowhere by loving your friends and family, those
> with whom you share kin and kind, those who are like you, of like
> kind. Such people already have their reward, Matthew has Jesus say.
> The only true reward comes of loving your enemies, those who are
> quite *unlike* you and who rather *dislike* you, and hating your kindred
> kind, your father and mother, brother and sister, hating those who
> love you. "Family values" in the kingdom, much to the chagrin of the
> Christian right today, are quite anarchic. Anybody can love the same;
> even the pharisees—or for that matter the mafia—have those "family
> values." It is hating the same and loving difference that counts in the
> kingdom.[133]

This is why Christ's "whole life was a horrible collision with the
merely human conception of what love is" (WL, 110).

Love for Kierkegaard, therefore, is the fulfilling of the law, the way
to keep the law merciful and just. Love gives life to the dead letter
of the law by making it serve human interests. To love in this Christian sense means sacrificing one's security in the world by adhering
to the "requirement of inwardness," which I have defined as the
critical posture adopted by the individual in relation to his or her

---

[133] Caputo, "Metanoetics," 13.

"natural" self, or the sense of self that one has before one becomes conscious of one's self as a being who relates to the God-man as one's highest ethical criterion.

Relating to God in this way, imitating him, obliges the individual to love every other, but especially those for whom the established order provides no welfare or security. This means that the ethical duty the prototype embodies is to "love the people we see." To give love, to give a gift of death (self-sacrifice), to show generosity and hospitality to the other by letting that other be (*Gelassenheit*) in his or her singularity, means pressing against the limits of the same, reaching out for the unexpected, for "the impossible." It demands that there be "no limit to love," for if "duty is to be fulfilled, love must be limitless" (WL, 167). For Kierkegaard, in other words, love does not amount simply to loving the perfect and the strong. It does, however, call for us to love the neighbor, which is everyone we see, despite his or her "weaknesses and imperfections":

> It is very soft and easy to wish the beloved to have all the possible perfections, and then if something is lacking it is in turn very soft and easy to sigh and sorrow and become self-important by one's presumably very pure and very deep sorrow. On the whole, it is perhaps a more common form of sensuality to want selfishly to make a show of the beloved or friend and to despair over every triviality. But would this be loving the people one sees? Ah, no, the people one sees, and likewise we ourselves when others see us, are not perfect; and yet it is very often the case that a person develops within himself this sentimental frailty that is designed only for loving the absolute epitome of perfections. And yet, although we human beings are all imperfect, we very rarely see the healthy, strong, capable love that is designed for loving the more imperfect persons, that is, the people we see. (WL, 167)

The way to become contemporaneous with the God-man is to love the other without limit, or "no matter how the object [of one's love] becomes changed." Christian love fulfills the law by responding, not only to those who are guaranteed protection under the law, but also to those who, as a result of their imperfections, are deemed outlaws (*hors texte*). One is called to love the other "just as you see him, with all his imperfections and weaknesses, to love him as you see him when he has changed completely" (WL, 174). Such "is a love without jealousy that would allow the other to be,"[134] for it is a surrendering to the impossible demand that we give without hope of return. Love can never be fulfilled, for like Derridean justice, love is always to come; love is always a task, something each individual must unremittingly strive to realize: "Christianity says it is a duty to remain in the debt, which means that it is an *action* and not an expression about, not a reflective view of, love. In the Christian sense, no human being has accomplished the highest in love, and even if this were so, this impossibility, there would at the very same moment still be, in the Christian sense, a new task" (WL, 188).

For Kierkegaard, the highest way to express Christian love is through "forgiveness"; that is, the act of forgiving is for this thinker the most genuine way to let the other be. For to forgive, to show mercy or justice, is to forget the wrongs of the past and to release the other from all accountability. It is on this point that we believe Kierkegaard anticipates Caputo and Derrida most fully. In order to see how this is so, let us briefly turn to the role played by forgiveness in the work of Caputo.

According to Caputo, the related categories of "repetition" and "reinvention," as I have defined them throughout this work, are both forms of forgiving. Forgiving, in Caputo's and Derrida's accounts, is a way to open up the past, to release it from the stranglehold of history. The process of repetition, that is, keeps us alert to the fact that all contexts—political, ethical, philosophical, and so forth—are formed contingently, since they are non-natural associations. Having no teleological course or predetermined heading, events are vulnerable to transformation and reinterpretation, what Derrida terms "iteration." Through such a process, "the past is transformed," rethought, and reassessed. Repetition is what one might call, following Nietzsche, "active forgetting," or a recalling of past events that aims not to consolidate the past through Hegelian recollection, but rather to free it up or release it. Forgiving, as defined by Caputo, is central to repetition because "it does not attempt to 'retrieve' (*wiederholen*) the past, even if you reconceive the past as what 'has been' (*das Gewesen*) (Heidegger), or to recycle the past and say yes to its endless return (Nietzsche), or to raise up the past to the eagle

---

[134] Derrida, "Sauf le nom," 74.

heights of the present or coming *parousia* (Hegel). It just forgets the past."[135]

In reference to Hannah Arendt's treatment of these same themes in *The Human Condition*,[136] Caputo argues that forgiving "keeps the web of relations loose and open-ended, making it possible for people to 'change their minds' and start all over again."[137] For if the passage to the impossible, to a future that is open-ended and free, was blocked, we would simply be caught in a vicious circle of retribution and vengeance, in which the logic of "an eye for an eye" would prevail:

> The opposite of forgiveness is vengeance, retribution, paying back, getting even, not letting go, clinging to events with a fury, drawing the strings and constraints of events still tighter, settling accounts, evening the score. Vengeance and retribution operate within a closed economy, with zero-sum accounting, in which there must be a balance of payments, balanced accounts, getting "even." Retribution makes good economic sense. But forgiveness belongs to the generalized economy of giving without getting back, without a payback, without a return on your investments. Forgiveness is more madness and bad economics.[138]

Forgiveness, therefore, is "letting go, *lassen,* a kind of *Gelassenheit.*"[139] Forgiveness is a merciful love.

Forgiving has much the same function for Kierkegaard. Through imitation of the God-man, or by imaginatively appropriating the Jesus-figure as ethical criterion and ideal, one is called not to wreak vengeance, but to have mercy and extend forgiveness. Underlying this is Kierkegaard's contention that the present and the past are the products of mere "explanation"; that is, the past is based on reports or explanations that are transmitted from generation to generation, reports we *choose* to believe. According to Kierkegaard, however, each of us has the capacity to read otherwise, to believe differently:

> With regard to another person's words, acts, and modes of thought, there is no certainty that to accept does not actually mean to choose.

---

[135] Caputo, *Against Ethics*, 110.
[136] See Hannah Arendt, *The Human Condition* (Chicago: University of Chicago Press, 1958), 236–43.
[137] Caputo, *Against Ethics*, 111.
[138] Ibid., 112.
[139] Ibid.

Therefore the view, the explanation, is a choice, just because a diversity of explanations is possible. But if it is a choice, it is always in my power, if I am one who loves, to choose the most lenient explanation. If, then, this more lenient or mitigating explanation explains what others light-mindedly, hastily, harshly, hardheartedly, enviously, maliciously, in short unlovingly explain summarily as guilt, if the mitigating explanation explains this in another way, it removes now one and now another guilt and in this way reduces the multitude of sins or hides it. (WL, 292)

In a manner strikingly similar to both Caputo and Derrida, Kierkegaard sees our capacity to reinvent and repeat the past through the power of forgiveness as the most passionate way to love the other in a Christian sense. To forgive is a matter of providing the most "mitigating explanation" that one can for the wrongdoings of one's forebears and neighbors. For him, the "servants of justice [*Ret*— 'right' or 'law']"—the lawmakers and "the judge"—should continue "to work at discovering guilt and crime"; "the rest of us," however, "are called to be neither judges nor servants of justice, but on the contrary are called by God to love, that is, with the aid of a mitigating explanation to hide a multitude of sins" (WL, 293). While the law mistakes explanations for facts, the one who strives through "the art of interpretation" to reduce the multitude of sins shows just "how acquainted he is with the human heart" (WL, 293). For in being guided by the heart, one learns how to forgive: "Keeping silent does not actually take away anything from the generally known multitude of sins. The mitigating explanation wrests something away from the multitude by showing that this and that were not sin. Forgiveness removes what cannot be denied to sin. This love strives in every way to hide a multitude of sins; but forgiveness is the most notable way" (WL, 294).

In making reference to "the human heart," Kierkegaard once again anticipates one of Caputo's central and ever-recurring notions, that of *metanoia*. For Caputo, making a judgment to suspend (reinvent) the law is not governed by "a strictly cognitive *nous*," but is rather determined "by a heart-based *nous*, a *nous* that in terms of the old physiology would have its seat not in the head but the breast."[140] *Metanoia*, that is, seeks mercy and compassion rather than strict ac-

---

[140] Caputo, "Metanoetics," 19.

countability; it means "to succumb to the demands of mercy, to let oneself be touched, be affected by the claims of the flesh laid low."[141] For this reason, "it is always and already implicated in forgiveness":

> Forgiving lets the web of human relations hang loose. It cuts the event loose, gives the Other space, room to breathe, to try again. Forgiving is letting go, *lassen*, a kind of *Gelassenheit*, not in the sense of *wesentliches Denken*, because it is not thinking at all, neither calculative nor meditative, not a matter of *nous* or *logos* at all, but a matter of *kardia*. Forgiveness does not enforce rules, does not exact payment. It does not let the law take its toll. It dismisses the law, suspends it, lifts it lets it hang in midair, in order to answer the call that wells up from the abyss of the Other. If someone "turns to you saying (*epistrepse pros se legon*) 'I have had a change of heart (*metanoo*),'" then you (we) should suspend the law, lift it off his/her back. Release them. Lift the law. Let them be. Lighten up.[142]

Through this process the ledger is wiped clean. For both Kierkegaard and Caputo, this active forgetting is a "wonder" because "in the moment of forgiveness" the content of the past is released and transformed "into something that is *not* in the past, not anymore";[143] that is, one has faith that "forgiveness takes the forgiven sin away" (WL, 294), or that "the one who loves by forgiveness *believes* away what is seen" (WL, 295). Forgiving, according to Kierkegaard, requires us to have "the miracle of faith," the miracle that what is seen, by being forgiven in love, "is blotted out" and "forgotten": "The one who loves forgives in this way: he forgives, he forgets, he blots out the sin, in love he turns toward the one he forgives; but when he turns toward him, he of course cannot see what is lying behind his back" (WL, 296).

To love, in Kierkegaard's radical "Christian" sense, is thus a form of self-denial to the extent that it is a process of releasing the other through the act of forgiveness (active forgetting, repeating the past with inventiveness), thereby "hid[ing] a multitude of sins." It is a matter of loving those whom we see—those, in other words, who call for mercy and compassion—for who does not at some stage require mercy? To love the other is to fulfill or give life to the law, for the

---

[141] Ibid.
[142] Caputo, *Against Ethics*, 112.
[143] Caputo, "Metanoetics," 22.

law was made for individuals and not vice versa. Through the God-relationship, or by becoming an imitator of the highest ethical proto-type, the individual strives to love as Christ loved and to forgive as he forgave. This means that one cultivates "leniency" toward the neighbor, that the self avoids "the resentment and revenge" that "pull the strings of the past ever tighter."[144] To love in this way is to have faith that the sin of the past can be erased. For *metanoia* "tells us to change our heart" and "to become merciful to a fault, to lift the strictures of the law and to let ourselves be laid claim to, to be besieged by the other one, by the others who suffer from their alterity."[145] If we respond to this claim by forgiving the other, accord-ing to Kierkegaard, we too will break free of the closed economy of vengeance and retribution in which balancing the accounts means "getting even": "Christianity's view is: forgiveness is forgiveness; your forgiveness is your forgiveness; your forgiveness of another is your own forgiveness; the forgiveness you give is the forgiveness you receive, not the reverse, that the forgiveness you receive is the for-giveness you give" (WL, 380). As such, judging the other is not the way to administer mercy or justice, for this presupposes that the individual who sits in judgment is not in need of reciprocal compas-sion. The message from both Kierkegaard and Caputo, and by impli-cation Derrida, is clear: "justice is attained by judging not."[146]

Alliances based on forgiveness and love of the Kierkegaardian sort amount to what Caputo and Derrida call a "weak community,"[147] or what Jean-Luc Nancy entitles "the inoperative community."[148] This is a community based upon a politics of emigration, of the émigré, and on an openness to the other no matter whom. This was Abra-ham's spiritual trial, his politics: to surrender the securities of *Sit-tlichkeit* to welcome the strange specter of the other—not the other I, but the near-dweller. Kierkegaard's community of neighbors is a kingdom of forgiveness, a "community in which the solitude of my accusation, my inescapable identity, the relentless recursivity of my being accused is relieved, lifted up, into a community of those who

---

[144] Ibid., 23.

[145] Ibid., 19.

[146] Caputo, *Against Ethics*, 112.

[147] Caputo, *Deconstruction in a Nutshell*, 124.

[148] Jean-Luc Nancy, *The Inoperative Community*, trans. Peter Connor et al. (Min-neapolis: University of Minnesota Press, 1991).

are forgiven and who forgive one another."[149] This is hospitality, generosity, genuine self-denial and sacrifice, or what Caputo calls "a mad economy or aneconomy of forgiving."[150] The only principle in such a "kingdom is to love," and this is love that *does not seek its own, for there are no* mine *and* yours *in love.*" Under the law, which caters to the universal and not to singularity or particularity, each has his or her own; that is, "justice (*Ret,* which translates as 'law' or 'right') pleads the cause of its own, divides and assigns, determines what each can lawfully call his own, judges and punishes if anyone refuses to make any distinction between *mine* and *yours*" (WL, 265):

> Thus there is community, perfect community in *mine* and *yours.* By being exchanged, *mine and yours* becomes *ours,* in which category erotic love and friendship have their strength; at least they are strong in it. But *ours* is for the community exactly the same as *mine* is for the solitary one, and *ours* is indeed formed—not from the contentious *mine* and *yours,* because no union can be formed from that—but is formed from the joined, the exchanged *yours* and *mine.* . . . [A]n exchange by no means abolishes the distinction "*mine* and *yours,*" because that for which I exchange myself then becomes mine again. (WL, 266–67)

The community of "mine and yours," a community founded on circular reappropriation of the same, is not an open quasi-community (democracy), but a "*communio,*" which, as John Caputo reminds us, "is a word for a military formation and a kissing cousin of the word 'munitions.' "[151] Such a structure is marked by the wall it erects "around the city to keep the stranger and the foreigner out."[152] This is why the word "community" frightens Kierkegaard and Derrida, why it is "just about the opposite of what deconstruction is."[153] For Kierkegaard, the logic of "mine and yours," or "ours," perpetuates such a *communio.* In order to challenge the hegemony of the "perfect" *communio,* Kierkegaard urges a surrendering or sacrificing of the self as "mine," for if there is such a "self-denying-in-all-things," then "in turn the specification 'yours' disappears entirely" (WL, 268). This is "the true love," or the impossible act of self-sacrifice

---

[149] Caputo, *Prayers and Tears,* 228.
[150] Ibid.
[151] Caputo, *Deconstruction in a Nutshell,* 107–8.
[152] Ibid., 108.
[153] Ibid.

that genuine hospitality requires. The giving up of the "mine" is a "letting go" of what I am owed, a rupturing of the logic of exchange in which "mine" and "yours" collapse into an "ours." It is the moment when "I push against this limit, this threshold, this paralysis, inviting hospitality to cross its own threshold and limit, its own self-limitation, to become a *gift beyond hospitality*."[154]

The one who truly loves, and who therefore "does not seek his own," has no conception of "community as friendship does," for friendship in the strictly classical sense is founded on a logic of exchange in which "like is now given for like." Self-denial requires the more fraught and challenging task of giving "everything away without getting the least in return" (WL, 269). Sacrifice of Abrahamic proportions is necessitated for the sovereignty of the *communio* to be disrupted by the incoming of the stranger. Kierkegaard explains:

> The truly loving person becomes the unconditionally injured one—which he in a certain sense makes himself by self-denial. But then the overturning of *mine* and *yours* has reached its highest point: and therefore love also has reached its highest blessedness within itself. No ingratitude, no misjudgment, no unappreciated sacrifice, no mockery as thanks, nothing, neither things present or things to come, is able to bring him sooner or later to understand that he has any *mine*, or make it appear that he had only for a moment forgotten the distinction "*mine* and *yours*," because he has eternally forgotten this distinction and has eternally been conscious of loving sacrificially, been conscious of being sacrificed. (WL, 269)

To let the other go through excessive hospitality, to love and forgive, is to unconditionally affirm the singularity of every other; the relationship with the other, in other words, "is released from the stricture and constricture, from a binding that binds up and confines."[155] Bookbinding is seen for what it is, a hilarious practice. The "distinctiveness" of the other is not under threat, but through love "is lifted up and given a new start."[156] "True love," that is, "loves every human being according to the person's distinctiveness," while "the rigid, the domineering person lacks flexibility, lacks the pliability to comprehend others; he demands his own from everyone, wants everyone to

---

[154] Ibid., 111.
[155] Caputo, *Prayers and Tears*, 228.
[156] Ibid., 229.

be transformed in his image, to be trimmed according to his pattern for human beings" (WL, 271). The domineering person is incapable of forgiving the other, of cutting the cord loose, of forgetting and letting "the past flow off without a trace."[157] Self-sacrificing love, on the other hand, "gives in such a way that the gift looks as if it were the recipient's property" (WL, 274). This generates a community that is "constituted by a paralogic of paradoxical gifts, gifts that are given only when we give everything away, even and especially our credit, when we for-give, give-forth, give away *everything*, unconditionally."[158]

"The greatest benefaction," according to Kierkegaard, "cannot be done in such a way that the recipient comes to know that it is to me that he owes it, because if he comes to know that, then it is simply not the greatest beneficence" (WL, 275). Real generosity does not seek to draw the other into a reciprocal alliance, but rather "to encourage a person to become himself, to become his own master" (WL, 278). In such a "weak community" the law is fulfilled only through love, through acts of forgiving in which the individual "gives away and renounces getting even." Through such active renunciation there is opened up "the possibility of a community of equals," in which all are "equally forgiven and equally detached from getting even." Those who love thus forget as they forgive:

> What can make the moment of forgiveness, the transition of agreement so natural, so easy, as this: that the one who loves . . . by abiding,

---

[157] Ibid., 227.

[158] Ibid., 228. Paul Ricoeur is gesturing in a somewhat similar direction when he says: "Forgiveness, in its full sense, certainly far exceeds political categories. It belongs to an order—the order of charity—which goes even beyond the order of morality. Forgiveness falls within the scope of an economy of the gift whose logic of superabundance exceeds the logic of reciprocity. . . . Insofar as it exceeds the order of morality, the economy of the gift belongs to what we would be able to term the 'poetics,' that is, the sense of creativity at the level of the dynamics of acting and the sense of song and hymn at the level of verbal expression. It is thus to this spiritual economy, to this poetics of the moral life that forgiveness essentially belongs. Its 'poetic' power consists in shattering the law of the irreversibility of time by changing the past, not as a record of all that has happened but in terms of its meaning for us today. It does this by lifting the burden of guilt which paralyses the relations between individuals who are acting out and suffering their own history. It does not abolish the debt insofar as we are and remain the inheritors of the past, but it lifts the pain of the debt." Ricoeur, "Reflections on a New Ethos for Europe," trans. Eileen Brennan, in *Paul Ricoeur: The Hermeneutics of Action*, ed. Richard Kearney (London: SAGE, 1996), 10. Can we still argue, after reading this, that the philosophies of Derrida and Ricoeur are irreconcilable?

has continually cleared away the past. Then from his side the agreement is indeed in effect, as if there had been no separation at all. When two people both have an idea of the past or of how long the separation has been, forgiveness is often a difficult collision, and the relationship is perhaps never fully established again. But the one who loves knows nothing about the past; therefore he does even this last thing in love; he absorbs the jolt [Stød] in such a way that there can be no collision—the transition of forgiveness cannot be made easier. How frequently has agreement been close to taking place between two people, but the one continued to feel hurt [stødt] as we say. When that is the case, then something from the past must have unlovingly emerged again. It is impossible, after all, to be offended by something that is softer than the softest, by love. (WL, 314)

Kierkegaard's notion of a community of neighbors, one founded on self-sacrificing love, challenges the inhospitable "perfect community" (communio) in which individuals, in loving the other, seek only their own. The former is a community in which universality gives way to the requirements of singularity, and one in which justice, compassion, and mercy keep the law from becoming unremitting and cruel. It is, to appropriate the words of Caputo once again, "constituted by bonds that do not bind up and constrain, by links of love that do not constrain, by the spontaneities of love, by which, over and above accusation, which puts me in the accusative of obligation, the least of God's children is the object of my love."[159] In such a community, "the law articulates with difficulty," but "love speaks the word plainly" (JP, 3:2404). For Kierkegaard, Derrida, and Caputo, the "infinite renunciation" which is Gelassenheit is the way "to love and trust and seek justice, to seek the kingdom, which is here and now, which is for the lame and the leper, the outcast and the sinner, the widow and the orphan."[160] Such indeed amounts to a politics of exodus, a politics of conviction and responsibility in the name of those whose only aspiration is for a room, no matter how modest, at the inn.

---

[159] Caputo, Prayers and Tears, 228.
[160] Caputo, "Instants, Secrets, and Singularities," 235.

AFTERWORD

Throughout this book I have highlighted a dimension of Kierkegaard's thought that has, in the main, been obfuscated by readings
that take it as a given that this thinker has little to contribute politically. While I acknowledge that there are many sides to this complex
thinker (the royalist and antidemocratic sentiments of the early
years, as distinct from the Kierkegaard of 1848 on—the Kierkegaard,
that is, of *Sickness unto Death, Practice in Christianity,* and *Attack
upon Christendom*) and his voluminous output, not all of which
would lend credence my thesis, I am confident that the reading of
Kierkegaard I have advanced is not without its merits.

In making a case for what I have chosen to call his "politics of
exodus," I have built upon certain studies that have dedicated themselves to identifying within Kierkegaard's work a genuine concern for
how to effectively tackle the plagues of the age. Commentators such
as George Pattison, David Gouwens, Merold Westphal, Martin Matustík, John Caputo, and James Marsh have in their respective ways
put forward convincing arguments for the inclusion of Kierkegaard
in contemporary political and ethical debate. This book has tried
to further advance that cause by arguing that the political spirit of
Kierkegaard's works anticipates in many important respects the ethico-political dynamic at the heart of Jacques Derrida's writings. In
driving home this conviction, I have sought to take the side of those
thinkers who consider Kierkegaard a postmodernist before his time,
while concomitantly steering clear of those who would blunt the
edge of Kierkegaard's work in this regard as a consequence of an
overemphasis on literary gimmicks and stylistic form. I have, that is,
a healthy respect for what we have come to call—rather infelici-
tously, it has to be said—"postmodernism," but only for that form
of postmodernism that prides itself on opening up structures and
institutions in the name of those whom they have silenced. For my
money, Derrida's work is laudably attentive to this task. So when I
argue in favor of the kinship that exists between Kierkegaard and

Derrida, my aim is not to reduce one author to the other, but just to demonstrate (*pace* Sylvia Walsh and Ronald Hall et al.) in which quarter I believe Kierkegaard's ideas are most alive and visible today.

As noted in the introduction to this work, I anticipate that many will find my conclusions unpalatable, especially those who have no truck with Derrida or deconstruction. In response, I wish to stress that even though I am convinced of Derrida's Kierkegaardian lineage, and even though I believe the type of comparison I have undertaken here is valuable, I am not of the opinion that deconstruction is the only contemporary movement to be influenced by Kierkegaard's politics of exodus. For example, I do not think it an exaggeration to claim that such a politics is at work in the liberation theology of Johann Baptist Metz, especially in the way he appropriates the *memoria passionis* as a steadying force on world history as a story of victory, as distinct from the often occulted histories of the crucified and the vanquished. Nor do I consider it a mistake to argue that the recent theology of Paul Ricoeur, founded as it is on the *imitatio Christi* as a way of taking the side of the least among us in concrete political affairs, is a practical unfolding of Kierkegaard's most radical impulses. Kierkegaard's stress on the role of the Cross, the suffering of the Christ-figure, and the way we are called to respond through imitation is the most powerful message emanating from his corpus. When we choose to ignore the social and political import of Kierkegaard's radical Christian ethics, his novel use of the God-man as paradigm and prototype, we lose the most essential element in his thought.

In short, while I have dedicated myself to showing how "postmodern" Kierkegaard's insights are, and thus, by implication, how indebted the best of postmodern thought is to his work, I think it true that any contemporary movement that appropriates, however inadvertently, the theology of the Cross as a symbol of solidarity with the poor and the hopeless is in debt to this remarkable thinker of the singular and the exception. My earnest hope is that many more will begin to probe this side of Kierkegaard, and that his intuitions regarding society's ills, and how we might respond to them, will be given the recognition they undoubtedly deserve.

BIBLIOGRAPHY

Adorno, Theodore. W. *Kierkegaard: Construction of the Aesthetic*. Trans. Robert Hullot-Kentor. Minneapolis: University of Minnesota Press, 1989.

————. *Negative Dialectics*. Trans. Knut Tarnowski and Frederic Will. New York: Seabury, 1973.

Agasinski, Sylviane. *Aparte: Conceptions and Deaths of Søren Kierkegaard*. Trans. Kevin Newmark. Tallahassee: University Press of Florida, 1988.

Altizer, Thomas J. J. *The Descent into Hell: A Study of the Radical Reversal of the Christian Consciousness*. New York: Seabury Press, 1979.

————. *Total Presence: The Language of Jesus and the Language of Today*. New York: Seabury Press, 1980.

Andic, Martin. "Confidence as a Work of Love." In *Kierkegaard on Art and Communication*, ed. George Pattison, 160–85. New York: St. Martin's Press, 1992.

Arendt, Hannah. *The Human Condition*. Chicago: University of Chicago Press, 1958.

Armstrong, Paul B. "Reading Kierkegaard—Disorientation and Reorientation." In *Kierkegaard's Truth: The Disclosure of the Self*, ed. Joseph H. Smith, 23–50. New Haven: Yale University Press, 1981.

Barnes, Hazel E. *Sartre*. London: Quartet Books Ltd., 1974.

Barrett, Lee. "An Immediate Stage on the Way to the Religious Life." In *The International Kierkegaard Commentary*, vol. 14, *"Two Ages: The Present Age and the Age of Revolution," A Literary Review*, ed. Robert L. Perkins, 53–71. Macon: Mercer University Press, 1984.

————. "Kierkegaard's Anxiety and the Augustinian Doctrine of Original Sin." In *The International Kierkegaard Commentary*, vol. 8, *"The Concept of Anxiety,"* ed. Robert L. Perkins, 35–62. Macon: Mercer University Press, 1985.

Beiser, Frederick C., ed. *The Cambridge Companion to Hegel*. Cambridge: Cambridge University Press, 1993.

Bejerholm, L. *Concepts and Alternatives in Kierkegaard*. Copenhagen: C. A. Reitzel, 1980.

Bell, Richard H. "On Being Sidetracked by the Aesthetic: Kierkegaard's Practical Paradox." In *Kierkegaard on Art and Communication*, ed. George Pattison, 55–63. New York: St. Martin's Press, 1992.

———. "On Trusting One's Own Heart: Scepticism in Jonathan Edwards and Søren Kierkegaard." In *History of European Ideas*, vol. 12, no. 1, ed. Ann Loades and George Pattison, 105–16. Oxford: Pergamon Press, 1990.

Bennington, Geoffrey. *Legislations: The Politics of Deconstruction*. London: Verso, 1994.

Bennington, Geoffrey, and Jacques Derrida. *Jacques Derrida*. Chicago: University of Chicago Press, 1993.

Bernasconi, Robert. "Deconstruction and the Possibility of Ethics." In *Deconstruction and Philosophy: The Texts of Jacques Derrida*, ed. John Sallis, 122–139. Chicago: University of Chicago Press, 1987.

———. "Politics beyond Humanism: Mandela and the Struggle against Apartheid." In *Working Through Derrida*, ed. Gary B. Madison, 94–120. Evanston: Northwestern University Press, 1993.

Bernstein, Richard J. "An Allegory of Modernity/Postmodernity: Habermas and Derrida." In *Working Through Derrida*, ed. Gary B. Madison, 204–29. Evanston: Northwestern University Press, 1993.

———. *The New Constellation: The Ethical-Political Horizons of Modernity/Postmodernity*. Oxford: Polity Press, 1991.

Bigelow, Pat. *Kierkegaard and the Problem of Writing*. Tallahassee: Florida State University Press, 1987.

Blanchette, Olivia. "The Silencing of Philosophy." In *The International Kierkegaard Commentary*, vol. 6, *"Fear and Trembling" and "Repetition,"* ed. Robert L. Perkins, 29–65. Macon: Mercer University Press, 1993.

Bloom, Harold, ed. *Kierkegaard*. New York: Chelsea House, 1989.

Boff, Leonard. *Jesus Christ, Liberator: A Critical Christology for Our Time*. Maryknoll, N.Y.: Orbis, 1978.

Brezis, David. *Temps et Presence: Essai sur la conceptualité kierkegaardienne*. Paris: J. Vrin, 1991.

Brown, James. *Kierkegaard, Heidegger, Buber, and Barth: Subject and Object in Modern Theology.* New York: Crowell-Collier, 1962.

Buber, Martin. *Good and Evil.* New York: Scribner, 1953.

———. *I and Thou.* Trans. Walter Kauffmann. Edinburgh: T. & T. Clark, 1970.

———. "The Question to the Single One." In *Between Man and Man,* 40–82. New York: Macmillan, 1965.

Cahoy, William John. "The Self in Community: Søren Kierkegaard's Thought on the Individual and the Church." Ph.D. diss., Yale University, 1989.

Caputo, John D. *Against Ethics: Contributions to a Poetics of Obligation with Constant Reference to Deconstruction.* Bloomington: Indiana University Press, 1993.

———. *Demythologizing Heidegger.* Bloomington: Indiana University Press, 1993.

———. "The Economy of Signs in Husserl and Derrida: From Uselessness to Full Employment." In *Deconstruction and Philosophy: The Texts of Jacques Derrida,* ed. John Sallis, 99–113. Chicago: University of Chicago Press, 1987.

———. *Heidegger and Aquinas: An Essay on Overcoming Metaphysics.* New York: Fordham University Press, 1982.

———. "Heidegger and Theology." In *The Cambridge Companion to Heidegger,* ed. Charles B. Guignon, 270–88. Cambridge: Cambridge University Press, 1993.

———. "Hermeneutics as the Recovery of Man." In *Hermeneutics and Modern Philosophy,* ed. Brice R. Wachtarhauser, 416–45. Albany: SUNY Press, 1986.

———. "Instants, Secrets, and Singularities: Dealing Death in Kierkegaard and Derrida." In *Kierkegaard in Post/Modernity,* ed. Martin J. Matustík and Merold Westphal, 216–38. Bloomington: Indiana University Press, 1995.

———. "Kierkegaard, Heidegger, and the Foundering of Metaphysics." In *The International Kierkegaard Commentary,* vol. 6, *"Fear and Trembling" and "Repetition,"* ed. Robert L. Perkins, 201–24. Macon: Mercer University Press, 1993.

———. "Metanoetics: Elements of a Postmodern Christian Philosophy." Forthcoming.

———. *The Mystical Element in Heidegger's Thought.* Athens: Ohio University Press, 1978; revised reprint, New York: Fordham University Press, 1986.

————. "On Being Inside/Outside Truth." In *Modernity and Its Discontents*, ed. John D. Caputo, James L. Marsh, and Merold Westphal, 45–63. New York: Fordham University Press, 1992.

————. "On Not Circumventing the Quasi-Transcendental: The Case of Rorty and Derrida." In *Working Through Derrida*, ed. Gary B. Madison, 147–69. Evanston: Northwestern University Press, 1993.

————. *The Prayers and Tears of Jacques Derrida*. Bloomington: Indiana University Press, 1997.

————. *Radical Hermeneutics: Repetition, Deconstruction, and the Hermeneutic Project*. Bloomington: Indiana University Press, 1987.

————. "Reason, History, and a Little Madness: Towards a Hermeneutics of the Kingdom." *Proceedings of the American Catholic Philosophical Association* 68 (1994): 27–44.

————, ed. and commentary. *Deconstruction in a Nutshell: A Conversation with Jacques Derrida*. New York: Fordham University Press, 1997.

Caputo, John D., James L. Marsh, and Merold Westphal, eds. *Modernity and Its Discontents*. New York: Fordham University Press, 1992.

Casey, Edward. "Imagination and Repetition in Literature." *Yale French Studies* 52 (1975): 250–66.

Cavell, Stanley. "Kierkegaard's *On Authority and Revelation*." In *Kierkegaard: A Collection of Critical Essays*, ed. Josiah Thompson, 373–92. New York: Anchor Books, 1972.

Caws, Mary, ed. *Textual Analysis: Some Readers Reading*. New York: Modern Language Association, 1986.

Champagne, Roland A. *Jacques Derrida*. New York: Twayne, 1994.

Clair, André. "Médiation et répétion: Le lieu de la dialectique kierkegaardienne." *Revue des Sciences philosophiques et théologiques* 59 (1975): 38–78.

————. *Pseudonymie et Paradoxe: Le Pensée Dialectique de Kierkegaard*. Paris: J. Vrin, 1976.

Clark, Lorraine. *Blake, Kierkegaard, and the Specter of the Dialectic*. Cambridge: Cambridge University Press, 1991.

Cole, Preston J. *The Problematic Self in Kierkegaard and Freud*. New Haven: Yale University Press, 1971.

Collins, James. "Kierkegaard's Imagery of the Self." In *Kierkegaard's*

Truth: The Disclosure of the Self, ed. Joseph H. Smith, 51–84. New Haven: Yale University Press, 1981.

Connell, George B. *To Be One Thing: Personal Unity in Kierkegaard's Thought.* Macon: Mercer University Press, 1985.

Connell, George B., and C. Stephen Evans, eds. *Foundations of Kierkegaard's Vision of Community: Religion, Ethics, and Politics in Kierkegaard.* Atlantic Highlands, N.J.: Humanities Press, 1992.

Cornell, Drucilla. *Philosophy at the Limit.* New York: Routledge, 1992.

————. "The Violence of the Masquerade: Law Dressed Up as Justice." In *Working Through Derrida*, ed. Gary B. Madison, 77–93. Evanston: Northwestern University Press, 1993.

————, ed. *Deconstruction and the Possibility of Justice.* New York: Routledge, 1992.

Coward, Howard, and Toby Foshay, eds. *Derrida and Negative Theology.* Albany: SUNY Press, 1992.

Creegan, Charles L. *Wittgenstein and Kierkegaard: Religion, Individuality, and Philosophical Method.* London: Routledge, 1989.

Critchley, Simon. *The Ethics of Deconstruction: Derrida and Levinas.* Oxford: Blackwell, 1992.

Crites, Stephen. "The Author and the Authorship: Recent Kierkegaardian Literature." *Journal of the American Academy of Religion* 38, no. 1 (1970): 37–54.

————. "'The Blissful Security of the Moment': Recollection, Repetition, and Eternal Recurrence." In *The International Kierkegaard Commentary*, vol. 6, *"Fear and Trembling" and "Repetition,"* ed. Robert L. Perkins, 225–46. Macon: Mercer University Press, 1993.

————. *In the Twilight of Christendom: Hegel vs. Kierkegaard on Faith and History.* Chambersburg, Pa.: American Academy of Religion, 1972.

————. "Pseudonymous Authorship as Art and Act." In *Kierkegaard: A Collection of Critical Essays*, ed. Josiah Thompson, 183–229. New York: Anchor Books, 1972.

————. *"The Sickness unto Death:* A Social Interpretation." In *Foundations of Kierkegaard's Vision of Community: Religion, Ethics, and Politics in Kierkegaard*, ed. George B. Connell and C. Stephen Evans, 144–60. Atlantic Highlands, N.J.: Humanities Press, 1992.

————. "Unfinished Figure: On Theology and Imagination." In *Un-*

finished: Essays in Honor of Ray L. Hart, ed. Mark C. Taylor, 155–83. Chico, Calif.: Scholars Press, 1981.

Crossan, John Dominic. *Jesus: A Revolutionary Biography*. San Francisco: Harper, 1994.

Cutting, Patricia. "The Levels of Interpersonal Relationships in Kierkegaard's *Two Ages*." In *The International Kierkegaard Commentary*, vol. 14, *"Two Ages: The Present Age and the Age of Revolution," A Literary Review*, ed. Robert L. Perkins, 73–86. Macon: Mercer University Press, 1984.

———. "The Possibility of Being-with-Others for Kierkegaard's Individual (*Den Enkelte*)." Ph.D. diss., University of New Mexico, 1976.

"The Deconstruction of Actuality: An Interview with Jacques Derrida." *Radical Philosophy* 68 (Autumn 1994): 28–41.

Deleuze, Gilles. *Difference and Repetition*. Bath: Athlone Press, 1994.

Derrida, Jacques. *Acts of Literature*. Ed. Derek Attridge. New York: Routledge, 1992.

———. *Adieu: à Emmanuel Lévinas*. Paris: Galilée, 1997.

———. *Aporias*. Trans. Thomas Dutoit. Stanford: Standford University Press, 1993. "Apories: Mourir-s'attendre aux limites de la vérité." In *Le Passage des frontières: Autour du travail de Jacques Derrida*, 309–38. Paris: Galilée, 1994.

———. *Archive Fever: A Freudian Impression*. Trans. Eric Prenowitz. Chicago: University of Chicago Press, 1996.

———. *Circumfession: Fifty-nine Periods and Periphrases*. In Geoffrey Bennington and Jacques Derrida, *Jacques Derrida*. Chicago: Chicago University Press, 1993. *Circonfession: Cinquante-neuf périodes et périphrases*. In Geoffrey Bennington et Jacques Derrida, *Jacques Derrida*. Paris: Éditions du Seuil, 1991.

———. *Cosmopolites de tous les pays, encore un effort!* Paris: Galilée, 1997.

———. "Deconstruction and the Other." In *Dialogues with Contemporary Continental Thinkers: The Phenomenological Heritage*, ed. Richard Kearney, 107–126. Manchester: Manchester University Press, 1984.

———. *A Derrida Reader: Between the Blinds*. Ed. Peggy Kamuf. New York: Harvester Wheatsheaf, 1991.

———. *Dissemination*. Trans. Barbara Johnson. London: Athlone Press, 1981. *La Dissémination*. Paris: Éditions du Seuil, 1972.

———. "Donner la mort." In *L'Éthique du don: Jacques Derrida et la Pensée du don*. Paris: Métailié-Transition, 1992.

———. "Force of Law: The 'Mystical Foundation of Authority.' " Trans. Mary Quaintance. *Cardoza Law Review* 11 (1990): 919–1078. Published also in *Deconstruction and the Possibility of Justice*, ed. Drucilla Cornell et al., 3–67. New York: Routledge, 1992. *Force de loi: Le "Fondement mystique de l'authorité."* Paris: Galilée, 1994.

———. *The Gift of Death*. Trans. David Wills. Chicago: University of Chicago Press, 1995.

———. *Given Time: I. Counterfeit Money*. Trans. Peggy Kamuf. Chicago: University of Chicago Press, 1992. *Donner le temps*. Paris: Galilée, 1991.

———. *Glas*. Trans. John P. Leavey, Jr., and Richard Rand. Lincoln: University of Nebraska Press, 1986. *Glas*. Paris: Galilée, 1974.

———. "How to Avoid Speaking: Denials." In *Derrida and Negative Theology*, ed. Howard Coward and Toby Foshay, 73–142. Albany: SUNY Press, 1992.

———. *Limited INC*. Evanston: Northwestern University Press, 1988.

———. *Mal d'archive: Une impression freudienne*. Paris: Galilée, 1994.

———. *Margins of Philosophy*. Trans. Alan Bass. New York: Harvester Wheatsheaf, 1982. *Marges de la philosophie*. Paris: Les Éditions de Minuit, 1972.

———. *Memoirs of the Blind: The Self-Portrait and Other Ruins*. Trans. Pascale-Anne Brault and Michael Naas. Chicago: University of Chicago Press, 1993. *Memoirs d'aveugle: L'autobiographie et autres ruines*. Paris: Éditions de la Réunion des musées nationaux, 1990.

———. *Of Grammatology*. Trans. Gayatri Chakravorty Spivak. Baltimore: Johns Hopkins University Press, 1974. *De la Grammatologie*. Paris: Les Éditions de Minuit, 1967.

———. *Of Spirit: Heidegger and the Question*. Trans. Geoffrey Bennington and Rachel Bowlby. Chicago: University of Chicago Press, 1989. *De l'esprit*. Paris: Galilée, 1987.

————. *On the Name.* Ed. Thomas Dutoit. Stanford: Stanford University Press, 1995.

————. *The Other Heading: Reflections on Today's Europe.* Trans. Pascale-Anne Brault and Michael B. Naas. Bloomington: Indiana University Press, 1992. *L'autre cap.* Paris: Éditions de Minuit, 1991.

————. "Passions." In *On the Name,* trans. David Wood, 1–31. Published also in *Derrida: A Critical Reader,* ed. David Wood, 3–35. Oxford: Blackwell, 1992. *Passions.* Paris: Galilée, 1993.

————. *Points . . . : Interviews, 1974–1994.* Ed. Elizabeth Weber. Trans. Peggy Kamuf et al. Stanford: Stanford University Press, 1995.

————. *Politiques de l'amitié.* Paris: Galilée, 1995.

————. *Positions.* Trans. Alan Bass. Chicago: University of Chicago Press, 1981.

————. *The Post Card: From Socrates to Freud and Beyond.* Trans. Alan Bass. Chicago: University of Chicago Press, 1987. *La carte postale: De Socrate à Freud et au-delà.* Paris: Flammarion, 1980.

————. *Psyché: Inventions de l'autre.* Paris: Galilée, 1987.

————. "Sauf le nom (Post-Scriptum)." In *On the Name,* trans. John P. Leavey, 33–85. *Sauf le nom.* Paris: Galilée, 1993.

————. *Specters of Marx: The State of the Debt, the Work of Mourning, and the New International.* Trans. Peggy Kamuf. New York: Routledge, 1994. *Spectres de Marx: État de la dette, le travail du deuil, et la nouvelle Internationale.* Paris: Galilée, 1993.

————. *Speech and Phenomena, and Other Essays on Husserl's Theory of Signs.* Trans. David B. Allison. Evanston: Northwestern University Press, 1973. *La voix et le phénomène.* Paris: Presses Universitaires de France, 1967.

————. *The Truth in Painting.* Trans. Geoff Bennington and Ian McLeod. Chicago: University of Chicago Press, 1987. *La vérité en peinture.* Paris: Flammarion, 1978.

————. *Writing and Difference.* Trans. Alan Bass. London: Routledge, 1978. *L'écriture et la différance.* Paris: Éditions de Seuil, 1967.

Desmond, William. *Art and the Absolute: A Study of Hegel's Aesthetics.* Albany: SUNY Press, 1985.

————. *Beyond Hegel and the Dialectic.* Albany: SUNY Press, 1992.

————. *Hegel and His Critics.* Albany: SUNY Press, 1989.

De Vries, Hent. "Adieu, à dieu, a-Dieu." In *Ethics as First Philosophy: The Significance of Emmanuel Levinas for Philosophy, Literature, and Religion*, ed. Adriaan T. Peperzak, 211–20. New York: Routledge, 1995.

Dooley, Mark. "Kierkegaard on the Margins of Philosophy." *Philosophy and Social Criticism* 21, no. 2 (1995): 85–107.

———. "Murder on Moriah: A Paradoxical Representation." *Philosophy Today* 39 (Spring 1995): 67–83.

———. "Playing on the Pyramid: Resituating the 'Self' in Kierkegaard and Derrida." *Imprimatur* 1, nos. 2–3 (1996): 151–62.

———. "The Politics of Exodus: 'Hospitality' in Derrida, Kierkegaard, and Levinas." In *The International Kierkegaard Commentary*, vol. 16, *"Works of Love,"* ed. Robert L. Perkins, 167–92. Macon: Mercer University Press, 1999.

———. "Private Irony vs. Social Hope: Derrida, Rorty, and the Political." *Cultural Values* 3, no. 3 (1999): 11–17.

———. "Risking Responsibility: A Politics of the *Emigré*." In *Kierkegaard: The Self in Society*, ed. George Pattison and Steven Shakespeare, 139–55. London: Macmillan, 1998.

Dreyfus, Hubert. *Being-in-the-World: A Commentary on Heidegger's "Being and Time," Division 1*. Cambridge: MIT Press, 1991.

———. "Heidegger on the Connection between Nihilism, Art, Technology, and Politics." In *The Cambridge Companion to Heidegger*, ed. Charles B. Guignon, 289–316. Cambridge: Cambridge University Press, 1993.

Dunning, Stephen N. *Kierkegaard's Dialectic of Inwardness*. Princeton: Princeton University Press, 1985.

———. "Kierkegaard's Systematic Analysis of Anxiety." In *The International Kierkegaard Commentary*, vol. 8, *"The Concept of Anxiety,"* ed. Robert L. Perkins, 7–34. Macon: Mercer University Press, 1985.

———. "Paradoxes in Interpretation: Kierkegaard and Gadamer." In *Kierkegaard in Post/Modernity*, ed. Martin J. Matustík and Merold Westphal, 125–41. Bloomington: Indiana University Press, 1995.

Dupré, Louis. *Kierkegaard as Theologian*. New York: Sheed and Ward, 1958.

———. "Of Time and Eternity." In *The International Kierkegaard Commentary*, vol. 8, *"The Concept of Anxiety,"* ed. Robert L. Perkins, 111–33. Macon: Mercer University Press, 1985.

Eagelton, Terry. *The Ideology of the Aesthetic*. Cambridge: Basil Blackwell, 1990.

Ellerby, Janet Mason. "Repetition and Redemption." Ph.D. diss., University of Washington, 1989.

Elrod, John W. *Being and Existence in Kierkegaard's Pseudonymous Authorship*. Princeton: Princeton University Press, 1975.

———. *Kierkegaard and Christendom*. Princeton: Princeton University Press, 1981.

———. "Passion, Reflection, and Particularity in *Two Ages*." In *The International Kierkegaard Commentary*, vol. 14, *"Two Ages: The Present Age and the Age of Revolution," A Literary Review*, ed. Robert L. Perkins, 1–18. Macon: Mercer University Press, 1984.

Evans, C. Stephen. "Faith as the Telos of Morality: A Reading of *Fear and Trembling*." In *The International Kierkegaard Commentary*, vol. 6, *"Fear and Trembling" and "Repetition,"* ed. Robert L. Perkins, 9–27. Macon: Mercer University Press, 1993.

———. *Kierkegaard's "Fragments" and "Postscript": The Religious Philosophy of Johannes Climacus*. Atlantic Highlands, N.J.: Humanities Press, 1983.

———. "Kierkegaard's View of the Unconscious." In *Kierkegaard in Post/Modernity*, ed. Martin J. Matustík and Merold Westphal, 76–97. Bloomington: Indiana University Press, 1995.

———. *Passionate Reason: Making Sense of Kierkegaard's "Philosophical Fragments."* Bloomington: Indiana University Press, 1992.

———, ed. *Foundations of Kierkegaard's Vision of Community: Religion, Ethics, and Politics in Kierkegaard*. Atlantic Highlands, N.J.: Humanities Press, 1992.

Fenger, Henning. *Kierkegaard: The Myths and Their Origins*. Trans. George C. Schoolfield. New Haven: Yale University Press, 1980.

Fenves, Peter. *Chatter: Language and History in Kierkegaard*. Stanford: Stanford University Press, 1993.

Ferguson, Harvie. *Melancholy and the Critique of Modernity: Søren Kierkegaard's Religious Psychology*. London: Routledge, 1995.

Ferreira, Jamie. *Transforming Vision: Imagination and Will in Kierkegaardian Faith*. Oxford: Clarendon Press, 1991.

Gasché, Rodolphe. *Inventions of Difference: On Jacques Derrida*. Cambridge: Harvard University Press, 1994.

———. *The Tain of the Mirror: Derrida and the Philosophy of Reflection*. Cambridge: Harvard University Press, 1986.

Gill, Jerry, ed. *Essays on Kierkegaard*. Minneapolis: Burgess, 1969.

Golomb, Jacob. *In Search of Authenticity: From Kierkegaard to Camus*. London: Routledge, 1995.

Gouwens, David J. *Kierkegaard as Religious Thinker*. Cambridge: Cambridge University Press, 1996.

———. *Kierkegaard's Dialectic of the Imagination*. New York: Peter Lang, 1989.

———. "Understanding, Imagination, and Irony in Kierkegaard's *Repetition*." In *The International Kierkegaard Commentary*, vol. 6, *"Fear and Trembling" and "Repetition,"* ed. Robert L. Perkins, 283–308. Macon: Mercer University Press, 1993.

Green, Ronald M. *Kierkegaard and Kant: The Hidden Debt*. Albany: SUNY Press, 1992.

———. "The Limits of the Ethical in Kierkegaard's *The Concept of Anxiety* and Kant's *Religion within the Limits of Reason Alone*." In *The International Kierkegaard Commentary*, vol. 8, *"The Concept of Anxiety,"* ed. Robert L. Perkins, 63–88. Macon: Mercer University Press, 1985.

Guarda, Victor. *Die Widerholung: Analysen zur Grundstruktur menschlicher Existenz im Verstandnis Søren Kierkegaard*. Konigstein/ Ts.: Forum Academicum in der Verlagsgruppe, 1980.

Guignon, Charles B. "Authenticity, Moral Values, and Psychotherapy." In *The Cambridge Companion to Heidegger*, ed. Charles B. Guignon, 215–39. Cambridge: Cambridge University Press, 1993.

———, ed. *The Cambridge Companion to Heidegger*. Cambridge: Cambridge University Press, 1993.

Habermas, Jürgen. "Communicative Freedom and Negative Theology." In *Kierkegaard in Post/Modernity*, ed. Martin J. Matustík and Merold Westphal, 182–98. Bloomington: Indiana University Press, 1995.

———. *The Philosophical Discourse of Modernity*. Trans. Frederick Lawrence. Cambridge: MIT Press, 1987.

Hall, Ronald L. "Language and Freedom: Kierkegaard's Analysis of the Demonic in *The Concept of Anxiety*." In *The International Kierkegaard Commentary*, vol. 8, *"The Concept of Anxiety,"* ed. Robert L. Perkins, 153–66. Macon: Mercer University Press, 1987.

———. *Word and Spirit: A Kierkegaardian Critique of the Modern Age*. Bloomington: Indiana University Press, 1993.

Hannay, Alastair. *Kierkegaard*. London: Routledge, 1991.

————. "Solitary Souls and Infinite Help: Kierkegaard and Wittgenstein." In *History of European Ideas,* vol. 12, no. 1, ed. Anne Loades and George Pattison, 41–52. Oxford: Pergamon Press, 1990.

Harrison, Robert P. "Heresy and the Question of Repetition: Reading Kierkegaard's *Repetition.*" In *Textual Analysis: Some Readers Reading,* ed. Mary Caws, 281–88. New York: Modern Language Association, 1986.

Hart, Kevin. *The Trespass of the Sign: Deconstruction, Theology, and Philosophy.* 2nd ed. New York: Fordham University Press, 2000.

Hartshorne, M. Holmes. *Kierkegaard, Godly Deceiver: The Nature and the Meaning of His Pseudonymous Writings.* New York: Columbia University Press, 1990.

Hegel, G. W. F. *Early Theological Writings.* Trans. T. M. Knox. Philadelphia: University of Pennsylvania Press, 1971.

————. *Faith and Knowledge.* Trans. H. S. Harris and W. Cerf. Albany: SUNY Press, 1977.

————. *Lectures on the History of Philosophy.* Trans. E. S. Haldane. 3 vols. New York: Humanities Press, 1968.

————. *Lectures on the Philosophy of Religion.* Trans. E. B. Speirs and J. B. Sanderson. 3 vols. New York: Humanities Press, 1968.

————. *Lectures on the Philosophy of Religion: The Lectures of 1827* (1-volume edition). Ed. Peter C. Hodgson. Trans. R. F. Brown et al. Berkeley: University of California Press, 1988.

————. *The Logic of Hegel.* Trans. W. Wallace. New York: Oxford University Press, 1968.

————. *Phenomenology of Spirit.* Trans. A. V. Miller. Oxford: Oxford University Press, 1977.

————. *Philosophy of History.* Trans. J. Sibree. New York: Dover, 1956.

————. *Philosophy of Mind.* Trans. W. Wallace and A. V. Miller. Oxford: Clarendon Press, 1971.

————. *Philosophy of Right.* Trans. T. M. Knox. London: Oxford University Press, 1967.

————. *Science of Logic.* Trans. A. V. Miller. New York: Humanities Press, 1969.

Heidegger, Martin. *The Basic Problems of Phenomenology.* Trans. Albert Hofstadter. Bloomington: Indiana University Press, 1982.

————. *Being and Time.* Trans. John Macquarrie and Edward Robinson. Oxford: Blackwell, 1962.

————. *The End of Philosophy.* Trans. John Stambaugh. London: Souvenir Press, 1975.

————. *Hegel's Concept of Experience.* Trans. Kenley Royce Dove. New York: Harper and Row, 1970.

————. *Hegel's Phenomenology of Spirit.* Trans. Parvis Emad and Kenneth Maly. Bloomington: Indiana University Press, 1994.

————. *Identity and Difference.* Trans. John Stambaugh. New York: Harper Torchbook, 1974.

Hoberman, John M. "Kierkegaard's *Two Ages* and Heidegger's Critique of Modernity." In *The International Kierkegaard Commentary,* vol. 14, *"Two Ages: The Present Age and the Age of Revolution," A Literary Review,* ed. Robert L. Perkins, 223–58. Macon: Mercer University Press, 1984.

Hodge, Johanna. *Heidegger and Ethics.* London: Routledge, 1995.

Hohlenberg, Johannes. *Søren Kierkegaard.* Trans. T. H. Croxaie. New York: Parthenon Books, 1954.

Huntington, Patricia J. "Heidegger's Reading of Kierkegaard Revisited: From Ontological Abstraction to Ethical Concretion." In *Kierkegaard in Post/Modernity,* ed. Martin J. Matustík and Merold Westphal, 43–65. Bloomington: Indiana University Press, 1995.

Husserl, Edmund. *Cartesian Meditations: An Introduction to Phenomenology.* Trans. Dorion Cairns. Dordrecht: Kluwer Academic Publishers, 1993.

Hyppolite, Jean. *Genesis and Structure of Hegel's "Phenomenology of Spirit."* Trans. Samuel Cherniak and John Heckman. Evanston: Northwestern University Press, 1974.

————. "Hegel's Phenomenology and Psychoanalysis." In *New Studies in Hegel's Philosophy,* ed. W. E. Steinkrauss, 57–70. New York: Holt, Rinehart and Winston, 1971.

Johnson, Howard A. "Kierkegaard and Politics." In *A Kierkegaard Critique,* ed. Howard A. Johnson and Niels Thulstrup, 74–84. New York: Harper, 1962.

Kant, Immanuel. *Critique of Practical Reason.* Trans. Lewis White Beck. Indianapolis: Bobbs-Merrill, 1977.

————. *Groundwork of the Metaphysic of Morals.* Trans. H. J. Paton. New York: Harper Torchbooks, 1964.

Kearney, Richard. "Between Tradition and Utopia: The Hermeneutical Problem of Myth." In *On Paul Ricoeur: Narrative and Interpretation,* ed. David Wood, 55–73. London: Routledge, 1991.

————. "Ideology and Religion: A Hermeneutic Conflict." In *Phenomenology of the Truth Proper to Religion,* ed. Daniel Guerrière, 126–45. Albany: SUNY Press, 1990.

————. "Kierkegaard's Concept of the God-Man." *Kierkegaardiana* 13 (1984) 105–21.

————. *Modern Movements in European Philosophy.* Manchester: Manchester University Press, 1994.

————. "Narrativity and Ethics." In *The Modern Subject,* ed. Otto M. Christensen and Siri Meyer, 48–62. Bergen: Centre for the Study of European Civilization, 1996.

————. *Poetics of Imagining from Husserl to Lyotard.* London: Harper Collins, 1991.

————. *Poetics of Modernity.* Atlantic Highlands, N.J.: Humanities Press, 1995.

————. *Poetique du Possible: Phenomenologie hermeneutic de la figuration.* Paris: Beauchesne, 1984.

————. *The Wake of Imagination.* London: Routledge, 1994.

————, ed. *Dialogues with Contemporary Thinkers: The Phenomenological Heritage.* Manchester: Manchester University Press, 1984.

————. *Paul Ricoeur: The Hermeneutics of Action.* London: SAGE, 1996.

————. *States of Mind: Dialogues with Contemporary Thinkers on the European Mind.* Manchester: Manchester University Press, 1995.

Keeley, Louise Carroll. "Subjectivity and World in *Works of Love.*" In *Foundations of Kierkegaard's Vision of Community: Religion, Ethics, and Politics in Kierkegaard,* ed. George B. Connell and C. Stephen Evans, 96–108. Atlantic Highlands, N.J.: Humanities Press, 1992.

Kierkegaard, Søren. *Armed Neutrality and An Open Letter.* Trans. Howard V. Hong and Edna H. Hong. Bloomington: Indiana University Press, 1968. (*Den Bevæbnede Neutralitet,* written 1848–49, publ. 1965; "Foranledigt ved en Yttring af Dr. Rudelbach mig betræffende," *Fædrelandet,* no. 26, January 31, 1851)

————. *Christian Discourses,* including *The Lilies in the Field and the Birds in the Air* and *Three Discourses at the Communion on Fridays.* Trans. Walter Lowrie. London: Oxford University Press,

1940. (*Christelige Taler*, 1848; *Lilien paa Marken og Fuglen under Himlen*, 1849; *Tre Taler ved Altergangen om Fredagen*, 1849)

————. *The Concept of Anxiety*. Trans. Reidar Thomte in collaboration with Albert B. Anderson. Princeton: Princeton University Press, 1980. (*Begrebet Angest*, by Vigilius Haufniensis, ed. S. Kierkegaard, 1844)

————. *The Concept of Irony*, together with "Notes on Schelling's Berlin Lectures." Trans. Howard V. Hong and Edna H. Hong. Princeton: Princeton University Press, 1989. (*Om Begrebet Ironi*, 1841)

————. *Concluding Unscientific Postscript to the Philosophical Fragments*. Trans. Howard V. Hong and Edna H. Hong. 2 vols. Princeton: Princeton University Press, 1992. (*Afsluttende uvidenskabelig Efterskrift*, by Johannes Climacus, 1846)

————. *The Corsair Affair*. Trans. Howard V. Hong and Edna H. Hong. Princeton: Princeton University Press, 1982.

————. *The Crisis [and a Crisis] in the Life of an Actress*. Trans. Stephen Crites. New York: Harper and Row, 1967. (*Krisen og en Krise i en Skuespillerindes Liv*, by Inter et Inter. *Fædrelandet*, nos. 188–91, July 24–27, 1848)

————. *De Omnibus Dubitandum Est*. Trans. Howard V. Hong and Edna H. Hong. Princeton: Princeton University Press, 1985.

————. *Early Polemical Writings*. Trans. Julia Watkin. Princeton: Princeton University Press, 1990.

————. *Edifying Discourses in Various Spirits*. Trans. Howard V. Hong and Edna H. Hong. Princeton: Princeton University Press, 1993. (*Obyggelige Taler i forskjellig Aand*, 1847)

————. *Eighteen Edifying Discourses*. Trans. Howard V. Hong and Edna H. Hong. Princeton: Princeton University Press, 1990. (*Opbyggelige Taler*, 1843, 1844)

————. *Either/Or*. Trans. Howard V. Hong and Edna H. Hong. 2 vols. Princeton: Princeton University Press, 1987. (*Enten/Eller 1–2*, ed. Victor Eremita, 1843)

————. *Fear and Trembling*. Trans. Howard V. Hong and Edna H. Hong. Princeton: Princeton University Press, 1983. (*Frygt og Bæven*, by Johannes de Silentio, 1843)

————. *For Self-Examination*. Trans. Howard V. Hong and Edna H. Hong. Princeton: Princeton University Press, 1990. (*Til Selvprøvelse*, 1851)

————. *The Journals of Søren Kierkegaard.* Trans. Alexander Dru. London: Oxford University Press, 1938. (From *Søren Kierkegaard's Papirer,* 1–11 in 18 vols., 1909–36)

————. *Judge for Yourself!* Trans. Howard V. Hong and Edna H. Hong. Princeton: Princeton University Press, 1990. (*Dømmer Selv!* 1852)

————. *Kierkegaard's Attack upon "Christendom."* Trans. Walter Lowrie. Princeton: Princeton University Press, 1944. (*Bladartikler* 1–21, *Fœderlandet,* 1854–55; *Dette skal siges; saa være det da sagt,* 1855; *Øieblikket,* 1–9, 1855; *Hvad Christus dømmer om officiel Christendom,* 1855)

————. *The Last Years.* Trans. Ronald C. Smith. New York: Harper and Row, 1965.

————. *Letters and Documents.* Trans. Hendrik Rosenmeier. Princeton: Princeton University Press, 1978.

————. *On Authority and Revelation, The Book on Adler.* Trans. Walter Lowrie. Princeton: Princeton University Press, 1955. (*Bogen om Adler,* written 1846–47, unpublished, *Papirer* 7^2 235; 8^2 B 1–27)

————. *Philosophical Fragments* and *Johannes Climacus.* Trans. Howard V. Hong and Edna H. Hong. Princeton: Princeton University Press, 1985. ("Johannes Climacus eller de omnibus dubitandum est," written 1842–43, unpublished, *Papirer* 4)

————. *The Point of View for My Work as an Author.* Trans. Walter Lowrie. London: Oxford University Press, 1939. (*Synspunktet for min Forfatter-Virksomhed,* posthumously published 1859; *Om min Forfatter-Virksomhed,* 1851)

————. *Practice in Christianity.* Trans. Howard V. Hong and Edna H. Hong. Princeton: Princeton University Press, 1991. (*Indøvelse I Christendom,* by Anti-Climacus, ed. S. Kierkegaard, 1850)

————. *Prefaces: Light Reading for Certain Classes as the Occasion May Require.* Trans. William McDonald. Tallahassee: Florida State University Press, 1989. (*Forord: Morskabslæsning for Enkelte Stænder efter Tid or Leilighed,* by Nicolaus Notabene, 1844)

————. *Repetition: A Venture in Experimenting Psychology.* Trans. Howard V. Hong and Edna H. Hong. Princeton: Princeton University Press, 1983. (*Gjentagelsen,* by Constantin Constantius, 1843)

————. *The Sickness unto Death.* Trans. Howard V. Hong and Edna H. Hong. Princeton: Princeton University Press, 1980. (*Sygdommen til Døden,* by Anti-Climacus, ed. S. Kierkegaard, 1849)

————. *Søren Kierkegaard's Journals and Papers*. Ed. and trans. Howard V. Hong and Edna H. Hong, assisted by Gregor Malantschuk. Bloomington: Indiana University Press, 1967–78.

————. *Stages on Life's Way*. Trans. Howard V. Hong and Edna H. Hong. Princeton: Princeton University Press, 1988. (*Stadier paa Livets Vej*, ed. Hilarius Bogbinder, 1845)

————. *Two Ages: The Age of Revolution and the Present Age: A Literary Review*. Trans. Howard V. Hong and Edna H. Hong. Princeton: Princeton University Press, 1978. (*En literair Anmeldelse: To Tidsaldre*, 1846)

————. *Works of Love*. Trans. Howard V. Hong and Edna H. Hong. Princeton: Princeton University Press, 1995. (*Kjerlighedens Gjerninger*, 1847)

Kirmmse, Bruce. "Call Me Ishmael—Call Everybody Ishmael: Kierkegaard on the Coming-of-Age of Modern Times." In *Foundations of Kierkegaard's Vision of Community: Religion, Ethics, and Politics in Kierkegaard*, ed. George B. Connell and C. Stephen Evans, 161–82. Atlantic Highlands, N.J.: Humanities Press, 1992.

————. *Kierkegaard in Golden Age Denmark*. Bloomington: Indiana University Press, 1990.

Klemke, E. D. *Studies in the Philosophy of Kierkegaard*. The Hague: Nijhoff, 1976.

Koh, Abraham Kwang. "The Grammar of the Self: Søren Kierkegaard." Ph.D. diss., Drew University, 1990.

Kojève, Alexandre. *Introduction to the Reading of Hegel: Lectures on the "Phenomenology of Spirit."* Trans. James H. Nichols, Jr. Ithaca: Cornell University Press, 1969.

Lacan, Jacques. *Four Fundamental Concepts of Psycho-Analysis*. Trans. Alan Sheridan. New York: Penguin, 1977.

Lawlor, Leonard. *Imagination and Chance: The Difference between the Thought of Ricoeur and Derrida*. Albany: SUNY Press, 1992.

Leitch, Vincent B. *Deconstructive Criticism: An Advanced Introduction*. London: Hutchinson, 1983.

Levin, David Michael. *The Listening Self: Personal Growth, Social Change, and the Closure of Metaphysics*. London: Routledge, 1989.

Levinas, Emmanuel. "Ethics of the Infinite." In *Dialogues with Contemporary Continental Thinkers: The Phenomenological Heritage*, ed. Richard Kearney, 47–69. Manchester: Manchester University Press, 1984.

―――. "Existence and Ethics." In *Kierkegaard: A Critical Reader*, ed. Jonathan Ree and Jane Chamberlain, 26–38. Oxford: Blackwell, 1998.

―――. *Noms Propres*. Paris: Fata Morgana, 1976.

―――. *Otherwise Than Being or Beyond Essence*. Trans. Alphonso Lingis. The Hague: Martinus Nijhoff, 1981.

―――. *Totality and Infinity: An Essay on Exteriority*. Trans. Alphonso Lingis. Pittsburgh: Duquesne University Press, 1969.

Likins, Marjorie. "The Concept of Selfhood in Freud and Kierkegaard." Ph.D. diss., Columbia University, 1963.

Lübcke, Poul. "Kierkegaard and Indirect Communication." In *History of European Ideas*, vol. 12, no. 1, ed. Ann Loades and George Pattison, 31–40. Oxford: Pergamon Press, 1990.

Lukács, Georg. *The Destruction of Reason*. Trans. Peter Palmer. London: Merlin, 1980.

―――. *The Young Hegel*. Trans. Rodney Livingstone. London: Merlin, 1975.

MacIntyre, Alasdair. *After Virtue*. Notre Dame: University of Notre Dame Press, 1984.

Mackey, Louis. *Kierkegaard: A Kind of Poet*. Philadelphia: University of Philadelphia Press, 1971.

―――. "The Loss of the World in Kierkegaard's Ethics." In *Kierkegaard: A Collection of Critical Essays*, ed. Josiah Thompson, 266–89. New York: Anchor Books, 1972.

―――. "The Poetry of Inwardness." In *Kierkegaard: A Collection of Critical Essays*, ed. Josiah Thompson, 1–102. New York: Anchor Books, 1972.

―――. *Points of View: Readings of Kierkegaard*. Tallahassee: Florida State University Press, 1986.

―――. "A Ram in the Afternoon: Kierkegaard's Discourse of the Other." In *Kierkegaard's Truth: The Disclosure of the Self*, ed. Joseph H. Smith, 193–234. New Haven: Yale University Press, 1981.

―――. "Slouching toward Bethlehem: Deconstructive Strategies in Theology." *Anglican Theological Review* 65 (1983): 255–72.

Madison, Gary. *The Hermeneutics of Post-Modernity: Figures and Themes*. Bloomington: Indiana University Press, 1988.

―――, ed. *Working Through Derrida*. Evanston: Northwestern University Press, 1993.

Magurshak, Dan. "*The Concept of Anxiety*: The Keystone of the

Kierkegaard-Heidegger Relationship." In *The International Kierke-gaard Commentary*, vol. 8, *"The Concept of Anxiety,"* ed. Robert L. Perkins, 167–95. Macon: Mercer University Press, 1985.

Malantschuk, Gregor. *Kierkegaard's Thought.* Trans. Howard V. Hong and Edna Hong. Princeton: Princeton University Press, 1971.

———. *Kierkegaard's Way to the Truth.* Trans. Mary Michelsen. Montreal: Inter Editions, 1987.

———, ed. *The Controversial Kierkegaard.* Trans. Howard V. Hong and Edna Hong. Waterloo: Wilfrid Laurier University Press, 1980.

Marcel, Gabriel. *Being and Having.* London: Collins, 1965.

Marsh, James L. *"The Corsair Affair* and Critical Social Theory." In *The International Kierkegaard Commentary*, vol. 13, *"The Corsair Affair,"* ed. Robert L. Perkins, 63–83. Macon: Mercer University Press, 1990.

———. "Kierkegaard and Critical Theory." In *Kierkegaard in Post/Modernity*, ed. Martin J. Matustík and Merold Westphal, 199–215. Bloomington: Indiana University Press, 1995.

———. "Marx and Kierkegaard on Alienation." In *The International Kierkegaard Commentary*, vol. 14, *"Two Ages: The Present Age and the Age of Revolution,"* A *Literary Review*, ed. Robert L. Perkins, 155–74. Macon: Mercer University Press, 1984.

———. *Post-Cartesian Meditations.* New York: Fordham University Press, 1988.

Martin, Mike W. *Self-Deception and Morality.* Lawrence: University Press of Kansas, 1986.

Marx, Werner. *Is There a Measure on Earth? Foundations for a Non-metaphysical Ethics.* Chicago: University of Chicago Press, 1965.

Matustík, Martin J. "Kierkegaard's Radical Existential Praxis, or: Why the Individual Defies Liberal, Communitarian, and Post-modern Categories." In *Kierkegaard in Post/Modernity*, ed. Martin J. Matustík and Merold Westphal, 239–64. Bloomington: Indiana University Press, 1995.

———. *Postnational Identity: Critical Theory and Existential Philos-ophy in Habermas, Kierkegaaard, and Havel.* New York: Guilford Press, 1993.

Matustík, Martin J., and Merold Westphal, eds. *Kierkegaard in Post/Modernity.* Bloomington: Indiana University Press, 1995.

McCarthy, Vincent A. *The Phenomenology of Moods in Kierkegaard.* The Hague: Martinus Nijhoff, 1978.

―――. "Psychological Fragments: Kierkegaard's Religious Psychology." In *Kierkegaard's Truth: The Disclosure of the Self*, ed. Joseph H. Smith, 235–66. New Haven: Yale University Press, 1981.

―――. "Schelling and Kierkegaard on Freedom and Fall." In *The International Kierkegaard Commentary*, vol. 8, *"The Concept of Anxiety,"* ed. Robert L. Perkins, 89–109. Macon: Mercer University Press, 1985.

McLane, Henry Earl. "Kierkegaard's Use of the Category of Repetition: An Attempt to Discern the Structure and Unity of His Thought." Ph.D. diss., Yale University, 1961.

Megill, Alan. *Prophets of Extremity: Nietzsche, Heidegger, Foucault, Derrida.* Berkeley: University of California Press, 1985.

Mooney, Edward. "Art, Deed, and System." In *The International Kierkegaard Commentary*, vol. 6, *"Fear and Trembling" and "Repetition,"* ed. Robert L. Perkins, 67–100. Macon: Mercer University Press, 1993.

―――. "Getting Issac Back: Ordeals and Reconciliations in *Fear and Trembling*." In *Foundations of Kierkegaard's Vision of Community: Religion, Ethics, and Politics in Kierkegaard,* ed. George B. Connell and C. Stephen Evans, 71–96. Atlantic Highlands, N.J.: Humanities Press, 1992.

―――. *Knights of Faith and Resignation: Reading Kierkegaard's "Fear and Trembling."* Albany: SUNY Press, 1991.

―――. *Selves in Discord and Resolve: Kierkegaard's Moral-Religious Psychology from "Either/Or" to "Sickness unto Death."* New York: Routledge, 1996.

Mueller, Paul. *Kierkehgaard's "Works of Love": Christian Ethics and the Maieutic Ideal.* Trans. C. Stephen and Jan Evans. Copenhagen: C. A. Reitzel, 1993.

Mullen, John Douglas. *Kierkegaard's Philosophy: Self-Deception and Cowardice in the Present Age.* New York: New American Library, 1981.

Muller, Rene J. *The Marginal Self: An Existential Inquiry into Narcissism.* Atlantic Highlands, N.J.: Humanities Press International, 1987.

Murdoch, Iris. *Metaphysics as a Guide to Morals.* London: Penguin, 1992.

―――. *Sartre: Romantic Rationalist.* London: Collins, 1972.

Nancy, Jean-Luc. *The Inoperative Community*. Trans. Peter Connor et al. Minneapolis: University of Minnesota Press, 1991.

Nathanson, Maurice. *Edmund Husserl: Philosopher of Infinite Tasks*. Evanston: Northwestern University Press, 1973.

———. *The Journeying Self: A Study in the Philosophy of Social Role*. Reading, Mass.: Addison-Wesley, 1970.

———. *Literature, Philosophy, and the Social Sciences: Essays in Existentialism and Phenomenology*. The Hague: Nijhoff, 1962.

Nicoletti, Michele. "Politics and Religion in Kierkegaard's Thought: Secularization and the Martyr." In *Foundations of Kierkegaard's Vision of Community: Religion, Ethics, and Politics in Kierkegaard*, ed. George B. Connell and C. Stephen Evans, 183–95. Atlantic Highlands, N.J.: Humanities Press, 1992.

Nordentoft, Kresten. *Kierkegaard's Psychology*. Trans. Bruce H. Kirmmse. Atlantic Highlands, N.J.: Humanities Press, 1972.

Norris, Christopher. *The Deconstructive Turn: Essays in the Rhetoric of Philosophy*. London: Methuen, 1983.

———. *Derrida*. London: Fontana, 1987.

O'Leary, Joseph. *Questioning Back: The Overcoming of Metaphysics in Christian Tradition*. San Francisco: Harper and Row, 1985.

———. *Religious Pluralism and Christian Truth*. Edinburgh: Edinburgh University Press, 1996.

Pattison, George. *Art, Modernity, and Faith: Towards a Theology of Art*. New York: St. Martin's Press, 1991.

———. "A Drama of Love and Death: Michael Pedersen Kierkegaard and Regine Olsen Revisited." In *History of European Ideas*, vol. 12, no. 1, ed. Ann Loades and George Pattison. Oxford: Pergamon Press, 1990. 79–93.

———. *Kierkegaard: The Aesthetic and the Religious: From the Magic Theatre to the Crucifixion of the Image*. London: Macmillan, 1992.

———, ed. *Kierkegaard on Art and Communication*. New York: St. Martin's Press, 1992.

Pattison, George, and Ann Loades, eds. *History of European Ideas*, vol. 12, no. 1. Oxford: Pergamon Press, 1990.

Pattison, George, and Steven Shakespeare, eds. *Kierkegaard: The Self in Society*. London: Macmillan, 1998.

Peperzak, Adriaan T. *To the Other: An Introduction to the Philosophy of Emmanuel Levinas*. West Lafayette, Ind.: Purdue University Press, 1993.

————, ed. *Ethics as First Philosophy: The Significance of Emmanuel Levinas for Philosophy, Literature, and Religion.* New York: Routledge, 1995.

Perkins, Robert L. "Abraham's Silence Aesthetically Considered." In *Kierkegaard on Art and Communication,* ed. George Pattison, 100–113. New York: St. Martin's Press, 1992.

————. "Envy as Personal Phenomenon and as Politics." In *The International Kierkegaard Commentary,* vol. 14, *"Two Ages: The Present Age and the Age of Revolution," A Literary Review,* ed. Robert L. Perkins, 107–32. Macon: Mercer University Press, 1984.

————. "Kierkegaard, a Kind of Epistemologist." In *History of European Ideas,* vol. 12, no. 1, ed. Ann Loades and George Pattison, 7–18. Oxford: Pergamon Press, 1990.

————. "Kierkegaard and Hegel: The Dialectical Structure of Kierkegaard's Ethical Thought." Ph.D. diss., Indiana University, 1965.

————. "Kierkegaard's Critique of the Bourgeois State." *Inquiry* 27 (1984): 207–18.

————. "The Politics of Existence: Buber and Kierkegaard." In *Kierkegaard in Post/Modernity,* ed. Martin J. Matustík and Merold Westphal, 167–81. Bloomington: Indiana University Press, 1995.

————. *Søren Kierkegaard.* London: Lutterworth Press, 1969.

————, ed. *The International Kierkegaard Commentary.* Vol. 8, *"The Concept of Anxiety."* Macon: Mercer University Press, 1985.

————. *The International Kierkegaard Commentary.* Vol. 13, *"The Corsair Affair."* Macon: Mercer University Press, 1990.

————. *The International Kierkegaard Commentary.* Vol. 6, *"Fear and Trembling" and "Repetition."* Macon: Mercer University Press, 1993.

————. *The International Kierkegaard Commentary.* Vol. 7, *"Philosophical Fragments" and "Johannes Climacus."* Macon: Mercer University Press, 1994.

————. *The International Kierkegaard Commentary.* Vol. 19, *"The Sickness unto Death."* Macon: Mercer University Press, 1987.

————. *The International Kierkegaard Commentary.* Vol. 14, *"Two Ages: The Present Age and the Age of Revolution," A Literary Review.* Macon: Mercer University Press, 1984.

————. *Kierkegaard's "Fear and Trembling": Critical Appraisals.* Tuscaloosa: University of Alabama Press, 1981.

Plato. *Collected Dialogues*. Ed. Edith Hamilton and Huntington Cairns. Princeton: Princeton University Press, 1978.

Plekon, Michael. "Kierkegaard the Theologian: The Roots of His Theology in *Works of Love*." In *Foundations of Kierkegaard's Vision of Community: Religion, Ethics, and Politics in Kierkegaard*, ed. George B. Connell and C. Stephen Evans, 2–17. Atlantic Highlands, N.J.: Humanities Press, 1992.

Pojman, Louis. *The Logic of Subjectivity*. University: University of Alabama Press, 1984.

Polka, Brayton. "Aesthetics and Religion: Kierkegaard and the Offense of Indirect Communication." In *Kierkegaard on Art and Communication*, ed. George Pattison, 23–54. New York: St. Martin's Press, 1992.

Poole, Roger. *Kierkegaard: The Indirect Communication*. Charlottesville: University Press of Virginia, 1993.

———. *Towards Deep Subjectivity*. London: Allen Lane, 1972.

———, ed. *A Kierkegaard Reader: Texts and Narratives*. London: Fourth Estate Limited, 1989.

Putnam, Hilary. *Renewing Philosophy*. Cambridge: Harvard University Press, 1992.

Pyper, Hugh. "The Lesson of Eternity: Christ as Teacher in Kierkegaard and Hegel." In *The International Kierkegaard Commentary*, vol. 7, *"Philosophical Fragments" and "Johannes Climacus,"* ed. Robert L. Perkins, 129–45. Macon: Mercer University Press, 1994.

Rapaport, Herman. *Heidegger and Derrida: Reflections on Time and Language*. Lincoln: University of Nebraska Press, 1989.

Ricoeur, Paul. *The Conflict of Interpretations: Essays in Hermeneutics*. Ed. Don Ihde. Evanston: Northwestern University Press, 1974.

———. "Fragility and Responsibility." Trans. Elizabeth Iwanowski. In *Paul Ricoeur: The Hermeneutics of Action*, ed. Richard Kearney, 15–22. London: SAGE, 1996.

———. *Freud and Philosophy: An Interpretation*. Trans. Denis Savage. New Haven: Yale University Press, 1970.

———. *From Text to Action*. Trans. Kathleen Balmey and John B. Thompson. London: Athlone Press, 1991.

———. *Hermeneutics and the Human Sciences*. Trans. John B. Thompson. Cambridge: Cambridge University Press, 1981.

————. *Interpretation Theory: Discourse and the Surplus of Meaning.* Fort Worth: Texas Christian University Press, 1976.

————. "Life in Quest of Narrative." In *On Paul Ricoeur: Narrative and Interpretation,* ed. David Wood, 20–33. London: Routledge, 1991.

————. "Love and Justice." Trans. David Pellauer. In *Paul Ricoeur: The Hermeneutics of Action,* ed. Richard Kearney, 23–37. London: SAGE, 1996.

————. *Oneself as Another.* Trans. Kathleen Blamey. Chicago: University of Chicago Press, 1992.

————. "Reflections on a New Ethos for Europe." Trans. Eileen Brennan. In *Paul Ricoeur: The Hermeneutics of Action,* ed. Richard Kearney, 3–13. London: SAGE, 1996.

————. *The Symbolism of Evil.* Trans. Emerson Buchana. Boston: Beacon Press, 1969.

————. "Two Encounters with Kierkegaard: Kierkegaard and Evil; Doing Philosophy after Kierkegaard." In *Kierkegaard's Truth: The Disclosure of the Self,* ed. Joseph H. Smith, 313–42. New Haven: Yale University Press, 1981.

————. "Universality and the Power of Difference." In *Visions of Europe: Challenging Ideas in Dialogue,* ed. Richard Kearney, 117–26. Dublin: Wolfhound Press, 1992.

Roberts, Robert C. *Faith, Reason, and History: Rethinking Kierkegaard's "Philosophical Fragments."* Macon: Mercer University Press, 1986.

Rogan, Jan. "Keeping Silent through Speaking." In *Kierkegaard on Art and Communication,* ed. George Pattison, 88–99. New York: St. Martin's Press, 1992.

Rorty, Richard. *Contingency, Irony, and Solidarity.* Cambridge: Cambridge University Press, 1989.

Rose, Gillian. *The Broken Middle: Out of Our Ancient Society.* Oxford: Blackwell, 1992.

Roth, Michael. *The Poetics of Resistance: Heidegger's Line.* Evanston: Northwestern University Press, 1996.

Rubin, Jane. "Too Much of Nothing: Modern Culture, the Self, and Salvation in Kierkegaard's Thought." Ph.D. diss., University of California, Berkeley, 1984.

Rudd, Anthony. *Kierkegaard and the Limits of the Ethical.* Oxford: Clarendon Press, 1993.

Rumble, Juliet Taylor. "Entangled Freedom: Self-Recognition and the Captivity of the Will in Kierkegaard's Thought." Ph.D. diss., Vanderbilt University, 1993.

Rumble, Vanessa. "Reflections of Immediacy: The Anatomy of Self-Deception in Kierkegaard's Early Writings." Ph.D. diss., Emory University, 1989.

———. "Sacrifice and Domination: Kantian and Kierkegaardian Paradigms of Self-Overcoming." *Philosophy and Social Criticism* 20, no. 3 (1994): 19–35.

———. "To Be as No-One: Kierkegaard and Climacus on the Art of Indirect Communication." *International Journal of Philosophical Studies* 3 (September 1995): 307–21.

Saatkamp, Herman J., ed. *Rorty and Pragmatism: The Philosopher Responds to His Critics.* Nashville and London: Vanderbilt University Press, 1995.

Sallis, John, ed. *Deconstruction and Philosophy: The Texts of Jacques Derrida.* Chicago: University of Chicago Press, 1987.

Santoro, Liberato, *The Dialectics of Desire.* Rome: Università degli Studi di Ferrara, 1995.

Sartre, Jean-Paul. *Being and Nothingness.* Trans. Hazel Barnes. New York: Philosophical Library, 1956.

———. "The Singular Universal." In *Kierkegaard: A Collection of Critical Essays,* ed. Josiah Thompson, 230–65. New York: Anchor Books, 1972.

Schleifer, Ronald, and Robert Markley, eds. *Kierkegaard and Literature: Irony, Repetition, and Criticism.* Norman: University of Oklahoma Press, 1984.

Schleifer, Ronald. "Irony, Identity, and Repetition." *Substance* 25 (1980): 44–54.

Schragg, Calvin O. *Existence and Freedom: Towards an Ontology of Human Finitude.* Evanston: Northwestern University Press, 1961.

———. "The Kierkegaard-Effect in the Shaping of the Contours of Modernity." In *Kierkegaard in Post/Modernity,* ed. Martin J. Matustík and Merold Westphal, 1–17. Bloomington: Indiana University Press, 1995.

———. *Philosophical Papers: Betwixt and Between.* Albany: SUNY Press, 1989.

Shmuëli, Adi. *Kierkegaard and Consciousness.* Trans. N. Handelman. Princeton: Princeton University Press, 1971.

Simpson, Lorenzo C. *Technology, Time, and the Conversations of Modernity.* New York: Routledge, 1995.

Smith, Joseph, and William Kerrigan, eds. *Interpreting Lacan.* New Haven: Yale University Press, 1993.

Smyth, John Vignaux. *A Question of Eros: Irony in Sterne, Kierkegaard, and Barthes.* Tallahassee: Florida State University Press, 1986.

Solomon, Robert C. *Continental Philosophy since 1750: The Rise and Fall of the Self.* Oxford: Oxford University Press, 1988.

Stack, George. "Kierkegaard and the Phenomenology of Repetition." *Journal of Existentialism* 7 (1966–67): 111–25.

———. *Kierkegaard's Existential Ethics.* University: University of Alabama Press, 1977.

———. "Repetition in Kierkegaard and Freud." *Personalist* 58 (1977): 249–61.

Stines, James. "Phenomenology of Language in the Thought of Søren Kierkegaard." Ph.D. diss., Duke University, 1970.

Stout, Jeffrey. *Ethics after Babel: The Languages of Morals and Their Discontents.* Boston: Beacon Press, 1988.

———. *The Flight from Authority: Religion, Morality, and the Quest for Autonomy.* Notre Dame: University of Notre Dame Press, 1981.

Strawser, Michael. "The Indirectness of Kierkegaard's Signed Writings." *International Journal of Philosophical Studies* 3 (March 1995): 73–90.

Sussman, Henry. *The Hegelian Aftermath: Readings in Hegel, Kierkegaard, Freud, Proust, and James.* Baltimore: Johns Hopkins University Press, 1982.

Taminiaux, Jacques. *Dialectic and Difference: Finitude and Modern Thought.* Atlantic Highlands, N.J.: Humanities Press, 1985.

———. *Poetics, Speculation, and Judgment: The Shadow of the Work of Art from Kant to Phenomenology.* Trans. Michael Gendre. Albany: SUNY Press, 1993.

Taylor, Charles. "Engaged Agency and Background in Heidegger." In *The Cambridge Companion to Heidegger,* ed. Charles B. Guignon, 317–66. Cambridge: Cambridge University Press, 1993.

———. *The Ethics of Authenticity.* Cambridge: Harvard University Press, 1991.

———. *Hegel.* Cambridge: Cambridge University Press, 1975.

———. *Hegel and Modern Society.* Cambridge: Cambridge University Press, 1979.

———. *Sources of the Self.* Cambridge: Harvard University Press, 1989.

Taylor, Mark C. "Aesthetic Therapy: Hegel and Kierkegaard." In *Kierkegaard's Truth: The Disclosure of the Self,* ed. Joseph H. Smith, 343–81. New Haven: Yale University Press, 1981.

———. *Altarity.* Chicago: University of Chicago Press, 1987.

———. *Deconstructing Theology.* New York: Crossroads, 1982.

———. *Erring A Postmodern A/Theology.* Chicago: University of Chicago Press, 1984.

———. "Journeys to Moriah: Kierkegaard vs. Hegel." *Harvard Theological Review* 70 (1977): 305–26.

———. *Journeys to Selfhood: Hegel and Kierkegaard.* 2nd ed. New York: Fordham University Press, 2000.

———. *Kierkegaard's Pseudonymous Authorship: A Study of Time and the Self.* Princeton: Princeton University Press, 1975.

———. "Refusal of the Bar." In *Lacan and Theological Discourse,* ed. Edith Wyschogrod, David Crownfield, and Carl A. Raschke, 39–59. Albany: SUNY Press, 1989.

———. "Self in/as Other." *Kierkegaardiana,* 13:63–71. Copenhagen: C. A. Reitzel, 1984.

———. *Tears.* Albany: SUNY Press, 1990.

Taylor, Mark L. "Ordeal and Repetition in Kierkegaard's Treatment of Abraham and Job." In *Foundations of Kierkegaard's Vision of Community: Religion, Ethics, and Politics in Kierkegaard,* ed. George B. Connell and C. Stephen Evans, 33–55. Atlantic Highlands, N.J.: Humanities Press, 1992.

Theunissen, Michael. *Das Selbst auf dem Grund der Verzweiflung.* Frankfurt am Main: Suhrkamp, 1991.

———. "Kierkegaard's Negativistic Method." In *Kierkegaard's Truth: The Disclosure of the Self,* ed. Joseph H. Smith, 381–425. New Haven: Yale University Press, 1981.

———. *The Other: Studies in the Social Ontology of Husserl, Heidegger, Sartre, and Buber.* Trans. Christopher Macann. Cambridge: MIT Press, 1984.

Thompson, Josiah. *Kierkegaard.* London: Victor Gollancz Ltd., 1974.

———. *The Lonely Labyrinth: Kierkegaard's Pseudonymous Works.* Carbondale: Southern Illinois University Press, 1967.

———. "The Master of Irony." In *Kierkegaard: A Collection of Critical Essays,* ed. Josiah Thompson, 103–63. New York: Anchor Books, 1972.

———, ed. *Kierkegaard: A Collection of Critical Essays.* New York: Anchor Books, 1972.

Thomte, Reidar. *Kierkegaard's Philosophy of Religion.* Princeton: Princeton University Press, 1948.

Thulstrup, Niels. *Kierkegaard's Relationship to Hegel.* Trans. George L. Stengeren. Princeton: Princeton University Press, 1980.

Tugendhat, Ernst. *Self-Consciousness and Self-Determination.* Trans. Paul Stern. Cambridge: MIT Press, 1986.

Veisland, Jorgen S. *Kierkegaard and the Dialectics of Modernism.* New York: P. Lang, 1985.

Vergote, Henri-Bernard. *Sens et répétition: Essai sur l'ironie kierke-gaardienne.* Orante: Éditions du cerf, 1982.

Vogel, Lawrence. *The Fragile "We": Ethical Implications of Heidegger's "Being and Time."* Evanston: Northwestern University Press, 1994.

Wahl, Jean. *Etudes kierkegaardiennes.* Paris: Librairie J. Vrin, 1938.

Walsh, Sylvia. "Kierkegaard: Poet of the Religious." In *Kierkegaard on Art and Communication,* ed. George Pattison, 1–22. New York: St. Martin's Press, 1992.

———. *Living Poetically: Kierkegaard's Existential Aesthetics.* University Park: Pennsylvania State University Press, 1994.

———. "On 'Feminine' and 'Masculine' Forms of Despair." In *The International Kierkegaard Commentary,* vol. 19, *"The Sickness unto Death,"* ed. Robert L. Perkins, 121–34. Macon: Mercer University Press, 1987.

Webb, Eugene. *Philosophers of Consciousness.* Seattle: University of Washington Press, 1988.

Weston, Michael. *Kierkegaard and Continental Philosophy.* London: Routledge, 1994.

Westphal, Merold. *God, Guilt, and Death: An Existential Phenomenology of Religion.* Bloomington: Indiana University Press, 1984.

———. "Johannes and Johannes: Kierkegaard and Difference." In *The International Kierkegaard Commentary,* vol. 7, *"Philosophical Fragments" and "Johannes Climacus,"* ed. Robert L. Perkins, 13–32. Macon: Mercer University Press, 1994.

———. *Kierkegaard's Critique of Reason and Society.* Macon: Mercer University Press, 1987.

————. "Kierkegaard's Sociology." In *The International Kierkegaard Commentary*, vol. 14, *"Two Ages: The Present Age and the Age of Revolution,"* A *Literary Review*, ed. Robert L. Perkins, 133–54. Macon: Mercer University Press, 1984.

————. "Kierkegaard's Teleological Suspension Religiousness B." In *Foundations of Kierkegaard's Vision of Community: Religion, Ethics, and Politics in Kierkegaard*, ed. George B. Connell and C. Stephen Evans, 110–29. Atlantic Highlands, N.J.: Humanities Press, 1992.

————. "Levinas's Teleological Suspension of the Religious." In *Ethics as First Philosophy: The Significance of Emmanuel Levinas for Philosophy, Literature, and Religion*, ed. Adriaan T. Peperzak, 151–60. New York: Routledge, 1995.

————. "The Transparent Shadow: Kierkegaard and Levinas in Dialogue." In *Kierkegaard in Post/Modernity*, ed. Martin Matustík and Merold Westphal, 265–81. Bloomington: Indiana University Press, 1995.

Wilde, Frank-Eberhar. *Kierkegaard and Speculative Idealism*. Copenhagen: C. A. Reitzel, 1979.

Wood, Allen W. *Hegel's Ethical Thought*. Cambridge: Cambridge University Press, 1990.

————. "Hegel's Ethics." In *The Cambridge Companion to Hegel*, ed. Frederick C. Beiser, 211–33. Cambridge: Cambridge University Press, 1993.

Wood, David. "Following Derrida." In *Deconstruction and Philosophy: The Texts of Jacques Derrida*, ed. John Sallis, 143–60. Chicago: University of Chicago Press, 1987.

————. *Philosophy at the Limit*. London: Unwin Hyman, 1990.

————, ed. *Derrida: A Critical Reader*. Oxford: Blackwell, 1992.

————. *On Paul Ricoeur: Narrative and Interpretation*. London: Routledge, 1991.

Wyschogrod, Edith. *Saints and Postmodernism*. Chicago: University of Chicago Press, 1990.

————. *Spirit in Ashes: Hegel, Heidegger, and Man-Made Mass Death*. New Haven: Yale University Press, 1985.

Wyschogrod, Edith, David Crownfield, and Carl A. Raschke, eds. *Lacan and Theological Discourse*. Albany: SUNY Press, 1989.

Wyschogrod, Michael. *Kierkegaard and Heidegger: The Ontology of Existence*. New York: Humanities Press, 1969.

INDEX

Abraham, xvii, xix, xxiii, 5, 51, 56, 59, 60, 61, 63, 64, 67, 67n13, 69, 70, 73, 76, 80, 83, 84, 96, 108, 109, 115, 117, 124, 127, 128, 129, 133, 135, 136, 147, 153, 163, 169, 171, 182, 183, 187, 198–205 passim, 215–48 passim
absurd, the, 66, 67, 137
Adorno, Theodore, xiii, xiiin1, 70
alterity, 111, 182, 206–9, 211, 213, 227, 233, 242
Andic, Martin, 231n128
Arendt, Hannah, 239, 239n136
Armstrong, Paul B., 57n6
Attridge, Derek, 192n59

Barrett, Lee, 2n3
Battaille, Georges, 147
belief, 102–15 passim, 126, 133, 169
Bennington, Geoffrey, 178, 179, 179n40, 188, 191, 199, 219n103
Bernstein, Richard J., 219n103
Blanchette, Olivia, 57n6
Bloom, Harold, 74n1
Boff, Leonardo, 21n24
Böhme, Jacob, 27
Book, the, 146–94 passim

Cahoy, William J., 1n2
Caputo, John D., xiv, xix–xxii, xxiv, 8n5, 19, 24n1, 57, 57n6, 58n7, 67n13, 74n1, 95n13, 99,

99n16, 100, 110, 117n1, 129–32, 134n11, 139, 144n1, 145, 145n2, 146, 155–57, 199, 199n66, 206, 206n77, 210n89, 216, 217n99, 219n103, 227n114, 229, 229n119 & n121, 230n122 & n125, 231n127, 232n129, 236, 236n133, 238–48 passim
Casey, Edward, 74n1
Chamberlain, Jane, xviin4
Christendom, xx, 18, 77, 140, 142, 143
Christ-figure, 12, 18, 20, 44n1, 51, 77, 106, 193, 236, 248; as "paradigm" or "prototype," 19, 56, 242
Christianity, xx, 115, 133, 134, 135, 140, 141, 230, 236, 238, 242; Christian thinker, xiv, xxii, 18, 30, 92, 142, 144, 145, 157, 206
Clair, André, 74n1
Climacus, Anti-, 11, 13, 18, 19, 45, 46, 47, 61, 62, 66, 71, 76, 80, 86–89, 91, 103–43 passim, 176, 179, 193, 221, 226 ; Johannes, 3, 4, 5, 7, 45, 54, 59, 75–116 passim, 159, 174, 176, 177, 184, 218
communication, 6, 10, 51, 70, 73, 170, 177–94 passim; direct, 6, 7, 69, 141, 169–71; indirect, 48, 91, 141, 144, 167, 169, 170, 177
Communism, 43